WORLD ECONOMIC OUTLOOK

May 1996

**A Survey by the Staff of the
International Monetary Fund**

**INTERNATIONAL MONETARY FUND
Washington, DC**

World economic outlook (International Monetary Fund)
World economic outlook: a survey by the staff of the International
Monetary Fund.—1980– —Washington, D.C.: The Fund, 1980–

    v.; 28 cm.—(1981–84: Occasional paper/International Monetary Fund
ISSN 0251-6365)
    Annual.
    Has occasional updates, 1984–
    ISSN 0258-7440 = World economic and financial surveys
    ISSN 0256-6877 = World economic outlook (Washington)
    1. Economic history—1971–   —Periodicals.   I. International
Monetary Fund.   II. Series: Occasional paper (International Monetary
Fund)
HC10.W7979   84-640155
                              338.5'443'09048—dc19
                                            AACR 2 MARC-S

Library of Congress   8507

    Published biannually.
ISBN 1-55775-567-1

The cover, charts, and interior of this publication
were designed and produced by the IMF Graphics Section

Price: US$34.00
(US$23.00 to full-time faculty members and
students at universities and colleges)

Please send orders to:
International Monetary Fund, Publication Services
700 19th Street, N.W., Washington, D.C. 20431, U.S.A.
Tel.: (202) 623-7430   Telefax: (202) 623-7201
Internet: publications@imf.org

recycled paper

Contents

Assumptions and Conventions

A number of assumptions have been adopted for the projections presented in the *World Economic Outlook*. It has been assumed that real effective exchange rates will remain constant at their average levels during February 16–March 14, 1996 except for the bilateral rates among the European exchange rate mechanism (ERM) currencies, which are assumed to remain constant in nominal terms; that established policies of national authorities will be maintained (for specific assumptions about fiscal and monetary polices in industrial countries, see Box 1 in Chapter 1); that the average price of oil will be $17.39 a barrel in 1996 and $16.12 a barrel in 1997, and remain unchanged in real terms over the medium term; and that the six-month London interbank offered rate (LIBOR) on U.S. dollar deposits will average 5.4 percent in 1996 and 5.6 percent in 1997. These are, of course, working hypotheses rather than forecasts, and the uncertainties surrounding them add to the margin of error that would in any event be involved in the projections. The estimates and projections are based on statistical information available on April 3, 1996.

The following conventions have been used throughout the *World Economic Outlook*:

. . .   to indicate that data are not available or not applicable;

—   to indicate that the figure is zero or negligible;

–   between years or months (for example, 1994–95 or January–June) to indicate the years or months covered, including the beginning and ending years or months;

/   between years or months (for example, 1994/95) to indicate a fiscal or financial year.

"Billion" means a thousand million; "trillion" means a thousand billion.

"Basis points" refer to hundredths of 1 percentage point (for example, 25 basis points are equivalent to $1/4$ of 1 percentage point).

Minor discrepancies between sums of constituent figures and totals shown are due to rounding.

*   *   *

As used in this report, the term "country" does not in all cases refer to a territorial entity that is a state as understood by international law and practice. As used here, the term also covers some territorial entities that are not states but for which statistical data are maintained on a separate and independent basis.

Preface

The projections and analysis contained in the *World Economic Outlook* are an integral element of the IMF's ongoing surveillance of economic developments and policies in its member countries and of the global economic system. The IMF has published the *World Economic Outlook* annually from 1980 through 1983 and biannually since 1984.

The survey of prospects and policies is the product of a comprehensive interdepartmental review of world economic developments, which draws primarily on information the IMF staff gathers through its consultations with member countries. These consultations are carried out in particular by the IMF's area departments together with the Policy Development and Review Department and the Fiscal Affairs Department.

The country projections are prepared by the IMF's area departments on the basis of internationally consistent assumptions about world activity, exchange rates, and conditions in international financial and commodity markets. For approximately 50 of the largest economies—accounting for 90 percent of world output—the projections are updated for each *World Economic Outlook* exercise. For smaller countries, the projections are based on those prepared at the time of the IMF's regular Article IV consultations with member countries or in connection with the use of IMF resources; for these countries, the projections used in the *World Economic Outlook* are incrementally adjusted to reflect changes in assumptions and global economic conditions.

The analysis in the *World Economic Outlook* draws extensively on the ongoing work of the IMF's area and specialized departments, and is coordinated in the Research Department under the general direction of Michael Mussa, Economic Counsellor and Director of Research. The *World Economic Outlook* project is directed by Flemming Larsen, Deputy Director, the Research Department, together with Graham Hacche, Chief of the World Economic Studies Division.

Primary contributors to the current issue are Francesco Caramazza, Robert F. Wescott, Staffan Gorne, Paula De Masi, James Haley, Mahmood Pradhan, Jahangir Aziz, John McDermott, and Cathy Wright. Other contributors include Liam Ebrill, Alain Feler, Oussama Kanaan, Manmohan S. Kumar, Douglas Laxton, Gabrielle Lipworth, Steven Symansky, and Anthony G. Turner. The authors of the annexes are indicated on the first page of each. The Fiscal Analysis Division of the Fiscal Affairs Department computed the structural budget and fiscal impulse measures. Sungcha Hong Cha, Toh Kuan, and Michelle Marquardt provided research assistance. Shamim Kassam, Allen Cobler, Nicholas Dopuch, Isabella Dymarskaia, Gretchen Gallik, Mandy Hemmati, and Yasoma Liyanarachchi processed the data and managed the computer systems. Susan Duff, Margarita Lorenz, and Margaret Dapaah were responsible for word processing. Juanita Roushdy of the External Relations Department edited the manuscript and coordinated production of the publication; Tom Walter coordinated production of the Arabic, French, and Spanish editions.

The analysis has benefited from comments and suggestions by staff from other IMF departments, as well as by Executive Directors following their discussion of the *World Economic Outlook* on March 27 and 29, 1996. However, both projections and policy considerations are those of the IMF staff and should not be attributed to Executive Directors or to their national authorities.

I

Global Economic Prospects and Policies

World economic growth has continued, on average, at a satisfactory pace, supported in particular by buoyant growth in many emerging market countries. However, growth slowed more markedly than expected during 1995 in western Europe and North America, leading to further increases in unemployment in some countries from already high levels and also to fears of a new economic downturn. In response, short-term interest rates have been reduced significantly and several countries have taken various fiscal and structural measures to revive confidence and stimulate job creation. While growth has clearly slowed below potential in some cases, the factors that appear to lie behind the slowdown are likely to prove temporary. There are also now clearer signs of an upturn in Japan. Overall, there do not seem to be grounds to expect a prolonged or generalized slowdown, and global growth is projected to pick up to around 4 percent a year in 1996 and 1997 from the rate of 3½ percent to which it slipped last year (Table 1).

The most pronounced deterioration in cyclical conditions since early 1995 has been in Germany, France, several other countries closely linked to the deutsche mark, and Switzerland. The timing and strength of the expected pickup in activity in these countries is somewhat uncertain, but the conditions appear to be in place for a quickening in the pace of economic growth during 1996. A strengthening of activity in these countries is essential to put unemployment securely on a downward path and to facilitate fiscal consolidation in accordance with the agreed timetable for Economic and Monetary Union (EMU). Conversely, a prolonged period of lackluster growth could exacerbate doubts about the EMU timetable and might lead to tensions in financial markets.

In other regions, the possibility of shifts in financial market sentiment in response to policy slippages also remains a potential downside risk. As witnessed on several occasions in the recent past, financial markets are highly sensitive to concerns about economic and financial imbalances, while the global economy has become more vulnerable to adverse market reactions (see the October 1995 *World Economic Outlook*). When doubt has arisen about the resolve of policymakers to tackle problems, markets have demonstrated their ability to force the necessary policy changes at substantial cost. Market discipline on economic policies, in contrast to self-discipline, often involves excessive volatility in asset prices, with seriously adverse consequences for activity and employment. Fortunately, it has become increasingly recognized that the global integration of markets requires greater policy discipline, and this recognition has been contributing to a strengthening of policy fundamentals in a growing number of countries in all regions.

In fact, a number of positive trends and developments point to the likelihood of continued, relatively solid world growth in the period ahead (Chart 1). Global inflationary pressures remain subdued. Notwithstanding an upturn in bond yields since January, real long-term interest rates are significantly lower than in most of the period since the early 1980s, owing in part to perceptions of stronger commitments to the reduction of fiscal imbalances in many industrial countries. Equity prices have continued to rise, reflecting strong profit performance as well as lower interest rates. And exchange rates among the major currencies have returned to levels more consistent with fundamentals, following the misalignments that arose in the spring of 1995. The correction of the overshooting of the yen has been particularly helpful in brightening the outlook for the Japanese economy.

Moreover, capital flows to emerging market countries have been generally well sustained following the containment of spillover effects from the Mexican crisis. Recoveries already seem to be under way in both Mexico and Argentina, and activity remains buoyant in many other emerging market countries where the danger of overheating appears to have subsided. In the transition economies of central and eastern Europe, the momentum of growth seems to have been stronger than projected last fall. There are also signs that output may have begun to recover in Russia. Some of the poorest countries, especially in Africa, have strengthened their growth performance and prospects as a result of intensified adjustment efforts. And world trade has continued to expand faster than past relationships between output and trade growth would seem to predict, reflecting the liberalization of trade and the trend toward current account convertibility in recent years together with the dynamic forces of globalization. Clearly, progress in implementing policies consistent with the global strategy set out by the Interim Committee three years ago, and reaffirmed in its

Table 1. Overview of the *World Economic Outlook* Projections

(Annual percent change unless otherwise noted)

	1994	1995	Current Projections 1996	Current Projections 1997	Differences from October 1995 Projections 1995	Differences from October 1995 Projections 1996
World output	**3.7**	**3.5**	**3.8**	**4.3**	**–0.2**	**–0.3**
Industrial countries	2.8	2.1	2.0	2.6	–0.2	–0.4
United States[1]	3.5	2.0	1.8	2.2	. . .	. . .
Japan	0.5	0.9	2.7	3.1	0.4	0.5
Germany	2.9	1.9	1.0	2.9	–0.6	–1.9
France	2.9	2.4	1.3	2.8	–0.5	–1.4
Italy	2.2	3.2	2.4	2.7	0.2	–0.4
United Kingdom	3.8	2.4	2.2	2.7	–0.3	–0.6
Canada	4.6	2.2	1.9	2.9	—	–0.7
Seven countries above	2.8	2.0	1.9	2.6	–0.1	–0.4
Other industrial countries	3.0	2.8	2.4	2.6	–0.4	–0.6
Memorandum						
European Union	2.8	2.6	1.8	2.7	–0.3	–1.0
Developing countries	6.4	5.9	6.3	6.4	–0.2	—
Africa	2.4	3.2	5.3	4.5	—	0.1
Asia	8.8	8.4	8.2	7.7	–0.3	0.3
Middle East and Europe	0.7	3.7	3.1	3.8	1.3	–0.1
Western Hemisphere	4.7	0.9	3.1	4.8	–1.0	–0.9
Countries in transition	–8.8	–1.3	2.5	3.8	0.8	–0.9
Central and eastern Europe	–2.9	1.4	3.0	4.2	1.2	–1.3
Excluding Belarus and Ukraine	3.4	5.2	4.5	4.6	1.2	0.1
Russia, Transcaucasus, and central Asia	–14.8	–4.3	1.9	3.3	0.3	–0.5
World trade volume (goods and services)	**9.0**	**8.7**	**6.4**	**7.0**	**0.7**	**–0.1**
Imports						
Industrial countries	9.1	7.3	4.8	5.0	0.2	–0.6
Developing countries	9.0	11.8	10.1	11.6	0.5	0.6
Countries in transition	4.3	10.9	11.6	10.1	. . .	. . .
Exports						
Industrial countries	8.2	7.1	4.8	5.4	0.2	–0.3
Developing countries	12.0	12.2	10.2	11.2	1.4	0.7
Countries in transition	5.3	11.8	8.9	7.2	. . .	. . .
Commodity prices in SDRs						
Oil[2]	–9.1	3.3	4.8	–7.2	2.2	10.9
Nonfuel[3]	10.8	2.4	2.0	–1.6	0.5	2.2
Consumer prices						
Industrial countries	2.3	2.4	2.3	2.5	–0.1	–0.3
Developing countries	48.0	19.9	12.6	9.8	0.4	–0.3
Countries in transition	264.8	128.2	38.2	13.6	–19.6	12.8
Six-month LIBOR (in percent)[4]						
On U.S. dollar deposits	5.1	6.1	5.4	5.6	–0.1	–0.8
On Japanese yen deposits	2.4	1.3	1.0	2.4	–0.1	–0.3
On deutsche mark deposits	5.3	4.6	3.3	4.5	—	–1.9

Note: Real effective exchange rates are assumed to remain constant at the levels prevailing during February 16–March 14, 1996, except for the bilateral rates among ERM currencies, which are assumed to remain constant in nominal terms.

[1]Exact comparison with the growth estimates in the October 1995 *World Economic Outlook* is not possible because of the change from a fixed-base-year method to a chain-weighted method of measuring real GDP, introduced in late 1995. In qualitative terms 1995 growth was somewhat weaker than estimated half a year ago, whereas the projection for 1996 is broadly similar to the one published in October.

[2]Simple average of spot prices of U.K. Brent, Dubai, and West Texas Intermediate crude oil. The average price of oil in U.S. dollars a barrel was $17.17 in 1995; the assumed price is $17.39 in 1996 and $16.12 in 1997.

[3]Average, based on world commodity export weights.

[4]London interbank offered rate.

October 1994 Madrid Declaration,[1] has brought significant results in many areas.

At the same time, it is apparent that many problems need to be addressed more adequately to strengthen growth in the medium to longer run, to reduce risks of adverse financial market reactions, and to enhance countries' resilience to economic disturbances. Despite some progress, budgetary imbalances in industrial countries remain a source of upward pressure on real interest rates and thus continue to crowd out private investment. Not only do these fiscal problems need to be addressed in a timely manner, but also early reforms of pension and health systems are needed to preempt even greater budgetary pressures in the future as populations age. There has been considerable progress since the early 1980s in the deregulation of financial markets and in other structural reforms, including further trade liberalization. In many countries, however, and especially in Europe, reforms of labor markets remain essential to reduce structural unemployment and to help alleviate fiscal imbalances.

Most developing countries have reduced fiscal imbalances substantially during the past decade. Together with trade liberalization and other structural reforms this has contributed to their robust economic performance in recent years. Many, however, continue to divert scarce resources from productive investment through large fiscal deficits. In addition, quasi-fiscal or off-budget involvement by governments in economic activity adversely affects economic incentives and growth in many countries. The transition countries also have achieved remarkable progress toward macroeconomic stability, and their budgetary imbalances have narrowed sharply. But in many cases fiscal deficits are still too large, and continuing government intervention in the economy on behalf of ailing sectors, including through off-budget operations, often remains a threat to the sustainability of recent reductions in inflation. Since such interventions are shielding enterprises and consumers from full exposure to market forces, these practices are also delaying the process of structural transformation and jeopardizing the prospects for sustained economic recovery.

Because many of these macroeconomic and structural policy challenges—which are often interrelated—are in the fiscal area, fiscal policy receives special attention in this issue of the *World Economic Outlook*.

Industrial Countries

Industrial country growth in 1995 was somewhat weaker than projected six months ago as the pace of expansion slowed significantly during the year in most countries. The slowdown, however, was far from uni-

Chart 1. World Indicators[1]
(In percent)

The global expansion is expected to continue with the growth of world output and trade above trend, while inflation should remain contained in industrial countries and slow further in developing countries.

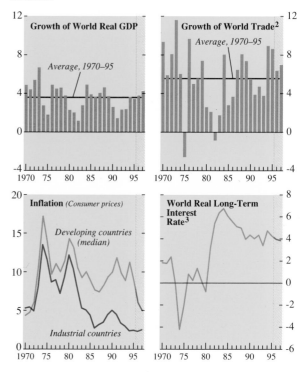

[1]Blue shaded areas indicate IMF staff projections.

[2]Goods and services, volume.

[3]GDP-weighted average of ten-year (or nearest maturity) government bond rates for the United States, Japan, Germany, France, Italy, the United Kingdom, and Canada. Excludes Italy prior to 1972.

---

[1]See page x of the October 1994 *World Economic Outlook*.

**Chart 2. Major Industrial Countries:
Unemployment Rates**
(Seasonally adjusted; in percent of labor force)

In continental Europe, unemployment rates have only fallen slightly since their cyclical peaks and have begun to edge up in recent months.

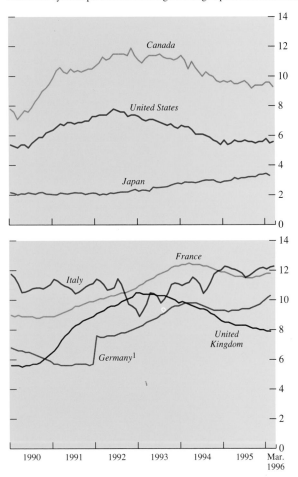

[1]Data through December 1991 cover west Germany only; data beginning with January 1992 are based on a revised methodology and are not comparable with earlier data.

form and was desirable in some cases to prevent the buildup of inflationary pressures. In the United States, although growth moderated to only 1¼ percent in the year to the fourth quarter of 1995, the economy, five years into its expansion, remained close to full capacity utilization; and by early 1996 there were signs of a renewed pickup. In Japan, activity remained lackluster under the influence of the strong yen and the uncertainties resulting from mounting problems in the financial sector, but by year-end, there were growing signs that the recovery was under way. In Europe, performance differed somewhat between the countries whose currencies have depreciated in recent years—including Italy, the United Kingdom, Sweden, and Spain—and the strong currency countries—Germany, France, other countries whose currencies have been kept closely linked to the deutsche mark, and Switzerland. In the former group—the "outer ring"—growth was better sustained and the slowdown that did occur was helpful in containing above-average inflation rates. In the hard currency group—the "inner core"—activity stagnated in the second half of 1995 and unemployment turned upward again before the recovery had made much headway (Chart 2).

Except in the United States and other countries at advanced stages of their recoveries, an economic slowdown during 1995 was not generally expected early in the year; and particularly in the inner core of Europe, the extent of the slowdown became apparent only quite recently. In retrospect, it appears that the substantial, worldwide rise of long-term interest rates during 1994 subsequently had a greater depressing effect on industrial country activity than expected. In addition, some of the effects of fiscal consolidation that were initially absorbed in some countries by private saving later materialized to reduce demand. Other developments unexpected at the beginning of 1995 also contributed to the slowdown: the sharp contraction in Mexico and the dramatic improvement in Mexico's trade balance had a significant negative impact on the U.S. economy early in the year; the large appreciation of the yen in the spring undercut the incipient Japanese recovery; and for the inner core countries of Europe, the appreciation of their currencies against the U.S. dollar and against other European currencies had a similar if less pronounced effect.

With the benefit of hindsight, it is also clear that the differences in performance between the inner core and the outer ring of European countries owe something to differences in the mix and stance of their economic policies. In the outer ring countries, relatively large fiscal imbalances have necessitated fairly restrictive fiscal stances, but monetary conditions have eased significantly during the past two to three years, especially taking into account not only the declines in short-term interest rates but also the depreciations of their currencies in the wake of the 1992–93 crises in the European Monetary System (EMS). In the hard currency group, not only have fiscal policies been restrictive, albeit to varying degrees—some countries did not take sufficient advantage of the 1994 recovery to reduce their fiscal deficits—but also monetary conditions—again broadly defined to take account of exchange rate developments—have remained relatively tight, at least until recent months. On balance, for western Europe as a whole, for which the movements in exchange rates had relatively little net effect on aggregate demand, the overall stance and mix of policies appear to have been more of a restraining factor than previously thought. The brunt of that restraint, however, has been borne by the strong currency countries, where it seems to have been amplified by unwarrantedly high wage settlements in Germany and confidence factors, including uncertainties about the future stance of policies and concern about the Maastricht convergence process. These forces have held back private consumption, as well as business investment, and have also led to reductions of inventories.

Economic policies, of course, reacted to these unexpected developments. However, economic policies, which always operate with a lag, could not have offset the unforeseen elements in the slowdown of activity in 1995. While monetary policies were generally eased as information became available about receding price pressures and slowing activity, for much of the year, assessments of the economic situation and prospects in Europe would not have justified a significantly faster easing than in fact occurred.

Looking ahead, however, there are good reasons to expect growth in Europe to pick up again in the course of 1996. The view that the recent weakness is temporary is supported by several developments. Most important, policy stances seem to be converging in a helpful way in the two groups of countries. Specifically, monetary conditions in the strong currency countries have eased markedly during the past year and fiscal consolidation efforts are also expected to strengthen, correcting the policy mix in a direction that is likely to be more conducive to growth. (The policy assumptions underlying the projections are set out in Box 1.) Moreover, progress toward fiscal consolidation in the outer ring has allowed risk premiums in interest rates to decline in most cases and has also helped to correct some of the undervaluation in currencies, although there is scope for further exchange rate appreciation as fiscal consolidation continues. Also, there are already some indications that the inventory adjustment process may have run its course. While the timing and strength of the expected pickup is somewhat uncertain, a prolonged period of weakness is unlikely.

Nevertheless, to facilitate a robust recovery in Europe, and to insure against downside risks, it is important that the available scope for further easing of monetary conditions in the hard currency countries be fully utilized without compromising the goal of medium-term price stability. Room for further de-

clines in short-term interest rates in these countries is suggested by their large margins of slack, subdued price pressures, the strength of their exchange rates, and modest growth of monetary aggregates in most cases during the past year. It is particularly important that the stance of monetary policy provides support for activity as fiscal consolidation efforts continue. Further fiscal consolidation must be actively pursued in the weak-currency countries as well; monetary policy in these countries needs to be firmly geared to achieving medium-term inflation objectives.

The continued need for fiscal consolidation reflects the paramount importance of re-establishing a more balanced policy mix conducive to stronger sustained growth in Europe. Further fiscal consolidation is also essential to allow the Maastricht process to proceed as planned. For these reasons and because of the implications for interest rates and financial market confidence if fiscal policy were eased, it is imperative to maintain adequate progress toward budgetary consolidation, particularly on the expenditure side of government budgets. Some quickening in the pace of expenditure consolidation would be in order in virtually all countries. If, contrary to the central projection in this report, there were a prolonged period of weakness, adequate progress in reducing structural imbalances would still allow fiscal policy to provide automatic stabilizers for activity. Further progress toward labor market reform also remains essential to tackle the root causes of high structural unemployment.

The weakening of activity in much of Europe and associated increases in fiscal deficits have prompted concerns about the feasibility of the timetable for EMU. Respect for the conditions for participation set out in the Maastricht Treaty is important and the achievement of the Maastricht fiscal criterion, given the projected pickup in growth during 1996, is clearly feasible and worthwhile for most EU members. At the same time, the historic decision to introduce a common currency, and the related decision on which countries will initially participate in this endeavor, presumably will reflect broader political and economic considerations. The introduction of a common currency and the establishment of an independent European central bank dedicated to the goal of price stability will bring potentially important long-run benefits in the form of greater financial and macroeconomic stability among the participants in the monetary union. For these benefits of monetary union to be realized, its participants will need to achieve and sustain a high degree of fiscal discipline. This suggests that the assessment of progress toward meeting the conditions for participation should be viewed in a longer-run context, taking into account the ability of governments to correct structural as well as actual fiscal imbalances and to make binding commitments to appropriate mechanisms for fiscal discipline beyond the test year of 1997 (see Appendix to Chapter II).

Box 1. Policy Assumptions Underlying the Projections

Fiscal policy assumptions for the short term are based on official budgets adjusted for any deviations in outturn as estimated by IMF staff and also for differences in economic assumptions between IMF staff and national authorities. The assumptions for the medium term take into account announced future policy measures that are judged likely to be implemented. In cases where future budget intentions have not been announced with sufficient specificity to permit a judgment about the feasibility of their implementation, an unchanged structural primary balance is assumed. For selected industrial countries, the specific assumptions adopted are as follows.

United States: For the period through FY 1999, fiscal revenues and outlays at the federal level are based on the average between those assumed in the administration's March 1996 budget proposal (using Congressional Budget Office assumptions) and the Congress's Balanced Budget Act of November 1995, after adjusting for differences between the IMF staff's macroeconomic assumptions and those of the Congressional Budget Office. From FY 2000 onward, the federal government primary balance as a proportion of GDP is assumed to remain unchanged from its projected FY 1999 level.

Japan: Measures that have already been announced are assumed to be implemented over the medium term. These measures include an increase in the consumption tax rate from 3 percent to 5 percent in 1997 and a simultaneous end to the temporary income tax cut, implementation of the 1994 pension reform plan, and achievement of the medium-term public investment plan.

Germany: The 1996 projection for the general government is based on the 1996 federal budget and recent official estimates for the other levels of government, adjusted for differences in macroeconomic projections. In 1997, the social security funds are assumed to close their

deficits mainly through higher contribution rates (as mandated by existing legislation), while other levels of government are assumed to follow unchanged policies. Projections for 1998 and beyond are predicated on an unchanged structural primary balance.

France: Projections incorporate the 1996 budget of the state and all policy measures announced by the authorities, including the FF 20 billion in additional expenditure cuts announced in March. The projections, however, do not include any measures (as yet unspecified and unannounced) that might be taken in connection with the 1997 budget. The reference point for social security is the reform package announced in November last year. Some of the measures in this package have already been implemented and are included in the projection; several other important measures, concerning mainly the control of medical expenditure, are also assumed to be implemented in 1996 and 1997; the relatively small number of measures that have been dropped by the government are excluded. However, the revenues of the social security system will be adversely affected by the slowdown in economic activity in the second half of 1995 and the relatively slow pace of economic growth in 1996. Projections for 1998 and beyond assume an unchanged structural primary balance.

Italy: Projections for 1996 are based on the official budget, adjusted for slippages from the authorities' estimates of the likely yield of the legislated measures and for known expenditures not provided for (current and back payments under the Constitutional Court sentences on pensions and the phased payment of tax refund liabilities postponed from 1995). Interest on zero-coupon bonds is included as it accrues, rather than when it is paid (as is the case in the official presentation). For 1997–98, it is assumed that the measures (*manovra*) announced in the three-year plan are fully implemented and yield the offi-

Budgetary problems are a threat to durable and satisfactory growth performance in almost all industrial countries. To be sure, many countries have worked in recent years to reduce excessive fiscal deficits, and policymakers continue to express their firm commitment to restoring better balance in public finances. But fiscal consolidation increasingly requires cuts in expenditure programs that are strongly supported by particular groups. Since the benefits of such cuts to society as a whole are not so visible and may be felt mainly in the longer run, the political difficulties associated with them—illustrated by recent social unrest in France, the budgetary stalemate in the United States, and the costly bailouts of some large enterprises in several European countries—may delay the progress needed. The risk of slippages in consolidation efforts is all the more disquieting since the fiscal burden of

public health and pension systems as presently structured is projected to increase considerably throughout most of the industrial world in the coming decades.

Increases in taxes are unlikely to provide a substantial part of the solution to the fiscal problems, because tax burdens are already very high in most countries and there is concern that higher levels of taxation may further distort resource allocation, adversely affect employment, and reduce long-term growth. There is also preliminary evidence, reported in Chapter III, that fiscal consolidation based on tax increases has been much less effective in achieving fiscal goals than measures to contain the growth in expenditures. Indeed, many industrial countries could probably strengthen their economic performance by reducing the shares of government expenditures and taxes in GDP. The additional pressures on public finances associated with

cially estimated amounts. Thereafter, the structural primary balance is presumed to remain unchanged.

United Kingdom: The budgeted three-year spending ceilings are assumed to be observed. Thereafter, noncyclical spending is assumed to grow in line with potential GDP. For revenues, the projections incorporate, through the three-year budget horizon, the announced commitment to raise excises on tobacco and road fuels each year in real terms; thereafter, real tax rates are assumed to remain constant.

Canada: Federal government outlays for departmental spending and business subsidies conform to the medium-term commitments announced in the March 1996 budget. Other outlays and revenues are assumed to evolve in line with projected macroeconomic developments. However, the unemployment insurance (UI) premium is assumed to fall in 1998/99 to a level that is consistent with an unchanged surplus in the UI account. The fiscal situation of the provinces is assumed to be consistent with their stated medium-term deficit targets.

Australia: Projections are based on the Commonwealth government's announced medium-term fiscal consolidation strategy in the 1995/96 budget and unchanged policies for the state and local governments.

Netherlands: Projections are based on the government's medium-term target expenditure path for the central government and social security. Only part of the room under the general government annual deficit ceilings is allocated to deficit reductions; the bulk is allocated to tax and social security premium reductions. From 1999 onward, the general government structural balance is assumed to remain constant.

Spain: Projections for 1996 are based on the rollover of the 1995 budget as modified by several decree laws, and adjusted for differences in macroeconomic assumptions

and similar slippages on budgeted expenditures as occurred in 1995. For 1997, revenue estimates are based on the assumption of an unchanged tax structure, but the personal income tax schedule and excise taxes are adjusted for inflation.

Sweden: The medium-term projections are based on the government's multiyear consolidation program approved by Parliament in 1995.

Switzerland: Projections for 1997–99 are based on official estimates for current services. Thereafter, the general government structural primary balance is assumed to remain constant.

* * *

Monetary policy assumptions are based on the established framework for monetary policy in each country, which in most cases implies a nonaccommodative stance over the business cycle. Hence, it is generally assumed that official interest rates will firm when economic indicators, including monetary aggregates, suggest that inflation will rise above its acceptable rate or range and ease when the indicators suggest that prospective inflation does not exceed the acceptable rate or range and that prospective output growth is below its potential rate. For the ERM countries, which use monetary policy to adhere to exchange rate anchors, official interest rates are assumed to move in line with those in Germany, except that progress on fiscal consolidation may influence interest differentials relative to Germany. On this basis, it is assumed that the London interbank offered rate (LIBOR) on six-month U.S. dollar deposits will average 5.6 percent in 1996 and 5½ percent in 1997; that the three-month certificate of deposit rate in Japan will average 1 percent in 1996 and 2.4 percent in 1997; and that the three-month interbank deposit rate in Germany will average 3.6 percent in 1996 and 4.6 percent in 1997.

aging populations underscore the need for fundamental reforms of public expenditure programs. In many cases, it will be necessary to rethink the role of the public sector in achieving key social objectives.[2] A particularly important area of reform is the broad range of social expenditure policies and regulations that impede the functioning of labor markets.

In contrast to the recent mixed growth performance of the industrial countries, low inflation remains a particularly encouraging aspect of current economic conditions in most of them. The countries most advanced in the expansion, including the United States and the

United Kingdom, began to tighten monetary conditions in 1994 to pre-empt potential inflationary pressures. This vigilance met with considerable success, and moderate inflation and growth have allowed these countries to ease monetary conditions in recent months. Elsewhere, success with inflation has allowed monetary authorities to respond to currency appreciations, rising unemployment, and moderate monetary growth by reducing official interest rates. In Japan, virtually all room for maneuver in easing monetary policy has now been used, and the accommodative stance established last summer is assisting in the recovery of activity; while there is little near-term risk of inflation, monetary conditions will obviously need to firm once the recovery is well established. In Germany and many other European countries, official interest rates have been lowered substantially in the past year

---

[2]See Vito Tanzi and Ludger Schuknecht, "The Growth of Government and the Reform of the State in Industrial Countries," IMF Working Paper 95/130 (December 1995).

because of mounting concerns about the sluggishness of monetary indicators and activity, and in the context of generally strong currencies. In the circumstances, this easing has involved no danger of stimulating inflation and thereby jeopardizing medium-term growth prospects.

With regard to prospects for individual countries, growth in the *United States* is expected to be sustained at rates close to potential in 1996–97 with inflation remaining subdued.[3] Fears of slower growth in 1996 have diminished with buoyant data, especially for employment, for the opening months of the year, and the economy will continue to be boosted by the easing of monetary conditions that has occurred since mid-1995. Evidence of a strengthening of activity has removed expectations of a further easing of monetary policy and has contributed to the recent rise in long-term interest rates. Nevertheless, long-term interest rates remain well below their level in early 1995. Further fiscal consolidation remains critical to strengthen national saving and improve long-term growth prospects.

Although the U.S. budget deficit has fallen sharply in recent years, it threatens to increase again in the absence of new measures. Unfortunately, the administration and Congress have so far failed to resolve their differences on specific measures to balance the budget over the medium term, and the proposals of both sides are disappointing with respect to the envisaged speed of consolidation. To justify and sustain confidence in financial markets, the debate over the budget should be resolved in a manner that ensures continued deficit reduction in 1996 and the next several years. A back-loaded deficit reduction program depending heavily on unspecified, future measures could raise fears that the promised deficit-reductions might not be delivered. Moreover, substantial tax cuts should be postponed until deficit reduction is substantially achieved.

In *Canada*, the pace of economic recovery slowed markedly in 1995 owing to the tightening of monetary conditions early in the year and the risk premiums in interest rates that resulted from political and economic uncertainties, as well as the slowdown in the United States. Following the referendum on Quebec in October, confidence improved and interest rates fell significantly, which should permit the pace of economic activity to pick up during 1996. Fiscal imbalances have diminished considerably in recent years but the federal and provincial governments will need to ensure that further consolidation is achieved in 1996 and over the medium term. Inflation has remained low,

which provides some flexibility for further easing of monetary policy if warranted by cyclical considerations and by further progress on the fiscal front. Overall, conditions are good for Canada's expansion to proceed at a healthy rate.

Economic activity now appears to be picking up in *Japan* after protracted sluggishness that has left the economy with considerable margins of unused resources. The supportive stance of both monetary and fiscal policies and the correction of the yen's excessive appreciation in early 1995 provide good reasons for expecting recovery to continue in 1996. Confidence in the financial system has begun to improve with the announcement of a strategy for resolving the financial problems of Japanese banks, steps to deal more effectively with failed institutions, and plans to strengthen banking supervision. Nevertheless, extricating financial institutions from their bad loans problem could act as a drag on the pace of recovery. Fiscal policy is appropriately aimed at providing continuing support in 1996 but budgetary consolidation will need to resume when the recovery gathers enough momentum to permit a withdrawal of stimulus.

In those European countries where the expansion has been marking time since mid-1995, evidence of a turnaround is still mixed even though conditions seem to be in place for a resumption of growth in the second half of 1996. In *Germany*, the strength of the exchange rate and the disappointing outcome of the 1995 wage round seem to have hurt the investment climate while export growth has also slowed. A related problem has been a drop in consumer confidence. Declines in interest rates and a buoyant equity market provide some basis for optimism with respect to chances of a pickup later in 1996, although the rise in real GDP is unlikely to be more than about 1 percent for the year. Even though growth in the key monetary policy indicator, M3, picked up somewhat in early 1996, subdued inflation and slack in the economy suggest room for further reduction of short-term interest rates. Following a larger-than-expected fiscal deficit in 1995, it is important to maintain discipline on the side of discretionary expenditures, although some allowance for the working of automatic stabilizers through the accommodation of weaker revenues would seem warranted. There is also a need to limit the deficits of state and local governments as well as pension funds; these were in fact the major source of the increase in the overall fiscal deficit last year.

Weakness of both consumer and investor confidence also contributed to the stagnation of activity in *France* in the second half of 1995 and to the downgrading of growth projections for 1996 to some 1–1½ percent. As in Germany, however, and as discussed earlier, activity is expected to strengthen during the year. Resistance to the government's fiscal and structural reform proposals, together with the renewed rise in unemployment to almost 12 percent of the labor force in early 1996, may

---

[3]On the new chain-weighted measure of real GDP, the potential growth rate is widely considered to be in the range of 2 to 2½ percent. Uncertainties about the level of the unemployment rate consistent with reasonable price stability mainly affect the level of potential output, not its growth rate. The reasons for the introduction of a chain-weighted measure of real GDP are discussed in Box 2.

Box 2. United States: Chain-Weighted Method for Estimating Real GDP

A "chain-weighted" procedure recently became the primary method used by the Bureau of Economic Analysis (BEA) of the U.S. Department of Commerce to separate nominal (or current-dollar) changes in GDP into their quantity-change and price-change elements. It thus became the primary method used to measure growth in the U.S. economy.[1] This method is free of the biases that tended to arise with the previously used "fixed-base-year" method because of structural shifts in the U.S. economy and, in particular, the sharp decline in the price of computers.

Under the fixed-base-year method, real GDP was estimated by using prices in a particular base year—most recently, 1987—to value each category of expenditure in the economy. Real GDP was calculated as the sum of the expenditure components valued at base-year prices; the growth in real GDP was simply the percent change in this sum. A major advantage of this technique was that real GDP could easily be decomposed into its parts (e.g., the major expenditure aggregates of private consumption, investment, government spending, and net exports) so that it was relatively straightforward to determine how each expenditure component contributed to growth.

Shifts in the structure of the U.S. economy, however, highlighted the sensitivity of GDP growth estimated by the fixed-base-year method to the choice of base year. The more distant in the past was the base year, the greater was the weight given to expenditure items where prices had subsequently been declining, or rising relatively slowly. These also tended to be the expenditures that had exhibited strongest growth, owing to substitution in demand away from goods whose relative prices were rising. As a result, the earlier was the base year, the more upwardly biased were estimates of subsequent real GDP growth. And when the base year was eventually updated—typically every five years—estimates of real GDP growth were revised downward. The sharp declines in computer prices beginning in the 1980s, and the dramatic expansion in the importance of this sector in the economy, highlighted this shortcoming of the fixed-base-year method. The BEA has estimated that the earlier change in the base year from 1982 to 1987 resulted in an average decline of 0.3 of 1 percentage point in GDP growth for the period 1982–88.

The chain-weighted method shifts the base year forward each year and therefore allows for continuous up-

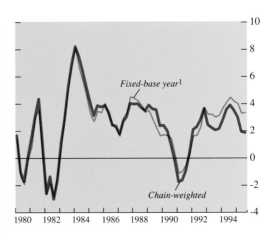

Chain-Weighted and Fixed-Base-Year Estimates of Real GDP
(Percent change from four quarters earlier)

Source: U.S. Department of Commerce, Bureau of Economic Analysis.
[1]Base year is 1987.

dating of weights. This has the advantage of eliminating the upward bias to real GDP growth that tended to be a feature of the fixed-base-year method (*see chart*). For example, the growth rate of real GDP for 1995 is calculated by averaging two estimates of growth: one with 1995 as the base year and the other with 1994 as base. Use of the chain-weighted method reduces the risk of potentially large revisions to historical estimates of real GDP. Although with the chain-weighted method it is not possible to decompose exactly the *level* of real GDP into its components, it is possible to decompose the *growth* of real GDP into the contributions of changes in the different (expenditure or output) components. It has been estimated that the change from 1987 fixed weights to the chain-weighted methodology lowered measured real GDP growth in 1995 by about ½ of 1 percentage point.

Beginning with this issue of the *World Economic Outlook*, national accounts data and projections for the United States are based on chain-weighted estimates.

---

[1]Among other industrial countries, Norway and the Netherlands also use the chain-weighted method to estimate real GDP.

have contributed to the waning of confidence. The government's firm stance has helped to re-establish market confidence, strengthen the franc, and permit an easing of short-term interest rates relative to Germany. Even though there is still a risk of slower growth with the possibility of renewed turbulence in the foreign ex-

change markets, this risk can be limited by the continuation of efforts to implement a more balanced policy mix.

Following vigorous expansion in 1994, the *United Kingdom* experienced a moderation of growth during 1995, which helped to alleviate inflationary pressures.

The economy is supported by gains in external competitiveness since 1992 and by recent declines in interest rates, and the outlook is for continued moderate growth, with inflation easing gradually now that earlier input cost increases appear to have worked through. The fiscal measures announced in the November budget were neutral, but mainly owing to shortfalls in revenue performance the path of medium-term fiscal consolidation has been shifted back a year. Little if any further easing of monetary conditions would seem warranted unless activity were to weaken markedly.

In *Italy*, the lira's sharp depreciation between 1992 and early 1995 led to gains in external competitiveness that helped buoy economic activity, while at the same time boosting inflation. Despite the difficulties affecting major trading partners and political uncertainties at home, growth was relatively high in 1995 because of exceptionally strong exports and is expected to remain stronger than in most other European countries in 1996. Visible progress in fiscal consolidation, together with favorable international market conditions, helped the lira to regain ground and to narrow the large interest-rate differentials relative to Germany. For the period ahead, it is essential to sustain fiscal consolidation to bring about a favorable cycle of deficit reduction, interest rate declines, a desirable firming of the lira, reduced inflation, and a more balanced economic expansion; however, there is a risk that political uncertainties and policy slippages may reverse recent improvements in economic and financial conditions.

Among the other industrial countries, *Sweden, Finland*, and *Spain* have also experienced both relatively rapid export growth following earlier gains in competitiveness and improvements in financial market confidence thanks to progress in reducing fiscal imbalances. In *Ireland*, the expansion has remained particularly buoyant with few signs of inflationary pressures. In *Denmark* and *Norway*, a slowing of growth since mid-1995 has alleviated the danger of overheating stemming from their relatively strong economic expansions since 1993. *Switzerland* has been particularly seriously affected by the strength of its currency—up by 20 percent in real effective terms since 1992—and by a loss of market shares at home and abroad. As a result, real GDP is projected to grow by less than 1 percent in 1996, not much better than in 1995. In response to the strength of the exchange rate and weakness of activity, official interest rates have been eased considerably and long-term interest rates have dropped to about 4 percent, the lowest in Europe.

While most other industrial countries continue to struggle with fiscal problems, *New Zealand* provides a remarkable contrast, with the budget having been in surplus since 1994. Helped by pathbreaking structural and institutional reforms, the disciplined fiscal policy pursued by New Zealand has contributed to above-average growth, declining unemployment, and price stability. *Australia*'s economic performance has also been very good in recent years, with a significant improvement in its fiscal position, although inflation edged up somewhat in 1995. For both countries, near-term prospects remain better than for most other industrial countries although fiscal and monetary policies will need to be alert to the challenge of maintaining growth in a way that avoids inflationary pressures and ensures a sustainable current account position.

Developing Countries

The growth momentum of many developing countries and the developing world's increased resilience to external disturbances, noted in earlier issues of the *World Economic Outlook*, are strong reasons to expect that the recent weakness in some industrial countries will not extend to a generalized global slowdown. The emerging market economies of Asia are likely to remain particularly buoyant, although growth is expected to moderate in several of them. This should help to alleviate inflationary pressures and reduce current account imbalances associated in part with large private capital inflows. Nevertheless, actions already taken in *Indonesia, Malaysia,* and *Thailand* to dampen domestic demand may need to be followed up by additional measures of restraint.

The *Chinese* economy appears to have achieved a soft landing after a prolonged period of overheating. Inflation has fallen to less than half the rate seen in 1994, and output growth has slowed to about 10 percent; continuing rapid monetary expansion, however, puts this progress at risk. The strength of the external sector provides a good opportunity for accelerating trade liberalization and for removing the remaining exchange restrictions on current transactions. Other policy priorities include the strengthening of public finances, the hardening of budget constraints on state-owned enterprises, and reforming the financial sector.

Elsewhere in Asia, *India*'s growth remained strong in 1995, reflecting a surge in investment and strongly growing exports, but is expected to moderate somewhat during 1996 as higher interest rates restrain domestic demand. Further progress with budgetary consolidation and structural reform after the elections are essential to sustain and strengthen growth. In the *Philippines*, economic recovery is expected to become more firmly established this year. Continued implementation of fiscal and structural reforms as well as a firm anti-inflationary monetary stance are needed to keep the economy on a sustainable growth path.

In Latin America, the consequences and spillovers from the financial crisis that engulfed Mexico in late 1994 and early 1995 have eased substantially. In *Mexico*, following a difficult year that saw real output contract by almost 7 percent, the recovery that has already begun is expected to gather strength during 1996. There are still risks arising from fragilities in the banking sector, and continuing fiscal discipline will be needed to maintain market confidence. In *Argentina* also, the adjustment efforts undertaken in the wake of the repercussions from the Mexican crisis should permit the recovery that appears to be under way to gain momentum in 1996. In *Brazil*, monthly inflation was brought down from 43 percent in the first half of 1994 to 1½ percent in 1995. This reflects the success of the Real Plan, which included the elimination of most forms of backward-looking indexation, the introduction of a new currency, and tight credit policy, which subsequently led to a nominal appreciation of the exchange rate. The fiscal situation weakened in 1995, however, and a strengthening of the public finances and structural reforms is critical to ensure the continued success of the Real Plan and stronger growth on a sustained basis. *Chile*, the strongest performer in Latin America, tightened its monetary policy late in 1995 amid signs of overheating. Growth is expected to slow from 8 percent in 1995 to a still impressive 6 percent in 1996, while inflation should moderate further.

Growth performance in Africa, especially in sub-Saharan Africa, is expected to continue to improve as a result of the implementation of stronger macroeconomic and structural policies in an increasing number of countries in recent years. Most countries of the CFA franc zone have seen continued recovery following the restoration of competitiveness by the devaluation of 1994 and supporting policies. In *South Africa*, activity, especially in manufacturing, is picking up with the country's reintegration into the global economy. Strong recovery is also under way in *Ghana*, *Kenya*, and *Uganda*. In a number of other countries, however, including *Nigeria* and *Zaïre*, economic conditions remain difficult. Further policy improvements will be needed for significant and sustained increases in living standards to be achieved.

In the Middle East and Europe region, economic performance and prospects have strengthened in several countries as a result of stronger macroeconomic and structural policies, as well as some overall improvement in regional stability (see Annex II). Growth in *Jordan* is expected to remain buoyant thanks to sustained structural adjustment policies. For many of the oil producing countries, however, large (albeit declining) fiscal deficits and weak oil prices continue to cloud the outlook. Economic activity in *Egypt* has continued to be constrained by structural impediments. *Turkey* saw rapid expansion in 1995, but sustained growth is threatened by continuing macroeconomic imbalances.

Notwithstanding many remaining problems, strengthened fiscal policies have played a key role in the solid economic performance of the developing countries in recent years. Overall, fiscal deficits at the level of central government have been cut by two thirds since the mid-1980s and currently average about 2 percent of GDP. In the Western Hemisphere, the remaining imbalances are relatively small, but the low national saving rates in that region point to the importance of further improvements in fiscal positions. In Asia, the overall picture has also improved although persistently large fiscal imbalances in some countries, particularly in the Indian subcontinent, continue to divert scarce resources from private investment. In several of the emerging market countries in Asia, some tightening of fiscal policies would help alleviate the risks associated with large capital inflows. In the Middle East, average fiscal deficits have fallen from over 12 percent of GDP in 1983–88 to 4 percent of GDP in 1995. But further efforts are clearly required, especially in some of the oil exporting countries. The average fiscal deficit in Africa has been halved since 1993 to also reach about 4 percent of GDP in 1995 (the median deficit has fallen from 7 percent of GDP in 1993 to 4½ percent of GDP in 1995).

Weaknesses in revenue mobilization, which reflect not only narrow tax bases but also inefficient tax administrations, are a serious problem in many developing countries. This hampers the ability of governments to provide basic public services and maintain adequate levels of investment in infrastructure. And in some cases it also contributes importantly to large fiscal deficits that undermine macroeconomic stability.

In many developing countries, the emphasis on expenditure reductions in fiscal consolidation may partly have reflected difficulties in mobilizing higher revenues, but there has been a general tendency toward reducing public expenditures in activities that can be carried out more efficiently by the private sector. The share of military expenditures in GDP has also fallen. If sustained, the declining share of public expenditures allocated to less productive activities should permit greater efforts in the areas of education, health care, and poverty alleviation. In addition, and important from a structural as well as a macroeconomic perspective, government intervention in the economy through quasi-fiscal activities has been substantially curtailed in many developing countries thanks to privatization, deregulation, and trade liberalization. Although the overall degree of government intervention in the economy is still often significantly higher than suggested by the ratio of government expenditure to GDP, and often constitutes a serious impediment to higher sustainable rates of economic growth, the general trend is very promising.

Transition Countries

Many of the transition countries have achieved considerable progress with macroeconomic stabilization and reform, and the fruits of their efforts to transform their economies are increasingly visible. Clearly, the transition process is working.

Following the turnaround in activity in 1994, the recovery in central and eastern Europe (excluding Belarus and Ukraine) gained further momentum in 1995. The region is expected to continue to grow at about the same pace in 1996–97 as last year—4 to 5 percent a year—with the potential for even stronger growth over the medium term if the policy challenges facing these countries are successfully addressed. *Poland*, the *Czech* and *Slovak Republics*, and *Slovenia* have achieved some of the most impressive results. Disciplined financial policies, structural reforms, trade liberalization, and rapid growth of trade, especially with western Europe, are important factors contributing to the rapid transformation that is taking place in these economies. Among the central Asian transition countries, *Mongolia*'s economic performance also shows the fruits of the country's reform efforts.

Many of the countries that are less advanced in the transition have made significant progress with structural reform, including price liberalization, privatization, and the dismantling of trade barriers. There has also been progress toward macroeconomic stability, although the sustainability of recent reductions in inflation is in doubt in some cases. Output appears to have bottomed out during 1995 in *Russia*, and a convincing recovery should emerge during 1996 provided policies stay on track. Economic prospects have also improved in *Kazakstan*, the *Kyrgyz Republic*, *Moldova*, *Armenia*, *Georgia*, and *Uzbekistan*. *Ukraine* made considerable progress with stabilization and systemic reform in 1995; in the absence of policy slippages, the decline in output should bottom out in 1996. In *Belarus*, *Tajikistan*, and *Turkmenistan*, where reform and stabilization efforts have been inadequate thus far, the contraction of output may well continue. Armed conflicts continue to delay the necessary reforms in several other countries, but throughout the former Yugoslavia prospects for recovery have now improved following the cessation of hostilities in *Bosnia and Herzegovina*.

Initial success with stabilization is no guarantee that inflation will not re-emerge. In some of the countries that are most advanced in the transition, capital inflows have helped to ease financing constraints, stimulate activity, and permit a more rapid replacement of obsolete capital equipment. Capital inflows also facilitate privatization and enterprise restructuring, thus promoting the role of market forces in the allocation of resources. However, as in other parts of the world, large-scale capital inflows may increase inflationary pressures unless macroeconomic policies are adjusted appropriately. Moreover, capital flows could prove to be disruptive outflows when domestic or external imbalances are large. To alleviate such risks, Hungary has implemented a program of fiscal consolidation that should put the ratio of external debt to GDP on a sustainable downward path, while Poland has allowed its currency to harden somewhat and the Czech Republic has widened its intervention band.

For the transition countries, achieving and sustaining macroeconomic stability is inextricably linked to the process of enterprise and bank restructuring and the reform of social safety nets. In many of these countries, standard fiscal indicators suggest that the reduction in fiscal imbalances has been accompanied by a substantial decline in government involvement in the economy. Further deficit reduction, however, is needed in most cases. There are also a number of indirect channels through which governments in some of these countries continue to influence resource allocation, including through directed credits and explicit or implicit loan guarantees, as well as by acquiescing in a dangerous accumulation of tax, wage, and inter-enterprise arrears. Moreover, there are likely to be budgetary implications from the substantial portfolios of problem loans in both the state-owned and private banks. Such problems, which vary in magnitude, constitute a potentially serious threat to macroeconomic stability and sustained recovery in some countries because of the possibility that the associated budgetary outlays will be monetized. Moreover, such practices are in many cases preventing or delaying the structural transformation of enterprises and therefore continue to distort economic incentives. The lack of respect for contractual commitments and reluctance of the authorities to enforce payments threaten to undermine the progress toward market-based economies. As emphasized by Adam Smith,

> Commerce and manufactures can seldom flourish long in any state which does not enjoy a regular administration of justice, in which the people do not feel themselves secure in the possession of their property, in which the faith of contracts is not supported by law, and in which the authority of the state is not supposed to be regularly employed in enforcing the payment of debts from all those who are able to pay.[4]

Social concerns are undoubtedly part of the reason for the continued and, in some instances, increased resort to quasi-fiscal measures of support to industry. To overcome this problem, it is necessary to put in place well-targeted unemployment and health insurance systems that will allow social responsibilities to be shifted away from enterprises. There is also an urgent need to reform pension systems. Because of particularly adverse demographic trends, many of the transition countries will need to reduce incentives for early retirement, increase contribution rates, and raise retirement ages in order to put pension systems on a sustainable footing.

---

[4]*Wealth of Nations, 1776* (New York; The Modern Library, 1937), p. 862.

II

World Economic Situation and Short-Term Prospects

In 1995, world economic growth weakened slightly to 3½ percent, which is marginally below both its long-term trend rate and the projection published in the October 1995 *World Economic Outlook* (see Table 1). This slight change in overall growth performance, however, masks a significant slowing of growth in the industrial countries and among the developing countries of the Western Hemisphere, and improved performance in Africa (especially the CFA countries), the Middle East, and the countries in transition.[5] Among the industrial countries, the slowdown in activity during 1995 was particularly marked in Germany, France, and a number of other countries in western Europe, while the poorer performance in the developing countries of the Western Hemisphere is essentially accounted for by output declines in Mexico, Argentina, and Uruguay. In the Asian developing countries, growth remained rapid although it moderated slightly, allaying concerns about overheating in some countries. Inflation remained low in industrial countries and declined significantly in developing countries and countries in transition. World trade again grew at more than double the rate of world output.

Although, as discussed in Chapter I, prospects are favorable for continuing world growth of around 4 percent this year and next, there are a number of potential threats to the global expansion. In Europe, growth performance and short-term prospects have deteriorated considerably since early last year, owing partly to (and contributing to) flagging consumer and business confidence. In the United States, failure to make expected progress toward balancing the budget risks unsettling financial markets. Elsewhere, shifts in investor sentiment, for instance in response to changed assessments of economic policies, may pose particular risks for those transition and developing countries with weak banking systems and limited capacities to intermediate large capital flows. While such concerns indicate downside risks to the near-term outlook, the tensions and imbalances that typically presage a downturn in activity are generally absent.

Economic Activity and Policy Stances in Industrial Countries

Average growth in the industrial countries of 2 percent in 1995 was somewhat below earlier projections. Moreover, the distribution across countries was markedly different from that expected in October, especially when considering developments within the year. Thus growth in North America, having weakened sharply in the first half of last year, rebounded in the third quarter but subsequently waned. In Japan, economic activity remained sluggish for most of 1995, but by the end of the year there were increasing signs that activity was beginning to pick up. In Europe, by contrast, growth generally weakened from early last year, although there were significant variations across countries.

In fact, in all the major industrial countries other than Japan, economic growth slowed during 1995 (Chart 3). The nascent recovery in Japan reflects the substantial easing of monetary and fiscal policies last summer and early fall, the reversal since last spring of the earlier sharp appreciation of the yen, and the authorities' announcement in late December of a strategy for resolving problems in the financial sector. For some countries where expansion has weakened, such as the United States, the United Kingdom, and Australia, the slowdown was from growth rates considerably above potential to rates more consistent with sustained noninflationary growth, and reflected the effects of monetary tightening and rising bond yields during 1994. But for countries where the recovery has made less headway and where there are still significant margins of slack, notably Germany, France, and several other European countries, the weakening of growth is of much greater concern.

The slowdown in Europe seems to reflect a number of adverse forces important to varying degrees in different countries, together with the high degree of integration and interdependence among the European economies. As discussed in Chapter I, there is a striking difference in recent growth performance between the strong currency countries and those countries whose currencies depreciated during and following the 1992/93 crisis in the European Monetary System. As partly mirrored in exchange rates, the difference appears to reflect differences in the stance and mix of fiscal and monetary policies between the two groups of

---

[5]As an indication of the progress that has been achieved among the countries that are most advanced in the transition, the Czech Republic became a member of the Organization for Economic Cooperation and Development (OECD), on December 21, 1995; Hungary, Poland, and the Slovak Republic (and also Korea) are also being considered for membership.

Chart 3. Selected Industrial Countries: Output Growth and Leading Economic Indicators[1]
(Percent change from four quarters earlier)

Leading indicators signal declines in output growth.

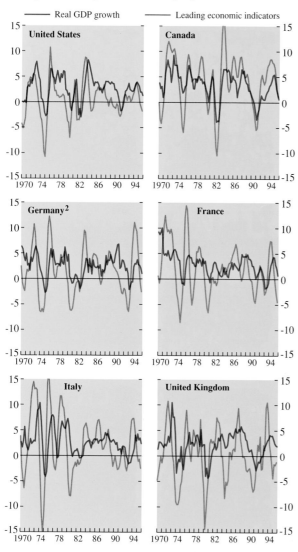

Sources: Bureau of Economic Analysis, Department of Commerce (United States); Statistics Canada (Canada); OECD, *Main Economic Indicators* (Germany, France, and Italy); and Central Statistics Office, *Economic Trends* (United Kingdom).

[1]The leading economic indicators are composite indices of variables that lead activity in the economic cycle. The indices differ by country, but typically include variables such as new orders, construction starts, hours worked, unfilled orders, producers' shipments, stock prices, money supply, and other variables. Japan is omitted because there is not a close relationship between output growth and the index of leading indicators.

[2]Data through 1991 apply to west Germany only.

countries. In addition, confidence factors may have played a role, particularly in France and Germany.

For Europe as a whole, relatively high real interest rates—especially given the generally considerable margins of slack—appear to have been a restraining factor. Both short-term and long-term real interest rates in Europe have remained significantly higher than in the United States during the comparable phase of its economic upswing and also much higher than in Japan (Chart 4). Real bond yields, in particular, have been consistently higher in Europe than in the United States and Japan. It is likely that Europe's fiscal deficits provide part of the explanation. In addition, the recurrent pressures within the exchange rate mechanism (ERM) of the European Monetary System and the fact that monetary policies in most countries have been constrained by the need to ensure exchange rate stability have meant that any additional policy support for economic activity would have to come from fiscal policy, thus adversely affecting the credibility of fiscal consolidation plans. This may have induced investors to demand higher interest rates on long-term bonds than they otherwise would have done.

Real interest rates do not explain the distribution of weakness within Europe, however. Short-term interest rates, in nominal and real terms, have been reduced significantly in most European countries since 1992, but in Germany, in some of the countries whose currencies have been closely tied to the deutsche mark, and in Switzerland, the stimulative effect on activity has been largely offset by rises in real effective exchange rates. And it is in these countries that export growth and business fixed investment have been weakest and the slowing of growth most marked. Meanwhile, exchange rate changes have provided added support for activity in the past few years in countries such as Italy, the United Kingdom, Spain, and Sweden. These contrasts are illustrated by movements in indices of monetary conditions that combine changes in short-term real interest rates and real effective exchange rates, weighted very approximately by their relative influences on aggregate demand.[6] Broadly measured in this way, it would appear that over the past three years the combined effects of changes in short-term interest rates and real effective exchange rates in Germany and France have been more of a restraining factor than in Italy and the United Kingdom (Chart 5).

___

[6]For a description of the construction, use, and limitations of such indices, see C. Freedman, "The Use of Indicators and of the Monetary Conditions Index in Canada," in Tomas J.T. Baliño and Carlo Cottarelli, eds., *Frameworks for Monetary Stability: Policy Issues and Country Experiences* (Washington: IMF, 1994). See also Direction de la prévision, Ministère de l'économie et des finances, *Note de Conjoncture Internationale* (Paris, December 1995), p. 10.

Some role in the slowdown may have also been played by the short-term negative effects on domestic demand of fiscal consolidation, especially in those countries where fiscal actions have not been sufficiently bold to induce marked and sustained declines in long-term interest rates or favorable expectations effects on private sector consumption and investment. There has also been a fairly general weakening of consumer and, especially, business confidence. Consumer confidence has seemingly been sapped by job insecurity and poor prospects for wage growth; and, in some countries, concerns about the implications for disposable incomes of proposals for reform of pension and social security systems and other measures related to budgetary consolidation efforts may have contributed as well. Business confidence may have been affected by uncertainties about countries' capacity to carry out necessary fiscal adjustments, and by concerns about high cost levels and the persistence of structural rigidities that impede the ability of firms to compete in international markets.

The easing of short-term interest rates in Europe during the past year—which may well continue in coming months given the weakness of inflationary pressures—together with further progress in the reduction of structural fiscal deficits should bring about both a more appropriate mix of policies and greater convergence of policies across Europe. Together with the significant decline in long-term interest rates since early 1995, the conditions would seem to be in place for growth to pick up again in the second half of 1996. The moderate pace of expansion that is projected, however, implies that little of the slack in labor markets will be absorbed over the next couple of years.

Growth in other industrial countries also will be supported in the period ahead by the declines in real interest rates over the past year. Real bond yields fell considerably during 1995, reversing much or all of the rise in the previous year, and despite the upturn in yields in early 1996, they remain relatively low by the standards of recent years. Real short-term interest rates have also come down, as subdued inflation and mounting evidence of weakening economic activity have led to monetary easing (Chart 6). Inflation in the industrial countries is expected to remain at around the lowest level in thirty years, permitting monetary policies to accommodate continuing expansion.

In most industrial countries, even in those cases where activity has recently weakened, fiscal policy can contribute most effectively to sustained recovery through the implementation of consolidation programs that address long-standing deficit and debt problems. Japan alone is implementing a substantially stimulative policy; and its fiscal consolidation will need to resume when recovery is firmly established. Most other countries seem likely to implement budgetary measures that reduce structural deficits this year and next (Table 2). In Europe, irrespective of the Maastricht

Chart 4. Industrial Countries: Real Interest Rates[1]
(In percent a year)

Real interest rates in Europe have remained considerably above those in the United States and Japan.

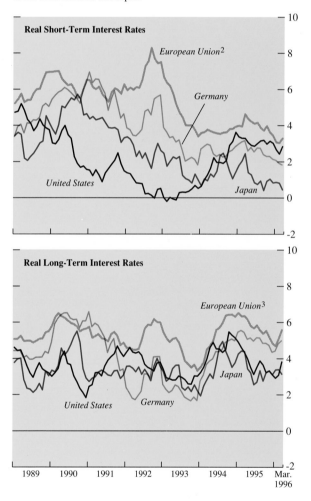

Sources: WEFA, Inc.; and Bloomberg Financial Markets.
[1]Real rates are nominal rates minus percent change of consumer prices from a year ago. Price data for January and February 1996 are partly estimated.
[2]Data prior to January 1990 exclude Luxembourg.
[3]Excludes Greece, and data prior to June 1993 exclude Finland.

Chart 5. Selected Major Industrial Countries: Monetary Conditions Index[1]

Broadly defined, monetary conditions in the United Kingdom and Italy have eased significantly more than in Germany and France, reflecting the real depreciation of sterling and lira.

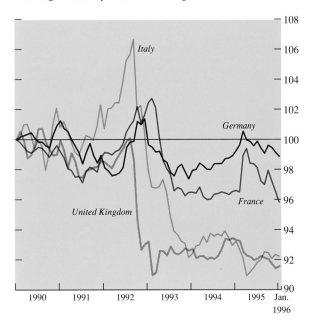

[1]For each country, the index is defined as a weighted average of the percentage point change in the real short-term interest rate and the percentage change in the real effective exchange rate from a base period (January 1990). Relative weights of 3 to 1 are used for France, Italy, and the United Kingdom, and of 2.5 to 1 for Germany. The weights are intended to represent the relative impacts of interest rates and exchange rates on aggregate demand; they should be regarded as indicative rather than precise estimates. For instance, a 3-to-1 ratio indicates that a 1 percentage point change in the real short-term interest rate has about the same effect on aggregate demand over time as a 3 percent change in the real effective exchange rate. Movements in the index are thus equivalent to percentage point changes in the real interest rate. The lag with which a change in the index may be expected to affect aggregate demand depends on the extent to which the change stems from a change in the interest rate or the exchange rate, and varies depending on the cyclical position; the lag also differs across countries. No meaning is to be attached to the absolute value of the index; rather, the index is intended to show the degree of tightening or easing in monetary conditions from the (arbitrarily chosen) base period. Changes in the relative weights used alter the value of the index but not the qualitative picture.

convergence process, most countries need to pursue fiscal consolidation not only to help lower real long-term interest rates and to alleviate the burden on monetary policy, but also to address the prospective budgetary costs of aging populations.

Turning to developments and prospects for individual countries, the *United States* saw a marked slowdown of growth in the first half of 1995, accounted for by a sharp inventory correction and a decline in real net exports that reflected the effects of the recession in Mexico (Table 3). Growth then rebounded strongly in the third quarter on the continued strength of investment demand and a pause in inventory adjustment, but slowed back to ½ of 1 percent at an annual rate in the fourth quarter. There seems to have been some renewed pickup in the early months of this year; in any event, growth is not expected to remain significantly below the growth of capacity for long. Thus, real GDP growth is expected to be 1¾ percent in 1996 as a whole and to rise to 2¼ percent in 1997, in line with the growth of potential output.[7] Several developments support this favorable assessment. Moderate wage increases and continuing productivity gains have contained cost pressures and resulted in a better-than-expected inflation performance. In turn, interest rates have fallen considerably. The Federal Reserve cut its target rate for the federal funds rate by a total of 75 basis points between July and January as the expansion weakened and inflation remained subdued. Bond yields also declined up to late January, seemingly helped by more optimistic market expectations of budget deficit reduction; they have subsequently risen back to the levels of mid-1995, but remain lower than in the preceding twelve months. And equity markets rose steeply up to early March, helped by strong corporate profits as well as interest rate developments; at the end of March they were more than 40 percent higher than at the beginning of 1995. High capacity utilization rates in manufacturing are another factor that should continue to support business fixed investment.

A significant risk to sustained expansion would seem to be posed by the vulnerability of financial markets to a possible failure to make significant early progress toward meeting announced fiscal goals. Although there is agreement between the Congress and the administration on the goal of a balanced federal budget by FY 2002, notable differences remain on measures needed to attain that objective. Moreover, under both of their proposals, much of the adjustment is delayed until the later years and depends on substantial further declines in interest rates.

In *Canada*, real GDP growth slowed from 4½ percent in 1994 to 2¼ percent in 1995. Domestic demand

[7]Data and projections for the United States are based on the new chain-weighted method for estimating real GDP (Box 2).

weakened sharply on higher interest rates, slow employment growth, falling real disposable incomes, high levels of consumer debt, and cutbacks in government consumption. The export sector, which had contributed substantially to the recovery, also weakened as the U.S. economy slowed, but net exports nevertheless continued to make a positive contribution to GDP growth. On several occasions last year, political uncertainties and concern about fiscal consolidation created tension in financial markets, pushing up interest rates and exerting downward pressure on the Canadian dollar. Following the Quebec referendum on October 30, interest rates declined substantially. Renewed market confidence in continued significant progress with budgetary consolidation was also a factor helping to lower interest rates. Both the federal and the provincial governments' fiscal deficits have narrowed appreciably in recent years. In early December, the federal government reaffirmed its commitment to the longer-term goal of a balanced budget and set a deficit target of 2 percent of GDP for FY 1997/98. The outlook is for continuing expansion, as lower interest rates and strong corporate profits support business fixed investment. Real GDP is expected to grow by 2 percent in 1996 and 3 percent in 1997.

In *Japan*, output expanded by only 1 percent in 1995, and despite weak labor force growth, the unemployment rate rose to 3.4 percent at year-end, a historical high. Although still low relative to other industrial countries, this unemployment rate understates the degree of slack in the labor market, given the nature of employment contracts in Japan and the tendency toward labor hoarding in periods of weak growth, as indicated by the decline in labor productivity in manufacturing in 1992–93. In the final quarter of 1995, growth picked up to 3½ percent at an annual rate, and conditions are in place for a convincing recovery to emerge in 1996 and to continue in 1997. The yen has depreciated by over 20 percent in real effective terms since its peak in April 1995 to a level that appears to be more consistent with economic fundamentals. Reflecting actions by the Bank of Japan, short-term interest rates declined from about 2¼ percent in early 1995 to below ½ of 1 percent in September, while growth in narrow money has picked up notably since about the middle of 1995. Furthermore, the implementation of the September 1995 supplementary budget and the extension into 1996 of the 1995 temporary tax cuts are expected to impart substantial fiscal stimulus during the year. These supportive policy measures and the steps taken to address the problems in the financial sector (Box 3) have improved consumer and business confidence and sparked a recovery in equity prices. On the strength of private consumption and capital investment, real GDP is expected to grow by 2¾ percent this year and over 3 percent in 1997. The decline in consumer prices experienced in 1995 will gradually be reversed, but with the large output gap and the modest

Chart 6. Three Major Industrial Countries: Policy-Related Interest Rates and Ten-Year Government Bond Yields[1]
(In percent a year)

Recent declines in policy-related interest rates should support economic activity.

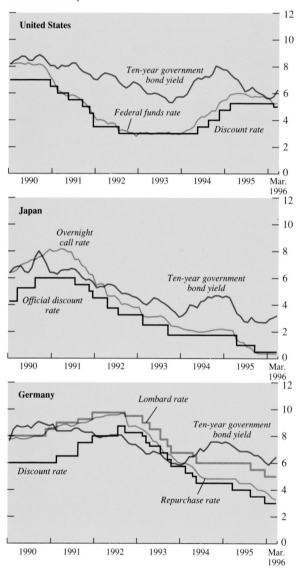

[1]The U.S. federal funds rate, Japanese overnight call rate, German repurchase rate, and all ten-year government rates are monthly averages. All other series are end of month.

17

Table 2. Industrial Countries: General Government Fiscal Balances and Debt[1]

(In percent of GDP)

	1980–89	1990	1991	1992	1993	1994	1995	1996	1997	2001
Major industrial countries										
Actual balance	−3.0	−2.1	−2.7	−3.8	−4.3	−3.5	−3.3	−3.1	−2.5	−1.3
Output gap	−0.4	2.7	0.5	−0.4	−1.8	−1.3	−1.5	−1.9	−1.6	—
Structural balance	−2.7	−3.3	−3.0	−3.5	−3.3	−2.7	−2.5	−2.1	−1.6	−1.3
United States										
Actual balance	−2.6	−2.7	−3.3	−4.4	−3.6	−2.3	−2.0	−1.7	−1.6	−1.0
Output gap	−0.7	2.8	−0.8	−0.5	−0.5	0.7	0.4	—	—	—
Structural balance	−2.3	−3.8	−3.1	−4.1	−3.4	−2.5	−2.2	−1.7	−1.6	−1.0
Net debt	34.7	44.8	48.3	52.0	54.4	55.3	56.4	56.6	56.4	53.4
Gross debt	48.0	57.5	61.3	64.0	66.2	66.1	66.7	67.6	67.5	63.8
Japan										
Actual balance	−1.5	2.9	2.9	1.4	−1.6	−2.1	−3.1	−4.1	−2.4	−2.5
Output gap	−0.2	3.2	3.2	0.8	−1.7	−3.5	−4.9	−4.6	−4.0	—
Structural balance	−1.4	1.7	1.8	1.1	−1.0	−0.8	−1.2	−2.2	−0.9	−2.5
Net debt	22.0	9.5	4.8	4.2	4.7	6.8	9.8	13.6	15.5	22.3
Gross debt	66.2	69.1	66.6	69.9	75.1	80.4	87.0	92.2	94.7	103.3
Memorandum										
Actual balance excluding social security	−4.3	−0.6	−0.8	−2.0	−4.8	−5.2	−6.2	−7.0	−5.2	−5.4
Structural balance excluding social security	−4.3	−1.6	−1.8	−2.2	−4.2	−4.1	−4.5	−5.5	−3.9	−5.4
Germany[2]										
Actual balance	−2.1	−2.0	−3.3	−2.9	−3.5	−2.6	−3.5	−3.9	−3.4	−1.3
Output gap	−1.6	2.1	3.4	2.0	−2.0	−2.0	−2.5	−3.8	−3.3	—
Structural balance	−1.3	−3.2	−5.6	−4.0	−2.4	−1.3	−2.1	−1.6	−1.4	−1.3
Net debt	20.8	21.6	21.4	27.7	35.0	40.3	48.7	51.3	52.7	51.9
Gross debt	39.8	43.4	41.1	43.7	47.8	50.1	57.7	60.1	61.1	58.8
France										
Actual balance	−2.0	−1.4	−2.0	−3.9	−6.0	−5.8	−5.0	−4.2	−3.6	−2.0
Output gap	−0.1	2.2	0.5	−0.5	−3.9	−3.1	−2.7	−3.5	−2.9	−0.1
Structural balance	−1.9	−2.6	−2.3	−3.5	−3.4	−3.6	−3.1	−1.8	−1.7	−2.0
Net debt[3]	21.5	25.1	27.1	30.2	34.4	40.3	43.3	45.8	46.9	47.6
Gross debt	29.0	35.4	35.8	39.7	45.4	48.4	52.3	55.0	56.4	57.1

pace of recovery, inflation is expected to be negligible in the next couple of years.

The pace of economic expansion in *Germany* slowed sharply, to a virtual halt, in the second half of 1995, and output growth is expected to remain well below its potential rate until the second half of this year. Output in 1996 as a whole is projected to be only 1 percent higher than last year. The slowdown stemmed from widespread weakness in demand. Private consumption and fixed investment have been sluggish, reflecting depressed consumer and business confidence; and export growth dwindled during 1995 partly because of the continued strength of the deutsche mark, relatively high unit labor costs, and the slowdown of growth elsewhere in Europe and in North America. Short-term interest rates were lowered substantially in late 1995 and early 1996 in response to weak monetary growth, low inflation, and the strong deutsche mark. The pickup in growth expected in the latter part of this year should be supported by lower interest rates and a strengthening of consumer spend-

ing as tax cuts raise real disposable income. However, the strong deutsche mark and relatively high unit labor costs could remain restraining factors, dampening business confidence. Moreover, rising unemployment may continue to depress consumer confidence.

Following the sharp deterioration in the fiscal position of the early 1990s, reflecting the costs of unification, impressive progress toward fiscal consolidation was achieved in 1992–94. However, beginning in 1995, the debt and debt-service obligations of the Treuhandanstalt (and of various other agencies) were taken over by the general government. This debt is equivalent to 8 percent of GDP, and the associated debt service amounts to between ½ percent and 1 percent of GDP. Although revenue shortfalls contributed to a larger-than-expected general government deficit of 3½ percent of GDP in 1995, another source of the worsened fiscal outturn was the larger deficits of the state and local governments and the pension funds. The structural deficit rose from 1¼ percent of GDP in 1994 to 2 percent of GDP in 1995. While some ac-

Table 2 *(concluded)*

	1980–89	1990	1991	1992	1993	1994	1995	1996	1997	2001
Italy[4]										
Actual balance	−10.9	−10.9	−10.2	−9.5	−9.6	−9.0	−7.2	−7.3	−5.9	−1.5
Output gap	2.1	2.9	1.8	—	−3.4	−3.3	−2.3	−2.1	−1.6	0.1
Structural balance	−11.7	−12.3	−11.1	−9.6	−7.9	−7.3	−6.0	−6.2	−5.1	−1.5
Net debt	71.2	92.8	96.2	103.0	112.0	117.2	114.4	112.0	109.5	94.5
Gross debt	77.1	97.8	101.3	108.4	119.4	125.4	122.9	121.4	119.5	103.8
United Kingdom										
Actual balance	−2.0	−1.2	−2.5	−6.3	−7.8	−6.8	−5.1	−3.8	−2.5	−0.3
Output gap	−0.9	2.0	−2.3	−4.5	−4.5	−2.9	−2.4	−2.0	−1.2	—
Structural balance	−1.0	−3.7	−2.7	−3.8	−4.4	−4.1	−3.2	−2.3	−1.4	−0.2
Net debt	41.6	27.2	26.7	28.1	32.5	37.7	40.8	43.2	43.0	38.5
Gross debt	49.3	34.4	33.6	34.9	40.4	46.0	48.8	49.7	49.5	45.0
Canada										
Actual balance	−4.5	−4.1	−6.6	−7.4	−7.3	−5.3	−4.2	−2.4	−1.3	0.4
Output gap	−0.1	1.2	−2.6	−3.7	−4.0	−2.1	−2.2	−2.5	−2.0	−0.2
Structural balance	−4.4	−4.9	−4.9	−4.8	−4.6	−3.8	−2.9	−0.9	−0.2	0.5
Net debt	28.7	44.0	49.7	56.9	61.9	64.4	66.7	68.0	66.5	57.3
Gross debt	59.5	73.1	80.4	88.0	93.8	95.6	98.3	99.7	97.3	83.4
Other industrial countries[5]										
Actual balance	−4.1	−2.4	−3.8	−4.8	−6.1	−5.1	−4.1	−3.0	−2.2	−1.4
Output gap	−0.3	2.4	0.9	−0.2	−2.4	−1.7	−1.3	−1.2	−1.1	—
Structural balance	−4.0	−4.2	−4.6	−4.6	−4.3	−3.6	−3.1	−2.1	−1.5	−1.4

[1]The output gap is actual less potential output, as a percent of potential output. Structural balances are expressed as a percent of potential output. The structural budget balance is the budgetary position that would be observed if the level of actual output coincided with potential output. Changes in the structural budget balance consequently include effects of temporary fiscal measures, the impact of fluctuations in interest rates and debt-service costs, and other noncyclical fluctuations in the budget balance. The computations of structural budget balances are based on IMF staff estimates of potential GDP and revenue and expenditure elasticities (see the October 1993 *World Economic Outlook*, Annex I). Net debt is defined as gross debt less financial assets, which include assets held by the social security insurance system. Estimates of the output gap and of the structural budget balance are subject to significant margins of uncertainty.

[2]Data before 1990 refer to west Germany. For net debt, the first column refers to 1986–89. Beginning in 1995, the debt and debt-service obligations of the Treuhandanstalt (and of various other agencies) were taken over by the general government. This debt is equivalent to 8 percent of GDP, and the associated debt service to ½ of 1 percent of GDP.

[3]Figure for 1980–89 is average of 1983–89.

[4]Fiscal balances for 1996 include interest accruing on zero coupon bonds first issued in 1995.

[5]For 1980–89, includes Australia, Austria, Belgium, Denmark, Ireland, the Netherlands, New Zealand, Spain, and Sweden; and for years thereafter also includes Finland, Greece, Norway, and Portugal. See Statistical Appendix Table A16 for details.

commodation of weaker revenues may be warranted in 1996, there seems to be no scope for relaxing discipline on discretionary expenditures. In late January, the government unveiled a package of supply-side measures aimed at raising economic efficiency and job creation over the medium to long term. They are not expected, however, to have any marked impact on employment in the near term.

The deterioration in consumer confidence during 1995 was especially marked in *France*. Consumption declined steeply in the second half of the year, especially in the fourth quarter because of public sector strikes. Although private consumption expenditure is expected to strengthen during this year, it will be restrained by relatively weak disposable income growth, while public consumption will be affected by budget cuts. Domestic demand should nonetheless be sustained by increases in business investment and other interest-sensitive expenditures. Owing to weak external demand, net exports are expected to make a negative contribution to real GDP growth in 1996, and

overall growth is expected to decline to only 1¼ percent from 2½ percent in 1995. As private consumption and exports recover in the second half of the year and through 1997, real GDP growth is expected to pick up to some 2½–3 percent next year. With the household saving ratio particularly high, growth prospects in France, as in a number of other European countries, depend importantly on an upturn in consumer confidence. The interest rate reductions on national savings instruments and other measures announced at the end of January are intended to boost consumer spending and the housing market.

In October, the French government announced a major reform of the social security system, intended to eliminate two thirds of the social security deficit in 1996 and achieve a small surplus in 1997. It also presented measures aimed at holding the 1995 central government deficit to its initial target. Despite a wave of strikes in response to the announced measures, and some concessions to public sector employees, the government adhered to the substance of its planned re-

Table 3. Industrial Countries: Real GDP, Consumer Prices, and Unemployment Rates

(Annual percent change and percent of labor force)

	Real GDP				Consumer Prices				Unemployment Rates			
	1994	1995	1996	1997	1994	1995	1996	1997	1994	1995	1996	1997
Industrial countries	**2.8**	**2.1**	**2.0**	**2.6**	**2.3**	**2.4**	**2.3**	**2.5**	**8.1**	**7.7**	**7.8**	**7.6**
Major industrial countries	2.8	2.0	1.9	2.6	2.2	2.3	2.2	2.5	7.2	6.9	7.0	6.9
United States[1]	3.5	2.0	1.8	2.2	2.6	2.8	2.6	3.0	6.1	5.6	5.8	5.9
Japan	0.5	0.9	2.7	3.1	0.7	-0.1	0.4	1.3	2.9	3.1	3.3	3.2
Germany	2.9	1.9	1.0	2.9	2.8	1.8	1.5	1.5	9.6	9.4	10.5	10.1
France	2.9	2.4	1.3	2.8	1.7	1.8	1.8	1.8	12.4	11.6	11.7	11.2
Italy	2.2	3.2	2.4	2.7	4.0	5.4	4.4	4.0	11.3	12.0	11.5	10.8
United Kingdom[2]	3.8	2.4	2.2	2.7	2.4	2.8	2.8	2.6	9.3	8.2	7.9	7.7
Canada	4.6	2.2	1.9	2.9	0.2	1.9	1.3	1.9	10.4	9.5	9.6	9.2
Other industrial countries	3.0	2.8	2.4	2.6	3.1	3.1	2.9	2.6	12.7	11.9	11.4	11.0
Spain	2.0	3.0	2.7	2.9	4.7	4.7	3.6	3.2	24.2	22.9	22.0	21.2
Netherlands	2.7	2.4	1.7	2.7	2.7	2.0	2.3	2.0	8.7	8.4	8.2	7.9
Belgium	2.2	1.9	1.4	2.5	2.4	1.5	2.0	2.0	13.0	13.0	13.1	12.8
Sweden	2.2	3.2	2.2	2.0	2.2	2.6	2.8	2.9	8.0	7.5	6.4	6.2
Austria	3.0	2.1	1.3	1.4	3.0	2.3	2.2	1.9	4.4	4.6	4.7	5.5
Denmark	4.4	2.9	1.9	2.2	2.0	1.9	2.4	2.6	12.1	10.0	9.5	9.5
Finland	4.4	4.2	2.8	2.5	1.1	1.0	2.0	2.0	18.4	17.2	16.0	15.0
Greece	1.5	2.0	2.3	2.5	10.9	9.3	7.4	5.6	9.6	9.5	9.4	9.2
Portugal	1.0	2.4	2.6	2.8	5.2	4.1	3.5	3.3	6.8	7.2	6.9	6.5
Ireland	6.7	7.4	5.9	4.3	2.3	2.5	2.3	2.7	15.3	13.2	12.6	12.0
Luxembourg	4.1	3.5	3.0	3.5	2.2	1.9	1.8	2.0	2.7	2.8	2.8	2.8
Switzerland	1.2	0.7	0.9	2.0	0.9	1.9	0.9	1.2	4.7	4.2	4.3	4.2
Norway	5.7	3.7	4.3	2.0	1.4	2.5	2.0	2.3	5.4	5.0	4.5	4.3
Iceland	2.8	2.6	3.2	2.6	1.6	1.6	2.7	3.2	4.8	5.0	4.4	4.2
Australia[3]	5.5	3.5	3.4	3.1	2.0	2.7	3.5	3.0	9.7	8.5	7.8	7.5
New Zealand[3]	3.8	3.2	3.5	4.4	1.8	2.3	1.9	1.4	8.1	6.4	6.1	5.4
Memorandum												
European Union	2.8	2.6	1.8	2.7	3.0	3.0	2.6	2.5	11.6	11.2	11.2	10.8

[1]The projections for unemployment have been adjusted to reflect the new survey techniques adopted by the U.S. Bureau of Labor Statistics in January 1994.

[2]Consumer prices are based on the retail price index excluding mortgage interest.

[3]Consumer prices excluding interest rate components; for Australia also excluding other volatile items.

forms. Financial markets responded positively with a strengthening of the franc, permitting an easing of monetary conditions and a narrowing of short-term interest differentials over Germany.

In *Italy*, real GDP growth of 3¼ percent in 1995 was stronger than projected in October and a full percentage point higher than in 1994. The expansion slowed through last year, however; and unemployment in early 1996 was unchanged from a year earlier. Export growth has been a key driving force behind the recovery, with the lira's depreciation during 1992–95 bringing further gains in market shares last year and boosting the current account surplus to 2½ percent of GDP. Fixed investment responded strongly to the export surge and robust profits. Private consumption was unusually sluggish, however, owing in part to the slow expansion of household income, while public consumption contracted. After declining to a 25-year low of less than 4 percent in mid-1994, inflation rose to 5½ percent in 1995, fueled by the depreciation of the lira and indirect tax increases. Underlying inflation,

however, has been contained by a cautious monetary policy and moderate wage growth.

Italy's generally favorable aggregate performance masks an unbalanced recovery: export volumes have grown at an average annual rate of over 11 percent in the past three years, while domestic demand has recovered only sluggishly from its steep decline of 1992–93. The short-term prospects are for more balanced, albeit more moderate, expansion. The relative contribution of domestic demand is expected to rise, and its composition is expected to shift toward consumption, in line with a pickup in the growth of real disposable income. After four successive years of decline, employment is expected to pick up and unemployment should gradually fall.

Italy's 1995 fiscal outturn was somewhat better than originally budgeted, owing to higher-than-expected inflation and stronger-than-expected growth. Fiscal adjustment has made appreciable progress in recent years: the general government fiscal deficit narrowed to 7¼ percent of GDP in 1995 from 9 percent in 1994;

the primary surplus widened to 3¾ percent; and the rise of the public debt-to-GDP ratio was halted. Also important, the improvement in recent years has stemmed from reductions in primary spending. The 1996 budget was passed by Parliament in late December, with favorable effects on bond yields and the lira, and the subsequent monetary easing across Europe should assist the fiscal situation, given the high cost of debt servicing in the Italian budget.

In the *United Kingdom*, economic expansion slowed to the more sustainable pace of 2½ percent in 1995, with unemployment continuing to fall at a moderate pace. Growth appears to have been below potential through most of last year, but underlying prospects remain favorable. Domestic cost pressures have remained subdued, household and corporate financial positions are strong, and income tax cuts will shortly take effect. The decline in long-term interest rates and the competitiveness of sterling should also support activity. Consumer confidence has improved, though it remains below the level seen in the late 1980s. In the wake of further signs of softening of demand, official interest rates were cut in three steps of 25 basis points each in December, January, and early March. The tax and spending measures announced in the November budget were neutral, but in view of the accommodation of the revenue shortfall in 1995, the downward path of the public sector borrowing requirement (PSBR) has been shifted back by one year.

Elsewhere in Europe, growth has also slowed in Belgium, Austria, Denmark, and Switzerland. In *Belgium*, a smaller contribution from net exports in 1995 more than offset a pickup in business investment. This year, consumer demand is expected to remain weak, partly because of uncertain employment prospects, and growth is expected to slow further. In *Austria*, much of the slowdown has been concentrated in the service sector, with tourism suffering from the appreciation of the schilling. A substantial tightening of fiscal policy is needed to meet deficit-reduction targets. In *Denmark*, investment is expected to grow less briskly, which, combined with slowdowns in consumption and exports, will reduce GDP growth in 1996 below potential. In *Switzerland*, projected growth has been revised downward quite substantially, reflecting the effect on exports of the large appreciation of the Swiss franc. The recent easing of monetary conditions should contribute to a gradual recovery in consumer spending and residential investment.

Growth of non-oil output in *Norway* slowed to 3¼ percent in 1995, still above its potential rate. All demand components are expected to contribute to a further slowing of the mainland economy in the next couple of years. With the output gap now closed, however, there is a risk of overheating if the pace of expansion remains significantly above its potential rate. In the *Netherlands*, the pace of economic expansion, which had been supported by a boom in business fixed investment, also slowed during 1995. The outlook is for continuing moderate growth, reflecting weak external demand, with continued low inflation and a declining fiscal deficit as a ratio to GDP. In *Ireland*, growth of around 5 percent is expected through 1996–97, owing to resurgent investment and continued buoyant export growth. In view of strong labor force growth and other demographic factors, however, declines in unemployment are likely to be limited without substantial labor market and tax reforms.

Moderate growth is projected for 1996 in Spain, Sweden, and Finland. In *Spain*, investment and exports are the driving forces of the recovery. Although labor market reforms introduced in the past couple of years have increased labor market flexibility somewhat, most of Spain's very high unemployment rate still appears to be structural. Continuing wage moderation should support further declines in inflation. *Sweden* and *Finland* have benefited from improved market confidence because of their successes in reducing fiscal deficits in 1995. In both countries, unemployment rates have remained very high, but the inflation outlook has improved, interest differentials with respect to Germany have narrowed, and currencies have strengthened.

Both Greece and Portugal are likely to see further improvements in growth performance in 1996. Further fiscal consolidation in *Greece* during 1995 bolstered market confidence and led to reduced interest rates, which, together with improved profitability, are expected to boost private investment in the coming year. The recovery in *Portugal*, which began in mid-1994, is projected to continue in 1996 as private consumption and investment strengthen. Reflecting a better-than-budgeted fiscal outcome in 1995, a 1996 budget that aims at further consolidation, and an ambitious privatization program, the escudo has remained stable and interest rate premiums have fallen appreciably.

In 1995, economic growth in both *Australia* and *New Zealand* slowed somewhat from 1994 reflecting the tightening of monetary conditions in both countries. In Australia, strong private consumption and business investment spending have continued to spur the economic expansion, which has been accompanied by a moderate increase in inflation. New Zealand's expansion, now in its fourth year, remains broadly based across production sectors and expenditure components. Unemployment declined further in 1995, reflecting this sustained growth and also significant progress with labor market reforms.

Economic Situation and Prospects in Developing Countries

In the *developing countries*, output increased by close to 6 percent in 1995 for the fourth consecutive year, and growth of 6–6½ percent is projected for 1996

Box 3. Resolving Financial System Problems in Japan

Japanese financial institutions face considerable asset-quality problems, arising both from the bursting of the bubble in land and equity prices since 1990 and the prolonged downturn in economic activity. The failure of several financial institutions during 1995, together with the lack of full disclosure of nonperforming loans and the absence of a transparent framework for disposing of failed institutions, contributed to market participants' sense of increasing risk of systemic crisis. This was reflected in the emergence, in late summer 1995, of a "Japan premium"—the amount of extra interest Japanese banks had to pay to borrow funds in the international interbank market. The premium widened considerably following the delayed revelation of large trading losses at the New York branch of Daiwa Bank. These developments strengthened the authorities' determination to tackle the difficulties in the financial sector: comprehensive plans have been announced for liquidating the *jusen* (housing loan corporations), improving bank supervision, and resolving the problem of failed institutions.

In November 1995, the Ministry of Finance released detailed estimates of problem loans in the financial sector based on a survey of individual institutions *(see table below)*.[1] These estimates, revised slightly in December, place total problem loans at ¥38.1 trillion (about 8 percent of GDP), of which ¥18.6 trillion is considered to be unrecoverable. While total problem loans are probably somewhat larger than the Ministry's figures suggest,[2] the latest estimates appear to have reduced uncertainty as to the magnitude of the problem.

A plan to liquidate the seven insolvent *jusen* was approved by the Cabinet in December 1995, following intense negotiation among the principal creditors.[3] While the agreement is yet to be ratified by the Diet, it represents a significant step forward in resolving the problems in the Japanese financial sector. The immediate losses associated with an estimated ¥6.4 trillion of unrecoverable assets are to be distributed among founding banks, other financial institutions, and agricultural cooperatives as shown in the table opposite.

In addition, ¥685 billion have been earmarked in the FY 1996 budget to cover the balance of the losses. The remaining *jusen* assets, amounting to about ¥6.8 trillion, are to be transferred to a loan-collecting firm, the Jusen Resolution Corporation (JRC). The founding banks, lender banks, and agricultural cooperatives are to extend

---

[1]Problem loans include nonperforming loans (loans to borrowers that have legally been declared bankrupt and loans on which interest has not been paid for 180 days) and restructured loans (loans on which interest rates have been reduced to below the official discount rate prevailing at the time).

[2]For instance, the official figure excludes an additional ¥3.1 trillion of problem loans of three institutions that collapsed during the summer, and the ¥5.5 trillion exposure of the agricultural cooperatives to the *jusen*. In addition, recapitalized loans and loans that have been restructured at above the official discount rate are excluded.

[3]There are eight *jusen*, of which seven are believed to be insolvent. The *jusen*, partially owned by banks (founding banks), insurance companies, and securities firms, were originally established to finance housing loans. During the second half of the 1980s, however, these institutions increased their borrowing from their shareholders, other financial institutions (lender banks), and the agricultural cooperatives to finance their rapidly expanding lending to real estate developers.

Estimated Problem Loans, as of the End of September 1995

	Twenty-One Major Banks	Regional Banks	Cooperative Institutions	Total
	(In trillions of yen)			
Problem loans	23.8	7.8	6.5	38.1
(In percent of GDP)	5.1	1.7	1.4	8.2
(In percent of assets)	3.1	2.9	2.4	2.9
Unrecoverable loans	. . .	. . .	. . .	18.6
Loan-loss reserves	4.9	1.3	0.8	7.0
Net operating profit (April–September 1995)	2.5	1.0	0.8	4.2

(Table 4) and 1997. Particularly positive aspects of the outlook for developing countries include the recoveries that have begun in Mexico and Argentina following the adjustment undertaken in 1995; stronger stabilization and reform efforts in many countries, particularly in Africa; and continued robust growth in Asia, despite the recent tightening of monetary policy in a number of countries to reduce excessive demand pressures.

Among the developing countries of the *Western Hemisphere*, aggregate output is expected to expand by 3 percent in 1996, substantially higher than the 1 percent growth seen in 1995. The improved outlook reflects successful adjustment efforts by countries affected by the Mexican crisis.

In Mexico, tight fiscal and monetary policies, brought about a major adjustment of the economy in

Distribution of Immediate Losses of Insolvent _Jusen_

	Loans	Losses	Losses/Loans
	(In trillions of yen)		*(In percent of loans)*
Founding banks	3.5	3.5	100
Other financial institutions	3.8	1.7	45
Agricultural cooperatives	5.5	0.5	10

low-interest loans to the JRC to finance the cost of assets purchased. Public money will be used to cover half of the possible losses incurred by the JRC; the commercial banks are expected to cover the remainder. The commercial banks are also to provide funds for the Deposit Insurance Corporation (DIC), amounting to around ¥1 trillion, and the investment income generated from these funds is to be used to make up part of the loss to be borne by the commercial banks.

The Financial System Stabilization Committee—set up in July 1995 to formulate a strategy for resolving the nonperforming loan problem—issued its final report at the end of December. The report recommended that deposit insurance premiums—currently 0.012 percent of insured deposits—be raised fourfold to recapitalize the DIC, whose funds are essentially exhausted. Moreover, financial institutions are to pay a special levy over the next five years, equal to three times the existing insurance premium, to establish "special funds" for financing the disposal of failed institutions beyond the payoff costs. To facilitate the disposal of failed credit cooperatives, the Committee recommended the establishment of the Resolution and Collection Bank—an institution similar to the Resolution Trust Corporation set up in the United States to restructure insolvent savings and loans in the late 1980s—(1) to take over failed institutions and handle their liquidation after deposit repayment and loan collection, in cases where other institutions cannot be found to take over the failed institutions; (2) to serve as a bridging bank until a takeover institution can be found; and (3) to collect those nonperforming loans that are not transferred to takeover institutions.

Measures to improve banking inspection and supervision have also been announced. To strengthen internal management controls, financial institutions will be ex-

pected to follow guidelines on in-house inspections and risk management, and will be inspected by external auditors and the Ministry of Finance to verify compliance with these criteria. Overseas branches also will be subject to greater scrutiny by the Ministry and the Bank of Japan. In addition, the authorities plan to strengthen the exchange of information with foreign supervisory authorities, in accordance with the Basle Concordat. Finally, there is to be greater coordination between the local and national supervisory authorities to strengthen the supervision of credit cooperatives.[4]

Banks' profitability improved in the first half of FY 1995. Net business profits rose to a record high, increasing by 66 percent over the same period in FY 1994, reflecting the decline in short-term interest rates and associated steepening of the yield curve.[5] In addition, the rise in overall equity prices boosted the banks' hidden reserves by close to 40 percent in the first half of FY 1995. Taking into consideration this increase in hidden reserves, the IMF staff estimates that the capital ratios as defined by the Bank for International Settlements (BIS) for the 21 major banks rose from 8.9 percent at the end of March 1995 to 9.3 percent at the end of September. The ratio is expected to decline, however, as loans to *jusen* will be written off in March 1996. Total operating profits of these banks have been around ¥3 trillion in recent years. Assuming that this level of profitability is maintained, that there is no further accumulation of problem loans, and that all profits are used to write down problem loans, the difficulties of the major banks can probably be resolved in about three years. However, given the uneven distribution of problem loans among smaller financial institutions, deposit insurance assistance or public money, or both, will likely be needed to wind up several failed institutions.

---

[4]Disclosure requirements for all classes of financial institutions are to be made more rigorous to promote market discipline, including sound management and depositor responsibility. These disclosure requirements will, however, not be made uniform across institutions.

[5]Bank equity prices rose sharply relative to the Nikkei 225 average in late 1995, reflecting strong profits in the first half of FY 1995 and expectations of a quick resolution of the difficulties in the banking sector. In early 1996, bank share prices retraced some of their previous gains, owing to uncertainties as to the pace at which problem loans are likely to be resolved—particularly in view of public opposition to the use of public funds to resolve the *jusen*—and the disproportionate burden to be borne by the major banks.

1995, promoted the recovery of investor and consumer confidence, and helped to stabilize financial markets. The external current account deficit was virtually eliminated as real GDP contracted by about 7 percent. Economic activity recovered somewhat in the latter part of the year, and with financial policies remaining tight, the restoration of confidence should lead to stronger growth in 1996. In Argentina, a significant

adjustment of the fiscal stance, together with a restructuring of the banking system, particularly the provincial banks, helped contain the spillover effects of the crisis in Mexico. Real GDP fell by 4½ percent in 1995 but is expected to recover gradually this year. In Brazil, output increased by 4 percent in 1995 and inflation slowed sharply, reflecting the continued success of the currency stabilization plan. In contrast,

Table 4. Selected Developing Countries: Real GDP and Consumer Prices

(Annual percent change)

	Real GDP			Consumer Prices		
	1994	1995	1996	1994	1995	1996
Developing countries	**6.4**	**5.9**	**6.3**	**48.0**	**19.9**	**12.6**
Median	**3.6**	**4.1**	**4.5**	**11.3**	**8.9**	**6.0**
Africa	**2.4**	**3.2**	**5.3**	**33.8**	**25.8**	**13.7**
Algeria	−0.9	3.9	5.8	30.5	16.3	8.5
Cameroon	−3.7	3.1	5.7	12.7	26.9	6.3
Côte d'Ivoire	1.8	6.5	6.5	26.0	14.2	6.8
Ghana	3.8	4.5	5.0	24.9	58.1	37.0
Kenya	3.9	5.0	5.0	28.8	1.7	5.0
Morocco	11.5	−6.0	9.1	5.1	6.6	5.0
Nigeria	1.3	2.9	3.1	57.0	73.5	28.0
South Africa	2.7	3.4	4.0	9.0	8.9	8.0
Sudan	2.2	4.2	2.0	120.0	85.0	60.0
Tanzania	3.1	4.5	5.5	29.0	22.0	11.3
Tunisia	3.4	3.5	6.7	4.7	6.2	5.0
Uganda	10.0	6.5	6.0	6.1	5.0	5.0
SAF/ESAF countries[1]	3.3	5.1	5.2	23.7	22.5	12.1
CFA countries	1.1	4.6	5.3	27.8	14.8	4.8
Asia	**8.8**	**8.4**	**8.2**	**13.5**	**10.9**	**8.4**
Bangladesh	4.4	4.7	5.1	6.3	8.9	9.0
China	11.8	10.2	10.0	21.7	14.8	10.0
Hong Kong	5.4	5.0	5.0	8.1	9.0	7.5
India	5.9	6.2	6.0	10.0	10.2	7.9
Indonesia	7.5	8.1	7.6	8.5	9.4	9.1
Korea	8.4	9.0	7.5	6.3	4.5	4.5
Malaysia	9.2	9.6	9.0	3.7	3.4	4.2
Pakistan	4.2	5.3	6.3	12.5	12.3	9.2
Philippines	4.4	4.8	6.1	9.1	8.1	8.0
Singapore	10.1	8.9	7.5	3.1	1.7	1.7
Taiwan Province of China	6.4	6.4	6.2	4.1	3.7	3.7
Thailand	8.6	8.6	8.3	5.0	5.8	5.7
Vietnam	8.9	9.5	9.5	14.5	13.1	9.0
Middle East and Europe	**0.7**	**3.7**	**3.1**	**32.0**	**33.1**	**23.8**
Egypt	2.7	3.2	4.8	9.0	9.4	7.2
Iran, Islamic Republic of	1.8	3.0	3.5	35.2	48.8	23.0
Israel	6.5	6.9	5.7	12.3	10.0	9.0
Jordan	5.9	6.4	6.5	3.5	3.0	3.5
Kuwait	1.1	−0.3	−2.4	4.7	5.4	2.1
Saudi Arabia	−0.1	−0.8	−0.1	0.6	5.0	2.4
Turkey	−4.7	7.4	3.0	106.3	93.6	80.3
Western Hemisphere	**4.7**	**0.9**	**3.1**	**223.7**	**37.9**	**19.0**
Argentina	7.4	−4.4	2.5	4.3	3.4	1.7
Brazil[2]	5.7	4.2	3.0	2,407.6	67.4	13.7
Chile	4.2	8.5	6.5	11.4	8.2	7.4
Colombia	5.7	5.3	4.5	22.8	20.9	18.5
Dominican Republic	4.3	4.8	5.0	8.3	12.5	7.1
Ecuador	4.0	2.5	3.0	27.3	23.0	18.4
Guatemala	4.0	5.0	4.5	12.5	8.6	7.0
Mexico	3.7	−6.9	3.0	7.1	35.0	28.9
Peru	12.8	6.9	3.5	23.7	11.2	10.3
Uruguay	5.1	−2.5	1.0	44.7	42.7	25.9
Venezuela	−2.8	2.2	−0.6	60.8	60.0	79.8

[1]African countries that had arrangements, as of the end of 1995, under the IMF's structural adjustment facility (SAF) or enhanced structural adjustment facility (ESAF).

[2]From December 1994 to December 1995, consumer prices increased by about 15 percent. Monthly inflation in February 1996 was about 0.8 percent.

economic conditions in Venezuela worsened over the past year, as confidence in government policies waned and investment stagnated. Prospects for an improvement in the economic situation in 1996 depend on the adoption of a credible exchange rate policy, the removal of controls, and measures to strengthen the fiscal position and deal with the problems of the banking sector. Countries with strong economic fundamentals, such as Chile and Peru, are continuing to see robust growth.

Economic growth in *Africa* is expected to improve further in 1996, reflecting continuing advances in macroeconomic and structural policies. Apart from the need to avoid policy slippages, weak commodity prices pose a downside risk for many countries in the period ahead. The South African economy grew by about 3½ percent in 1995, despite declines in the agricultural sector owing to a drought and in the gold mining sector because of labor disputes. In manufacturing, meanwhile, output expanded vigorously and is expected to continue to do so in 1996. In Uganda, continuing gains in the credibility of policies, as well as higher coffee prices, boosted real GDP by 6½ percent last year; weaker coffee prices are expected to moderate growth in 1996. In Kenya, with the implementation of prudent polices, the deepening of structural reforms, and the resumption of normalized relations with the donor community, the expansion is projected to continue in 1996. Tight financial discipline in Algeria, supported by rescheduling agreements with official and commercial creditors, has promoted macroeconomic stability; the 5½–6 percent growth rate projected for 1996 is subject to downside risks, however. In Nigeria, growth picked up during 1995 but remains low compared with other major African countries, because of ongoing political uncertainties. Recently, however, oil production rose and foreign exchange market liberalization has been boosting non-oil exports.

In most countries in the CFA franc zone, buoyant commodity prices in 1994 and early 1995, and improved external competitiveness following the devaluation in 1994, supported the continued recovery in 1995. Real GDP grew by 4½ percent, the strongest growth in ten years. Restrained fiscal and wage policies have been essential to the recovery process. In Côte d'Ivoire, coffee and cocoa production increased, while in Senegal groundnut production registered strong growth. With continued liberalization and prudent financial policies, growth is expected to continue to strengthen in 1996 despite a downward revision in projected commodity export prices.

Despite a tightening of financial policies in a number of countries in the region, growth in *Asia* is expected to slow only slightly in 1996, to about 8 percent. After a prolonged period of overheating, a restrictive credit policy in China should help to hold economic growth to a more sustainable rate of 10 per-

cent in 1996. Economic expansion in India remained strong during 1995 but is projected to moderate during 1996, partly because of higher interest rates that are restraining domestic demand. Further progress is expected in the area of structural reform after the elections, and this should help to boost investor confidence. Growth in Korea is expected to moderate to 7½ percent this year from 9 percent in 1995. In Malaysia, overheating should ease in 1996 as a result of the recent tightening of monetary policy, but the economy is still likely to grow by about 9 percent. In Thailand, tighter monetary policies helped to reduce demand pressures in the second half of 1995, and growth should slow marginally in 1996. Growth is also expected to slow somewhat in 1996 in Taiwan Province of China. Economic activity in the Philippines is continuing to recover following the implementation of a successful stabilization program. In Indonesia, rapid growth of bank lending and surging foreign investment continue to support economic activity. Strong industrial expansion sustained economic growth above 9 percent in Vietnam in 1995; a similar growth rate is expected in 1996.

Improved regional stability in the *Middle East and Europe* is expected to stimulate confidence and activity in a number of countries in 1996, but large government deficits and weakening oil prices continue to cloud the outlook for several oil producers. In Saudi Arabia, continued tight fiscal policies are expected to restrain growth again in 1996. In Turkey, following a severe recession and the initiation of substantial adjustment policies during 1994, output increased by 7½ percent in 1995, owing to strong exports, consumption, and investment. The economic outlook for 1996 is quite uncertain, however, and rests on the strengthening of public finances. In Egypt, growth in 1995 was sustained by increases in industrial production and construction that offset a decline in cotton production. In the Islamic Republic of Iran, growth and investment remain weak owing to tight credit and import controls, and a slowdown in non-oil exports. In Jordan, economic recovery is expected to continue, supported by substantial stabilization efforts.

Developments and Prospects in Transition Countries

Most of the *countries in transition* made substantial further progress toward low inflation and market-based economic structures in 1995, and most also saw improved growth performance or smaller output declines than in the preceding years (Table 5). Output growth has remained most robust in countries that began earliest and that have persevered longest with macroeconomic stabilization and structural reforms. In Poland, output expanded by about 6½ percent in 1995, fueled by strong export performance and a re-

Table 5. Countries in Transition: Real GDP and Consumer Prices

(Annual percent change)

	Real GDP			Consumer Prices		
	1994	1995	1996	1994	1995	1996
Countries in transition	**−8.8**	**−1.3**	**2.5**	**265**	**128**	**38**
Median	**1.1**	**1.6**	**3.9**	**130**	**40**	**21**
Central and eastern Europe	**−2.9**	**1.4**	**3.0**	**153**	**75**	**27**
Excluding Belarus and Ukraine	3.4	5.2	4.5	46	26	17
Albania	9.4	8.6	7.0	23	8	8
Belarus	−12.6	−10.2	−3.5	2,220	709	56
Bulgaria	1.4	2.5	3.0	96	62	27
Croatia	0.8	5.0	5.0	97	2	3
Czech Republic	2.6	5.0	5.0	10	9	9
Estonia	3.0	4.0	4.0	48	29	20
Hungary	2.9	1.9	1.4	19	28	21
Latvia	2.2	0.4	2.1	35	25	21
Lithuania	1.7	5.3	5.0	72	36	19
Macedonia, Former Yugoslav Rep. of	−8.2	−3.0	3.0	123	16	7
Moldova	−31.2	−3.0	4.0	330	30	22
Poland	6.0	6.5	5.5	32	28	19
Romania	3.9	6.9	4.0	137	32	23
Slovak Republic	4.9	7.4	5.5	13	10	7
Slovenia	5.3	4.8	5.0	20	12	6
Ukraine	−23.7	−11.4	−1.7	891	376	70
Russia	**−15.0**	**−4.0**	**2.3**	**302**	**190**	**51**
Transcaucasus and central Asia	**−14.2**	**−5.7**	**0.4**	**1,611**	**263**	**52**
Armenia	5.4	5.0	6.5	5,273	176	20
Azerbaijan	−20.8	−13.2	−4.4	1,664	412	28
Georgia	−11.4	−5.0	8.0	17,272	169	50
Kazakstan	−25.0	−11.0	0.4	1,880	176	39
Kyrgyz Republic	−20.1	1.3	2.4	278	43	20
Mongolia	2.3	6.3	5.0	88	57	37
Tajikistan	−21.4	−12.5	−7.0	350	635	901
Turkmenistan	−20.0	−13.9	3.7	1,748	1,262	106
Uzbekistan	−4.2	−1.2	−1.0	1,568	305	46

covery in investment spending. With somewhat less strong growth projected for 1996, real GDP is poised to reach its pretransition peak. Economic recovery continued during 1995 in the Czech and Slovak Republics, Estonia, and Lithuania. In Latvia and Lithuania, the authorities have acted to contain the effects of serious banking sector problems that emerged during 1995. In Hungary, the need to restrain domestic demand to correct large macroeconomic imbalances slowed output growth in 1995 to 2 percent. In Mongolia, despite policy slippages earlier in the year, output expanded by about 6 percent in 1995 and, provided that appropriate policies are kept in place, robust growth is expected to continue.

Among the countries in transition that have implemented stabilization and reform policies more slowly or less consistently, growth performance and prospects are mixed. Even though output rose in 1995 in Armenia, Bulgaria, and Romania, future growth prospects for these countries are somewhat uncertain. Future economic growth in Armenia critically depends on the lifting of the blockade along the west and east trade routes and also on the timely resolution of tax arrears and banking sector problems. In Bulgaria, serious delays in implementing structural reforms threaten the sustainability of macroeconomic stabilization and therefore the outlook for growth. In Romania, the further quickening of growth in 1995 was accompanied by rapidly expanding bank credit, falling external reserves, and a deteriorating current account. Corrective macroeconomic policy measures have been implemented, but any further policy slippages could jeopardize sustained growth.

Progress with stabilization during 1995 arrested the steep declines in output in a number of other countries, creating the conditions for the resumption of growth in 1996. In Russia, output, which declined by 4 percent in 1995 as compared with 15 percent in 1994, has shown signs of an emerging recovery since early last year. One of the essential preconditions for growth began to be put more securely in place last year with the significant progress made in reducing inflation. In the Kyrgyz Republic, noteworthy progress with macroeconomic stabilization and structural reforms laid the foundation for the modest growth seen in 1995, and stronger expansion is projected for the medium term. Economic prospects have also become more favorable in Georgia and Uzbekistan; both countries have made considerable progress with stabilization over the last year, and should begin to see clearer results of their efforts in the period ahead.

In other transition countries, progress in achieving macroeconomic stability has been insufficient to prevent further steep declines in output. Although tight financial policies have been implemented in Azerbaijan and Kazakstan, they have not been in place long enough to translate into growth. Meanwhile, in Belarus, Ukraine, and Tajikistan policy slippages in 1995 have undermined any prospect for recovery in the year ahead.

Inflation and Commodity Prices

Generally subdued inflation in much of the world economy is a particularly encouraging aspect of the current global expansion. At the root of this success seems to be a greater understanding among voters that inflation is harmful to growth and economic welfare. As a result, there appears to have been a general strengthening of policymakers' mandates and determination to address macroeconomic imbalances and especially of monetary authorities' resolve to resist inflationary pressures. The fact that progress toward price stability is shared by so many countries testifies to the important role of peer pressure in countries' common fight against inflation. Moreover, rapid trade integration and enhanced global competition are helping to transmit efficiency gains across countries and to diminish the scope for excessive increases in wages and other costs to be shifted to consumers. Although there is no room for complacency, there would seem to be grounds for optimism with respect to the chances of safeguarding the progress that has been achieved on the inflation front.

Among the *industrial countries*, earlier fears of an increase in inflationary pressures in the countries most advanced in the expansion have largely subsided. The strong anti-inflationary commitment and pre-emptive actions of monetary authorities in these countries have played a key role. In the United States, modest wage increases and slower growth in nonwage labor costs—in particular, employer-provided health insurance costs—have helped to keep inflation in check despite the high level of resource utilization (Chart 7). In Canada, inflation rose to the top half of the authorities' official target range of 1–3 percent in the first half of 1995, owing in part to the earlier depreciation of the Canadian dollar, but it has since subsided to below 2 percent. In the United Kingdom, inflation firmed as

Chart 7. Major Industrial Countries: Output Gaps[1]
(Actual less potential, as a percent of potential)

Output gaps in most major industrial countries remain negative.

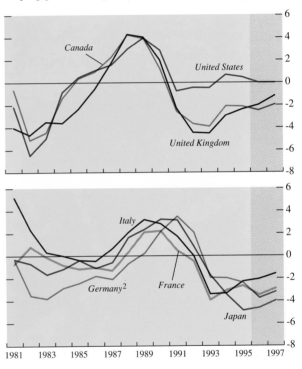

[1]Blue shaded areas indicate IMF staff projections. The gap estimates are subject to a significant margin of uncertainty. For a discussion of the approach to calculating potential output, see the October 1993 *World Economic Outlook,* p. 101.

[2]Data through 1991 apply to west Germany only.

27

a result of input price increases following the depreciation of sterling, but domestic cost pressures have remained moderate, and headline inflation should edge down slowly in 1996 from its present level close to 3 percent. In New Zealand, underlying inflation has mostly been maintained within the 0–2 percent target band, while in Australia, underlying inflation has edged up to just over 3 percent, reflecting continued wage pressures and indirect tax increases.

In most of continental Europe, inflationary pressures have continued to diminish partly due to currency appreciations and continuing sizable margins of slack. High unemployment has contributed to the containment of wage pressures in many countries, including France, although its influence was less apparent in the 4½ to 5 percent increase in hourly earnings in Germany's manufacturing industry in 1995. Wage pressures in Germany are likely to have been a significant factor behind recent increases in unemployment, particularly given the strength of the deutsche mark during 1995. Unit labor costs, however, have been contained by rapid productivity growth and labor shedding. Rigidities in labor markets suggest some potential for inflation rates in Europe to rise if activity were to pick up strongly. However, with the recent downscaling of growth prospects for Europe, many countries may well continue to experience weaker-than-projected inflation during the next couple of years.

Even some of the countries with weak currencies have been quite successful in containing inflation at relatively moderate levels. These include Finland and Sweden, in particular, while Spain and Portugal registered significant declines in inflation during 1995. Italy has had greater difficulty in controlling the inflationary impulses associated with the depreciation of the lira during 1992–95, and consumer price inflation rose to 5½ percent last year. However, provided recent progress in the fiscal area continues at an adequate pace, Italy's inflation rate should again begin to converge toward the moderate inflation performance of its main trading partner countries.

Japan has been facing the unusual problem of a declining price level as a result of a period of protracted economic weakness and the sharp appreciation of the yen in the first half of 1995. Price declines have exacerbated the weakness of demand and added to difficulties in the financial sector. However, the prospect of moderate recovery in 1996 supported by stimulatory fiscal and monetary policies should help prevent further reductions in the price level. While the prospect of stagnating wages in 1996 should help the recovery of industrial profitability after recent years' deterioration in external competitiveness, it also carries adverse implications for consumer confidence and private consumption.

In the *developing world*, although inflation remains generally higher than in the industrial countries, the large majority of countries have also experienced a moderation of price increases in recent years. This is the case in several countries that had earlier experienced very high inflation rates. Among the countries in the Western Hemisphere, for example, Argentina, following hyperinflation in the late 1980s, has successfully kept inflation in low single-digit rates since 1993.[8] Brazil has also seen a sharp decline in inflation since the introduction of the real in 1994, and the maintenance of strong stabilization efforts should hold inflation at 15 percent in 1996, the lowest rate since 1973. In Mexico, the steep decline in the value of the peso contributed to a sharp rise in inflation during 1995 in spite of the tightening of financial policies, but inflation is expected to decline substantially during 1996. In Venezuela, on the other hand, strong stabilization policies will need to be implemented to prevent further acceleration of prices.

Inflation in most *African* countries is expected to decline further in 1996, as these economies reap the benefits of the recent strengthening of stabilization efforts. Inflation in Algeria declined in 1995 despite the depreciation of the dinar and reductions of subsidies on cereals. In Uganda, inflationary pressures last year were subdued, as the monetary impact of the coffee price boom was successfully contained. In South Africa, although drought reduced domestic corn production, inflation was stable at 9 percent. Inflation in countries of the CFA franc zone is also expected to ease in 1996. Nigeria is one of the relatively few African countries to have seen a rise in inflation, to above 70 percent, in 1995; but there has been a substantial tightening of fiscal and monetary policies since the latter part of last year, and provided that these are kept in place, inflation is expected to decline in 1996.

Inflation in *Asia* is also expected to moderate in 1996, owing to monetary tightening in many countries. A tightening of financial policies in China contributed to a reduction of inflation to 15 percent in 1995, and a further decline is expected in 1996. In Southeast Asia, several countries, including Malaysia and Thailand, experienced problems of overheating in 1995, which were reflected mainly in widening current account deficits while inflation increased only moderately. With recent measures of restraint, these problems, linked to rapid capital inflows, should abate somewhat in 1996. In Pakistan, inflation is likely to ease in 1996, but to remain above 9 percent owing mainly to the depreciation of the rupee.

In the *Middle East and Europe* region, inflation is expected to remain relatively moderate during 1996 in most countries. In Israel, strong growth in recent years

---

[8]At the end of 1995, Argentina's inflation rate stood at only 1½ percent, the lowest in fifty years.

has led to concerns about overheating, but a nonaccommodating monetary stance should help to ease inflationary pressures. In contrast, inflation in Turkey is expected to remain high at about 80 percent owing to loose financial polices and continued currency depreciation.

Hard-earned progress in bringing down inflation has been sustained in most of the *countries in transition*. For the countries more advanced in the transition process, strong growth does not pose an immediate threat of overheating in most cases because of continuing large output gaps and the opportunities for improved productivity, particularly through enterprise restructuring (Chart 8). Although the Czech and Slovak Republics, as well as Albania and Croatia, have contained inflation to under 10 percent, other countries such as Poland, Hungary and the Baltic countries have had greater difficulty in reducing inflation below the 20–40 percent range. The persistence of inflation in these countries may be attributable in varying degrees to continued large relative price adjustments, the use of indexation mechanisms (particularly in Poland), and in some cases to capital inflows that have led to marked increases in official reserves and rapid monetary growth.

Progress in 1995 in reducing inflation is also noteworthy in many countries less advanced in the transition process (Chart 9). Russia made substantial headway, reducing monthly inflation from 18 percent in January 1995 to 3¼ percent by year-end, through tighter financial policies. Inflation in January 1996 edged up to about 4 percent, partly as a result of adjustments to administered prices for public transportation and utilities; in addition, however, there was considerable pressure in late 1995 and early 1996 to ease financial policies, and this pressure will need to be resisted effectively for the projected further progress in lowering inflation to be secured. In Armenia, Azerbaijan, Bulgaria, Kazakstan, the Kyrgyz Republic, Moldova, and Uzbekistan, monthly inflation has been maintained in the low single-digit range, but more progress is needed in strengthening monetary and credit policies. After some progress earlier in the year, inflation worsened in Turkmenistan and Ukraine, and most notably in Tajikistan, owing to slippages in financial policies.

Prices for all major categories of primary *commodities* rose between 1994 and 1995 in U.S. dollar terms although most of the increase reflected the weakness of the U.S. currency. In real terms, commodity prices fell slightly, continuing their long-term trend.[9] In 1996–97, average commodity prices are expected to continue to decline in real terms.

Chart 8. Selected Countries More Advanced in Transition: Inflation
(Twelve-month percent change in the consumer price index)

Inflation has come down but remains high generally.

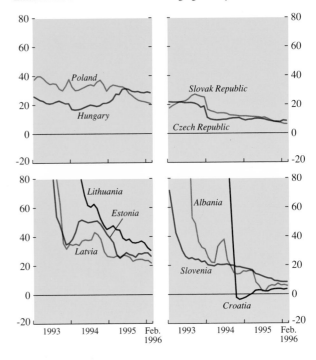

---

[9]See Statistical Appendix, Table A26.

Chart 9. Selected Countries Less Advanced in Transition: Inflation

(Monthly percent change in consumer price index)

Inflation in most countries slowed down considerably during 1995.

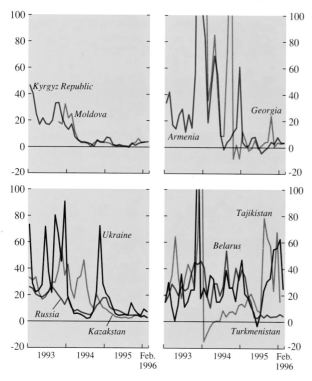

The average price of crude *petroleum* rose by 9.5 percent in 1995 in terms of U.S. dollars,[10] reflecting unexpectedly high demand in the first five months of the year and constrained supply, which was due in part to adherence by most OPEC (Organization of Petroleum Exporting Countries) members to their agreed quotas. Prices weakened from about midyear, but the ensuing decline was significantly offset later in the year and in early 1996 when prices rose, owing to a number of factors, including a drop in Mexican production; low stocks of heating oil in both North America and Europe, which coincided with unusually cold weather; and the disruption of Russian supplies to western Europe. Current indications are that the crude price will on average rise somewhat in 1996 but decline in 1997.

After increasing sharply during 1994 and the first quarter of 1995, the Fund's index of *nonfuel commodity prices* in U.S. dollar terms declined gradually through the remainder of 1995 and is expected to continue to decline in 1996.[11] During 1995, a decline in coffee prices was largely offset by increases in the prices of other commodities, notably cereals, soybeans, and soybean meal. Poor cereal and soybean crops in the United States coincided with low world carryover stocks and resulted in substantial increases in prices beginning in May 1995. Prices of cereals in the final quarter of 1995 were about 30 percent higher than in the first quarter. In the last few weeks of the year, a tax on wheat exports imposed by the European Union may have exacerbated price increases. Although prices for cereals, soybeans, and soybean meal are expected to be higher in 1996 than in 1995, expanded cereals acreage—as a result of higher prices and the lifting of government restrictions in the United States and the European Union—is expected to increase production and thereby lower prices during the year.

Foreign Exchange and Financial Markets

In the industrial countries, developments in foreign exchange and financial markets since the last *World*

---

[10]The Fund's revised indicator petroleum price increased from $15.68 in 1994 to $17.17 in 1995. This price is an average of the prices for U.K. Brent, Dubai, and West Texas Intermediate crudes. (The indicator price was modified during 1995 to replace the price of the Alaska North Slope crude c.i.f. U.S. Gulf of Mexico by the price of West Texas Intermediate crude; the volume of shipments of Alaska crude to the Gulf had fallen sharply and spot trading had become very thin.)

[11]The index covers a basket of 35 nonfuel primary commodities with weights based on average world exports of these commodities during 1987–89. The coverage and weights for this index were revised in 1995 to reflect recent information on world trade in commodities. See Box 2 in the October 1995 *World Economic Outlook*, p. 23.

Economic Outlook have in a number of respects been conducive to improved economic growth performance. In most countries, reflecting the actions of monetary authorities, short-term interest rates have declined substantially. Long-term interest rates generally continued to decline up to late January, and although they have risen more recently they have remained below the levels seen in most of 1994 and 1995. Exchange rate movements have generally been moderate and have brought the currencies of the three major countries into better alignment, relative to fundamentals. There has also been an appropriate appreciation of the Italian lira, and tensions in the exchange rate mechanism of the European Monetary System have eased. In addition, most equity markets have remained buoyant.

Since the end of September, monetary authorities in most industrial countries, faced with continuing low inflation and weakening growth, have allowed *short-term interest rates* to decline (Chart 10). In Japan—the only notable exception—short-term market rates have remained stable at very low levels since the official discount rate was reduced to its historic low of ½ of 1 percent in early September.

Among the seven major industrial countries, short-term rates have declined most since September in France (by about 2 percentage points) and Canada (by about 1½ percentage points), partly reflecting the easing of currency pressures related to political and fiscal policy concerns.[12] Downward pressure on the Canadian dollar receded in the period immediately following the Quebec referendum at the end of October. Pressures on the French franc were also relieved from late October, following renewed commitment to fiscal discipline in France and the easing of tensions over prospects for EMU. Pressure on the franc and in French financial markets re-emerged in early December amid strikes in protest against the authorities' reform proposals, but subsequently receded. In Italy, short-term rates declined substantially between October and January as confidence strengthened with the enactment of the 1996 budget. Subsequently, renewed political uncertainties led to an upturn in rates, but at the end of March they were still about 1 percentage point lower than in September.

In many other industrial countries, short-term rates have declined by 50–80 basis points since September. In mid-December, key official interest rates were lowered by 50 basis points in Germany and by 25 basis points in the United States and the United Kingdom, amid increasing evidence of weakening growth in these countries. Further reductions of 25 basis points followed in January in the United Kingdom and the

Chart 10. Major Industrial Countries: Nominal Interest Rates
(In percent a year)

Interest rates have declined in most industrial countries.

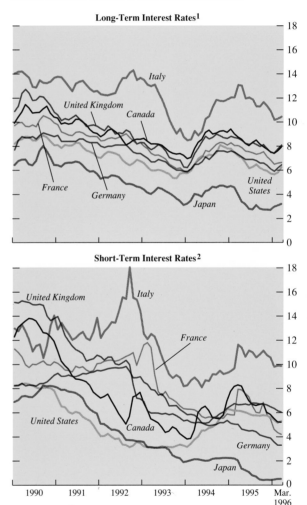

Sources: WEFA, Inc.; and Bloomberg Financial Markets.
[1]Yields on government bonds with residual maturities of ten years or nearest.
[2]Three-month maturities.

---

[12]Movements in interest rates, exchange rates, and equity markets discussed in this section refer to the period from the end of September 1995 through the end of March 1996.

Chart 11. Major Industrial Countries: Effective Exchange Rates

(1990 = 100; logarithmic scale)

The main counterpart to the continued recovery of the U.S. dollar in recent months has been the depreciation of the Japanese yen.

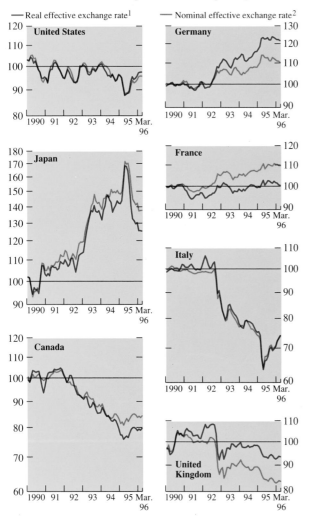

—— Real effective exchange rate[1]   —— Nominal effective exchange rate[2]

[1]Defined in terms of relative normalized unit labor costs in manufacturing, as estimated by the IMF's Competitiveness Indicators System, using 1989–91 trade weights.

[2]Constructed using 1989–91 trade weights.

United States, and again in early March in the United Kingdom, while Germany also eased monetary conditions further. The decline in short-term rates in Germany helped further to relieve tensions in the ERM and contributed to a general lowering of short-term interest rates in participating countries.

The general decline in *long-term interest rates* that began in late 1994 continued in most countries other than Japan up to the latter part of January 1996. By that time, the increases in long-term rates that had occurred in 1993–94 had been almost fully reversed in a number of countries, including the United States. The declines between September and January may be attributed to the downgrading of projections for growth and inflation, the reductions in short-term interest rates permitted by monetary authorities, and also improved prospects for fiscal consolidation in the United States and a number of other countries. Among the major industrial countries, only in Japan, where prospects of economic recovery improved and projected fiscal deficits widened, did long-term rates rise in this period. Between mid-January and mid-March, however, bond yields moved upward in the other industrial countries as well. This reversal appears to have stemmed partly from revised market expectations about near-term monetary policy adjustments in the light of some relatively buoyant economic and monetary indicators in key countries, but less optimistic assessments of fiscal prospects may also have played a role. In Europe, concerns that slow growth might place medium-term fiscal targets in jeopardy, and related uncertainties about EMU, may have contributed to upward movements in long-term rates.

At the end of March, long-term rates were higher than six months earlier in the United States (by about 15 basis points) as well as Japan (by about 40 basis points), and they were virtually unchanged in the United Kingdom. But they were still about 90 basis points lower than at the end of September in France and Italy, partly reflecting improved budget prospects in these countries. In Germany and Canada, long-term rates declined by around 15 basis points over the six months. In all the major industrial countries, long-term rates at the end of March remained lower than in most of 1994 and 1995. The likelihood of further declines in long-term rates would be improved by the implementation of strong fiscal consolidation plans and by the reduction of risks of slippages in fiscal policies arising from weak growth and rising unemployment.

In *foreign exchange markets*, the U.S. dollar's recovery from the historic lows reached in spring 1995 against the Japanese yen and the deutsche mark, and also in effective terms, continued up to late January, but the dollar weakened slightly in February and stabilized in March. Since the end of September, the U.S. dollar has risen by a further 8½ percent against the yen, by around 3 percent against the mark, the French franc, and the pound sterling, by 1 percent against the

Canadian dollar, and by 3 percent in nominal effective terms. The yen has declined further against all other major currencies, depreciating by 6½ percent in nominal effective terms in this period. The nominal effective value of the yen is now more than 20 percent below its peak of April 1995, and estimates of Japan's real effective exchange rate indicate that its international cost competitiveness has improved to early 1993 levels (Chart 11). Only a few currencies have strengthened against the dollar since September. They include the Italian lira and Swedish krona, both of which have benefited from increased confidence in progress with fiscal consolidation in their respective countries.

Equity markets have risen further since the end of September in most industrial countries, reflecting declines in interest rates and, in a number of cases, strong profit growth (Chart 12, top panel). Since the beginning of 1995, equity prices have risen particularly strongly in the United States, recording gains of about 40 percent. In contrast to the situation in 1987, when a sharp rise in the U.S. stock market opened up a large premium of bond yields over equity yields prior to the October crash, the growth of corporate profits and the decline in U.S. bond yields since 1994 have been such that the premium has actually fallen to relatively low levels (Chart 13). In Japan, the corresponding yield gap has remained low in recent months, by historical standards, in spite of the sharp recovery in equity prices from their low of July 1995. Equity markets generally remain vulnerable both to reversals in bond markets—and thus to disappointments about progress with fiscal consolidation—and also to any significant weakening of profit performance.

In the developing world, movements in currency and financial markets since September 1995 reflect a wide range of country-specific economic and political factors. However, for a number of countries, a common underlying element has been the continuation of large capital inflows, which gathered momentum in the closing months of last year and January of this year. This led to pressures on exchange rates, large accumulations of foreign exchange reserves, and increases in domestic liquidity.

Capital flows to developing economies recovered strongly in 1995, topping levels seen in earlier years (Table 6). To alleviate upward pressures on exchange rates resulting from these inflows, authorities in several countries responded by intervening in currency markets that boosted foreign exchange reserves and domestic liquidity. In Latin America, Brazil's reserves increased by over $15 billion in the second half of the year, with broad money increasing concomitantly, and there has been significant downward pressure on interest rates. In Argentina, a significant inflow of capital during December returned international reserves and monetary aggregates to their pre-crisis levels before the Mexican crisis, while annual yields on bench-

Chart 12. Equity Prices
(In U.S. dollars; logarithmic scale; January 1990 = 100)

Equity prices have risen in most industrial countries but have been more volatile in many developing countries.

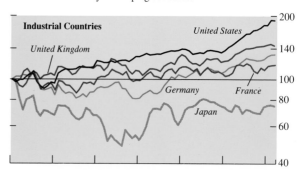

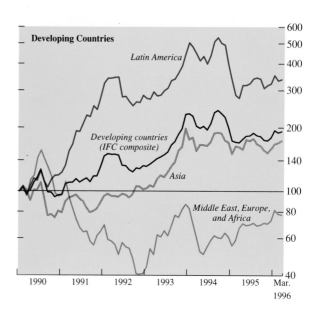

Sources: WEFA, Inc.; and International Finance Corporation, Emerging Markets data base.

Chart 13. United States and Japan: Equity Yield Gap and Stock Market Prices

Despite strong gains in equity prices, bond yields have declined in relation to equity yields in both the United States and Japan.

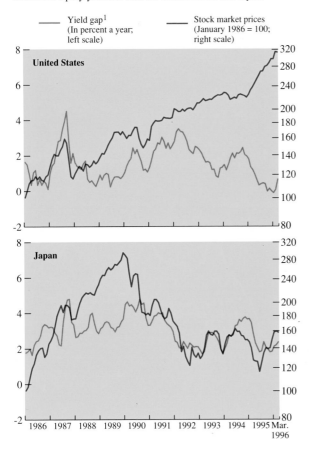

Sources: WEFA, Inc.; and Morgan Stanley, *Capital International Perspective.*

[1]The equity yield gap is defined as the difference between the yield on ten-year government bonds and the inverse of the price-earnings ratio of stocks.

mark bonds dropped by about 5 percentage points in the last few weeks of the year. In the first three months of the year, deposit and loan rates began to follow long-term rates down.

Several financial markets in Latin America experienced considerable volatility in October and November following market turbulence in Mexico. Beginning at the end of September private sector concerns about prospects for an early recovery in Mexico and the health of its banking system exerted downward pressure on the peso (Chart 14). By mid-November, the Mexican peso had depreciated by 27 percent against the U.S. dollar, and short-term interest rates had more than doubled. A mildly favorable response to the 1996 budget, the announcement of stepped-up efforts to support troubled commercial banks, occasional intervention by the Bank of Mexico in the foreign exchange market, and successful international bond placements contributed to improving market sentiment at year-end. However, the peso came under renewed pressure in early February on concerns about inflation. Nevertheless, the peso was still stronger in real and nominal terms than it was last autumn; and peso interest rates, although still high, are well down from their peaks in September and October. Venezuela lowered the official value of its currency by 41 percent relative to the dollar in mid-December, in the face of dwindling reserves. The devaluation unified all administered exchange rates and eliminated a two-tier system in place since October. In Brazil, at the end of January the trading band for the real against the U.S. dollar was lowered by 7 percent because of concerns about deteriorating trade competitiveness, but the actual exchange rate only depreciated by 1½ percent over the three months to the end of March 1996. Also, in response to a surge in capital inflows and strong growth of reserves, the authorities announced a number of restrictions on short-term capital flows. In Ecuador, the currency has depreciated against the dollar by over 10 percent since September because of uncertainty about inflation and stabilization policies.

In Asia, the desire to enhance the effectiveness of monetary policy prompted the Indonesian central bank in January to widen (to 3 percent) the intervention band within which the currency may fluctuate in response to market forces. In Thailand, to prevent currency appreciation in the face of large inflows, the central bank intervened substantially in the foreign exchange market; despite measures to sterilize the resulting increase in liquidity, downward pressure on interest rates emerged in early 1996. Following a two-year period in which the exchange rate of the Indian rupee had been held stable in the face of heavy capital inflows, it depreciated by over 15 percent against the U.S. dollar between September and January, reflecting rapid import growth, a widening of the trade deficit, and political uncertainties. After falling to a record low of nearly 38 rupees to the dol-

Table 6. Developing Countries: Capital Flows[1]

(Annual average, in billions of U.S. dollars)

	1973–77	1978–82	1983–88	1989–95	1994	1995
Developing countries						
Net private capital flows[2]	10.2	26.0	11.6	114.3	149.0	166.4
Net direct investment	3.6	9.0	12.6	39.8	61.3	71.7
Net portfolio investment	0.2	1.7	4.3	41.5	50.4	37.0
Other net investments	6.4	15.3	–5.2	33.1	37.3	57.8
Net official flows	11.0	25.5	29.5	11.7	2.6	27.3
Change in reserves[3]	–20.2	–21.7	–9.6	–56.8	–57.9	–75.7
Africa						
Net private capital flows[2]	4.5	4.3	0.5	4.9	11.9	9.8
Net direct investment	1.0	0.3	1.1	2.1	2.2	2.1
Net portfolio investment	0.1	–0.3	–0.4	–0.3	1.1	0.1
Other net investments	3.4	4.3	–0.1	3.0	8.6	7.6
Net official flows	2.4	7.2	6.6	2.0	1.5	2.8
Change in reserves[3]	–1.4	0.4	–0.4	–2.1	–5.1	–1.4
Asia						
Net private capital flows[2]	4.3	13.9	11.2	45.7	75.1	98.2
Net direct investment	1.4	3.0	5.6	24.4	41.9	52.4
Net portfolio investment	0.1	0.2	0.9	10.1	16.0	18.5
Other net investments	2.8	10.7	4.7	11.2	17.1	27.3
Net official flows	4.0	7.4	6.4	7.2	6.0	5.9
Change in reserves[3]	–6.9	–7.0	–18.0	–38.9	–61.6	–50.0
Middle East and Europe						
Net private capital flows[2]	–10.3	–21.1	1.9	29.7	11.4	19.0
Net direct investment	–1.3	–0.1	1.2	0.9	–0.5	0.0
Net portfolio investment	0.0	–0.2	5.0	13.6	15.9	8.4
Other net investments	–9.1	–20.8	–4.3	15.2	–4.1	10.5
Net official flows	2.3	6.6	6.6	–2.6	–1.4	–3.8
Change in reserves[3]	–14.2	–17.6	9.5	–4.4	–0.2	–2.6
Western Hemisphere						
Net private capital flows[2]	11.7	28.9	–2.0	34.0	50.7	39.5
Net direct investment	2.5	5.8	4.7	12.4	17.7	17.1
Net portfolio investment	0.0	2.0	–1.2	18.1	17.4	10.0
Other net investments	9.2	21.1	–5.6	3.6	15.6	12.3
Net official flows	2.3	4.4	9.8	5.1	–3.5	22.4
Change in reserves[3]	2.2	2.5	–0.7	–1.4	9.0	–21.7

Sources: IMF, Balance of Payments Statistics data base; and IMF staff estimates.

[1]Net capital flows comprise net direct investment, net portfolio investment, and other long- and short-term net investment flows, including official and private borrowing.

[2]Because of data limitations other net investment may include some official flows.

[3]A minus sign indicates an increase.

lar in early February, the currency stabilized after the Indian authorities announced measures aimed at reversing the lags in repatriation of export receipts, which have affected flows in the thin foreign exchange market. It has traded in a narrow range of around Rs 34 to the U.S. dollar since then. At the end of October, the Pakistan rupee was devalued by 7 percent, following concerns over external competitiveness and a sharp fall in the country's foreign exchange reserves. Since then the currency has been relatively stable.

In Turkey, the lira came under significant pressure amid uncertainties in the run-up to the general election in December, leading to considerable exchange market intervention and reserve losses. The currency stabi-

lized in January, but continued to fall in February and March as the central banks allowed the Turkish lira to depreciate in line with inflation expectations. At the end of March, the lira had depreciated against the dollar by about 18 percent since December. Finally, the South African rand fell sharply against the U.S. dollar in mid-February amidst concerns that government plans to relax foreign exchange controls would trigger flows of capital out of the country. The currency remained under pressure on uncertainties about economic policies and by the end of March was trading around R 4 to the U.S. dollar compared with a six-month average up to mid-February of around R 3.65.

Equity markets in developing countries have been volatile in recent months. In general, prices have risen substantially, especially since December when a cut in U.S. interest rates raised hopes of increasing equity flows to emerging markets (see Chart 12, bottom panel). In Latin America, equity prices fell in both Argentina and Mexico in September and October; the markets rallied from November onward, with a significant surge in January. However, there was a marked correction in February, with a rebound in Mexico in March. By the end of March, equity prices in Argentina were only slightly higher than at the beginning of the year, while in Mexico they were over 10 percent higher. The equity markets in Brazil and Peru, which were adversely affected by the events in Mexico in October, have also rebounded since then, with the market in Colombia increasing sharply in February but then giving up most of the gains in March. The Venezuelan market rose by over 50 percent in local currency terms in the last three months of the year on investor optimism concerning the government's economic reform and liberalization plans; the market rose another 65 percent in the first three months of this year. The gradual slowing of growth and political uncertainties contributed to a decline in the Korean stock market by over 10 percent in November and December; the decline subsequently slowed and prices increased slightly in March. Tighter financial policies and moderating growth in China contributed to a reduction in equity prices by over 25 percent from September to January. In Indonesia, Malaysia, the Philippines, and Thailand, markets have been buoyant since December, although there was some reversal in Thailand in March. Equity prices in India continued to fall in October and November on concerns about high interest rates and political uncertainty, but a significant pickup has occurred since then; in the first three months of this year, prices increased by over 10 percent. In Pakistan, equity prices bounced back sharply in December after the announcement of the package of measures to stabilize the economy. Prices continued to increase until March, when there was a correction. Equities in South Africa rose substantially during November to January, buoyed by large portfolio inflows and a small upward revision by Standard & Poor's of the country's long-term foreign currency rating. The market was, however, adversely affected by political and exchange market uncertainties in February and March. In Turkey, equity prices in local currency terms have risen by over 50 percent since the beginning of the year amidst healthy earnings expectations and receding political uncertainties.

Chart 14. Selected Developing Countries: Bilateral Exchange Rates Against the U.S. Dollar and Real Effective Exchange Rates[1]

(January 1992 = 100; logarithmic scale)

The Mexican peso experienced considerable volatility in 1995 and early 1996.

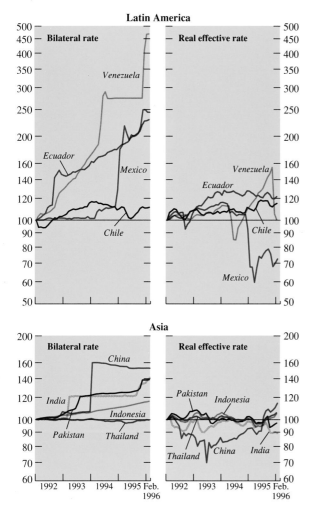

[1]Bilateral exchange rates are in domestic currency units per U.S. dollar, so that a rise indicates depreciation of the domestic currency. The real effective exchange rate indices show changes in the real value of the domestic currency in terms of a basket of currencies of trading partners, with consumer price indices used as deflators; here a rise indicates appreciation (in real effective terms) of the domestic currency.

External Payments, Financing, and Debt

As in 1994, world trade in goods and services grew by about 9 percent in 1995, more than twice the rate of growth of world output. Despite the recent economic

Table 7. Selected Countries: Current Account Positions

(In percent of GDP)

	1993	1994	1995	1996	1997
United States	−1.5	−2.2	−2.1	−2.0	−2.0
Japan	3.1	2.8	2.2	1.9	2.0
Germany	−0.9	−1.0	−0.7	−0.5	−0.5
France	0.8	0.7	1.2	0.8	0.8
Italy	1.1	1.7	2.4	2.4	2.6
United Kingdom	−1.8	−0.3	−0.8	−0.3	−0.0
Canada	−4.0	−3.0	−1.7	−0.6	−0.6
Australia	−3.7	−4.8	−5.3	−4.6	−4.5
Austria	−0.4	−0.9	−1.8	−1.4	−0.8
Belgium-Luxembourg	5.4	5.6	6.0	6.1	6.3
Denmark	3.5	1.8	1.5	1.2	1.3
Finland	−1.3	1.3	3.5	2.9	2.6
Greece	−0.7	−0.1	−2.3	−2.1	−2.0
Netherlands	4.0	4.1	4.4	3.4	3.8
Norway	3.1	2.4	3.5	4.9	5.3
Spain	−0.8	−0.8	1.3	0.5	0.2
Sweden	−2.2	0.4	2.2	3.2	3.5
Switzerland	8.4	7.1	6.5	5.9	5.5
Algeria	1.6	−4.3	−7.3	−4.4	−3.6
Argentina	−2.9	−3.5	−1.3	−1.6	−1.7
Brazil	−0.2	−0.3	−2.7	−2.2	−2.2
Cameroon	−5.6	−3.1	−3.6	−1.6	−2.3
Chile	−4.6	−1.4	0.2	−2.8	−2.6
China	−2.0	1.5	2.3	1.0	0.3
Côte d'Ivoire	−8.9	−2.1	−3.1	−3.6	−5.0
Egypt	4.7	0.4	2.7	−0.3	−3.2
India	−0.4	−0.6	−1.5	−1.9	−2.1
Indonesia	−1.6	−1.7	−3.7	−4.1	−4.2
Israel	−2.1	−3.5	−5.6	−4.7	−6.1
Korea	0.1	−1.2	−2.0	−1.5	−1.5
Malaysia	−4.6	−5.9	−8.5	−7.9	−7.7
Mexico	−6.4	−7.7	−0.1	−0.9	−1.0
Nigeria	−2.9	−2.4	−0.7	−1.7	−2.7
Pakistan	−4.9	−3.3	−3.8	−4.3	−3.9
Philippines	−5.5	−4.4	−3.3	−2.7	−2.3
Saudi Arabia	−14.6	−7.5	−4.0	−2.2	−4.3
Singapore	9.1	17.3	18.3	14.7	13.1
South Africa	1.5	−0.5	−2.3	−2.5	−2.4
Taiwan Province of China	3.0	2.6	1.6	1.8	1.9
Thailand	−5.4	−5.7	−7.1	−7.0	−6.4
Turkey	−3.5	2.0	−1.0	−1.9	−1.6
Uganda	−1.6	−0.8	−3.0	−3.3	−3.0
Czech Republic	2.2	−0.1	−3.3	−4.9	−4.3
Hungary	−9.0	−9.5	−5.5	−3.9	−2.9
Poland[1]	−0.1	2.3	2.9	0.4	−1.2
Russia	3.4	1.2	1.2	−0.4	−1.3

[1]Based on data for the current balance, including a surplus on unrecorded trade transactions, as estimated by IMF staff.

slowdown in Europe and the softening of domestic demand in the United States, world trade is expected to increase by 6½–7 percent a year in 1996 and 1997. The rapid growth of world trade can be traced to a number of factors, including achievements in trade liberalization, especially the increased openness of many developing countries and countries in transition; increasing international diversification of production, including outsourcing by multinational corporations; and the dynamic growth of trade among developing countries, especially in Asia and Latin America. The implementation of the Uruguay Round agreements under the aegis of the World Trade Organization should ensure further dismantling of trade barriers and promote continued growth.

Recent developments in economic activity, and shifts in external competitiveness, are expected to help reduce current account imbalances significantly in a number of countries over the next couple of years (Table 7). Current account deficits that widened substantially in 1994 and 1995 in a number of rapidly growing Asian economies are expected to narrow or stabilize owing mainly to the implementation of corrective policy measures. In Latin America, however, economic recovery is likely to widen current account deficits in some countries. In the industrial countries, the economic slowdown in Europe is expected to be associated with weaker import and export volumes across countries, resulting in only modest shifts in current account positions in 1996. Japan's current account surplus, which has narrowed considerably in recent years, is expected to remain at around 1995 levels as a percent of GDP, as the effects of improved competitiveness stemming from exchange rate realignments since mid-1995 are offset by a strengthening of economic activity. For the United States, stronger growth in some important trading partners, particularly Japan and Mexico, together with continuing strong competitiveness, is expected to be countered by relatively strong import growth.

Among other industrial countries, Canada is expected to register a further narrowing of its current account deficit, which declined by about 1 percent of GDP in both 1994 and 1995. This projected continued improvement reflects increased competitiveness—resulting from earlier declines in the dollar, gains in productivity, and industrial restructuring—as well as the moderate growth of domestic demand. Within Europe, in Germany and the United Kingdom, export volumes are likely to slow owing to the weakness of growth in other European countries, but declining import volumes will prevent any significant erosion in their external balances. In France, a small decrease in the current account surplus is expected because of a pickup in the growth in import volumes later in 1996 when domestic demand is projected to improve. Current account surpluses are expected to increase during 1996–97 in Italy and Sweden, reflecting strong growth in exports bolstered by earlier depreciations of their currencies, and also in Norway because of a continuing increase in exports of oil and gas. Current account deficits are expected to persist in Austria, partly due to weakness in the tourism balance, and in Greece because of the increase in imports of investment goods, including for publicly funded infrastructure projects.

Among the developing countries of Asia, robust growth during 1995 in Malaysia and Thailand spurred import demand, particularly for machinery and equipment. In Indonesia, supply shocks contributed to sharp growth in food imports. As a result, current account deficits in these countries widened by 1½–2½ percentage points of GDP. Tightened financial policies are expected to cause these imbalances to stabilize or decline slightly in 1996. In China, the current account surplus is expected to narrow because of both strong import growth and moderating export growth.

In a number of countries in the Western Hemisphere, current account deficits narrowed in 1995. Imports declined substantially in response to the adjustment policies implemented in the wake of Mexico's financial crisis and the resulting slowdown in economic activity. Export earnings increased owing, among other factors, to exchange rate depreciation, and in some cases, favorable terms of trade movements. In Mexico, the current account deficit was virtually eliminated in 1995, after reaching a deficit of about 8 percent of GDP in 1994. The sharp real depreciation of the peso over the last year will continue to spur exports in the coming year. With gains in competitiveness through falling wages and prices in the tradable goods sector, the current account deficit in Argentina also narrowed substantially during 1995. Chile, which was largely unaffected by Mexico's crisis, also registered a narrowing current account deficit owing to exceptionally high copper prices. Current account deficits in these countries are expected to widen in 1996 as growth continues to recover in most countries of the region and as commodity prices decline somewhat.

For Africa, notwithstanding the recovery-related increase in imports and the projected decline in commodity prices, current account balances are expected to improve somewhat in 1996 as further trade liberalization boosts export volumes. The current account deficit in South Africa widened slightly to over 2 percent of GDP in 1995, despite the expansion of exports, as domestic demand for manufacturing and food imports increased. In Uganda, the doubling of coffee prices in late 1994 and early 1995 boosted export earnings, but this was insufficient to prevent a widening of the current account deficit. With the projected decline in coffee prices the current account deficit is expected to widen somewhat in 1996. In Cameroon, increases in cotton and timber production are expected to improve the current account position this year.

Net capital flows to emerging market countries recovered strongly during the second half of 1995 following the sharp decline in the wake of the Mexican financial crisis. Although some countries have not recovered fully from the fallout of the Mexican crisis—especially countries where weaknesses in domestic financial markets were exposed by the crisis—aggregate net capital flows to developing countries in 1995 were higher than in the previous year. Interest rate declines in the major industrial countries helped capital flows to recover, as did the favorable reaction of financial markets to policy tightening in many emerging market countries. In Latin America, with the two main exceptions of Mexico and Argentina, private inflows exceeded the levels attained in 1994, with particularly sharp increases to Brazil. The Asian countries continued to attract large flows, and flows surged to South Africa and Turkey and central Europe. Official flows to developing and transition countries were unusually high during 1995. In particular, use of IMF resources surged to about $26.8 billion in 1995—more than triple its 1994 level—reflecting in part loans of $13 billion to Mexico and $5 billion to Russia, to support comprehensive adjustment programs.

The rapid recovery in capital flows to developing countries, despite the widespread contagion effects earlier in 1995, suggests that for most of the large recipient countries, these inflows are attracted largely by prudent macroeconomic policies and prospects for strong growth. Provided policymakers in developing countries continue to contain inflationary pressures, aggregate capital flows should be sustained at relatively high levels over the medium term. Capital flows to all developing country regions are expected to increase gradually. The composition of aggregate inflows, however, is expected to vary considerably among the different regions. Asian and Latin American countries will continue to receive most private capital inflows, especially as the pace of privatization activity picks up in a number of the larger countries, such as Brazil and Thailand. By contrast, official flows, which were unusually high in 1995, are expected to decline further in 1996 and 1997. For some African countries, such as the CFA countries and Uganda, the decline in external assistance is expected to be partly offset by a gradual increase in private capital inflows, but for the region as a whole aggregate inflows will only be marginally higher than in 1994 and 1995.

The burden of debt for the developing countries and the countries in transition is projected to ease further during 1996 reflecting the increased share of non-debt-creating flows in net external financing observed since 1994. The external debt burden of developing countries is projected to decline to 30 percent of GDP, and 107 percent of export earnings, the lowest levels since 1982 (Chart 15). In sub-Saharan Africa, however, despite some improvement, debt and debt service are still a cause for concern even though debt-servicing ratios are relatively low, and a large portion of debt is concessional and supported by official transfers. In response to these concerns, the World Bank and the IMF are assisting countries to implement appropriate policies and develop strategies in the event of future financial difficulties. For the countries in transition, the growth of debt in 1996 is projected to slow to about 6 percent and to diminish thereafter.[13]

Since the last *World Economic Outlook*, a number of countries have completed debt and debt-service agreements with commercial banks, and other countries have made substantial progress toward resolving their commercial bank debt problems. Completed agreements as of February 1996 brought total restructured bank debt for 25 countries to $173 billion. In October 1995, Panama completed a debt and debt-service-reduction agreement with commercial banks covering

Chart 15. Developing Countries and Countries in Transition: External Debt and Debt Service[1]
(In percent of exports of goods and services)

Debt and debt-service ratios are expected to decline in 1996.

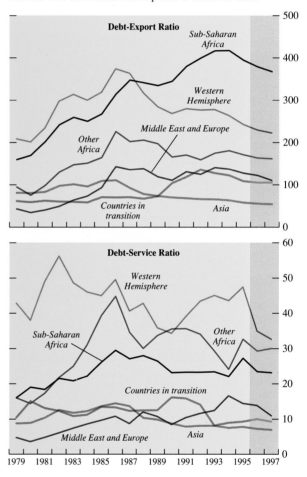

[1]Debt service refers to actual payments of interest on total debt plus actual amortization payments on long-term debt. The projections (blue shaded areas) incorporate the impact of exceptional financing items.

---

[13]For the transition countries, the ratios of debt to output and debt to exports of goods and services are projected to decline in 1996 to 27 percent and 105 percent, respectively.

about $2 billion of principal and $1.5 billion of past due interest, and Algeria concluded an agreement to reschedule $3.2 billion of a total of $4.2 billion commercial bank debt outstanding. Peru made further progress in normalizing relations with commercial banks and announced an agreement in principle, and Vietnam and Côte d'Ivoire continued discussions with their commercial bank creditors. Albania, Ethiopia, Nicaragua, and Sierra Leone completed buybacks of commercial bank debt at steep discounts, with support from the World Bank–IDA Debt Reduction Facility. In November 1995, discussions between Russia and the London Club resulted in an agreement to reschedule $25.5 billion of commercial bank debt inherited from the former Soviet Union, and approximately $7 billion in interest arrears. Slovenia and commercial bank creditors reached agreement on the country's share of the unallocated portion of the former Socialist Federal Republic of Yugoslavia's debt. A bond exchange for the debt is likely to take place by the end of May 1996.

Paris Club creditors also made progress with debt restructuring under the Naples terms since the last *World Economic Outlook*. Agreement was reached with Bolivia on a stock-of-debt operation; with Cameroon, Honduras, and Zambia on flow reschedulings; and with Gabon on a nonconcessional flow rescheduling. The international financial institutions are continuing to work on finding ways to alleviate the debt problems of the heavily indebted poor countries.

Appendix

The Maastricht Convergence Process

On December 16, 1995, at the conclusion of the European Council meeting in Madrid, the member countries of the European Union confirmed that the third and final stage of Economic and Monetary Union will begin on January 1, 1999. They agreed that the Council, meeting at the level of heads of state or government, will decide as early as possible in 1998, on the basis of performance indicators for 1997, which member states fulfill the conditions laid out in the Maastricht Treaty for participation in the monetary union. It was also agreed that the European Central Bank (ECB) will be created early enough (once the decision on stage three is taken) to allow preparations to be completed and full central bank operations to start on January 1, 1999. As stipulated in the Treaty, the primary objective of the European System of Central Banks (ESCB)—the ECB together with national central banks—will be to maintain price stability and, without prejudice to that objective, support the general policy goals of sustainable growth and high levels of employment.

The third stage will start with the irrevocable fixing of exchange rates among the currencies of participat-

ing countries and against the *Euro*—the name chosen for the single currency. For these countries, monetary policy will be formulated and implemented by the ESCB, while the general orientation for foreign exchange policy may be formulated by the Council.[14] Monetary and foreign exchange policy decisions will be carried out in Euros and all new tradable public debt will be issued in Euros by the participating member states. Under the changeover scenario to the single currency, it is envisaged that by the start of 2002, at the latest, Euros banknotes and coins will begin to circulate as legal tender alongside national currencies, and that at most six months later (by mid-2002) the national currencies will have been completely replaced by the Euro.

Notwithstanding the strong political commitment to EMU in most member states, it has proven much more difficult than expected to meet the conditions for participation set out in the Treaty. To qualify for the third stage, countries must satisfy convergence criteria for inflation, government budget deficits and debt, long-term interest rates, and exchange rate stability within the ERM. While there has been significant progress in most areas, so far only one country, Luxembourg (which shares a currency with Belgium) is within all the stipulated reference values (Table 8). Others are attempting to comply and most EU countries have at least some chance of qualifying by 1997. However, qualification by a sufficiently large number of countries is by no means assured. Setbacks may result not only from policy slippages but also from adverse economic or financial disturbances beyond the immediate control of governments.

For the countries whose ability to qualify is in doubt, the most critical obstacle is satisfying the Treaty's fiscal criterion, which incorporates deficit and debt considerations. Several countries also have difficulties meeting other convergence criteria but tackling the fiscal problems would go a long way toward increasing convergence with respect to inflation and long-term interest rates.[15] For countries with fiscal deficits of 3 percent or more of GDP, the Treaty stipulates that the fiscal criterion can still be satisfied if there has been a substantial and continuous decline of the fiscal deficit to a level close to the reference value, or if the excess over the reference value can be con-

---

[14]According to Article 109 of the Treaty, the Council may, acting unanimously, and after consulting the ECB in an effort to achieve consensus consistent with the objective of price stability, conclude formal agreements on an exchange rate system for the Euro in relation to non-Community currencies. In the absence of such a system, the Council may, acting by a qualified majority, adopt general orientations for exchange rate policy in relation to non-Community currencies. These orientations must not conflict with the goal of price stability.

[15]It is unclear how the criterion on exchange rate stability will be applied given the widening of fluctuation margins in the ERM that occurred in mid-1993 at the height of the EMS crisis.

Table 8. European Union: Convergence Indicators for 1995, 1996, and 1997

(In percent)

	Consumer Price Inflation			General Government Balance/GDP				Gross Government Debt/GDP[2]			Long-Term Interest Rates[3]
	1995	1996	1997	1995	1996	1997	1997[1]	1995	1996	1997	March 1996
Germany	1.8	1.5	1.5	−3.5	−3.9	−3.4	...	57.7	60.1	61.1	6.5
France	1.8	1.8	1.8	−5.0	−4.2	−3.6	−3.0	52.3	55.0	56.4	6.7
Italy	5.4	4.4	4.0	−7.2	−6.8	−5.9	−4.4	122.9	121.4	119.5	10.4
United Kingdom[4]	2.8	2.8	2.6	−5.1	−3.8	−2.5	...	48.8	49.7	49.5	8.1
Spain	4.7	3.6	3.2	−5.9	−4.7	−3.9	−3.0	64.7	65.5	65.4	9.9
Netherlands	2.0	2.3	2.0	−3.8	−3.5	−2.5	...	79.0	79.5	78.5	6.5
Belgium	1.5	2.0	2.0	−4.5	−3.4	−3.7	−2.5	133.8	132.7	130.6	6.8
Sweden	2.6	2.8	2.9	−6.8	−4.5	−2.5	−2.5	80.3	79.5	78.6	8.8
Austria	2.3	2.2	1.9	−6.1	−5.1	−4.0	−3.0	66.7	69.3	71.3	6.6
Denmark[5]	1.9	2.4	2.6	−1.7	−1.0	−0.6	—	81.6	81.6	78.3	7.6
Finland	1.0	2.0	2.0	−5.6	−3.0	−0.5	−0.5	60.3	62.5	62.0	7.7
Greece[6]	9.3	7.4	5.6	−9.0	−7.9	−6.5	−4.2	113.2	113.3	113.1	13.3
Portugal	4.1	3.5	3.3	−5.2	−4.5	−4.2	−3.0	72.6	72.6	72.3	9.1
Ireland	2.5	2.3	2.7	−2.1	−2.6	−2.5	...	85.3	80.0	76.0	8.0
Luxembourg	1.9	1.8	2.0	0.4	—	—	...	6.3	6.7	6.8	6.8
All EU[7]	3.0	2.6	2.5	−5.1	−4.6	−3.6		72.0	73.0	72.9	7.9
Maastricht convergence criteria reference range/value	**2.5–3.3**	**3.0–3.3**	**3.0–3.4**	**−3.0**	**−3.0**	**−3.0**		**60.0**	**60.0**	**60.0**	**8.5–8.8**

Sources: National sources; and IMF staff projections.

Note: The table shows the convergence indicators mentioned in the Maastricht Treaty, except for the exchange rate criterion. The relevant convergence criteria are (1) consumer price inflation must not exceed that of the three best performing countries by more than 1½ percentage points; (2) interest rates on long-term government securities must not be more than 2 percentage points higher than those in the same three member states; (3) the financial position must be sustainable. In particular, the general government deficit should be at or below the reference value of 3 percent of GDP. If not, it should have declined substantially and continuously and reached a level close to the reference value, or the excess over the reference value should be temporary and exceptional. The gross debt of general government should be at or below 60 percent of GDP or, if not, the debt ratio should be sufficiently diminishing and approaching the 60 percent reference value at a satisfactory pace. The exchange rate criterion is that the currency must have been held within the normal fluctuation margins of the ERM for two years without a realignment at the initiative of the member state in question.

[1]Official targets or intentions. The staff's fiscal projections shown in the two preceding columns are in some cases based on different growth, inflation, or interest rate assumptions from those used by national authorities and do not take into account further consolidation measures that are planned by EU governments in accordance with their convergence programs but which have not yet been announced. For Germany, the authorities intend to respect the Maastricht fiscal deficit criterion, as noted in the *Annual Economic Report of the Government*, January 1996. The target for Italy is that contained in the government's three-year fiscal plan of May 1995. The U.K. authorities' objective is to bring the public sector borrowing requirements back toward balance over the medium term. The authorities project the general government deficit in 1996/97 (April–March) to be close to the 3 percent Maastricht reference value and to fall substantially below that level in subsequent years. The Netherlands has no official deficit target, but the authorities have established an upper limit for the central government deficit that translates to a central government deficit of less than 3 percent of GDP. The targets for Austria, Greece, Portugal, and Spain are derived from the convergence plans presented to the EU. For Denmark, the target is that contained in *Budgetoversigt*, Ministry of Finance, December 1995. For Ireland, the authorities' objective is to keep the general government deficit comfortably within the Maastricht reference value. Luxembourg has no formal objective; the authorities expect to keep the general government accounts close to balance in 1996 and 1997.

[2]Debt data refer to end of year. They relate to general government but may not be consistent with the definition agreed at Maastricht.

[3]Ten-year government bond yield or nearest maturity.

[4]Retail price index excluding mortgage interest.

[5]Government deposits with the central bank, government holdings of nongovernment bonds, and government debt related to public enterprises amounted to some 20 percent of GDP in 1995.

[6]General government balance includes capitalized interest; long-term interest rate is 12-month treasury bill rate.

[7]Average weighted by 1994 GDP shares, based on the purchasing power parity (PPP) valuation of country GDPs for consumer price index, general government balances, and debt.

sidered to be temporary and exceptional. It also stipulates that if the debt-to-GDP ratio is not less than 60 percent, the criterion can still be satisfied if it is approaching the benchmark at a satisfactory pace. In the annual excessive deficit exercise—which assesses compliance with the Treaty's fiscal requirements—Ireland's fiscal imbalance has not been deemed excessive; although the debt ratio is significantly above 60 percent of GDP, it is considered to be falling at a satisfactory pace (the fiscal deficit has been comfortably below 3 percent since 1989).

Over the next two years, the EU member states are expected to intensify their efforts to meet the convergence requirements. Moreover, as reflected in the offi-

Chart 16. European Union: General Government Budget Positions[1]
(In percent of GDP)

Expected progress toward reducing underlying budgetary imbalances is masked to some extent by large cyclical components in fiscal deficits.

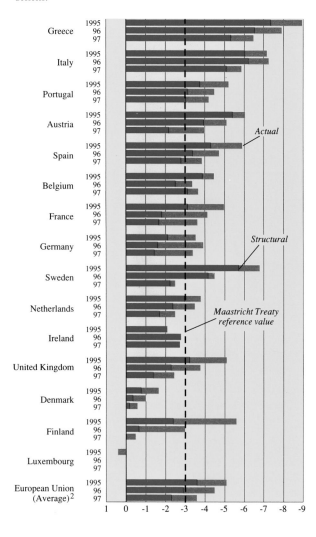

Note: The ordering of countries is based on the projected actual budget position in 1997.

[1]Structural budget positions are not shown for Luxembourg (1995–97) because data are unavailable, and for Finland (1997) because the structural balance is in surplus. Actual budget positions are not shown separately for Ireland (1995–97) because they are about equal to structural deficits, reflecting the high level of resource utilization. The actual budget position for Luxembourg is expected to be in approximate balance in 1996–97.

[2]Excludes Luxembourg.

cial targets for fiscal deficits in 1997 shown in Table 8, most member states have declared their intention to go the extra mile to satisfy the fiscal criterion in particular. Given the measures announced so far, further efforts do indeed seem to be required in most cases. In this respect, the recent deterioration in cyclical conditions in much of continental Europe has further complicated the convergence process although by 1997 a number of countries are still projected to be within striking distance of the 3 percent reference value for fiscal deficits.

As discussed earlier in this chapter, there are good reasons to expect growth to pick up in Europe by the second half of 1996 and in 1997. On these prospects, the additional effort required to meet the Maastricht criterion in 1997 would seem feasible and worthwhile, especially in certain key cases, given the more general need to strengthen fiscal consolidation in these countries. If activity turns out to be significantly weaker than expected, it would be difficult for many countries to fully meet the fiscal criterion. It would be important in such circumstances that progress in reducing structural budget deficits be sustained even while allowing the automatic stabilizers to cushion activity.

Despite the difficulties in meeting the fiscal deficit criterion, which refers to the actual deficit, the fiscal situation and prospects are somewhat more encouraging on a cyclically adjusted or structural basis (Chart 16). In fact, most of Europe still has not fully recovered from the recessions of 1992–93, and margins of slack—the shortfall of actual from potential output—are likely to remain significant at least through 1996 and possibly longer. Levels of potential output are difficult to measure precisely, partly because of uncertainty regarding the level of unemployment that is consistent with nonaccelerating inflation. Nevertheless, the staff's assessment is that margins of slack in 1995 may have amounted to roughly 2½ percent of potential GDP in the European Union as a whole. This would imply, on average, a cyclical component in EU countries' budget deficits of about 1½ percent of GDP, as indicated in the lowest set of bars in the chart. The cyclical components of deficits are likely to widen somewhat in 1996 in those countries that have seen the sharpest slowdowns, especially Germany and France, but should begin to decline in 1997, eventually disappearing with Europe's assumed recovery in future years.

The Treaty does not address whether cyclical factors might be considered to justify "exceptional and temporary" excesses from the agreed fiscal reference value. However, although the Treaty seems to allow for some flexibility in interpreting its provisions, the common view is that the 3 percent reference value should be high enough to take account of normal cyclical fluctuations.

The vulnerability of the convergence process to cyclical conditions underscores the need to reduce cyclically adjusted fiscal deficits well below the 3 percent reference value over the medium term. It is therefore encouraging that member states generally have expressed their support, at least in principle, for a Stability Pact along the lines proposed by the German authorities. According to this proposal, the participants in EMU would aim to keep fiscal deficits at no more than 1 percent of GDP in "normal times."[16] To allow automatic stabilizers to operate during cyclical slowdowns, such a rule would imply that government budgets would register moderate surpluses at peaks of the business cycle. The possibility of sanctioning countries with fiscal deficits above 3 percent of GDP through non-interest-bearing deposits and eventually fines is already envisaged in the Maastricht Treaty. A key additional feature of the German proposal is to make such sanctions automatic, unless overridden by a qualified majority of the Council.

The Treaty stipulates that if by the end of 1997 a date has not been set for the start of the third stage, then the third stage will start on January 1, 1999. Some observers, however, have suggested that the starting date for EMU be postponed to give countries more time to meet the fiscal criterion. Even though it seems likely that some of the existing members of the EU would join the monetary union at a later stage, which presumably also would be the case for the potential future member states,[17] a postponement is seen by many as likely if only a very small number of countries are considered to qualify by early 1998. Most EU governments, however, have emphasized that there could be serious drawbacks to postponing the starting date since that might lead to a relaxation of convergence efforts and adversely affect financial market confidence.

* * *

From a longer-term perspective—and irrespective of the decision that will be taken in early 1998—achieving a high degree of fiscal discipline is essential for macroeconomic stability, for ensuring reasonable price stability without overburdening monetary policy, and for allowing adequate levels of investment and growth. In addition, fiscal policy in Europe is facing a major challenge because of the potential future pressures on government budgets associated with the aging of Europe's population (see Chapter III). Fiscal discipline is also necessary to permit a countercyclical role for fiscal policy, at least by allowing automatic stabilizers to operate over the business cycle. In fact, since the exchange rate instrument would no longer be available to help individual member countries adjust in exceptional circumstances, a countercyclical role for fiscal policy may be needed to a greater extent than before. This could be the case particularly in response to adverse disturbances with asymmetric effects across member states, although of course, the incidence of policy-induced asymmetric shocks could well be lower than before. Overall, the success of the monetary union may well hinge on the ability of governments to make binding commitments to appropriate mechanisms for fiscal discipline beyond the test year of 1997.

Both the fiscal outlook and the long-run economic performance of the monetary union will also depend on the success with which countries tackle the many impediments to job creation and job search that characterize European labor markets. Despite some progress in several countries in enhancing labor market flexibility, levels of structural unemployment, particularly among the unskilled and the young, remain much higher in Europe than in most other industrial countries. In response to this problem, many European countries have attempted to lower unemployment through early retirement and work sharing, that is, through reductions in hours worked. However, while there is nothing objectionable in early retirement and reduced working hours freely agreed between employers and employees that exploit the trade-off between income and leisure, there is little evidence to suggest that such measures are likely to reduce unemployment significantly. In fact, because such measures may raise the cost of labor, they are more likely to increase unemployment.

Instead, fundamental reforms are urgently needed in most countries to reduce the gap between wage costs and productivity for the most vulnerable groups, including measures that better achieve social objectives without impeding job creation and job search. As in the case of fiscal discipline, such reforms should not be viewed as policy requirements that are necessary only because of the planned monetary union: they are essential in their own right in order to address the serious problems of unemployment and social exclusion, to enhance the flexibility of wages and prices, to promote greater economic dynamism in the European economies, and to help alleviate fiscal imbalances. Indeed, there are many reasons why economic performance in the monetary union would be much better, and the potential drawbacks associated with the loss of the exchange rate instrument much smaller, if European labor markets were more flexible.

---

[16]For countries participating in the third stage of EMU, the permanent locking of exchange rates would presumably help to reduce risk premiums in interest rates and, hence, government debt-servicing costs. This should help to lower budget deficits further in accordance with the objective of the proposed Stability Pact.

[17]The December 1995 Madrid meeting of the European Council confirmed the intention of the EU to consider the membership applications of the countries of central and eastern Europe, Malta, and Cyprus.

III

Fiscal Challenges Facing Industrial Countries

The ballooning of public debt in industrial countries over the past two decades of relative world peace and prosperity is unprecedented. Increasingly, this is a problem. Higher levels of government debt boost real interest rates, retard the accumulation of private capital, and limit gains in living standards. Perhaps most worrisome is that populations will age noticeably over the coming decades, exacerbating budgetary pressures because of pension and health care demands. As a result, future public debt paths on current policies appear unsustainable in most industrial countries. Most governments recognize the problems of persistently high deficits and debt; some progress with fiscal consolidation has been made; and further progress is expected over the latter part of the 1990s. Still, North American and most European countries have made only limited progress to date in putting their ratios of public debt to GDP on downward trajectories; and debt in Japan, which has been most concerned about the fiscal implications of its aging population, seems poised to rise sharply in the coming years.

This chapter analyzes the factors that underlie this trend toward higher public debt levels in the industrial countries, including such factors as the growth of the modern welfare state. The strains that population aging are likely to place on government budgets are also assessed. Finally, the experiences of countries that have moved to reduce their budget deficits are reviewed. The analysis shows that fiscal consolidation does not always have harsh consequences for economic activity, as many have assumed. In particular, when fiscal consolidation is concentrated on the expenditure side rather than the revenue side, the odds improve that both the ratio of public debt to GDP will fall and that economic growth can be maintained. Democratic governments, aware that difficult fiscal consolidation is necessary but worrying about the next election, may find some reassurance in this. Indeed, delaying corrective action usually will ensure only that adjustment will ultimately be imposed by financial markets, and that the consequences may be more severe and more prolonged.

A Short History of Fiscal Trends

Over the past one hundred and fifty years, public sector budgets in industrial countries have rarely been

Chart 17. Selected Industrial Countries: Ratio of Average Budget Balance to GDP[1]
(In percent of GDP)

Large deficits have typically only occured during periods of war.

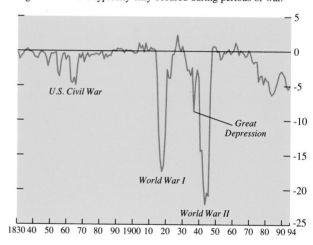

Source: Paul Masson and Michael Mussa, "Long-Term Tendencies in Budget Deficits and Debt," IMF Working Paper 95/128 (December 1995), p. 4a.

[1]Simple average of Canada, France, Italy, Japan, the United Kingdom, and the United States.

in serious deficit except in extreme circumstances.[18] The key periods when budget deficits mushroomed were during the two World Wars and during the Great Depression of the 1930s (Chart 17). Other special events, such as the U.S. Civil War in the 1860s, the Russo-Japanese War in the early 1900s, and German unification in the early 1990s, have also increased deficits sharply. These large but temporary budget deficits increased ratios of public debt to GDP abruptly (Chart 18). But such debt spikes have generally been transitory, because in the wake of these episodes, governments have tightened their belts and even run surpluses. Given the historical experience, the continuous and sustained rise in budget deficits and debt ratios in most industrial countries over the past couple of decades, a period of general peace and economic prosperity, is especially striking.

In the period from the end of World War II until about 1970, expenditures and revenues increased more or less in parallel, and governments' fiscal positions were kept close enough to balance to ensure that public debt ratios were flat or declining. Large deficits then emerged following the first oil crisis in the mid-1970s, and budget deficits in almost all industrial countries widened dramatically after 1980. Revenue collections do not seem to have been the problem. The ratio of revenue to GDP has increased for nearly every industrial country over the past couple of decades, and for these countries taken together, revenues have increased from a simple average of 28 percent of GDP in 1960 to 44 percent in 1994 (Chart 19). Some countries, including Denmark, Finland, and Sweden, currently have revenue-to-GDP ratios that exceed 50 percent. Even "low-revenue" countries, such as Australia, Japan, and the United States, have seen their ratios of revenue to GDP rise from the 18 to 25 percent range in 1960 to the 30 to 35 percent range today. For the most part, these higher revenues have been generated through higher direct taxes—often via high marginal tax rates—and through higher social security contributions. The result is that effective tax rates on income have become so high in some countries that they discourage work and create other distortions in labor markets and in the economy more generally.[19]

Rather than being a revenue problem, modern fiscal imbalances stem from the fact that expenditures have increased even more dramatically. Government expenditures in industrial countries jumped from a simple average of 28 percent of GDP in 1960 to 50 percent in

Chart 18. Selected Industrial Countries: Ratio of Gross Debt to GDP
(In percent of GDP)

Debt ratios have soared during periods of war, but the increases over the past couple of decades are unusual for a period of relative world peace and prosperity.

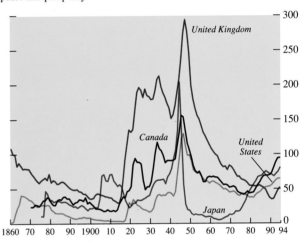

Source: Paul Masson and Michael Mussa, "Long-Term Tendencies in Budget Deficits and Debt," IMF Working Paper 95/128 (December 1995), p. 4b.

---

[18]For a comprehensive review of long-term fiscal trends, see Paul Masson and Michael Mussa, "Long-Term Tendencies in Budget Deficits and Debt," IMF Working Paper 95/128 (December 1995).

[19]See for example, Martin Feldstein, "The Effect of Marginal Tax Rates on Taxable Income: A Panel Study of the 1986 Tax Reform Act," *Journal of Political Economy*, Vol. 103 (June 1995), pp. 551–72.

Chart 19. Major Industrial Countries: Revenues and Expenditures as a Share of GDP

(In percent of GDP, all countries with equal weight)

Although revenues have increased steadily as a share of GDP, expenditures have increased even more rapidly, causing substantial budget deficits since the mid-1970s.

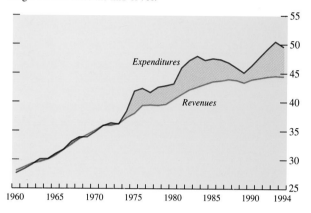

Sources: Data for 1964–76 are from OECD, *Historical Statistics 1960–1993* (Paris, 1995); for 1977–94 the data are from OECD, *Economic Outlook* (Paris, December 1995).

Chart 20. Major Industrial Countries: Government Expenditure on Transfers and Subsidies

(In percent of GDP)

Spending on transfers and subsidies has been one of the fastest growing components of government expenditure.

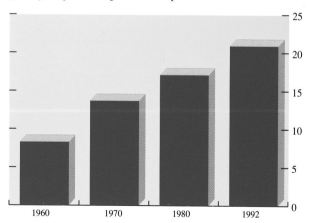

Source: Vito Tanzi and Ludger Schuknecht, "The Growth of Government and the Reform of the State in Industrial Countries," IMF Working Paper 95/130 (December 1995), p. 11.

1994, a year in which the ratio hit 69 percent of GDP in Sweden and roughly 55 percent of GDP in Belgium, France, Italy, and the Netherlands. Government consumption spending increased sharply over the period from 1960 to 1980, but has been roughly flat as a percentage of GDP since 1980. The really big increases have been in transfers (including public pensions), subsidies, and interest payments. In 1960, transfers and subsidies averaged just 8 percent of GDP in the industrial countries, but they jumped to 17 percent of GDP in 1980 and 21 percent in 1992 (Chart 20). Such payments now account for roughly one third of GDP in France, Italy, Norway, and Sweden. Interest payments in the industrial countries roughly tripled as a share of GDP between 1970 (1½ percent) and 1992 (4¼ percent). Even the so-called peace dividend that was supposed to result from the end of the Cold War has not helped much. Defense budgets, especially in the United States, have been cut noticeably over the past decade, but the average savings in industrial countries have amounted to only a little over a percentage point of GDP. The peace dividend therefore has been more than absorbed by the increase in transfer payments over this period.

As a result of these growing imbalances between expenditures and revenues, public debt has increased sharply in relation to GDP in almost all industrial countries. Between 1980 and 1995, the average gross public debt in these countries swelled from about 40 percent of GDP to about 70 percent. Most countries, including Belgium, Canada, Denmark, France, Germany, Italy, Japan, the Netherlands, Sweden, and the United States experienced roughly a doubling of their gross public debt ratios over this period, while Greece and Spain saw debt ratios increase by a factor of four or five. Among the highest debt countries, Belgium, Canada, Greece, and Italy had gross debt ratios near or over 100 percent of GDP in 1995. The debt situation in the industrial countries is even more worrisome if the unfunded liabilities of public pensions are included.

Causes of Modern Fiscal Problems

What forces have been behind these adverse budgetary developments? First and foremost has been the growth of public pensions, social spending, and other transfers. In most cases, governments have found it easier to increase revenues to try to cover these spending increases, or to allow deficits to widen, than to tackle underlying problems. In some cases, this spending growth has been related to the transformation of targeted social safety nets into universal benefits. A particular problem has been that as well-intentioned social support programs have become more generous and widely available, the number of beneficiaries has increased sharply.[20] Special interest lobbying has compounded these problems and made reform extremely difficult. Indeed, these problems have led democracies, which seem to have intrinsic difficulties in saying no to well-organized groups, to search for new policy approaches.[21] Balanced budget amendments, fiscal responsibility acts, stability pacts, and similar measures and proposals are all attempts to deal with constitutional and institutional arrangements recognized to be detrimental to fiscal discipline (Box 4).

Meanwhile, unemployment benefits that replace high proportions of previous earnings and that last for long periods have contributed to structural unemployment, and this has had a doubly negative impact on budget deficits. The exclusion of more and more people from the labor force means that fewer workers are supporting growing numbers of unemployed and retirees through higher tax burdens. European countries in particular face difficult budget challenges because a large and growing share of their populations are simply not participating in economic production. Indeed, just as tackling entitlement spending in the United States will be important in solving its budget deficit problems, achieving significant reductions in structural unemployment would greatly assist in the improvement of fiscal positions in Europe.

The productivity slowdown since the early 1970s has imposed a harsher budget constraint than policymakers and voters expected or seem to have realized (Chart 21). It took a long time to appreciate that there was a trend break in productivity in the early 1970s, and the result has been a smaller tax base than was expected. By the reckoning of many, voters and politicians still have not reduced their expectations about the level of benefits that governments can afford to provide for their citizens. Meanwhile, real interest rates, which would normally have been expected to decline in the face of slower productivity growth, have moved substantially higher in the 1980s and 1990s, creating another squeeze on government budget positions. Furthermore, any option of reducing the real level of government debt by generating unanticipated inflation has largely been removed by supersensitive investors who quickly exact a risk premium.

Increased exchange rate flexibility since 1973 and the growth and increasing integration of world capital markets also may have made it easier to run larger budget deficits. While there is some empirical evidence that openness of financial markets has disciplined governments with very large fiscal imbalances,

Chart 21. Selected Major Industrial Countries: Productivity Growth in Manufacturing and Average Budget Balance[1]
(Annual percent change)

As productivity growth slowed down in the 1970s and 1980s in many industrial countries, average budget balances worsened.

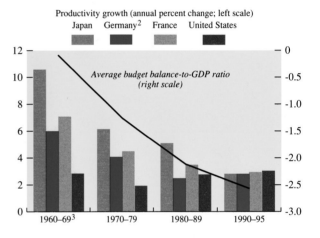

Source: U.S. Department of Labor, Bureau of Labor Statistics.
[1]Average budget balances-to-GDP ratios weighted by GDP (PPP basis).
[2]The value for Germany in the last set of columns is based on 1990–94 data.
[3]Average budget balances for 1960–69 exclude Japan and France.

---

[20]For further discussion, see Assar Lindbeck, "Hazardous Welfare-State Dynamics," *American Economic Review, Papers and Proceedings*, Vol. 85 (May 1995), pp. 9–15.

[21]For a discussion of why democracies have such difficulties, see Mancur Olson, *The Logic of Collective Action: Public Goods and the Theory of Groups* (Cambridge, Massachusetts: Harvard University Press, 1971).

Box 4. New Zealand's Fiscal Responsibility Act

The Fiscal Responsibility Act passed by New Zealand in 1994 represents an innovative approach to the promotion of prudent fiscal policy.[1] The Act is intended to increase the transparency of the fiscal and economic implications of government policy, to ensure independent assessment and reporting of fiscal policy, to facilitate parliamentary and public scrutiny of fiscal developments, and to encourage a longer-term focus in budgeting. To these ends, the Act legislates principles of responsible fiscal management and includes measures aimed at improving the flow of information on the public finances.

The principles of responsible fiscal policy defined by the Act include the achievement of "prudent levels" of government debt through operational budget surpluses; the maintenance of prudent debt levels, once achieved, through balanced budgets on average over reasonable periods of time; the achievement and maintenance of adequate levels of government net worth to provide a buffer against future adverse developments; the prudent management of fiscal risks, including pension liabilities; and the pursuit of expenditure policies consistent with stable and predictable tax rates. The Act avoids the problems of balanced budget rules that would preclude automatic stabilizers from operating. The requirement that tax rates be stable and predictable reinforces the long-term orientation of fiscal policy and the need to budget for future liabilities.

The Act also requires the government to specify short- and long-term fiscal objectives that are consistent with the principles laid out. It allows the government to depart temporarily from these principles, provided they explain why and specify how and when they plan to return to them. The government has specified prudent levels of public sector debt to be below 30 percent of GDP in the short term and below 20 percent in the longer term.

The Act also improved the quality of information flows about the public finances. A major innovation was the requirement that all of the financial reporting and forecasts be prepared on a basis consistent with the private sector's generally accepted accounting practice. This was done to enhance the credibility of public sector accounts and also to take advantage of the synergies and economies that result from aligning public and private sector accounting practices.

The change in accounting practice implied a shift from cash to accrual accounting and also required a consolidated presentation for the "Crown," which covers core government, the Reserve Bank, state-owned enterprises, and other public sector entities. A standard set of the Crown's financial reports is comparable to what a publicly listed company is required to publish. The reports include a balance sheet statement of the Crown's financial position, an operating statement, a statement of cash flows, and notes that show contingent liabilities and known risks. The frequency of reporting has increased and now includes an annual budget report on the government's fiscal strategy (discussing the likely development of crucial variables ten years into the future), a half-year economic and fiscal update, a fiscal update toward the end of the financial year, as well as an economic and fiscal update report before any general election, and monthly statements for the financial year to date. The update reports project

---

[1]For a detailed description, see New Zealand, The Treasury, *Fiscal Responsibility Act 1994—An Explanation* (1995); and also *New Zealand—Recent Economic Developments*, IMF Staff Country Report 96/14 (February 1996).

especially in more recent periods, it seems likely that on balance over the 1970s and 1980s, open financial markets for creditworthy potential borrowers allowed industrial-country governments to run larger deficits than they otherwise would have done.

Possible Justifications for Budget Deficits

Some might argue that it might be justifiable for governments to run budget deficits if the growth in government spending contributes to attaining broader economic and social objectives.[22] Increasing public

investment as a share of GDP, for example, by improving physical infrastructure, might raise the rate of return on private capital or produce a good or service that the private sector would not provide because of externalities. Higher spending on education or health care, perhaps deficit financed, might also be argued to enhance a nation's human capital. Such spending for both physical and human capital could be said to represent a good national investment that should pay for itself through higher productivity, higher incomes, and hence, higher tax revenues. But it is difficult to use this argument to justify the growth of public deficits and debt in the past couple of decades, because, as indicated earlier, virtually all of the growth of government spending has been in the areas of transfers (including public pensions), subsidies, and interest payments, not public investment or education. Between 1960 and 1990, for example, public investment shrank as a share of GDP in most industrial countries. It is not even clear that high levels of overall government

---

[22]For a survey of the relationship between government involvement and economic performance, see Joel Slemrod, "What Do Cross-Country Studies Teach About Government Involvement, Prosperity, and Economic Growth?" *Brookings Papers on Economic Activity: 2* (1995), The Brookings Institution (Washington), pp. 373–415.

revenues and expenditures three years out, and in addition assess the main risks to the outlook.

These reporting requirements are intended to ensure that any changes in the government's fiscal position become quickly apparent to the public, including the financial markets. It is no longer possible to move spending off-budget; arrears show up as an increase in the value of payables; neglected maintenance would be reflected in a decline of the value of public assets shown on the balance sheet; and sales of public assets leave government net worth unchanged. Capital expenditures show up on the balance sheet for the full amount at the time of commitment, preventing the buildup of hidden future financing needs. Decisions that increase future liabilities are shown to reduce net worth.

New Zealand's Crown balance sheet for 1994/95 (*see table*) illustrates the type of information required by the new approach. It contains items typically found on a company's balance sheet (such as advances and borrowings), as well as some items unique to governments (state highways, currency issued).

One problem in producing such a public sector balance sheet is the valuation of public assets and liabilities that are not easily marketable (such as highways, specialist military equipment, and state parks) or, even if marketable, lack an observable market price. However, most assets and liabilities are valued in line with private sector practice. For example, fixed assets are recorded at their depreciated replacement cost. Unfunded components of future commitments under the government employees' pension scheme (Government Superannuation Fund) are included among liabilities, since it is a scheme members contribute to in return for contractually defined benefits. However, public pensions and other welfare payments are not shown on the balance sheet, since they are noncontractual commitments, but are shown in the fiscal strategy reports. Nor is the Crown's power to tax included among its assets.

In interpreting the balance sheet, it should be noted that large changes in net worth can be occasioned by valuation changes in assets, such as land and foreign exchange reserves, which the government has no immediate intention of liquidating. This is one of the reasons why net worth is not a suitable indicator for near-term fiscal policy; its impact is better assessed on the basis of the operating and cash flow statements.

With the passage of its Fiscal Responsibility Act, New Zealand took a practical step to increase the fiscal transparency of its government decisions and to promote responsible fiscal management. Similar approaches could be worth considering in other countries.

New Zealand: Crown Balance Sheet, 1994/95
(In millions of New Zealand dollars; fiscal year ended June)

Assets		Liabilities	
Marketable securities	6,523	Liabilities	57,646
Advances	4,782	Payables and	
State-owned		provisions	3,824
enterprises	16,420	Currency issued	1,620
Physical assets	13,432	Borrowings	44,096
State highway	7,454	Pension liabilities	8,106
Other assets	5,876		
		Net worth[1]	−3,159
Total	**54,487**	**Total**	**54,487**

Source: New Zealand, The Treasury, *Economic and Fiscal Update* (Wellington, December 1995).

[1]The Crown's net worth had become positive by December 1995.

spending are effective in promoting economic or social goals.[23]

Budget deficits can sometimes be appropriate because of the benefits of tax smoothing. If government spending has to be high today because of, say, a natural disaster, a balanced budget policy might require extremely high tax rates today that could be very distortionary. If instead, a budget deficit is used as a buffer, the distortionary effects of taxation, including disincentives to work, could be minimized. This argument is clearly relevant to such national imperatives as paying for wars, natural disasters, or nation-building.

For example, it was clearly sensible for the German authorities to resort to temporary deficit spending to finance certain aspects of the unification with the eastern Länder.

Fiscal policy, including budget deficits, also has an important role in helping to stabilize economies and dampen business cycles. Fiscal policy in all countries incorporates automatic stabilizers, such as unemployment benefits, the outlays on which are countercyclical, and taxes on income and spending, the revenues from which are procyclical. These automatic stabilizers tend to generate budget deficits during an economic slowdown even if the budget is balanced over the cycle as a whole. Such deficits may clearly be considered desirable, however, because they help to dampen cyclical fluctuations.

The active use of fiscal policy as an instrument of demand management, including measures generating fiscal deficits to boost aggregate demand, is generally considered today to have a great risk of being counter-

---

[23]While an increased size of government historically has been associated with significant improvements in social indicators, a recent study suggests that when the government share of the economy exceeds about one third, diminishing returns set in. See Vito Tanzi and Ludger Schuknecht, "The Growth of Government and the Reform of the State in Industrial Countries," IMF Working Paper 95/130 (December 1995).

productive, except in exceptional circumstances where a country is faced with particularly adverse domestic or external shocks. This is partly because of the difficulty of ensuring that such policies are timed appropriately, given the inevitable decision and implementation lags. It is also because deficits resulting from discretionary policy actions may be hard to unwind and may lead to adverse financial market reactions. Even when there may appear to be a case for policy stimulus, large existing deficits have increasingly eliminated fiscal policy as a countercyclical policy instrument.

Why Persistent Budget Deficits Are a Problem

Some observers contend that it does not really matter if countries run persistent budget deficits or if levels of public debt to GDP rise, because private savers, anticipating larger future tax liabilities, will compensate for government dissaving and leave national saving unaffected. But the preponderance of research suggests that while there is some tendency for private savers to compensate for changes in public sector saving, the offset is far from complete. This means that government dissaving hurts national saving and lowers future living standards because either domestic investment is reduced or borrowing from abroad is increased, and with it, future obligations to service foreign debt out of future national income.

With internationally integrated financial markets, larger budget deficits and higher levels of public debt may have more widespread damaging consequences for investment and economic growth (Annex I). It seems likely, in particular, that there is a positive and significant link between industrial countries' public debt levels and global real interest rates. While the magnitude of estimates varies, some studies suggest that the run-up in public debt over the last fifteen years has increased real interest rates globally by 100 to 250 basis points or more.[24] Higher real interest rates are likely to have led to lower investment spending globally, and over time to lower capital stocks, lower capital-labor ratios, smaller increases in labor productivity, and hence slower real income growth. These losses can cumulate over time into major reductions in living standards.

Large budget deficits and debt burdens also have negative implications for economic policymaking, which can reduce welfare. If fiscal policy is disabled

as a stabilization instrument, because of the priority that has to be given to fiscal consolidation, then monetary policy may become overburdened as an instrument if there is more than one policy objective. Many would argue that this is the case in Europe today, since in the ERM countries a major task of monetary policy is to stabilize exchange rates. Large deficits can also influence exchange rates and may contribute to misalignments (see the October 1995 *World Economic Outlook*). As real debt and debt-service payments mount, so do risk premiums. This in turn increases the pace of debt accumulation and could generate a self-reinforcing cycle that becomes difficult to break.

High levels of government spending can also give the wrong microeconomic signals and incentives, and thereby reduce the rate of sustainable economic growth. Government subsidies, for example, reduce economic efficiency by shielding enterprises from competition, distorting price signals, and encouraging rent-seeking activities. The result is a misallocation of resources from their most productive uses. As governments try to garner more revenues, higher tax rates can reduce entrepreneurial initiative and encourage tax evasion, the growth of underground economic activity, and special pleading by organized interest groups. This suggests the possibility of a vicious circle whereby increased expenditures result in higher deficits, which lead to higher taxes, which in turn further blunt incentives and reduce output.

Sustainability of Public Debt and Generational Fairness

Persistent budget deficits may also result in a growth path for public debt that is simply not sustainable in the long run. Debt sustainability depends on the interest rate, the growth rate of the economy, and the ratio of the primary balance—the budget balance excluding interest payments—to GDP.[25] As long as the rate of interest on the public debt exceeds the economy's nominal growth rate, public debt will tend to grow faster than GDP unless a country runs a primary surplus. The larger the wedge between the interest rate and the nominal growth rate, the larger the primary surplus needed to stabilize the debt-to-GDP ratio.

---

[24]See, for example, Thomas Helbling and Robert Wescott, "The Global Real Interest Rate," in *Staff Studies for the World Economic Outlook* (IMF, September 1995), pp. 28–51; and Robert Ford and Douglas Laxton, "World Public Debt and Real Interest Rates," IMF Working Paper 95/30 (March 1995).

[25]Debt dynamics are described by the equation $\Delta d = [(r - g)/(1 + g)]d_{-1} - pb$, where Δ indicates the change from the previous period, d is the debt-to-GDP ratio, pb is the primary balance-to-GDP ratio, r is the nominal interest rate on public debt, and g is the growth rate of nominal GDP. There are two conventional measures of public debt: general government gross liabilities (gross debt) and the corresponding net liabilities (net debt). Net debt is the measure used to calculate the fiscal adjustment required to meet specific debt objectives since it comes closest to the correct measure of government net worth that should be used in sustainability calculations. Elsewhere in this chapter gross debt is used because it plays an important role in financial markets in many countries.

Table 9. Industrial Countries: Sustained 15-Year Changes in Primary Government Balance Required to Stabilize Net Debt to GDP

(In percent of GDP)

	Net Debt		Primary Balance 1995	Required Change in Primary Balance[1]	
	Average 1978–80	1995		Scenario 1	Scenario 2
Austria	35.7	54.6	−2.6	4.8	5.2
Belgium	62.7	127.9	4.7	4.3	6.4
Canada	12.6	66.7	1.8	4.2	3.0
Denmark	2.3	54.5	1.7	3.4	1.5
France[2]	−0.6	35.1	−2.0	5.7	3.7
Germany[2]	11.0	49.1	−0.3	4.2	2.9
Ireland[2,3]	71.6	86.3	2.3	−1.7	1.1
Italy[2]	54.4	108.9	3.3	6.0	7.6
Japan[4]	14.4	9.8	−2.5	2.5	1.5
Netherlands	21.9	60.5	0.8	3.6	3.0
Norway	8.8	−21.5	−4.1	1.8	0.4
Spain[2]	5.2	50.3	−0.5	5.9	4.2
Sweden[2]	−19.5	27.0	−5.3	9.9	6.6
United Kingdom	46.3	40.8	−2.5	3.0	4.1
United States	25.6	56.4	0.5	2.3	2.0

Source: World Economic Outlook data base.

[1]Scenario 1 shows the increase in the primary balance, starting in 1995, that would return the ratio of net debt to GDP to the average of the 1978–80 level by 2010. Scenario 2 shows the increase in the primary balance required for net debt to become 30 percent of GDP by 2010.

[2]For these countries net debt data are taken from the OECD, Economic Outlook data base.

[3]For Ireland, gross debt is used as a proxy for net debt.

[4]Due to the large asset position of the Japanese social security fund, gross debt, and net debt of the government are vastly different. The average gross debt over the period 1978–80 was 46.9 percent of GDP, while in 1995 it was 87.0 percent of GDP. Using these figures in the calculations would imply that the required change in the primary balance to meet the objectives of scenarios 1 and 2 would be 7.9 and 9.0 percent of GDP, respectively.

Given these debt dynamics, it is clear that even though public net debt ratios were stabilizing in 1995 in a number of industrial countries, albeit at imprudently high levels in many cases, reducing debt ratios will require major efforts.

Table 9 shows the sustained improvements in primary balances that would be required to return net public debt ratios in the industrial countries from 1995 levels to their average 1978–80 levels or to move them to an arbitrary common target level of 30 percent of GDP by 2010.[26] These mechanical calculations assume that interest rates and nominal GDP growth rates remain constant at their average 1993–95 levels. For Canada to reduce its net debt ratio from 67 percent of GDP today to its 1978–80 level of 13 percent, for example, would require a sustained increase in its primary surplus of 4.2 percent of GDP over and above its 1995 level. If there were a common debt target of 30 percent of GDP for all industrial countries then Italy would have to make the strongest adjustment: to

meet this target in 15 years, Italy would have to increase its primary surplus by 7.6 percentage points of GDP above its 1995 primary surplus to 10.9 percent of GDP. While lower interest rates and faster GDP growth would work in the direction of lowering ratios of debt to GDP, most of the correction would have to be achieved by running larger primary balance surpluses.

Generational accounting highlights the distributional implications of fiscal policies across generations and provides an innovative alternative approach for assessing the sustainability of fiscal policies (Box 5). The basic idea is to quantify the way government benefits and tax burdens fall upon various age cohorts. A key concept in generational accounting is the net tax payment, which is defined as taxes paid minus transfers received. The present value of expected lifetime transfer receipts for each age group—pensions, sick pay, unemployment benefits, and so on—is subtracted from the present value of expected lifetime tax payments, such as income taxes, property taxes, and social security contributions.

Although generational accounts depend upon a number of important assumptions about such factors as future productivity and real wage growth and the real discount rate, they can be viewed as a way to

[26]This numerical exercise represents an upper bound to the required primary surplus, because it does not assume a narrowing in risk premiums arising from the reduction in the ratio of debt to GDP, nor any growth benefits from lower interest rates.

Box 5. Uses and Limitations of Generational Accounting

Generational accounts may be used to assess the distributional implications across generations or age cohorts of changes in fiscal policies. They often highlight the fact that policy changes can shift resources among generations without affecting the present fiscal deficit at all. The definition of generational accounts is straightforward.[1] Using present-value calculations and imposing the intertemporal zero-sum constraint that future generations must pay with interest for government purchases for which past and current generations have not paid, generational accounts seek to answer the question of how much each generation would pay in net taxes—that is, taxes and contributions paid minus transfers received—if fiscal policies were to remain unchanged. The difference between the lifetime net tax rates of newborn and future generations provides an indicator of the sustainability of present fiscal policies, because it provides estimates of the adjustment in taxes or benefits, or both, of future generations that will be needed to ensure that the intertemporal zero-sum constraint is satisfied. For example, for the United States it is estimated that assuming annual labor productivity growth of 0.75 percent and a real discount rate of 6 percent, lifetime net tax rates of newborn and future generations would amount to 37 and 78 percent of labor income, respectively (see table), clearly indicating that under the assumptions made, present fiscal policies in the United States are unsustainable.[2]

While generational accounts provide a useful perspective on the fiscal sustainability issue, their empirical implementation imposes heavy data demands and requires specific assumptions relating to a number of difficult conceptual and theoretical issues, which raise questions about their ultimate usefulness. More specifically:

• They are highly sensitive to the specific assumptions adopted about the determination of private consumption. It is typically assumed that private consumption is determined by standard life-cycle considerations, implying, inter alia, the absence of liquidity constraints and of a bequest motive: with bequests, the transfer of the burden of paying for government spending from this generation to the next could be reversed. The numerical parameters adopted within this approach have an important impact on the calculations, as would the adoption of more fundamentally different assumptions about consumption behavior.

United States: Lifetime Net Tax Rates Under Alternative Macroeconomic Assumptions
(In percent of lifetime labor income)

Real Discount Rate	Labor 0.25	Productivity 0.75	Growth Rate 1.25
Newborn generation			
3	28	26	25
6	40	37	34
9	47	43	39
Future generations			
3	60	49	41
6	94	78	63
9	154	126	103
Difference in lifetime net tax rate of newborn and future generations (in percentage points)			
3	32	23	16
6	54	40	29
9	107	83	63

Note: The newborn generation refers to people born next year. Future generations refer to people born thereafter.

Source: John Sturrock, *Who Pays and When?* Table 5, p. 30. Variant based on intermediate population projection.

• They require agreement on a single discount rate for all generations that would capture both the cost of waiting and the risk premium for uncertainty.

• They require assumptions on the incidence of a range of taxes, with the incidence of capital taxes especially uncertain.

• They do not, as presently constructed, assume that there are intergenerational benefits from public consumption or capital expenditure.

• They assume an arbitrary time period for the implementation of the intertemporal budget constraint.

• They ignore the long-run effects that fiscal policy can have on expected future income, including its distribution between capital and labor.

In addition to these issues, generational accounts, like any other long-term projections, are subject to uncertainty as regards future demographic changes, the rate of technical progress, and hence future growth. In the particular case of the United States, sensitivity analyses indicate that the difference between lifetime net tax rates of newborn and future generations could range between 16 and 107 percentage points for real discount rates ranging from 3 to 9 percent and annual labor productivity growth rates ranging from 0.25 to 1.25 percent (see table). In light of these implementation difficulties, generational accounts are likely to be useful mainly as a conceptual tool of policy analysis and as a supplement to customary budget presentations.

---

[1]For recent reviews of the merits and limitations of generational accounts, see John Sturrock, *Who Pays and When? An Assessment of Generational Accounting* (Washington: Congressional Budget Office, 1995); and the *Journal of Economic Perspectives*, Vol. 8 (Winter 1994), which devotes the volume to generational accounting.

[2]These assumptions, used in the Congressional Budget Office study, are based on average labor productivity growth since the 1973 oil shock and the historical average real rate of return on equities.

judge the intergenerational fairness of changes in present fiscal policies. Generational accounting studies for countries including the United States, Italy, Norway, and Sweden, for example, suggest that today's young workers will have to pay $200,000 or $300,000 more in taxes over their lifetimes than they receive in benefits, if current benefit levels are to be kept unchanged, while current retirees in these countries may each receive up to $100,000 or more in benefits than they will have paid in taxes.[27] Another way of expressing generational accounting estimates is through effective lifetime tax rates. According to some estimates, for example, future generations of U.S. workers would face effective lifetime tax rates of over 70 percent of income if current spending patterns remained unchanged, compared with rates of 20 to 30 percent for current retirees, and 30 to 35 percent for current workers.[28] Such wide discrepancies in net tax payments or lifetime tax rates across age cohorts suggest that current benefit levels are inequitably high, and that they may therefore not be politically sustainable. That is, faced with the prospect of such punitive taxes, younger generations are likely to press the political system for reduced benefit levels, especially for retirees, to make intergenerational balances more equal.

There is a linkage between the degree of cross-generational "unfairness" in a country's fiscal policies as quantified by generational accounting and the magnitude of a country's overall fiscal problems. Generational accounting studies have shown that Italy, for example, has one of the largest discrepancies between the net tax burden due to be placed on current newborns and that to be placed on future generations, while this imbalance in countries like Norway, Sweden, and the United States appears to be much smaller. It is not coincidental that Italy also faces a much worse debt problem than these other countries.

While generational accounting has been criticized for being heavily dependent upon arbitrary assumptions, including about the distant future, it does have the advantage of presenting in shorthand form the unfair fiscal windfall that certain generations gain, or the unfair burden that other age cohorts will suffer. It also could serve an educational purpose by stimulating debate among younger and older voters about the proper level of transfer program generosity. In the end, this type of analysis strongly suggests that transfer programs and public pension systems will require major

overhauls to make them more equitable across generations, and thereby more sustainable.

Population Aging, Invisible Debt, and Needed Pension Reforms

Unfortunately, the weak budget positions of most countries today are not the end of the fiscal story. Governments also have explicit and implicit liabilities that will shape their future budget positions, such as promises to pay public pensions and health care benefits to retirees. With the expected aging of industrial countries' populations, there will be more elderly people to support, a smaller share of the population to work and pay taxes on labor income, and much higher medical care bills that most governments have promised to fund. When these future liabilities, together with likely future tax revenues, are taken into account, the budget prospects of industrial countries look dramatically worse. This is sometimes referred to as the invisible debt problem.

Broadly speaking, demographic developments in industrial countries over the period from 1950 to 1990 were quite favorable for budget positions. The key development was the postwar baby boom's entry into the labor force, which to date has had to support relatively few retirees. Elderly dependency ratios, defined as the population aged 65 and over as a percentage of the working age population, aged 15 to 64, have drifted slightly upward over the past four decades, but are expected to increase sharply over the next fifty years (Chart 22). Between 1995 and 2030, for example, elderly dependency ratios in most industrial countries are expected to double to the 35 to 50 percent range. By 2050, elderly dependency ratios in countries that are expected to face the worst demographic squeezes, including Germany, Italy, and Japan, will probably be in the 50 to 60 percent range, meaning that there will be less than two people of working age to support each retiree, compared with roughly five today. The situation is expected to be only somewhat better in the other industrial countries.

This dramatic aging of populations has powerful implications for public pension plans, most of which are funded on a pay-as-you-go basis. IMF staff have recently estimated that in net present value terms, public pension liabilities in 1994 exceeded 68 percent of GDP in all major industrial countries except the United Kingdom and the United States, assuming that key pension plan parameters continue as under current law (Chart 23).[29] These net pension liabilities exceed

---

[27]See Robert P. Hagemann and Christoph John, "The Fiscal Stance in Sweden: A Generational Accounting Perspective," IMF Working Paper 95/105 (November 1995).

[28]See, for example, Alan J. Auerbach, Jagadeesh Gokhale, and Laurence J. Kotlikoff, "Generational Accounting: A Meaningful Way to Evaluate Fiscal Policy," *Journal of Economic Perspectives*, Vol. 8 (Winter 1994), pp. 73–94.

[29]See estimates in Sheetal K. Chand and others, *Aging Populations*.

Chart 22. Selected Industrial Countries: Elderly Dependency Ratios

(In percent)

Elderly dependency ratios have drifted up modestly over the past four decades but will soon begin to jump dramatically.

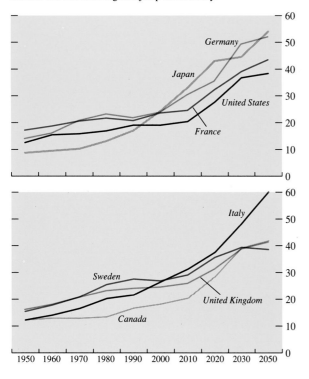

Sources: Data for 1950–80 are from OECD, *Demographic Trends, 1950–90* (Paris, 1979); data for 1990–2050 from Eduard Bos and others, *World Population Projections 1994–95* (World Bank: Johns Hopkins University Press, 1994).

the visible government debt in most of these countries; France, Germany, and Japan are expected to face the largest imbalances between inflows and outflows. Many of the smaller European industrial countries, including Belgium, Denmark, Greece, Luxembourg, the Netherlands, Portugal, and Spain, face pension system imbalances of a similar magnitude.[30] The situation looks even worse when commitments to provide future health care benefits for retirees are taken into account. The United States, which is in better shape than many other countries in terms of pension liabilities, appears to be in a particularly unfavorable position in this regard. In sum, public pension programs are much more generous than governments seem likely to be able to support financially. Future generations of workers will face either much higher tax burdens to maintain such levels of transfers or sharply reduced benefits levels. Modest reductions in youth dependency ratios over this period will provide only a small budgetary offset to the effects of aging.

There are various ways to make current public pension plans more sustainable. The key parameters that characterize a public pension plan are the contribution rate (i.e., the rate of social security taxation), the replacement rate (i.e., the average pension benefit as a percentage of a country's average gross wage), the retirement age, and the indexing formula used to adjust benefits for inflation. The simplest way to gauge the scale of adjustment needed to make a pension plan sustainable is to look at the contribution gap.[31] This gap is the difference between a constant sustainable contribution rate that over a long period of time would lead to no buildup of pension debt above an initial level and the expected average contribution rate likely to prevail under current law (Table 10).[32] For the German pension plan's net asset position in 2050 to be the same as the initial net asset position in 1995, for instance, a sustainable contribution rate of 13.7 percent would be required each year. Assuming average contribution rates remain unchanged at just 10.3 percent of GDP over this period, Germany would appear to face a contribution gap of 3.4 percent of GDP.

All industrial countries face contribution gaps over this period, with the typical major industrial country projected to have an annual gap of 1.8 percent of GDP if nothing is changed. Some countries are relatively well off, while others seem to face a critical situation. The United Kingdom should experience almost no

---

[30]See Jan B. Kuné and others, "The Hidden Liabilities of the Basic Pensions System in the Member States," Center for European Policy Studies Working Paper (Brussels, November 1993).

[31]In this analysis of the contribution gap, the contribution rate is a percentage of GDP.

[32]This contribution gap analysis therefore does not show what steps would be required to reduce net pension liabilities to a uniform benchmark across countries. As shown in Chart 23, there were large differences in net pension liabilities across countries in 1995.

contribution gap, and for the United States and Sweden, the gap is expected to be less than 1 percent of GDP a year. Countries such as Japan, Germany, and France, however, face contribution gaps of nearly 3½ percent of GDP a year. To avoid a further buildup of pension debt over the next fifty-five years, these countries need either to permanently increase social security tax collections by roughly 3½ percent of GDP, or scale back benefits by a similar amount, or implement a combination of tax increases and payout reductions of this magnitude.

Table 10 also shows illustrative IMF staff estimates of the fiscal impact of various changes in pension plan parameters that would reduce payouts: a 5 percentage point reduction in the replacement rate for all pensioners; a cutback of the present indexation arrangements of pension benefits to 80 percent of the CPI inflation rate; and a uniform and immediate increase in the retirement age to 67. For most countries, increasing the retirement age can be a powerful tool for closing the contribution gap. In countries like France, and especially Italy, where retirement often takes place at a relatively early age, raising the retirement age to 67 could completely close large contribution gaps. Prompt attention is important, however, since postponing action is costly. For the average industrial country, a delay of ten years in addressing pension plan imbalances will permanently increase the contribution rate that will eventually be needed by 0.7 percent of GDP; a 30-year delay would increase the gap to almost 5 percent of GDP. The earlier an adjustment is made, the smaller the adjustment needed.

Governments should therefore move quickly to address not only high current (nonpension) deficits but also large future pension liabilities. The two problems are related because both contribute to high and increasing tax burdens (Box 6). What broad, long-run public pension system reforms might make the most sense for the industrial countries? As a basic principle, benefit levels must be realistic and plans should be financially sustainable. Given that in many industrial countries raising already high contribution rates has become increasingly controversial in terms of both equity and efficiency, the emphasis of reforms will clearly have to shift to adjustments in benefits and retirement ages, the latter because of steady gains in average lifespans. Modifications could include reductions in the replacement ratio in countries where it is high, and some slowing in the inflation indexing formula. In addition, governments could aim at linking individual pension contributions more closely to benefits—for example, by investing part of contributions in individual retirement accounts—and at fostering increased personal responsibility for retirement support. Multipillared approaches that incorporate a blend of solutions have appeal, because they can combine a basic social protection element with a scheme establishing a tighter link between contributions and bene-

Chart 23. Major Industrial Countries: Net Present Value of Public Pension Liabilities[1]
(In percent of GDP)

For many industrial countries, net pension liabilities exceed current overall national debt.

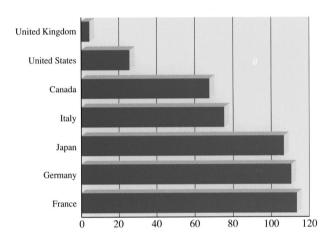

Source: Sheetal K. Chand and others, *Aging Populations and the Fiscal Consequences of Public Pension Schemes with Particular Reference to the Major Industrial Countries*, IMF Occasional Paper (forthcoming).

[1]Net present value of difference between projected primary expenditure and revenue of public pension fund during 1995–2050, adjusted for net asset position of public pension systems at end-1994. These estimates and relative rankings are sensitive to the methodology chosen and to discount rate and productivity assumptions.

Table 10. Selected Industrial Countries: Sustainable Contribution Rates and Contribution Gaps, 1995–2050

(In percent of GDP)

	Projected Average Contribution Rate 1995–2050	Sustainable Contribution Rate 1995–2050[1]	Contribution Gap[2]	Effects of Reforms on Contribution Gap				
				Reforms postponed by 10 years	Reforms postponed by 30 years	Reduction in replacement rate by 5 percentage points	80 percent indexation	Retirement at age 67
Major industrial countries	**6.5**	**8.3**	**1.8**	**0.7**	**4.5**	**−1.1**	**−0.8**	**−1.4**
United States	4.7	5.5	0.8	0.2	1.5	−1.2	−0.2	−0.3
Japan	3.9	7.2	3.3	1.4	8.9	−0.7	−1.5	−1.6
Germany	10.3	13.7	3.4	1.3	9.5	−1.4	−2.3	−1.2
France	12.1	15.4	3.3	1.3	7.9	−1.3	−1.4	−3.7
Italy	16.0	18.5	2.5	1.1	6.5	−0.7	−0.2	−5.7
United Kingdom	4.2	4.3	0.1	0.1	0.3	−0.8	−0.5	−1.1
Canada	3.8	5.8	2.0	0.5	3.4	−1.2	−0.4	−0.7
Sweden	7.1	8.0	0.9	0.2	1.5	−1.2	−0.6	−1.0

Source: This table is based on Sheetal K. Chand and others, *Aging Populations and the Fiscal Consequences of Public Pension Schemes with Particular Reference to the Major Industrial Countries*, IMF Occasional Paper (forthcoming).

[1]The sustainable contribution rate is defined as the constant contribution rate over 1995–2050 that equalizes the net asset position in 2050 with the initial net asset position in 1995.

[2]Defined as the difference between the sustainable contribution rate and projected overall contribution rate.

fits. However, any shift from current pay-as-you-go pension systems to fully funded, defined contribution systems could involve substantial transition costs.[33] Moreover, any substantive reform of current unsustainable systems may entail some social tension and, depending on the specific reform measures, impose higher burdens on certain age cohorts. Still, in view of the long lead times for changing pension arrangements, the earlier the need for appropriate public pension reforms is addressed the better.

Economics of Fiscal Consolidation

Given the heavy public debt burdens in most industrial countries, a broad move toward fiscal consolidation seems inevitable and appears to be gaining political support. Many governments resist such corrective actions not only because they may hurt particular groups, but also because they fear that budget contraction will cause a recession or erode established social achievements. But need it do so? Several highly publicized episodes of fiscal contraction over the past decade, including Denmark (1983–87) and Ireland (1987–89), demonstrate that it is simultaneously possible for budget deficits to be cut, ratios of public debt to GDP to decline, and economic performance to improve.[34] But are these cases exceptions rather than

the rule? Perhaps most important, is it possible to pare a budget in such a way as to enhance growth prospects?

The simple "Keynesian" view of fiscal consolidation is that lower government purchases or higher taxes reduce aggregate demand and income, and have a multiplied negative impact on output. More complete analysis allows for "crowding-in" effects through lower interest rates and currency depreciation, but these have usually been considered to provide only partial offsets to the negative multiplier effect. There are other transmission mechanisms, however, by which government budget deficits affect an economy, including wealth effects and expectations effects, and it is possible for these to outweigh the negative Keynesian effect relatively quickly. A smaller budget deficit could reduce interest rates significantly by reducing the default premium on public debt, and this could lead to positive wealth effects. Especially in countries that have suffered from extremely high fiscal imbalances and where the action is viewed as necessary to restore government solvency and reduce the probability of default, this could sharply increase the market value of wealth held by the private sector and stimulate economic growth. Or consumers and businesses could view deficit reduction as signaling a permanent reduction in their future tax burden and feel that their permanent income had been increased, something that could also trigger higher spending and stimulate economic growth. In short, the impact on an economy of fiscal contraction depends on a number of factors, some of which are mutually offsetting. The question of whether deficit reduction will raise or lower output, and especially how long it will take be-

---

[33]For a discussion of multipillared approaches, see World Bank, *Averting the Old Age Crisis* (New York: Oxford University Press for the World Bank, 1994), pp. 101–63.

[34]See Box 2 in the May 1995 *World Economic Outlook*, pp. 24–25.

fore positive effects materialize, may therefore be considered an empirical one.

To study the economic effects of fiscal consolidation, the experiences of a wide range of industrial countries over the past twenty-five years were examined.[35] The study sought to identify episodes of fiscal consolidation, determine which ones were successful in reducing the debt ratio, and then examine the consequences for a series of economic performance measures, such as GDP, employment, the unemployment rate, interest rates, and exchange rates, during and after the fiscal action. Episodes of fiscal consolidation were identified by looking at changes in the primary structural budget balance.[36] These cyclically adjusted primary balances remove two components from the government budget balance: (1) interest payments, which cannot be directly influenced in the short run by fiscal policy; and (2) that part of the government balance that is a result of the economy's deviation from potential output over the business cycle. Fiscal impulse measures were then developed as the change in the primary structural balance scaled by potential GDP. To isolate those periods of fiscal consolidation that seemed to reflect aggressive policy actions that were sustained, only those periods when the fiscal impulse measure showed a tightening in two successive years, amounting to at least 1½ percentage points of GDP in total, were labeled as episodes of fiscal consolidation. Table 11 lists all 74 episodes that satisfy this definition of fiscal consolidation over the period 1970 to 1995. Included are several well-known episodes of multiyear fiscal adjustments, such as Denmark from 1983 to 1986, Ireland from 1982 to 1984 and 1986 to 1989, and New Zealand from 1985 to 1987 and in the early 1990s.

Successful cases of fiscal consolidation were defined as those that resulted in a reduction of at least 3 percentage points in the ratio of gross public debt to GDP by the second year after the end of the two-year fiscal tightening. Using this yardstick, there were 14 episodes of successful fiscal consolidation and 48 unsuccessful cases out of the 62 episodes for which debt

Table 11. Industrial Countries: Episodes of Fiscal Consolidation[1]

	Last Year of Two-Year Periods of Fiscal Consolidation
Australia	81, 82, 87, 88
Austria	78, 81
Belgium	83, 84, 85, 86, 87, 93
Canada	81, 87, 95
Denmark	84, 85, 86
Finland	76, 89
France	80, 84
Germany[2]	77, 82, 83, 93, 94
Greece	83, 87, 91, 92, 93, 94, 95
Ireland	83, 84, 87, 88, 89
Italy	77, 83, 92, 93
Japan	81, 82, 84, 85, 87
Netherlands	82, 83, 88
New Zealand[3]	86, 87, 92, 95
Norway	85, 86, 95
Portugal	70, 80, 85, 86, 95
Spain	84, 87
Sweden	76, 84, 87, 95
United Kingdom	80, 81, 82, 95
United States	77

Source: OECD, *Economic Outlook*.

[1]A structural government balance must increase by at least 1.5 percent of potential GDP over two years, and be positive in both years, to register as a fiscal consolidation.

[2]Data before 1990 refer to west Germany.

[3]Calculations based on World Economic Outlook data base.

data were available.[37] Table 12 shows that for all 62 episodes of fiscal consolidation, real GDP growth on average outpaced average industrial country GDP growth slightly in the year before the fiscal contraction was undertaken but fell somewhat below average growth over the two-year fiscal consolidation phase and the year after. Employment growth also tended to drop and the unemployment rate increased, again relative to what was happening in the industrial countries as a whole. But in the 14 episodes in which countries were successful in reducing their ratios of public debt to GDP, economic growth and job creation increased in the adjustment phase and in the following year, the unemployment rate declined, both short- and long-term real interest rates declined, and the currency appreciated in real terms. Thus, successful fiscal consolidation tended to be associated with successful economic performance.

Given the complexity of the interactions among economic growth, interest rate movements, and reductions in debt ratios, no study can definitively establish clear

---

[35]For a background study with additional empirical support, see John McDermott and Robert Wescott, "An Empirical Analysis of Fiscal Adjustment," IMF Working Paper (forthcoming). This follows work described in several recent papers, including Alberto Alesina and Roberto Perotti, "Reducing Budget Deficits," paper presented at Conference on Growing Government Debt: International Experiences, Economic Council of Sweden, Stockholm, June 12, 1995, and Francesco Giavazzi and Marco Pagano, "Non-Keynesian Effects of Fiscal Policy Changes: International Evidence and the Swedish Experience," paper presented at IMF Research Department seminar, November 16, 1995.

[36]A blend of IMF and OECD data was used to provide the broadest possible country coverage and the longest possible historical perspective. The results did not appear to be very sensitive to the choice of structural balance methodology.

---

[37]Because the definition of success depends on the change in the public debt two years after the consolidation, 9 episodes of fiscal consolidation that occurred after 1993 cannot be classified. In addition, 3 episodes are not classified because data on public debt were not available (Australia 81 and 82; New Zealand 86).

Box 6. Paths to Sustainable Budgets and Pension Schemes in Industrial Countries

As discussed in the text, fiscal adjustment is needed to address both high overall deficits today (related primarily to nonpension spending) and upward pressures on deficits in the future caused by an excess of pension costs over receipts. In this box, four scenarios illustrate the magnitude of the combined problem for the average industrial country and various ways of addressing it are discussed. The average industrial country[1] has an initial net debt-to-GDP ratio of 45 percent and a general government deficit of 4 percent of GDP, despite a small surplus in the pension system equal to ½ of 1 percent of GDP. Public pension plans typically do not have any substantial accumulated reserves; on average, they amount to only 8 percent of GDP. It should be emphasized that a number of countries have more serious fiscal problems than the average; in particular, for most countries in continental Europe the size of both existing debt and unfunded future liabilities is greater than average (Chart 23 in Chapter III). In addition, other government spending is expected to rise because of population aging, especially spending on health care, but that aspect is not considered here.

The magnitude of the problem is illustrated in a *baseline scenario (see chart)* where general government revenues and nonpension expenditures maintain constant ratios to GDP, and pension benefits per retiree, based on the country-specific pension rule, generally rise in line with per capita nominal GDP. The deficit and debt levels start to explode in the first few decades of the next century, and by 2050 they are in excess of 20 percent and 400 percent of GDP, respectively (not shown). This is obviously not sustainable.

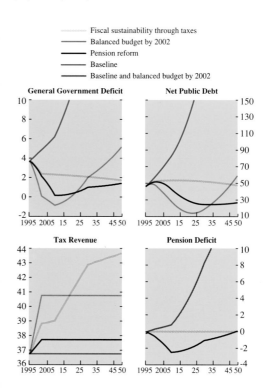

Fiscal Adjustment Scenarios
(In percent of GDP)

Source: IMF staff estimates.

[1]All data used in this box are based on PPP-weighted averages for the seven major industrial countries in 1995.

---

lines of causality. Instead, the results presented here report on broad patterns in the movements of these variables and are meant to be suggestive. Caution in interpreting the results is necessary, especially because, as the data indicate, trends in world growth and interest rates help to determine whether an episode of fiscal consolidation will succeed in reducing the ratio of public debt to GDP. Good timing in relation to the world business cycle clearly helps. Many of the episodes of fiscal contraction in which reductions in debt ratios were sustained occurred in the late 1980s—a period of solid industrial country growth and generally flat interest rates. Of the 30 cases of fiscal consolidation over the 1984–89 period, for example, 12 were successful. On the other hand, it is difficult to reduce debt ratios in the midst of a global recession, especially if interest rates are increasing sharply at the same time. None of the 7 efforts at fiscal consolidation over 1980–81, including the highly visible efforts in the United Kingdom, was successful in lowering debt ratios, be-

cause of these economic headwinds. The study partially corrects for some of these factors by using a two-year period of fiscal consolidation and by looking at how economic variables such as real GDP growth and real interest rates moved relative to average industrial country movements. Even so, given the expected link between growth and debt reduction, it remains an interesting question why, even within the period of broad economic expansion in the mid-1980s, a clear majority of fiscal consolidation efforts failed to put debt ratios on sustained downward trajectories.

What factors seem to have contributed to the success of fiscal consolidation?[38] The size of the fiscal

---

[38]Many of the hypotheses tested were suggested by Alesina and Perotti, "Reducing Budget Deficits," and Giavazzi and Pagano, "Non-Keynesian Effects of Fiscal Policy Changes." As these authors point out, using these simple statistics, one cannot rule out an episode being deemed successful, where an exogenous increase in growth, possibly due to an easing of monetary conditions, facilitated the budget consolidation process.

To some extent these results are due to the working of debt dynamics from a starting point where the debt level is high and the primary surplus is not great enough to offset the excess of the real interest rate over the real growth rate.[2] Eliminating the immediate deficit problem, however, in particular by reducing it to zero in seven years through a permanent increase in tax rates, can be seen from the chart in a second scenario (*balanced budget by 2002*) as not solving completely the long-run problem associated with adverse demographics and debt dynamics. Nevertheless, it is a good start, and it causes the ratio of public debt to GDP to decline for an extended period of time. However, by 2020 it is again on an explosive path, and the debt ratio is approaching 60 percent of GDP by 2050, with the overall deficit at 5 percent of GDP in that year. As the chart shows, in this scenario as well as in the baseline, the pension deficit as a ratio to GDP widens alarmingly as a result of demographic trends, if benefit and contribution rates are left unchanged.

One possible solution would involve raising contribution rates to balance pension expenditures and revenues, which would make the pension system strictly pay-as-you-go. This is illustrated in a third scenario (*fiscal sustainability through taxes*) where in addition to the increase in contribution rates, other taxes are raised so as to stabilize the public debt ratio. However, the magnitude of the increase in tax revenues is such that this scenario is unlikely to be either desirable or feasible; it involves massive increases in

pension contribution rates and the overall tax burden. Higher taxes would involve increasing labor market distortions, and a decline in long-run output. It also would be viewed as inequitable because the burden of sustainability would be borne by the working population and not retirees—associated with extremely skewed generational accounts.

The solution to the joint fiscal problem needs to involve expenditure reductions, including reductions in the generosity of pension benefits. Though the details of desirable measures vary from country to country, they are likely to include increasing retirement ages and declines in replacement ratios. Some increases in contribution rates may be necessary as well. The timing of the introduction of measures is likely to depend on a balance of considerations, some of them political; it needs to be recognized, however, that delaying adjustment, though politically expedient, has serious drawbacks. These include greater uncertainty, which makes it difficult for individuals to plan their retirement rationally, and exacerbating the fiscal problem, which would require a larger eventual adjustment. An illustration of a possible adjustment path where early action is taken is shown in the fourth scenario (*pension reform*); the path includes gradual increases in retirement ages from 63 to 67 and reductions in replacement ratios by 8¼ percentage points. The increase in contribution rates required to put the pension and overall fiscal position on a sustainable path is much smaller than in the third scenario. The net public debt stock falls below 30 percent of GDP and remains at this lower level through 2050, and the increase in tax revenues is only about 1 percentage point of GDP, with correspondingly smaller distortions of labor supply. The higher retirement age in itself increases potential output through an increase in the labor force.

---

[2]All simulations assume an inflation rate of 3 percent, labor productivity growth of 1½ percent a year, labor force growth dictated by demographic trends, and a real interest rate of 3½ percent a year.

---

consolidation may have played a role. The average magnitude of the two-year fiscal contraction was 4.0 percent of potential GDP for the successful cases, but only 3.2 percent for unsuccessful cases. A more timid commitment to fiscal consolidation may be more likely to fail than a strong one. This may be partly due to a nonlinear relationship between fiscal policy and output growth, whereby small reductions in budget deficits may reduce aggregate demand, while large adjustments may revive confidence and expectations so that growth is given a boost. Also, in many of the successful cases the fiscal consolidation was undertaken as part of a broader adjustment and reform program that may have enhanced the overall credibility of government commitment to the consolidation.

Real short-term interest rates tended to decline in the successful cases, whereas they increased in the unsuccessful cases (again, relative to movements in a weighted average of real short-term interest rates in the major industrial countries). It is possible that the

larger fiscal action in successful cases may have been a factor in restoring financial market confidence and allowing monetary authorities to ease monetary conditions. Real long-term interest rates moved lower in both successful and unsuccessful cases, but probably for very different reasons. Perhaps these rates declined because of improved financial confidence in the successful cases where the policy initiatives were more vigorous, but because of weaker economic growth in the unsuccessful cases.

The composition of the fiscal consolidation also seems to have played a role. The 62 episodes of fiscal consolidation were divided into two categories: those in which the deficit was cut mainly (at least 60 percent) through revenue increases, and those in which it was reduced mainly (at least 60 percent) through expenditure cuts (Table 13).[39] Of the 17 cases where most of

---

[39]Actually noninvestment government expenditure cuts.

Table 12. Industrial Countries: Macroeconomic Effects of Fiscal Consolidation

Macroeconomic Variables	Type of Fiscal Consolidation	Time Frame		
		One year before	Two years during	One year after
Real GDP[1]	All episodes	0.05	−0.39	−0.11
(percent change)	Successful	−0.18	0.10	0.65
	Unsuccessful	0.11	−0.71	−0.97
Employment[1]	All episodes	0.01	−0.53	−0.61
(percent change)	Successful	−0.18	0.10	0.65
	Unsuccessful	0.06	−0.71	−0.97
Unemployment rate[1]	All episodes	0.91	1.08	1.47
(percent of labor force)	Successful	2.12	1.90	0.30
	Unsuccessful	0.55	0.84	1.52
Real interest rates short[2]	All episodes	0.63	0.88	1.52
(percent a year)	Successful	2.44	2.06	1.86
	Unsuccessful	0.09	0.52	1.42
Real interest rates long[3]	All episodes	0.41	0.02	−0.01
(percent a year)	Successful	1.34	1.06	1.08
	Unsuccessful	0.15	−0.27	−0.33
Exchange rates, real effective	All episodes	96.59	96.42	97.20
(1990 = 100)	Successful	92.42	93.69	97.44
	Unsuccessful	97.88	97.27	97.13

Sources: OECD, *Economic Outlook;* IMF, World Economic Outlook data base, and *International Financial Statistics.*

[1]Differential with industrial country average.

[2]The real rate differential with respect to the major industrial country average is constructed using the short rates as defined in Table 36 of the OECD *Economic Outlook* less the annual percentage change in the GDP deflator.

[3]The real rate differential with respect to the major industrial country average is constructed using the long rates as defined in Table 36 of the OECD *Economic Outlook* less the three-year average of the annual percentage change in the GDP deflator.

the policy action was achieved through expenditure reductions, 7 were successful, while among the 37 cases where the consolidation was achieved mainly on the revenue side, only 6 had successful outcomes. The message is reinforced by the fact that the average expenditure cut in the episodes with successful outcomes was 3¾ percent of GDP, whereas in the unsuccessful cases it was just 2 percent. There was a particularly large difference in how government wage outlays were handled in the two cases. In the successful cases, the government wage bill was cut by nearly 1 percent of GDP, while the cuts averaged just ⅓ of 1 percent in the unsuccessful cases. Social security payments and government consumption excluding wages were also cut much more sharply in the successful episodes than they were in the unsuccessful cases.

A few factors that might be expected to be important for predicting the success or failure of fiscal consolidation did not appear to be significant in this study. Whether the pace of real economic growth was above the average growth rate in the industrial countries in the year before the fiscal contraction did not seem to be related to whether the action was successful or not.

In fact, a larger share of fiscal contraction cases that were launched in the face of subpar growth, as opposed to above average growth, ended up succeeding. This suggests that some sense of economic crisis might have been necessary to convince governments to make tough choices—especially larger budget cuts and cuts more focused on expenditures. Finally, real exchange rate movements do not appear to have played a major role in explaining why cases of fiscal consolidation succeeded.[40] Between the year before the fiscal consolidation and the end of the two-year contraction, the real exchange rate appreciated slightly in the successful cases and depreciated slightly in the unsuccessful cases.[41] This would suggest that on average, the successful cases did not benefit from a depreciation-driven export surge.

---

[40]A notable exception may have been Ireland in the late 1980s, where the currency depreciated sharply in real terms before and during its consolidation period.

[41]It is interesting to note that in the year after the two-year contraction, the real exchange rate appreciated sharply in the successful cases.

Table 13. Industrial Countries: Characteristics of Fiscal Consolidation

Characteristics	All Episodes	Successful	Unsuccessful
Type of consolidation[1]			
Revenue increasing	37	6	31
Expenditure cuts[2]	17	7	10
Of which:			
Average expenditure cut[3]	−3.22	−3.73	−2.12
Average government wage cut[4]	−0.60	−0.86	−0.33
Average transfers cut[4]	0.19	0.05	0.28
Average subsidies cut[4]	−0.26	−0.26	−0.24
Average social security cut[4]	−0.28	−0.83	0.18
Average government consumption less wage[4]	−0.34	−0.64	−0.07

Sources: IMF, World Economic Outlook data base, and *International Financial Statistics;* and OECD, Economic Outlook data base.

[1]Eight episodes are excluded because they involve almost an equal mix of revenue and expenditure measures.

[2]Negative sign indicates expenditure cuts.

[3]Structural expenditure cuts as a percent of potential GDP.

[4]As a percent of GDP.

Lessons from Fiscal Consolidation Experiences

Although it is difficult to disentangle the complex relationships among fiscal contraction, economic growth, and public debt reduction, a few lessons do seem to emerge. First, a policy of tight fiscal consolidation does not necessarily lead to recession. There have been many cases where countries have experienced strengthening economic growth during and following a contractionary fiscal policy phase. There may even be a virtuous circle between economic growth and debt-ratio reduction. If growth is maintained, aided, say, by lower interest rates or strong economic expansion among trading partners, then fiscal tightening is more likely to produce a declining ratio of debt to GDP. Conversely, if the fiscal consolidation looks credible and likely to reduce the debt ratio, then domestic interest rates are more likely to decline, both through financial market forces and through monetary policy action, and this will help to ensure that growth is maintained. Fiscal contractions of larger magnitude may be viewed as more credible than smaller ones, and therefore, may increase the odds of such a virtuous circle.

Second, the composition of the fiscal consolidation seems to influence the chances for success. More emphasis on spending cuts than on revenue increases appears to help. In particular, cuts in the government wage bill, in other government consumption, and in social security payments seem to help generate a sustained downward movement in the ratio of public debt to GDP. This may be related to the fact, referred to earlier, that the key driving force behind governments' fiscal woes over the past fifteen years seems to have been expenditure growth—often tied to generous indexing formulas for government employees' wages and pensions or transfer recipients—not a decline in revenues. When governments try to solve their budget problems by raising taxes and not by braking spending in these hard-to-rein-in categories, the higher revenues tend to be absorbed and the government share of the economy continues rising. That is, fiscal improvements are more likely to be fleeting unless the overall size of the government sector is capped. This is not to say that revenue increases may not be appropriate in certain cases—indeed, the worst outcome is probably to leave a deficit problem unaddressed. Rather it is to say that outcomes tend to be more successful when authorities tackle the roots of the budget problem, which often appear to be on the spending side. Financial markets may play a role in the higher success rate for spending-cut cases. Market participants may be aware of what actions address most effectively the intractable budget problems that governments face, especially the political difficulties of paring the government workforce, subsidies, and transfers, and may reserve their rewards—improved business confidence and lower risk premiums, for example—for only the boldest policy actions.

* * *

Budget deficits in almost all industrial countries have in the past two decades become too big, out of bounds by peacetime standards, and in many cases unsustainable. This is especially true when invisible debt is taken into account, because demographic forces in most countries over coming years will reveal severely unbalanced pension plans. The concept of generational accounting is helpful in thinking about the fairness of current pension and benefit schemes and suggests that current plans may not be politically sustainable. Major pension system reforms are clearly needed.

Large and persistent deficits have a series of negative macroeconomic and microeconomic consequences for national economies and for the world economy. Interest rates are biased upward, investment is reduced, and the growth of living standards is less than it could be. But contrary to conventional belief, fiscal consolidation need not be contractionary for an economy, at least not for very long. There are many cases where economies have actually experienced accelerating economic growth during and following a phase of fiscal contraction. The chances of a successful fiscal consolidation, where the ratio of public debt to GDP is put on a steadily declining path, seem to be higher if the deficit reduction occurs mainly on the spending side, especially if financial markets perceive that policymakers have tackled the root causes of the fiscal imbalance. When the emphasis is placed on the revenue side, policies are often viewed as less credible. Countries should take this into account as they craft their policies.

Reforming programs that transfer income or that subsidize certain activities will be particularly difficult to implement because many benefit programs have now come to be considered as entitlements or *acquis sociaux*. To be successful, reforms may have to change habits, social norms, and attitudes, which is unlikely if reforms are timid and piecemeal. Recent experiences of countries that have successfully reversed expansionary trends in public expenditures in general, and in transfers and subsidies in particular, have one common feature: the reforms represented fundamental changes in the underlying policy regime.

IV

Fiscal Policy Issues in Developing Countries

The strengthening in the growth performance of many developing countries in recent years has reflected fundamental changes in economic policies. A major role has been played by fiscal policies, which have been re-oriented toward the objectives of a more stable macroeconomic environment, stronger domestic saving and investment, and market-oriented structural reform. This re-orientation has required not only greater discipline in containing fiscal imbalances but also a scaling back of the role of government in the economy to ensure that state intervention does not impede private sector development. Addressing fiscal imbalances has also facilitated economic liberalization and structural reform by reducing governments' budgetary dependence on distortionary taxes and controls.

Policy improvements, however, have been uneven across countries, and this is reflected in significant variations in economic performance. Some developing countries have made limited progress with fiscal consolidation, which has hindered their growth and increased their vulnerability to changes in external conditions. For these countries, policy measures on a number of fronts, including public sector reform, privatization of state-owned enterprises, trade and financial liberalization, and strengthening tax administration, would help raise living standards, increase the pace of development, and reduce the risk of falling further behind other developing countries that have made greater progress in adjustment and reform. All developing countries, however, face the challenge of sustaining improvements in policies to safeguard financial stability, to promote efficient resource allocation and growth, and thus to maximize the benefits and minimize the risks associated with increasingly globalized financial and product markets.

Fiscal Trends

There has been a marked improvement in the fiscal positions of a large number of developing countries since the 1980s. For the developing countries as a group, the central government deficit-to-GDP ratio declined by 2½ percentage points between 1983–89 and 1990–95 (Table 14).[42] For most countries, fiscal ad-

---

[42]The fiscal data discussed in this section refer to activities of the central government because of the lack of internationally comparable data for a broader definition of the public sector.

Table 14. Developing Countries: Budgetary and Economic Indicators

(Annual averages; in percent of GDP unless otherwise noted)

	1975–82	1983–89	1990–95
Central government fiscal balance[1]	–3.4	–5.5	–3.0
Central government revenue[1]	20.7	19.2	18.1
Central government expenditure	23.7	24.4	20.9
Current expenditure	16.6	18.0	16.5
Private saving	19.6	21.6	24.6
Private investment	14.1	14.3	17.3
Current account balance	–0.8	–1.5	–1.5
Terms of trade[2]	1.7	–0.6	—
External debt	24.4	38.0	36.9
Real GDP[2]	4.5	4.9	5.7
Consumer prices[2]	21.7	38.7	40.3
Consumer prices (median)[2]	11.8	8.7	10.1

[1]Including grants.
[2]Annual percent change.

justment has been achieved primarily through the containment of expenditure, with a marginally greater reduction in capital expenditure relative to GDP than in current expenditure. With regard to revenue, for developing countries as a group the ratio of central government revenue to GDP has followed a downward trend since around 1980 (Chart 24). This mainly reflects the impact on oil producers of weakening oil prices and difficulties in revenue mobilization, although there has also been a trend in some countries toward lower taxation as a means of improving incentives for private sector activity and thereby promoting growth. Although saving and investment levels have been affected by a number of factors, including the availability of external finance, fiscal consolidation since the late 1980s and associated improvements in the economic environment are likely to have been a key factor contributing to the increase in private saving and investment in the developing countries as a group. Compared with the 1983–89 period, both the ratio of private saving to GDP and the ratio of private investment to GDP were about 3 percentage points higher in 1990–95; and between the same periods average annual GDP growth in the developing countries increased by almost 1 percentage point.

The decline in fiscal deficits in developing countries as a group conceals significant variations both among and within regions (Table 15). In Africa, despite sub-

Chart 24. Developing Countries: Fiscal Deficits
(In percent of GDP)

Deficits have fallen in most regions, although improvements in Africa, and the Middle East and Europe are more recent.

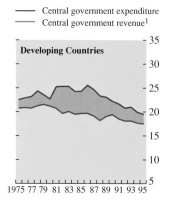

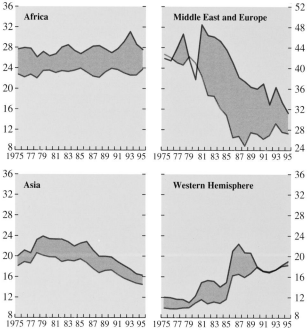

[1]Including grants.

stantial improvements in macroeconomic and structural policies in a number of countries, such as Kenya, Uganda, and more recently the CFA countries, the average fiscal deficit for the region widened in the early 1990s.[43] Many African countries faced unfavorable external conditions for much of this period, with falling commodity prices and lower industrial country growth leading to substantial declines in the terms of trade, especially for sub-Saharan African countries. While some of these countries have managed to make modest progress in reducing fiscal deficits, in part because of external debt rescheduling agreements in the late 1980s and early 1990s, which altered the time profile of interest payments, most of the adjustment has been in the form of lower capital expenditure. In fact, for Africa as a whole, the ratio of current government expenditure to GDP increased by over 2 percentage points in the 1990–95 period, while the ratio of capital expenditure to GDP was marginally lower than in the mid-1980s. The average fiscal deficit declined in 1995 to just under 4 percent of GDP, but for most African countries the fiscal situation remains fragile, with many countries still heavily dependent on grants to finance large fiscal imbalances.

In the Middle East and Europe, although there has been a marked reduction in fiscal deficits since the mid-1980s—a decline of 5 percentage points in the deficit-to-GDP ratio—the average deficit, at over 7 percent of GDP, is still substantially larger than in other developing country regions. Many countries in the region were characterized by excessive growth of government outlays during the 1980s, following the jumps in oil prices and revenues of the 1970s and early 1980s. The subsequent fall in oil prices and the associated decline in government revenues left many countries with unsustainable expenditure programs and clearly unsustainable fiscal imbalances. The significant reduction in government expenditures that has since occurred is primarily due to lower capital spending: the ratio of current expenditure to GDP has been broadly stable at about 26 percent since the 1970s. There are, however, some notable differences from these average developments among the more diversified economies of the region. In Egypt, for example, a broadening of the tax base in recent years has led to increased tax revenues. Jordan, on the other hand, has been able to increase its capital expenditures as a percentage of GDP since 1992 by reducing current spending.[44]

The strongest improvement in fiscal balances has been among the developing countries in the Western Hemisphere, where several large countries, including Argentina, Brazil, and Mexico achieved fiscal sur-

---

[43]Uganda's successful adjustment was discussed in Box 3 of the October 1995 *World Economic Outlook*, p. 54.

[44]Annex I provides a detailed assessment of progress with macroeconomic stabilization and structural reforms in the Middle East and North Africa region.

pluses in the early 1990s. For the region as a whole, fiscal deficits fell from almost 4½ percent of GDP in the mid-1980s to under ½ of 1 percent of GDP in 1990–95. In contrast to the period after the debt crisis of the early 1980s, when declining world interest rates and rising industrial country growth helped to lower the region's fiscal deficits, progress with fiscal consolidation in the 1990s has been primarily due to stronger budgetary policies. Substantially lower inflation in the 1990s has also led to a marked reduction in central government interest payments in countries such as Argentina and Mexico. Reductions in central government expenditure and increases in public sector saving did not, however, lead to a corresponding increase in national saving, because of an offsetting decline in saving by the private sector. A continuing concern for a number of countries in the region is the extent to which capital inflows have substituted for shortfalls in the domestic saving-investment balance, which arguably may call for further improvements in fiscal positions to strengthen national saving.

The aggregate data for developing countries in Asia reflect the fact that many countries in the region have a long track record of prudent macroeconomic policies. For most of the period since the mid-1970s, fiscal deficits in many of the high-performing Asian economies have been maintained at levels well below those observed in other developing country regions. Most Asian countries have also managed to maintain relatively high private saving rates, which have helped them avoid resorting to monetary financing of fiscal deficits. Moreover, fiscal deficits declined further, on average, in the 1990–95 period, and in contrast with many other developing countries, this fiscal adjustment has been achieved largely by reducing current expenditure. This aggregate picture, however, again masks considerable variations within the region. In Pakistan, for example, persistent fiscal imbalances have contributed to low national saving and investment, thereby impeding growth performance, while in other South Asian countries, such as Bangladesh, although there has been some improvement in fiscal positions in recent years and domestic saving rates are higher than in many developing countries, they are substantially below saving rates in the faster growing economies of Asia.

Underlying Causes of Fiscal Deficits

For many developing countries, widening fiscal deficits in the 1970s and 1980s were largely a result of public expenditure expanding unsustainably fast— much faster than the tax revenue base of the economy. This unsustainable growth of *public expenditure* can be traced to a number of causes, including external factors such as increases in global interest rates, which raised the cost of servicing these countries' growing

Table 15. Developing Countries: Budgetary and Economic Indicators by Region

(Annual averages; in percent of GDP unless otherwise noted)

	1975–82	1983–89	1990–95
Africa			
Central government fiscal balance[1]	–4.4	–4.8	–5.3
Central government revenue[1]	22.8	23.0	23.2
Central government expenditure	27.2	27.8	28.5
Current expenditure	17.1	19.6	21.9
Private saving	20.5	16.5	16.8
Private investment	16.5	13.5	13.5
Current account balance	–4.7	–2.6	–3.8
Terms of trade[2]	–0.3	0.4	–0.8
External debt	30.5	59.5	86.5
Real GDP[2]	2.6	2.6	1.8
Consumer prices[2]	16.1	16.0	26.6
Consumer prices (median)[2]	12.5	9.4	12.5
Asia			
Central government fiscal balance[1]	–3.1	–3.4	–2.3
Central government revenue[1]	19.3	18.2	15.6
Central government expenditure	22.4	21.6	17.9
Current expenditure	17.5	15.9	13.1
Private saving	22.1	26.4	33.1
Private investment	13.8	15.0	20.1
Current account balance	–1.4	–0.9	–0.5
Terms of trade[2]	0.8	—	0.3
External debt	19.3	25.8	26.2
Real GDP[2]	5.8	7.7	8.0
Consumer prices[2]	7.3	7.9	9.2
Consumer prices (median)[2]	8.5	6.7	8.6
Middle East and Europe			
Central government fiscal balance[1]	–3.2	–12.2	–7.2
Central government revenue[1]	40.3	28.9	27.3
Central government expenditure	43.5	41.1	34.5
Current expenditure	26.6	26.3	26.2
Private saving	14.6	16.1	19.5
Private investment	13.2	13.3	16.2
Current account balance	7.7	–3.4	–2.7
Terms of trade[2]	4.7	–2.4	–0.8
External debt	22.5	35.9	41.0
Real GDP[2]	3.5	2.7	3.8
Consumer prices[2]	19.0	22.1	26.9
Consumer prices (median)[2]	11.4	6.0	8.3
Western Hemisphere			
Central government fiscal balance[1]	–2.3	–4.4	–0.3
Central government revenue[1]	10.2	14.1	17.5
Central government expenditure	12.6	18.4	17.8
Current expenditure	10.9	15.5	15.4
Private saving	19.9	21.0	16.2
Private investment	14.0	14.2	15.7
Current account balance	–3.8	–1.0	–2.1
Terms of trade[2]	1.3	–0.4	0.4
External debt	29.6	53.1	42.0
Real GDP[2]	4.2	2.0	2.7
Consumer prices[2]	47.2	160.6	198.3
Consumer prices (median)[2]	13.2	12.5	14.0

[1]Including grants.
[2]Annual percent change.

external debt. But in many cases, upward trends in public spending were associated with government attempts to accelerate the process of development and industrialization through state involvement in economic activities that, as became increasingly apparent, could have been carried out more efficiently by the private sector. During the 1980s, governments in many African countries, in particular, provided extensive fiscal subsidies to loss-making enterprises, including those involved in activities such as the marketing and distribution of agricultural products—activities where there is little evidence of genuine market failure—as well as quasi-fiscal support to central banks involved in the allocation of subsidized foreign exchange and credit to domestic enterprises. State intervention in the allocation of credit was also prevalent among many of the successful Asian countries during the early 1980s; although in countries such as Korea subsidized credit was allocated largely to export industries that had to meet the test of international competition, while in Indonesia credit controls were significantly reduced.

For some developing countries, civil wars, political instability, and regional tensions limited the extent to which military expenditures could be reduced during the 1980s, a period when global military spending fell by over 20 percent in real terms. In comparison with the 1970s and early 1980s, the ratio of military spending to GDP in all developing countries—over 5½ percent in 1972–85—declined to under 4½ percent in the second half of the 1980s, although in sub-Saharan Africa it increased by ½ of 1 percentage point of GDP.[45] More recently, military spending has declined further in most regions, including sub-Saharan Africa.

In many countries, poor governance and a lack of accountability of the public sector have contributed to inadequate control of government expenditure and failure to ensure that expenditures are allocated efficiently and equitably to serve society's priorities. Expenditure on prestige projects, or spending that rewards politically powerful groups or benefits only a small minority—often to the detriment of expenditure on basic social services—stems largely from asymmetries in the political costs and benefits associated with taxation and spending. In countries that have democratic governments, expansionary fiscal policies have tended to be synchronized with the electoral cycle, especially on the expenditure side.[46] Such politically motivated increases in spending may be difficult to reverse, especially when they result in higher employment in the public sector or in quasi-public institutions.

Among the countries with relatively successful growth performance, such as many Asian and Latin American countries, fiscal imbalances have often reflected increasing needs for investment in infrastructure, investment in human capital through health and education spending, and improvements in public services, including through public sector wage expenditures. Spending in these categories, when well-designed and efficiently allocated, can enhance the productivity of the private sector and promote growth. In some cases, private sector involvement in the provision of infrastructure and other public services may help moderate demands on public expenditure, but fiscal imbalances will usually call for expenditures elsewhere to be contained or reduced.

In many developing countries, losses of public sector enterprises have frequently added to the government's fiscal deficit: this is one reason why the central government's accounts may flatter the public sector's financial position, especially in the short run. In Kenya, for example, losses of the National Cereals and Produce Board during the 1980s—equivalent to about 5 percent of GDP a year—were eventually, though not contemporaneously, borne by the central government. In India, the cost to the central government of financing losses incurred by public enterprises amounted to almost 1½ percent of GDP a year in the early 1990s; subsequently, budgetary support to public enterprises was limited to just under 1 percent of GDP in 1995 and their access to subsidized bank loans was significantly curtailed. Public enterprises are often inefficient monopolies that are subsidized at the expense of the taxpayer, and whose activities do not need to be conducted in the public sector; their monopoly power frequently stems from entry restrictions on potential private sector competitors.

For a large number of public sector activities, such as central bank operations, and implicit subsidies in the form of government guarantees for borrowing by public enterprises, there are often no contemporaneous budgetary outlays; such quasi-fiscal operations frequently entail the creation of contingent or unfunded liabilities. This is another reason why the ratio of central government expenditure to GDP, which is typically about half that in industrial countries, may significantly understate the extent of public sector involvement in the economy. Difficulties in raising tax revenue through the budgetary process often help to explain why governments pursue fiscal objectives partly through quasi-fiscal means.[47] Some activities of central banks and other public financial institutions, such as foreign exchange market operations and subsidized loans to public sector enterprises, although non-

---

[45]For an analysis of trends in military expenditure and estimates of the associated effects on economic growth, see Malcolm Knight, Norman Loayza, and Delano Villanueva, "The Peace Dividend: Military Spending Cuts and Economic Growth," *Staff Papers*, IMF, Vol. 43 (March 1996); and Tamim Bayoumi, Daniel Hewitt, and Steven Symansky, "The Impact of Worldwide Military Spending Cuts on Developing Countries," IMF Working Paper 93/86 (November 1993).

[46]For an empirical assessment of political fiscal policy cycles in developing countries, including countries with IMF-supported structural adjustment programs, see Ludger Schuknecht, "Political Business Cycles and Expenditure Policies in Developing Countries," IMF Working Paper 94/121 (October 1994).

[47]For an extensive discussion of the range of policy instruments that are often used to pursue fiscal objectives, see Vito Tanzi, "Government Role and the Efficiency of Policy Instruments," IMF Working Paper 95/100 (October 1995).

transparent and difficult to quantify fully, can entail considerable costs to the public sector as a whole. In Jamaica, for example, central bank losses from exchange rate guarantees exceeded 5 percent of GDP in the early 1990s. And in Mexico, the decline in the deficit of the nonfinancial public sector in the early 1990s overstated the improvement in the true fiscal position, partly because it did not reflect the quasi-fiscal costs of the large expansion in lending by the public sector development banks.

Apart from the losses of public enterprises and the costs of quasi-fiscal activities, expenditures may be devolved from central to local governments without corresponding financing. For all these reasons, improvements in the central government's fiscal balance may misrepresent the true evolution of the public sector's overall financial position. Reductions in central government expenditures may simply reflect a shift to quasi-fiscal activities and implicit government liabilities, rather than a genuine retrenchment of the public sector's involvement in the economy. In Senegal, for example, while direct operational subsidies provided by the central government declined between 1985 and 1989, there was a large rise in central government overdrafts with quasi-public financial institutions. In such cases, the appearance of fiscal discipline in the central government's accounts may be illusory, and an apparent improvement in the fiscal position may not promote macroeconomic stability simply because the public sector's long-term financing requirement may fail to improve or may even deteriorate.

Difficulties in Revenue Mobilization

In a large number of developing countries, fiscal problems have been exacerbated by the presence of large sectors of informal (or "underground") economic activity. Typically the result of the prevalence of price controls in many areas of the economy, high tax rates, and weak institutional and administrative structures, such informal activity often adds dynamism to an economy, but it also narrows the tax base. The lack of sufficiently developed tax administration and collection capabilities also limits the extent to which the formal as well as the informal sector can be taxed.

As a result of these difficulties, most developing countries have been heavily dependent on taxes on international trade and on domestic product markets (Chart 25). For developing countries as a group, trade taxes accounted for almost 30 percent of total tax revenue during the period 1975–90, compared with only 3 percent for industrial countries.[48] In many of the more successful developing countries, especially in

---

[48]See Howell H. Zee, "Some Simple Cross-Country Empirics of Tax Revenue Ratios," paper presented at the International Seminar on Fiscal Reforms in Developing Countries, Seoul National University, Seoul, Korea, October 1994.

Chart 25. Developing Countries: Sources of Tax Revenue

(In percent of total tax revenue)

Trade taxes still account for a large proportion of tax revenue in developing countries.

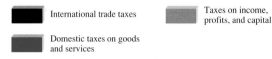

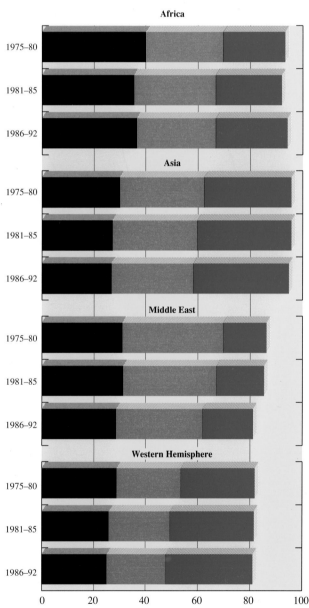

Source: IMF, *Government Finance Statistics.*

Chart 26. Developing Countries: Commodity Prices and Tax Revenues of Commodity Exporters

Revenues of commodity exporters have been strongly affected by swings in commodity prices.

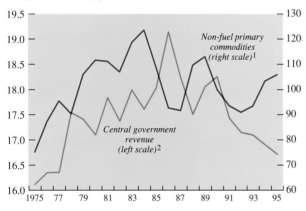

[1]In SDRs: 1990 = 100.
[2]In percent of GDP.

Asia and in Latin America, the relative importance of customs duties on imports and export taxes has declined in recent years, reflecting progress with trade liberalization and also domestic reforms. In many other developing countries, however, despite the negative economic effects of inward-oriented policies, trade barriers have been removed only gradually, in part because governments have remained dependent on trade taxes to finance spending programs.

For countries that are heavily dependent on commodity exports, tax revenues are strongly affected by movements in commodity prices (Chart 26). When commodity prices rise—such as during the early and late 1980s—government revenues are boosted both directly in countries where commodity-producing sectors are state owned and indirectly through increased revenues from trade and income taxes. Governments in a number of commodity-exporting countries have tended to use these windfall gains to finance procyclical expenditures with the result that when commodity prices have declined, these countries have been left with unsustainable fiscal deficits. For some coffee-producing countries, such as Kenya and Tanzania, expansions induced by the coffee price booms of the late 1970s and early 1980s led to enduringly higher domestic and external debt burdens, largely because the windfall gains were used to fund public sector expenditures that yielded little or no return. Experience in many oil exporting countries has been similar. In fact, in Mexico, Nigeria, and Venezuela, following the oil price hike of the late 1970s, external borrowing increased long before oil prices began to fall.

Consequences for Economic Growth and Development

The relationship between fiscal policies and longer-term economic performance depends on a number of factors. Whether fiscal policies promote economic growth depends on the extent to which government expenditure is directed toward increasing the stock of productive physical and human capital; on the extent to which the provision of government services complements private sector activity; on the extent to which fiscal deficits crowd out private sector investment; on the effect of deficits on macroeconomic stability; and also on the parallel structural reforms needed to elicit the private sector's supply response. In many countries, fiscal imbalances are the prime cause of low national saving and investment rates, while the development and efficiency of domestic financial systems frequently suffer from interest rate and credit controls, part of whose function is to facilitate the financing of fiscal deficits. In some instances, governments may be able to resort to foreign saving, often for relatively long periods, but the buildup of external imbalances with no counterpart in productive domestic investment

Table 16. Developing Countries: Fiscal Deficits and Economic Performance[1]

(Annual averages; in percent of GDP unless otherwise noted)

	Small Fiscal Deficit			Moderate Fiscal Deficit			Large Fiscal Deficit		
	1975–82	1983–89	1990–95	1975–82	1983–89	1990–95	1975–82	1983–89	1990–95
Central government fiscal balance[2]	–0.2	–1.4	–1.2	–6.7	–6.0	–3.5	–5.5	–12.1	–6.0
Real GDP[3]	5.1	6.4	6.9	3.0	2.6	5.0	4.6	3.2	3.1
Consumer prices[3,4]	13.2	12.2	14.4	34.5	51.5	33.8	15.4	29.3	16.6
Consumer prices (median)	11.0	7.5	9.2	12.6	8.2	8.4	12.0	10.4	13.0
Current expenditure	13.4	14.9	14.9	18.9	17.6	17.5	22.0	27.3	21.9
Private saving	19.7	23.3	29.0	20.2	18.4	16.3	19.1	18.9	13.9
Private investment	16.0	16.6	19.9	10.0	12.6	15.6	14.9	12.4	14.9
Current account balance	–2.0	–0.3	–0.1	–2.1	–2.8	–3.3	1.6	–3.1	–3.6
Terms of trade[3]	1.1	–0.5	0.4	0.7	–1.0	–0.4	3.4	–0.4	–1.0
Real effective exchange rate[3]	0.7	–3.8	2.5	–0.8	–1.1	2.0	1.1	–2.5	–3.5
External debt	21.8	30.8	27.6	26.3	46.8	48.9	27.3	47.4	52.2

[1]The classification of small, moderate, and large fiscal deficit countries is based on the average deficit-to-GDP ratio for the period 1983–89.
[2]Including grants.
[3]Annual percent change.
[4]Excluding Brazil.

increases a country's vulnerability to sudden reversals of capital inflows with their disruptive consequences for domestic policies and economic activity.

Impeding Growth Prospects

A comparison of developing countries ranked by the size of fiscal deficits during the mid-1980s shows that the group of countries characterized by small fiscal deficits (or surpluses) had markedly higher growth rates than countries that had moderate or large deficits (Table 16). Large fiscal deficits may of course be partly a result of slow economic growth, especially over short periods. Moreover, both large deficits and slow growth may in some cases be partly due to difficult external conditions, such as weak terms of trade or high global interest rates. Nevertheless, the experience of many developing countries suggests that weak fiscal discipline, indicated by persistent fiscal deficits, does reduce growth over the longer term. Countries that had large deficits in the 1980s experienced real GDP growth of only about 3 percent in the 1990–95 period compared with growth of almost 7 percent in small deficit countries. However, within the group of countries that had large deficits during the 1980s, a number of countries that undertook strong fiscal adjustment programs that were sustained, such as Chile and Uganda, shifted to markedly steeper growth paths. In many other countries where fiscal adjustment programs were not sustained, growth declined in the 1990s.

An important channel through which fiscal deficits damage growth performance is by reducing national saving and crowding out domestic investment, through effects not only on the cost and availability of finance but also on the real exchange rate and international competitiveness. Tables 14 and 16 suggest that fiscal discipline may have helped to boost not just na-

tional saving, but private saving: for example, in small deficit countries, the ratio of private saving to GDP was almost 4½ percentage points higher than in the large deficit countries during the 1980s. Moreover, these differences in private saving rates have increased markedly during the 1990s. There may have been a number of forces at work here, including the longer-term effects of structural reforms on economic incentives and the confidence-building effects of greater macroeconomic stability. Fiscal consolidation has also helped to reduce governments' dependence on financial repression, thereby stimulating private saving. The usual conclusion of econometric work in this area is rather different: it is that reductions in fiscal deficits increase national saving by less than the decline in public sector dissaving, because of a partly offsetting decline in private saving.[49] This still carries the implication that a smaller fiscal deficit is likely to promote private investment. The extent to which this raises productivity and growth then depends on the productivity of private investment relative to the productivity of the public spending that is displaced. Providing that public spending is not reduced in key areas where there are significant market failures—such as those arising from externalities to the provision of basic health care, education, and essential public services—overall productivity and growth are likely to benefit.[50]

---

[49]This so-called Ricardian effect is attributed to the private sector's reduced need to save to meet expected future tax liabilities. For recent estimates of the extent to which changes in public saving are offset by changes in private saving, see Paul R. Masson, Tamim Bayoumi, and Hossein Samiei, "Saving Behavior in Industrial and Developing Countries," in *Staff Studies for the World Economic Outlook* (IMF, September 1995), pp. 1–27.

[50]For an extensive discussion of inefficiencies of public expenditure, see Fiscal Affairs Department, *Unproductive Public Expenditures: A Pragmatic Approach to Policy Analysis*, IMF Pamphlet Series 48 (1995).

The contribution of public expenditure to growth and welfare naturally depends on its composition. Expenditure on improving the provision of primary education and basic health services, on productive investment in such areas as transport and communication, and on essential government services, can be very effective in enhancing growth in developing countries, whereas increasing civil service employment to expand governmental administrative functions, or expenditure on military equipment, may reduce the productive capacity of the economy by limiting resources available to the private sector. The broad classification of public expenditure into current and capital categories, although convenient, does not always convey the productive potential of different kinds of spending. The provision of health services, for example, through the wages of nurses and doctors, is part of current expenditure, while construction projects—including prestige projects with low productive potential—are classified as capital expenditures irrespective of their contribution to productive capacity, as are purchases of commercial property. These examples help to indicate why recent studies that have compared the effects on growth of current and capital public expenditures have arrived at ambiguous results, although it has been found that growth has tended to be higher in countries that have increased the share of certain kinds of capital expenditure—such as infrastructure investment—in total government expenditure.[51] Furthermore, if it is debt financed, public capital expenditure may crowd out private capital expenditures. In India and Senegal, for example, increases in public investment were associated with significant declines in private investment during the 1980s.

Macroeconomic Instability

In many developing countries, fiscal imbalances have been the underlying cause of macroeconomic instability, which, in turn, has impeded growth prospects. In countries where fiscal imbalances are large and perceived to be unsustainable, the uncertainty about impending policy changes, including higher taxes, expenditure cuts, and changes in interest rates and exchange rates, is likely to weaken the private sector's confidence and reduce private sector investment expenditures. In India, for example, during the foreign exchange crisis of the early 1990s that was caused largely by a rapid buildup of domestic and external imbalances, gross fixed investment declined by 4 percent in 1991–92 and recovered only gradually over the next two years.[52]

Large fiscal deficits in developing countries have also been associated with rapid inflation, essentially because they are typically financed to a large extent by monetary growth. During the 1980s, many Latin American countries, such as Argentina, Brazil, and Mexico, experienced very high rates of inflation largely as a result of substantial fiscal deficits that could not be financed by borrowing on either domestic or international financial markets. Although some countries are still characterized by relatively high inflation, average inflation in the developing countries has declined significantly in recent years, owing largely to strong fiscal consolidation programs. Impressive achievements in this regard are those of Argentina, whose 12-month inflation rate by late 1995 had been reduced to 1½ percent, from over 2000 percent early in the decade, and Brazil, which lowered average monthly inflation from over 40 percent in the first half of 1994 to about 1½ percent in 1995.

Fiscal policy and inflation are also related by the fact that rapid inflation can provide an important, though unsustainable, source of budgetary revenue, through seigniorage, which consists primarily of the "inflation tax."[53] In the 1980s, a number of developing countries, including Ghana and Zambia, relied on the inflation tax as a significant source of revenue to finance their budgets. Over the longer term, however, higher inflation reduces the attractiveness of domestic monetary assets and this eventually limits the amount of revenue that can be generated. The decline of inflation has reduced the amount of revenue derived from inflation since the 1970s (Table 17).

Governments in many developing countries have intervened in financial markets in attempts to finance deficits at below-market interest rates; this has been a major factor impeding the development of financial sectors and limiting intermediation in financial markets and the availability of credit to the private sector. Although some regulatory controls on financial markets are motivated by prudential concerns, many controls in developing countries, such as interest rate ceilings and statutory underrenumerated reserve and

---

[51]See, for example, Robert Barro, "Economic Growth in a Cross-Section of Countries," *Quarterly Journal of Economics*, Vol. 106 (May 1991), pp. 407–43, which finds that higher current expenditure lowers per capita growth; but also Shantayana Devarajan, Vinaya Swaroop, and Heng-fu Zou, "The Composition of Public Expenditure and Economic Growth," World Bank Working Paper (1995), which finds that higher current expenditure increases growth while higher capital expenditure reduces growth. William Easterly and Sergio Rebelo, "Fiscal Policy and Economic Growth: An Empirical Investigation," NBER Working Paper 4499 (October 1993), which examines components of capital expenditure, find a strong positive association between growth and expenditure on transport and communication.

[52]See Ajai Chopra, Charles Collyns, Richard Hemming, and Karen Parker, *India: Economic Reform and Growth*, IMF Occasional Paper 134 (December 1995).

[53]Seigniorage comprises the inflation tax—the reduction in the purchasing power of private sector holdings of high-powered money balances due to inflation—and autonomous changes in the level of real high-powered money balances.

Table 17. Developing Countries: Indicators of Financial Repression[1]

(Annual averages; in percent of GDP unless otherwise noted)

	Small Fiscal Deficit			Moderate Fiscal Deficit			Large Fiscal Deficit		
	1975–82	1983–89	1990–95	1975–82	1983–89	1990–95	1975–82	1983–89	1990–95
Real interest rate[2]	–2.1	2.9	1.6	–5.6	0.8	1.3	–4.8	–2.2	–2.5
Seigniorage[3]	2.4	2.6	1.9	3.0	3.5	2.8	2.4	2.7	1.7
Government borrowing from central bank	1.9	1.7	1.5	2.3	1.9	2.1	3.3	4.9	2.1
Broad money	34.3	50.4	64.9	36.4	45.5	45.6	25.4	39.2	36.7
Private sector credit	29.7	41.7	53.7	20.8	29.7	32.5	15.4	21.8	20.7

[1]The classification of small, moderate, and large fiscal deficit countries is based on the average deficit-to-GDP ratio for the period 1983–89.
[2]The real interest rate is defined as the nominal interest rate on short-term bank deposits discounted by actual inflation, in percent a year.
[3]Seigniorage is calculated as the change in high-powered money balances as a percent of GDP.

liquidity requirements on financial institutions, are primarily intended to ensure the provision of funding to governments at below-market rates (Box 7). It is difficult to estimate the revenue effectively generated by these policies since the extent of the subsidy depends on the differential between controlled interest rates and the interest rates that would prevail in the absence of controls, but in many countries, revenue from financial repression can be substantial.[54]

Many developing countries have managed to sustain relatively large fiscal deficits—in some cases averaging almost 10 percent of GDP over a number of years. Such deficits are unlikely to be sustainable, however, because government debt cannot grow faster than the economy in the long term.[55] Moreover, delays in implementing adjustment measures can lead to substantial output losses when fiscal adjustment is forced upon governments by financial markets. During the 1980s, the fiscal deficit in Pakistan averaged over 7 percent of GDP and was financed largely through extensive controls on financial markets, relatively strong monetary growth, and external borrowing; growth also averaged about 6 percent a year in the 1980s. But in the early 1990s, adverse supply conditions increased the fiscal deficit to over 9 percent of GDP, and the growing external debt burden eventually led to a fi-

nancial and exchange market crisis in 1993, followed by a sharp decline in growth to about 2½ percent. Large fiscal imbalances also contributed to the financial crisis in Turkey in 1994, which brought about a sharp decline in the availability of external finance and a deep recession; output declined by over 4½ percent in 1994 compared with over 8 percent growth in the previous year.

Benefits and Challenges of Fiscal Adjustment

In contrast with the 1970s and most of the 1980s, there is now widespread consensus on the need for fiscal discipline, on the associated benefits in terms of monetary and financial stability, and economic growth and development, and on the need for constraints to be placed on the size and role of the public sector. As the experience of many successful performers among developing countries illustrates, a key requirement for the promotion of growth is often to scale down the role of the state. For many developing countries, this requires reducing overemployment and increasing efficiency in the public sector, and implementing extensive privatization programs. But in many developing countries there is also scope—much more so than in industrial countries—to enhance revenues without worsening distortions and reducing efficiency, especially by broadening the revenue base and improving tax collection and administration. Some important reforms, however, including the liberalization of trade and the financial system, may have short-term negative implications for revenue that may need to be offset. For developing countries that have benefited from substantial foreign investment, both safeguarding financial stability and maintaining the momentum of reforms are essential for growth to be sustained.

Economic growth has been considerably higher in developing countries that have addressed fiscal imbalances decisively and implemented strong fiscal con-

---

[54]See William Easterly and Klaus Schmidt-Hebbel, "Fiscal Adjustment and Macroeconomic Performance: A Synthesis," in *Public Sector Deficits and Macroeconomic Performance*, ed. by William Easterly, Carlos A. Rodriguez, and Klaus Schmidt-Hebbel (New York: Oxford University Press for the World Bank, 1994), for estimates of government revenue from financial repression in selected developing countries during the late 1970s and 1980s.

[55]In fact, if public debt grows at a rate faster than the difference between the real growth rate of the economy and the real interest rate, the fiscal deficit will not be sustainable. It is difficult to evaluate the sustainability of fiscal deficits in many developing countries because nominal interest rates are often controlled at below-market rates so that real interest rates do not reflect the opportunity cost of financing debt. See also section on Sustainability of Public Debt and Generational Fairness in Chapter III for a formal analysis of fiscal sustainability in the industrial countries.

Box 7. Quasi-Fiscal Activities in Developing Countries

In a large number of developing countries, economic policy objectives are frequently pursued through operations of central banks and other public sector financial institutions that may have important fiscal implications.[1] Central bank lending to the public sector, including foreign exchange lending at below-market interest rates, and subsidized loans and loan guarantees extended by public sector financial institutions to specific sectors and groups of borrowers affect the public sector's net financial position even though they may not show up in the central government budget as specific expenditure or revenue items.

Central banks lend to governments by providing overdraft facilities or directly purchasing government securities. When interest rates on loans to central governments and other public sector bodies are set at below-market rates, public expenditures will not be evaluated at their true opportunity costs, and this can lead both to excessive expenditure and to the selection of projects for which the true economic costs exceed their benefits. Apart from direct lending to governments, central banks frequently compel commercial banks to hold short-term government securities at below-market rates, by imposing statutory liquidity requirements. Central banks may also pay below-market rates on commercial banks' reserve assets. These devices essentially represent taxes on the banking system, which tend to restrict the development of financial intermediation, increase the spread between borrowing and lending rates, and reduce saving and investment in the economy. Such forms of financial repression can also yield substantial revenue to the government. Between 1984 and 1987, for example, the Mexican government extracted close to 6 percent of GDP, or about 40 percent of total tax revenue, from controls on financial markets.[2]

In many developing countries, subsidized lending by development banks and other public sector financial institutions to specific groups, often without adequate collateral, is the most common form of quasi-fiscal operations. In India, for example, the central bank requires that government-owned commercial banks lend about 40 percent of their assets to small-scale farmers and other small businesses. To finance such lending, nonfinancial public sector undertakings are required to maintain deposits at below-market interest rates with the commercial banks and other public sector financial institutions. Extensive problems of loan recovery have plagued public sector banks that engage in such implicit subsidization since it promotes adverse selection. In some cases, the central bank has to step in by either providing funds to recapitalize bankrupt banks or assuming nonperforming assets. When faced with serious financial difficulties, state banks in Brazil have frequently raised overdrafts on the collateral of their legal reserves and taken large rediscount loans from the central bank. In early 1991, to improve the central bank's portfolio, the government swapped such loans with its own securities to the extent of about 2 percent of GDP.

Despite a strong trend toward exchange market unification in developing countries, central banks in a number of countries still engage in multiple exchange rate practices, with different exchange rates applying to various categories of activities. A frequently used variation of this

---

[1]For a more detailed discussion on the use of different quasi-fiscal instruments, see George A. Mackenzie and Peter Stella, *Quasi-Fiscal Operations of Public Financial Institutions*, IMF Occasional Paper (forthcoming).

[2]For further details see Alberto Giovannini and Martha De Melo, "Government Revenue from Financial Repression," *American Economic Review*, Vol. 83 (September 1993), pp. 953–63.

---

solidation measures. A classification of developing countries based on the magnitude of fiscal adjustment—the change in the fiscal balance as a percent of GDP—between 1980–85 and 1990–95 shows that in the group of countries where fiscal balances improved the most, output was on average over 40 percent higher in 1990–95 than in 1980–85 (Chart 27). Although the strengthening of fiscal policies in these countries was in part attributable to favorable growth performances, prudent policies played a key role in sustaining relatively high growth. By contrast, in countries where fiscal balances worsened, growth has been significantly lower, and in some cases output has barely grown over the last fifteen years.

When faced with the need to reduce *government expenditures*, policymakers in many developing countries have frequently chosen the politically easier paths of cutting capital spending or allowing real wages in the public sector to be eroded by keeping nominal wage levels unchanged while prices are rising. Rarely have governments reduced public sector employment.[56] In a number of African countries, the growth of value added by government, measured primarily by increases in public sector employment, has exceeded the growth of private sector activity for long periods and sometimes by significant margins.[57] In Kenya and Zimbabwe, growth in the private sector during most of the 1980s and early 1990s was almost 2 percentage points lower than the growth of the government sector.

---

[56]See Aart Kraay and Caroline Van Rijckeghem, "Employment and Wages in the Public Sector—A Cross-Country Study," IMF Working Paper 95/70 (July 1995).

[57]See James P. Gordon, "Can Increasing the Government Payroll Boost Growth? Evidence from Africa," IMF Working Paper (forthcoming) for an assessment of the public sector's contribution to growth in selected African countries.

practice is to set the official exchange rate (cost of foreign exchange in terms of domestic currency) at a lower level than the market rate. All official transactions, such as debt-service payments on external debt owed by the government and public enterprises, along with payments for imports of state-owned enterprises, such as government-owned oil and electricity companies, are conducted at the official rate. The government may also require the surrender or repatriation of export proceeds of some or all commodities—in many countries, in fact, all exports are subject to surrender and repatriation requirements—and allow private sector imports of necessities (e.g., medicine) and capital goods at the official rate. Apart from distorting the allocation of resources and understating expenditure on public sector imports and debt-service payments in domestic currency terms, this also obscures the effective levels of taxation on exports and imports. During 1979–82, the Costa Rican central bank provided foreign exchange for certain imports at a lower rate than the rate it had paid for the foreign currency. In 1981 alone, these subsidies amounted to about 4½ percent of GDP. In 1987–88, the parallel market exchange rate of the Ugandan shilling ranged between U Sh 200 and 400 per U.S. dollar, although the Coffee Marketing Board was surrendering its export receipts to the central bank at the official exchange rate of U Sh 60 per U.S. dollar.

Governments also, through development banks and other public sector financial institutions, often provide exchange rate guarantees or subsidize exchange risk insurance. As a result of these subsidies, a strong incentive is created for the beneficiaries to increase their foreign currency liabilities, especially in countries where inflation is higher than in the main trading partner countries. While the impact of these subsidies on the fiscal deficit may not be immediate, the increase in the contingent liabilities of public sector financial institutions and ultimately those of the government may result in substantial

fiscal expenditures during times of macroeconomic instability. In Chile, following the devaluation of 1982 in the aftermath of the debt crisis, the central bank provided subsidized foreign exchange to the private sector for external debt-service obligations, equivalent to almost 2 percent of GDP a year in 1983–85. At the same time, exchange rate guarantees amounted to about ½ of 1 percent of GDP a year.

In recent years, central banks in many countries that have experienced large capital inflows have opted to increase reserves and sterilize them rather than let the domestic currency appreciate freely. As a consequence, the domestic interest in such cases has often risen to levels higher than the return on foreign reserves, giving rise to losses for the central bank. In the early 1990s, quasi-fiscal costs of such sterilization operations were as high as ½ of 1 percent of GDP a year for some Latin American countries.[3]

Quasi-fiscal operations are typically undertaken to circumvent legislative and political constraints on fiscal policy, but they frequently have important fiscal consequences and, in general, reduce efficiency by distorting relative prices in the economy, thus impeding development. While it may be difficult to quickly eliminate many of the subsidies implicitly provided through quasi-fiscal operations, acknowledging such activities in central government budget statements would enhance the transparency of fiscal policy. Over the longer term, however, reliance on such subsidies, whether provided implicitly or explicitly, should be phased out in combination with the implementation of other structural reforms that enhance resource allocation and long-term growth.

---

[3]See Miguel A. Kiguel and Leonardo Leiderman, "On the Consequences of Sterilized Intervention in Latin America: The Case of Colombia and Chile" (World Bank: Washington 1993).

Real wage reductions in the public sector, however, like capital spending cuts, can be counterproductive. They may reduce public sector efficiency, especially in key areas such as tax administration, the enforcement of tax regulations, law and order more generally, and the operation of state-owned utilities. To the extent that declining real wages of civil servants lead to a widening of differentials with respect to private sector pay, this expedient may also foster corruption and rent-seeking activities.[58] In Tanzania, for example, real wages of civil servants had declined by 1980 to

one fifth of their 1970 level, and this was widely regarded as a major factor contributing to absenteeism and corruption in the public sector. In contrast, among many of the relatively successful developing countries, such as Chile, Korea, and Singapore, public sector wages have been maintained at levels that are broadly comparable with the private sector.

Although reductions in public sector employment may be politically difficult, especially in countries where alternative employment opportunities appear limited in the short term, a number of countries have managed to implement extensive civil service retrenchment programs by providing severance payments and job-search assistance to departing workers. Between 1987 and 1991, Ghana reduced its civil service workforce—including through the elimination of "ghost workers"—by about 10 percent, offering severance payments of two months' salary for every year of

---

[58]For a formal analysis of the effects on tax evasion and corruption of widening wage differentials between the public and private sectors, see Nadeem Ul Haque and Ratna Sahay, "Do Government Wage Cuts Close Budget Deficits? A Conceptual Framework for Developing Countries and Transition Economies," IMF Working Paper 96/19 (February 1996).

Chart 27. Developing Countries: Fiscal Adjustment and Growth

(Changes between 1980–85 and 1990–95)

Developing countries that have addressed fiscal imbalances have experienced large output gains.

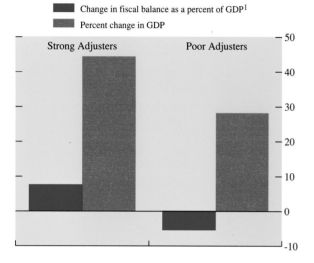

¹The magnitude of fiscal adjustment is evaluated as the change in the average fiscal balance between the period 1980–85 and 1990–95. Countries are ranked on the basis of the size of the fiscal adjustment.

service and additional assistance, including employment counseling and food-for-work programs, for those who failed to secure alternative employment. In some cases, in the short term, net budgetary savings from such civil service retrenchment programs may be small but over the medium term the efficiency gains and savings can be substantial.

In most developing countries, reducing employment in state-owned enterprises is a prerequisite for their restructuring and privatization. A large number of such enterprises engage in activities that the private sector could undertake more efficiently. In many African and Middle Eastern countries, such as Senegal and Egypt, state-owned enterprises are engaged in food production, while in India, state-owned enterprises are extensively involved not only in heavy industry and mining but also in the production of consumer goods. For the developing countries as a group, nonfinancial state-owned enterprises account for over 10 percent of GDP.[59]

There has been relatively little progress in most developing countries in introducing more competition and easing entry restrictions on potential private sector competitors to state-owned enterprises. In spite of some large privatizations, the number of enterprises run by the state has not declined markedly. In some countries, policymakers have sought to improve the efficiency of state-owned enterprises by instituting performance contracts for managers. In most cases, however, such measures have led to little or no improvement in efficiency and profitability, in part because the enterprises, being state owned, continue to face conflicting objectives. In Senegal, for example, performance contracts for managers of the state-owned electricity company detailed more than 20 criteria on which performance would be judged, but the government lacked the power to enforce penalties if the criteria were not met. In fact, profitability declined because the government did not force other state-owned enterprises to pay for their electricity consumption on a timely basis. By contrast, in countries where state-owned utility companies have been sold to the private sector, as with the privatization of telecommunications in Argentina, Chile, Malaysia, and Mexico, productivity has increased, in part because of higher investment.

Among many commodity-exporting countries, the motivation for state intervention in commodity-producing sectors has frequently been macroeconomic stabilization. In the face of volatile export revenues, governments are concerned about the impact of foreign exchange flows on the real exchange rate and the international competitiveness of the traded goods sec-

[59]See World Bank, *Bureaucrats in Business: The Economics and Politics of Government Ownership* (Washington: Oxford University Press for the World Bank, 1995).

tor. Intervention has taken a variety of forms, including export taxes imposed when commodity prices are high, requirements on exporters to hold foreign exchange earnings at the central bank, and investing proceeds from commodity price booms to promote diversification of exports. Experience suggests, however, that such intervention has tended to introduce further distortions and instability into the economy. Moreover, public sector management of windfall gains from commodity price booms frequently entails dealing with competing claims, such as from government ministries, special interest groups, and state-owned enterprises, which are not always resolved in such a way that the increase in revenues is invested in programs that enhance longer-term growth performance.

Since the 1980s, fiscal consolidation programs in many developing countries have also entailed improvements in the structure of *taxation* and in *tax administration systems*. A number of countries have rationalized and consolidated tax structures to reduce distortionary taxes, especially taxes on international trade, and have moved toward broad-based consumption taxes. In India, for example, the maximum tariff on imports was reduced from 400 percent in 1990 to 50 percent in 1995, and average tariff rates fell from well over 80 percent to under 30 percent over the same period. In Indonesia, prior to the introduction of the value-added tax (VAT) in 1985, revenue from indirect taxes amounted to about 1 percent of GDP, whereas by the late 1980s such revenue was equivalent to over 3 percent of GDP. Reforms of tax structures have also included marked reductions in personal and corporate income tax rates. In Thailand, the maximum personal income tax rate was reduced from 65 percent in 1980 to under 40 percent in 1993. While there is widespread acceptance that such reforms help improve allocative efficiency, and can therefore lead to higher revenue over the longer term, their success depends on limiting ad hoc exemptions that tend to narrow the tax base and reduce efficiency. Lower personal income tax rates can also help to promote a more equitable tax system in countries where, because of poor tax administration, high marginal tax rates are applied in an ad hoc and discriminatory fashion. Improving tax enforcement and compliance can allow countries to lower tax rates and at the same time increase tax revenue. In Chile, the difference between estimated potential revenue from indirect taxes and actual revenue declined from almost 25 percent in 1981 to 17 percent in 1993 as a result of more efficient tax administration.[60]

Concerns about inadequate tax revenues have also slowed the pace of *trade* and *financial liberalization* in some developing countries. Countries that have traditionally been dependent on trade taxes for a significant portion of revenues have dismantled trade barriers only gradually, despite the potential long-term benefits of liberal trade regimes. Although trade liberalization may lead to shortfalls in revenue in the short term— and in these cases expenditure reductions may be difficult to avoid—some trade liberalization measures can be implemented without significant declines in revenue. In fact, lifting quantitative restrictions may well increase revenue as the imports liberalized would most likely be subject to tariffs. Moreover, even in the case of tariff reductions, the fall in revenue may be small. In countries that have liberalized exchange markets, especially where official and unofficial exchange rates have been unified, the higher domestic currency price of imports at the liberalized market exchange rate may well allow tariff rates to be reduced with no loss of revenue.[61]

Developing countries that are at a relatively advanced stage in liberalizing trade regimes and implementing market-oriented structural reforms have attracted large *capital flows* in recent years. In some cases, however, the capital inflows may be attracted primarily by high domestic interest rates stemming from an unbalanced mix of monetary and fiscal policy. For these countries, fiscal tightening will help to safeguard financial stability by improving the domestic saving-investment balance. For all such recipient countries, however, large-scale capital inflows have been accompanied by higher domestic spending and higher imports, which have increased fiscal revenues. Such increases in revenue may well be unsustainable, and as suggested by Mexico's experience, policymakers may need to aim for structural fiscal surpluses to provide a buffer that can be used in the event of large outflows. The experience of Mexico also underscores the role of fiscal policies in determining the credibility, and ultimately the sustainability, of pegged exchange rates. Devaluations that are not accompanied by strong fiscal measures are unlikely to gain credibility or deliver effective adjustment.[62]

While fiscal policies can bring substantial longer-term growth benefits, fiscal consolidation measures such as reductions in public sector employment, tax increases, and the privatization of state-owned enterprises can have adverse effects on the economically weaker social groups in the short term. The removal of generalized subsidies on basic necessities, the relaxation of price controls, and currency devaluations can

---

[60]See World Bank, *Lessons of Tax Reform* (Washington, 1991).

[61]See Box 3 of the October 1994 *World Economic Outlook*, pp. 26–27, for details of exchange market reforms in a number of African countries.

[62]See the October 1994 *World Economic Outlook* for extensive discussions of the recent surge in capital flows to developing countries and Annex I of the May 1995 *World Economic Outlook* for an evaluation of the causes of the sharp reversal of capital flows to Mexico in early 1995.

cause real incomes of domestic consumers to decline in the short term. The adverse effects of adjustment and reform on the poor and vulnerable need to be addressed through well-targeted and cost-effective *social safety nets*. In a number of countries, such as Mozambique and Zambia, cash compensation schemes have shielded vulnerable groups during periods of rising prices and at the same time permitted a strengthening of budgetary positions. In Jordan, a generalized subsidy for selected food items was replaced in 1990 with a food coupon scheme that allowed coupon recipients to purchase fixed quantities of basic necessities at below market prices; the budgetary costs of food subsidies declined from over 3 percent of GDP in 1990 to about 1 percent in 1994. These examples illustrate the fact that, despite practical difficulties, especially in poorer countries, of targeting the most vulnerable groups—difficulties that often arise from weak administrative capacity and in some cases from inadequate political support—social safety nets can help alleviate many of the short-term adverse consequences of fiscal consolidation.

In comparison with many industrial countries, where the unfunded liabilities of publicly provided *pension schemes* currently imply considerable increases in future tax burdens, developing countries are at a relatively early stage of establishing extensive pension programs for the elderly. In some rapidly growing developing countries, however—especially many Asian countries with aging populations—the need to offer sufficient security to retired persons is likely to place growing demands on public sector expenditures. The experiences of public sector provision of pensions in a number of countries suggest that developing countries in the process of implementing pension programs should encourage greater private sector participation to avoid excessive fiscal burdens, which frequently arise from poor public sector administrative capabilities. During the 1980s, the rate of return on publicly managed funds in Egypt, Peru, Venezuela, and Zambia ranged between −12 percent and −37 percent a year; in Zambia, more than half the contributions were used for administrative expenses. The establishment of sound privately managed systems, however, will often require a strengthening of the financial system and of the official regulatory and supervisory capability. Pension reforms in many Latin American countries, such as Chile in the early 1980s, and more recently Argentina, have been designed to overcome the problem of rising contributions required to finance overextended benefit commitments. In addition to the fiscal burden, excessive contributions—higher than could possibly be realized in future benefits—will tend to discourage formal sector employment and to reduce saving and capital accumulation.

* * *

Many developing countries have made substantial progress with economic policies since the 1980s and are now much better placed to reap the benefits of increased integration of goods and financial markets in the global economy. The resilient growth performance of developing countries in the 1990s is indicative of the progress that has been made. Although domestic policies have improved in a number of areas, improved fiscal policies have been a prime source of greater macroeconomic stability and increased confidence for investment. Compared with the 1980s, fiscal imbalances are markedly smaller in a large number of countries, despite significant differences in the underlying causes of fiscal deficits. For some countries, deficits have stemmed largely from inappropriate policy responses to terms of trade shocks, but in most cases, fiscal deficits reflect a legacy of excessive and unnecessary state involvement in economic activities, which in turn has impeded growth of both the economy and tax revenue bases. Among the more successful performers, rapid and sustained economic growth has increased the need for public sector provision of infrastructure to keep pace with private sector development. Despite differences in the underlying causes of deficits, fiscal consolidation measures have consisted primarily of expenditure cuts, reflecting a widespread consensus among policymakers on the adverse effects on growth of higher taxation. In some developing countries, rapid growth has also enabled governments to reduce taxation without reducing expenditures on essential public services.

While sound fiscal policies have been established in a number of countries, in many others it is necessary to speed up the process of fiscal consolidation and ensure that programs already initiated stay on track. And in parallel with disciplined fiscal policies, radical structural reforms are still needed in many countries to elicit the private sector supply response and raise growth performance. With more open trade regimes and increased integration of capital markets, the costs of macroeconomic imbalances are likely to be even greater than in the past. Indeed, as some countries have already seen, adjustment forced by financial markets can require sharp changes in expenditure policies and lead to large output losses. All countries need constantly to evaluate expenditure priorities and to limit the extent of public sector intervention and the associated distortions that may hinder private sector activity. For many of the strong performers, it will be imperative to ensure that public sector commitments to extend social security programs, including pension schemes, do not give rise to excessive fiscal burdens. These countries have the opportunity to avoid the costly mistakes of many industrial countries where pension entitlements have contributed to increasingly unsustainable fiscal burdens.

V

Fiscal Challenges of Transition: Progress Made and Problems Remaining

With the collapse of central planning, the transition countries confronted daunting fiscal challenges.[63] The key objective for economic policy was to transform the role of the state in support of market-based economic systems, and fiscal policy had a leading role in reducing the share of output claimed by the public sector and in the reform of transfers to households and enterprises. In addition, fiscal policy, together with monetary and exchange rate policies, had to ensure a reasonable degree of macroeconomic stability. Continued instability would jeopardize the transition to a market economy because of the distorted relative price signals and poor incentives associated with rapid inflation. Macroeconomic stabilization was also essential to foster adequate levels of saving and investment, especially given the need to replace the substantial share of the capital stock that was obsolete.

Achieving macroeconomic stability was complicated by the unavoidable initial jump in prices as they were liberalized. Inflation was also fueled early on by significant overhangs of liquidity, the legacy of past financial imbalances whose inflationary consequences had been suppressed by price controls. In addition, the collapse of the command system, which led to large terms of trade shocks and the loss of external markets in many countries, contributed to a sharp drop in output. As a result, enormous strains were put on budgets owing to declines in revenues and new demands for subsidies, transfers, and credits to cushion the effects on employment and living standards.

Given the magnitude of the challenges, most transition countries have by now made remarkable progress toward macroeconomic stability. In some cases, fiscal deficits have been reduced to levels below those prevailing in most industrial countries. Fiscal discipline

has played a key role in reducing inflation and in the recovery of output among the countries more advanced in the transition. There has also been in many cases a major reduction in the role of the government in the economy, partly owing to widespread privatization of previously state-owned assets. In many areas, however, the role of the state remains significant, even in some of the most advanced transition countries.

Continued involvement in the economy occurs not only through activities directly reflected in budgets, but also through a number of off-budget or quasi-fiscal channels involving loan guarantees and other contingent liabilities, directed credits, and the tolerance of systemic nonpayment. Often the motivation for such practices is to safeguard employment by preventing the closure of unprofitable enterprises, but the distinction between social concerns and commercial and other objectives is often blurred. Whatever their purpose, many of these activities represent actual or contingent government fiscal liabilities, which may constitute a threat to macroeconomic stability. In addition, these practices continue to distort the allocation of resources and therefore worsen the chances of recovery. In several countries, these effects are exacerbated by a serious and growing problem of nonperforming bank loans, which threatens to impose a large financial burden on governments through the need for budgetary resources to compensate depositors and to restructure banking systems.

Progress in Fiscal Consolidation

Many transition countries have made substantial progress toward reducing the excessive fiscal imbalances that characterized the initial phase of the transition, although individual country experiences differ considerably. In reviewing this progress, it is useful to distinguish between two groups of countries, one more advanced and the other less advanced in the transition process (Table 18).[64] It must be borne in mind, how-

---

[63]The country classification in the *World Economic Outlook*, which is described in the Statistical Appendix, places in the group of transition countries ten countries in central and eastern Europe, the three Baltic countries, the Russian Federation, the other eleven countries of the former Soviet Union, and Mongolia. Two additional countries, Bosnia and Herzegovina and the Federal Republic of Yugoslavia, are also classified in the group of transition countries, but they are not yet included in the *World Economic Outlook* because their data are incomplete. Asian countries that are also in transition from central planning are classified as developing countries; these countries differ in certain important respects from the transition countries as defined here, although they also share important similarities with respect to issues discussed in this chapter.

[64]Methodological problems plague national accounts data in most transition countries. These problems are thought to be more severe in countries of the former Soviet Union, given their earlier stage in the transition, as well as the more limited capacity of their statistical agencies. The fiscal balance, revenue, and expenditure figures cited below should therefore be viewed as indicative of broad trends, rather than as a precise accounting of fiscal developments.

Table 18. Countries in Transition: General Government Budget Balance[1]

(In percent of GDP)

	1989	1990	1991	1992	1993	1994	1995
Countries more advanced in transition							
Albania[2,3]	–8.6	–15.4	–30.7	–21.5	–16.0	–13.0	–13.1
Croatia	...	...	–5.0	–3.8	–0.7	1.7	–1.5
Czech Republic	...	...	...	–2.2	0.6	–1.3	–1.6
Estonia	...	...	5.2	–0.3	–0.7	1.3	0.3
Hungary[2]	–1.3	0.9	–3.0	–6.8	–6.7	–8.6	–6.7
Latvia[2]	...	...	6.3	–0.8	0.6	–4.0	–3.4
Lithuania[2]	...	...	...	...	–0.1	–2.0	–1.3
Macedonia, former Yugoslav Rep. of	...	...	–4.4	–9.6	–13.6	–3.1	–1.5
Mongolia	...	...	–9.7	–12.7	–14.6	–24.6	–11.1
Poland	–8.0	3.3	–6.7	–8.0	–4.0	–2.0	–2.7
Slovak Republic	...	...	...	–11.9	–7.1	–1.3	–0.4
Slovenia	...	...	2.6	0.2	0.3	–0.2	–0.5
Countries less advanced in transition							
Armenia	...	...	...	–31.0	–56.1	–16.4	8.7
Azerbaijan	...	...	...	2.8	–15.3	–10.5	–5.4
Belarus	...	...	...	0.1	–4.2	–2.8	–2.6
Bulgaria	–1.4	–12.8	–14.7	–15.0	–15.7	–7.0	–6.0
Georgia	...	...	...	–25.4	–26.2	–16.3	–5.7
Kazakstan	...	...	...	–7.3	–1.2	0.3	–3.3
Kyrgyz Republic	...	...	...	–17.4	–13.5	–8.4	–10.4
Moldova	...	...	...	–26.2	–7.4	–9.0	–5.5
Romania	8.4	1.1	–1.7	–4.6	–0.1	–1.0	–2.5
Russia	...	...	...	–18.9	–7.6	–10.1	–4.8
Tajikistan	...	...	...	–30.5	–23.6	–2.7	–12.0
Turkmenistan	...	...	...	13.2	–0.4	–1.4	–1.6
Ukraine	...	...	...	–29.3	–10.3	–8.8	–3.5
Uzbekistan	...	...	...	–12.2	–17.5	–7.0	–4.2

Sources: National authorities; and IMF staff estimates.

[1]Defined as total revenue and grants minus total expenditure (including extrabudgetary funds) plus net lending.

[2]Central government balance.

[3]Excludes concessional external financing of development projects on the order of 6–8 percent of GDP.

ever, that such a dichotomy is necessarily an imperfect simplification, since in fact the degrees of progress made by different countries are closer to a continuum. The classification is not based on any one criterion—the rate of inflation, or the fiscal balance, say—but on a range of indicators of the progress made in macroeconomic stabilization and structural reforms. Thus a few countries classified as more advanced in transition still have large fiscal imbalances financed from noninflationary sources, as in the case of Mongolia. To the extent that such imbalances reflect the costs of structural reform, they are not necessarily indicative of a weak adjustment effort. Indeed, because broad-ranging structural reforms are necessary to revive and sustain growth in transition economies, the situation may point to improved public finances in the future. Conversely, some countries classified as less advanced in transition have only modest imbalances, but have generally made less progress in terms of structural reforms, particularly enterprise restructuring. The slow pace of structural reforms in these countries undermines the sustainability of fiscal adjustment and

threatens the progress made toward financial stabilization. In addition, because structural reforms typically entail significant budgetary costs that have yet to be reflected in fiscal balances, the progress made by less-advanced transition countries toward fiscal consolidation may be less secure.

Among the countries more advanced in transition, Poland undertook a massive fiscal adjustment early in its transition. This effort proved not to be fully sustainable, however, and the fiscal balance deteriorated again in 1991–92, but fiscal restraint has subsequently narrowed the deficit significantly. Reflecting the relatively sound macroeconomic situation in the former Czechoslovakia, the Czech Republic moved from a small deficit in 1992 to a slight surplus in 1993 and has since remained close to approximate balance. The Slovak Republic initially incurred large budgetary imbalances, but strong fiscal consolidation efforts in 1994–95 virtually eliminated the deficit. Estonia and Lithuania have pursued cautious fiscal policies and the authorities have contained budget deficits at modest levels or achieved small surpluses. Good progress toward fiscal balance has also been made by Croatia, while Slovenia's budgetary position has been close to balance for several years.

Substantial fiscal imbalances remain, however, in some of the other countries that are relatively advanced in the transition. During the early 1990s, Hungary's fiscal position deteriorated markedly, with the deficit increasing to 8½ percent of GDP in 1994. The fiscal deterioration was mirrored in a growing external current account deficit financed by official borrowing and capital inflows, and corrective actions became necessary. In early 1995, fiscal austerity measures were introduced that helped to contain the deficit to about 6½ percent of GDP last year, but further measures are necessary to put the fiscal balance on a sustainable, long-term footing; the 1996 budget is an important step in this direction. The fiscal deficit in Albania remained high in 1995, at about 13 percent of GDP, although this represents a considerable improvement from the early 1990s. Large fiscal imbalances also remain in Mongolia, financed from noninflationary sources.

The improved fiscal positions in most of the advanced transition countries reflect both expenditure control and, following an initial drop at the outset of transition, relatively stable revenues in relation to GDP (Chart 28).[65] In Poland, revenues totaled 47 percent of GDP in 1995, about 5 percentage points above the level that prevailed at the outset of transition (Table 19). Early in the reform process, however, revenues were steady in relation to GDP, while the severe compression of expenditures implemented in 1990 could not be sustained (Table 20). In the Czech and Slovak Republics, revenues declined as a share of GDP early in the transition largely because of discretionary cuts in the rates of corporate income tax and turnover taxes, but this was more than offset by spending restraint. Somewhat atypically, Croatia managed to raise the share of revenues in GDP from about 32 percent in 1991 to 55 percent in 1995, much of this increase being matched by higher expenditures. In contrast, Albania suffered a severe decline in revenues—from almost 50 percent of GDP in 1990 to about 25 percent in 1995; although expenditures also fell sharply over this period, a large deficit remains as indicated earlier.

The fiscal situation has also improved in the countries that are less advanced in the transition. In most cases, macroeconomic imbalances inherited from

---

[65]It should be noted that, as a result of steep declines in real GDP, the revenue-to-GDP figures cited here mask, in many cases, very significant declines in real revenues. To the extent that these revenue declines stem from the transition process, particularly the collapse of central planning and the dismantling of direct controls over resource allocation, they may be both inevitable and desirable provided they are matched by concomitant reductions in expenditures achieved by reducing the role of government in the economy.

Chart 28. Selected Countries More Advanced in Transition: General Government Expenditure, Revenue, and Balance[1]
(In percent of GDP)

Fiscal discipline has been maintained in most of these countries.

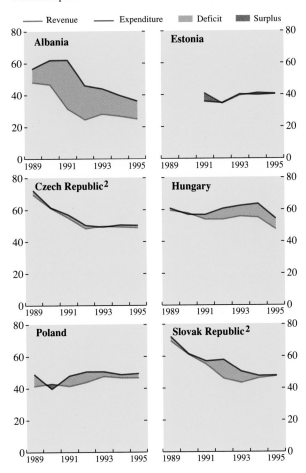

[1]Expenditure equals total expenditure (including extrabudgetary funds) plus net lending; revenue equals total revenue plus grants. Data for 1995 are IMF staff projections.
[2]Prior to 1992, former Czechoslovakia.

Table 19. Selected Countries in Transition: General Government Revenue
(In percent of GDP)

	1989	1990	1991	1992	1993	1994
Armenia: Total revenue	...	...	...	26.7	23.5	27.6
Profit tax	...	...	...	7.1	4.5	5.7
Personal income tax and social security contributions	...	...	...	2.4	1.6	1.2
VAT and excises	...	...	...	8.5	6.2	3.2
Other taxes and nontax revenue	...	...	...	8.7	11.2	17.5
Bulgaria: Total revenue	59.8	51.6	40.4	38.3	35.2	38.0
Profit tax	23.2	17.9	16.5	8.4	5.4	7.2
Wage tax and social security contributions	13.7	13.8	12.0	16.1	15.1	12.8
VAT, excises, and customs duties	12.0	10.0	8.2	8.3	10.3	13.1
Other taxes and nontax revenue	10.9	9.9	3.7	5.5	4.4	4.9
Czech Republic: Total revenue[1]	69.5	61.1	55.0	48.3	50.4	51.2
Profit tax	11.0	12.2	13.7	10.6	7.7	6.2
Wage tax, and social security contributions	21.9	21.2	17.0	17.9	19.5	22.5
VAT, excises, and customs duties	19.5	21.2	13.8	12.5	13.3	14.4
Other taxes and nontax revenue	17.1	6.7	10.5	7.1	9.9	8.1
Estonia: Total revenue	...	...	...	34.6	39.6	41.2
Profit tax	...	...	...	5.9	4.8	3.4
Personal income tax and social security contributions	...	...	...	16.5	20.4	20.7
VAT, excises, and customs duties	...	...	...	9.4	11.6	13.5
Other taxes and nontax revenue	...	...	...	2.8	2.8	3.6
Hungary: Total revenue	59.6	57.9	53.9	53.9	55.8	53.3
Profit tax	8.1	8.2	5.6	2.5	2.0	2.0
Wage tax and social security contributions	19.8	19.8	19.9	21.0	21.9	20.7
VAT, excises, and customs duties	18.9	15.6	14.0	14.9	15.8	14.9
Other taxes and nontax revenue[2]	12.8	14.3	14.3	15.5	16.1	15.7
Poland: Total revenue	41.5	43.0	41.5	44.0	47.6	46.7
Profit tax	9.7	14.0	6.1	4.6	4.2	3.4
Wage tax[3] and social security contributions	10.8	10.4	15.9	18.2	19.0	18.6
Turnover tax, excises, and customs duties	8.9	6.9	9.5	11.3	14.2	14.8
Other taxes and nontax revenue	12.1	11.7	10.0	9.9	10.1	9.9
Romania: Total revenue	51.0	39.7	39.3	37.6	33.6	31.4
Profit tax	...	7.3	5.0	5.3	3.8	3.8
Wage tax and social security contributions	13.0	13.2	17.6	19.7	17.3	15.7
VAT, excises, and customs duties	18.8	12.1	9.1	8.3	9.4	7.6
Other taxes and nontax revenue	19.2	7.1	7.6	4.3	3.1	4.3
Russia: Total revenue[4]	...	...	...	16.7	13.7	10.5
Profit tax	...	...	...	3.9	3.4	2.7
Wage tax and social security contributions	...	...	...	—	—	—
VAT, excises, and customs duties	...	...	...	11.7	8.5	7.6
Other taxes and nontax revenue	...	...	...	1.1	1.9	—

Sources: National authorities; and IMF staff estimates.
[1]For 1989–91, former Czechoslovakia.
[2]Excludes privatization receipts.
[3]Including tax on excess wage increases.
[4]Federal government operations.

central planning were aggravated by a lack of fiscal control early in the transition process.[66] The resulting deterioration of fiscal positions has been followed by

substantial consolidation. The deficit of the Russian Federation, for example, declined from almost 20 percent of GDP in 1992 to about 5 percent in 1995. Several other countries also contained fiscal imbalances to about 5 percent of GDP in 1995, including Azerbaijan, Kazakstan, Moldova, Romania, Uzbekistan, and

[66]This problem is attributable to the poor institutional capacity of key central agencies at the outset of the transition process. In most countries, government spending units independently pursued individual objectives without central control or coordination of spending decisions. The problem of poor expenditure control was exacerbated by weak tax administration, as the procedures used under central planning (sequestration of bank accounts, for example) were

abandoned because of their incompatibility with market reforms. Although important progress has been made in introducing or augmenting treasury and tax administration functions, additional efforts in these areas are required in most transition countries.

Table 20. Selected Countries in Transition: General Government Expenditure[1]

(In percent of GDP)

	1989	1990	1991	1992	1993	1994
Armenia: Total	...	...	...	...	85.0	44.0
Goods and services	...	...	...	...	34.8	15.4
Interest	...	...	...	...	0.7	1.9
Subsidies	...	...	...	...	16.7	12.8
Social security benefits	...	...	...	...	7.3	4.0
Capital expenditures	...	...	...	...	25.5	9.8
Bulgaria: Total	61.5	60.4	55.0	53.4	50.9	45.0
Goods and services	24.1	22.5	17.6	18.7	17.5	15.2
Interest payments	3.1	5.6	17.9	15.9	14.2	14.1
Social security benefits	10.4	12.0	13.7	14.3	15.2	12.9
Subsidies	15.5	14.9	4.1	1.8	2.2	1.3
Other current expenditures	2.9	2.3	—	—	—	—
Capital expenditures	5.5	3.1	2.0	2.8	1.9	1.5
Czech Republic: Total[2]	72.3	61.5	57.1	47.5	49.4	50.7
Goods and services	25.2	24.6	24.4	20.2	24.0	25.1
Interest payments	—	0.2	0.5	1.0	1.6	1.4
Social security benefits	13.6	13.6	16.1	14.0	13.8	13.7
Subsidies	25.0	16.2	7.7	5.0	3.9	3.4
Capital expenditures	8.5	6.9	8.4	7.3	6.7	7.1
Estonia: Total	...	...	...	34.9	40.3	39.9
Goods and services	...	...	...	22.1	23.0	21.9
Social security benefits	...	...	...	9.3	11.1	10.4
Subsidies	...	...	...	0.8	0.9	0.8
Other current expenditures	...	...	...	1.3	2.9	2.8
Capital expenditures	...	...	...	1.4	2.4	4.0
Hungary: Total	60.9	57.0	56.9	60.7	62.5	62.0
Goods and services	20.5	18.7	18.5	18.8	20.3	18.3
Interest payments	4.5	5.4	5.9	5.5	5.0	6.8
Social security benefits	14.4	15.7	18.2	18.3	18.1	17.6
Subsidies	12.1	9.5	7.4	5.5	4.3	4.5
Other current expenditures	2.9	3.1	1.2	4.8	7.9	8.2
Capital expenditures	6.6	4.6	5.8	7.7	6.9	6.6
Poland: Total	48.8	39.8	48.0	50.6	50.6	48.7
Goods and services	10.3	10.3	13.1	12.7	12.4	10.4
Interest payments	—	0.4	1.6	3.2	3.4	4.2
Social security benefits	11.2	10.6	17.3	18.7	19.5	20.7
Subsidies	12.9	7.3	5.1	3.2	2.2	2.2
Other current expenditures	11.1	8.4	7.2	9.3	9.7	8.2
Capital expenditures	3.3	2.8	3.7	3.4	3.3	3.1
Romania: Total	42.6	38.8	38.7	42.2	33.7	32.4
Goods and services	9.8	12.4	14.4	14.2	11.4	12.4
Interest payments	0.1	...	...	0.2	0.9	1.3
Social security benefits	9.5	10.6	10.1	9.1	8.9	10.5
Subsidies	5.7	7.9	8.1	12.9	5.5	3.8
Capital expenditures	17.6	7.8	5.9	5.8	7.0	4.4
Russia: Total[3]	...	...	...	27.8	20.6	21.6
Interest	...	...	...	0.1	2.1	1.9
Noninterest	...	...	...	27.2	18.5	19.7
Of which:						
Defense	...	...	...	1.0	4.4	4.4
Law enforcement and public order	...	...	...	1.1	1.5	1.8
Industry, energy, and construction	...	...	...	6.1	2.8	2.9
Net lending	...	...	...	3.9	1.9	2.2
Intergovernment transfers	...	...	...	1.7	2.7	3.5

Sources: National authorities; and IMF staff estimates.

[1]Expenditures include extrabudgetary funds and net lending except for Bulgaria and Poland, where net lending is excluded.

[2]For 1989–91, former Czechoslovakia.

[3]Federal government operations.

Chart 29. Selected Countries Less Advanced in Transition: General Government Expenditure, Revenue, and Balance[1]

(In percent of GDP)

Falling revenues exacerbated the need for expenditure restraint in these countries.

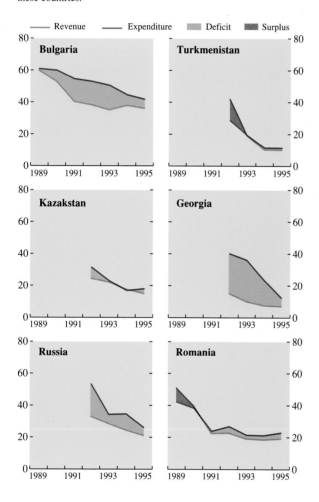

[1]Expenditure equals total expenditure (including extrabudgetary funds) plus net lending; revenue equals total revenue plus grants. Data for 1995 are IMF staff projections.

Ukraine. Armenia and Georgia have made remarkable progress as well, given the size of their initial imbalances. Less progress in fiscal consolidation has been made by the Kyrgyz Republic and Tajikistan.

In contrast, Belarus, which has lagged behind other countries in terms of structural reforms and where the use of direct controls remains widespread, did not suffer an initial sharp deterioration in its fiscal position. Fiscal imbalances there have remained at relatively low levels.

While fiscal consolidation in countries less advanced in transition has also reflected expenditure reductions, the need for expenditure compression has been exacerbated by poor revenue performance (Chart 29). This is the case in Romania, in particular, and also in most countries of the former Soviet Union, where the ratio of revenues to GDP fell by 5 to 10 percentage points in the early 1990s. The decline in revenues occurred, in part, as a result of the implementation in most countries of market-based tax reforms designed to enhance economic efficiency. These efforts included replacing Soviet-era turnover taxes with value-added taxes, as well as enterprise profit taxes, which included wages in the tax base, with a genuine corporate income tax having a narrower tax base. Together with declining output, the latter accounts for the decline in profit tax receipts. Unlike the complex systems of taxes, profit remittances and cross-sectoral subsidies and price controls that characterized the command economy, the new tax instruments were designed to be transparent, consistent, and have some degree of permanence. The objective was to ensure that saving, investment, and production decisions reflected the underlying risk and return associated with each activity, and that residual profits would not be appropriated by capricious changes in the tax code. At the same time, several tax reforms were intended to reduce the tax burden to increase the posttax returns to productive activities.

In the initial stages of transition, rapid inflation allowed many transition countries to rely extensively on seigniorage and the implicit inflation tax on cash balances as sources of revenue.[67] Inflation also boosted conventional tax revenues as enterprises reported large profits from the valuation of inventories (which were very large under central planning) whereas depreciation allowances were not indexed to inflation. Additional revenues were obtained from requirements that commercial banks hold undercompensated reserves with the central bank.

Reliance on inflation-related revenues quickly became unsustainable. At high rates of inflation, currency substitution (or dollarization) became wide-

---

[67]Access to seigniorage and the inflation tax might have been an important incentive for many countries of the former Soviet Union to withdraw from the ruble area and to introduce their own currencies.

spread, as individuals and enterprises sought secure, stable stores of value. As a result, seigniorage revenues declined. More important, inflation had to be reduced for the health of the economy. The fiscal illusion arising from inflation-related revenues had reduced the pressure on many governments to undertake the fundamental structural changes to the economy and public finances that were needed to secure sustainable fiscal consolidation. The subsequent progress in reducing inflation revealed the underlying weakness in real tax revenues.[68]

The poor performance of revenues and the unsustainability of seigniorage and the inflation tax implied that progress with fiscal consolidation required a substantial curtailment of public expenditure. This requirement was consistent with the reforms needed to reduce government intervention in the economy and enhance the role of market forces.

Transforming the Role of the State

Efforts to reduce and redefine the role of the state in the economy have been based on three broad kinds of measures—price liberalization, enterprise reform and privatization, and the implementation of effective social safety nets suited to a market economy. Price liberalization, together with opening the economy to international trade and payments, was required to ensure that relative prices accurately reflect demand and supply considerations. However, because relative prices cannot promote efficient resource use if productive assets are controlled by state-owned enterprises pursuing noneconomic objectives, privatization was needed to ensure that enterprises would respond to market signals and, for loss-making enterprises, to facilitate their restructuring or closure and the transfer of assets to owners who would utilize them more productively. Of course, the restructuring and closure of enterprises entails substantial dislocation as workers are dismissed, while the inflation associated with price liberalization erodes living standards of individuals on fixed incomes. This underscored the need for, and the importance of, an effective social safety net that would assist individuals adversely affected in the short term by transition while avoiding distortions of labor supply decisions.

In most transition countries, there has been good progress with the liberalization of prices although con-

trols have generally remained on housing and utility prices, especially heating and electricity. Price liberalization and increases in administered prices have permitted substantial reductions in the budgetary costs of subsidies in most advanced transition countries. In the Czech Republic, Hungary, and Poland, subsidies were reduced from 12–25 percent of GDP prior to transition to less than 5 percent of GDP in 1994. At these levels, subsidy rates in more advanced transition countries are comparable to or below those in industrial countries; in fact, in some instances, subsidies have been imposed or advocated to compete with subsidies in industrial countries. Subsidies have also been cut significantly in countries less advanced in transition; they were virtually eliminated in Armenia and Georgia in 1995. Focusing on budgeted subsidies may be misleading, however. In many countries less advanced in transition, direct subsidies have been replaced by a number of off-budget measures that have many of the same effects as direct subsidies, but which lack the transparency of budgeted policy instruments. In these countries, budgeted subsidies may not reflect accurately the extent of government intervention in the economy.

There has also been significant progress in the sale of state-owned enterprises, which, together with the emergence of new enterprises and service establishments, has fostered private sector development (Table 21). In most countries more advanced in transition, small enterprises have been largely transferred to the private sector.[69] Among the less-advanced transition countries, only the Russian Federation and the Kyrgyz Republic have achieved this measure of success. Less progress has been made, however, in the privatization of large enterprises. And only Croatia, the Czech Republic, Estonia, Hungary, and the Kyrgyz Republic have so far transferred more than 50 percent of state enterprise assets to the private sector. The slow progress made in privatizing large enterprises is worrisome and seems to reflect continuing reluctance to expose these enterprises fully to market forces.

The slow pace of privatization of large enterprises may reflect concerns regarding the social effects of restructuring in the absence of effective and adequately financed social safety nets. At the outset of the transition process, the former centrally planned economies were confronted with the challenge of replacing their comprehensive systems of income and job security with social support structures compatible with a market economy. The importance of putting in place cost-effective social safety nets was reinforced by the need to protect those most affected by the inevitable short-term decline in output and national income. Progress in

---

[68]Revenue performance in the transition countries is reviewed in two recent studies: Gérard Belanger, "Eastern Europe—Factors Underlying the Weakening Performance of Tax Revenues," IMF Working Paper 94/104 (September 1994); and Richard Hemming, Adrienne Cheasty, and Ashok K. Lahiri, "The Revenue Decline," in *Policy Experiences and Issues in the Baltics, Russia and Other Countries of the Former Soviet Union* ed. by Daniel A. Citrin and Ashok Lahiri, IMF Occasional Paper 133 (December 1995).

[69]For a detailed discussion of the status of privatization and enterprise restructuring, see European Bank for Reconstruction and Development, *Transition Report: Investment and Enterprise Development* (London, 1995).

Table 21. Privatization Indicators in Selected Transition Countries

	Private Sector Share of GDP[1] (In percent)	Privatization Receipts[2] (In percent of GDP)			
		1992	1993	1994	1995
Countries more advanced in transition					
Albania	60	1.1	0.8	1.3	0.2
Croatia	45	0.4	0.2	0.4	0.7
Czech Republic	70	—	0.8	1.8	1.1
Hungary	60	2.3	3.8	0.8	7.9
Latvia	60	—	0.1	0.4	0.4
Lithuania	55	0.9	0.8	0.3	0.1
Macedonia, former Yugoslav Rep. of	40	0.1	0.5	—	0.1
Poland	60	0.4	0.5	0.8	0.8
Slovak Republic	60	—	1.3	2.2	1.6
Countries less advanced in transition					
Belarus	15	—	0.1	0.3	0.1
Bulgaria	45	—	0.1	1.5	1.1
Georgia	30	...	...	...	0.1
Kazakstan	25	—	2.5	0.3	0.4
Russian Federation	55	0.6	0.2	0.1	0.2
Turkmenistan	15	...	...	...	—
Ukraine	35	...	0.1	0.2	0.2

[1]European Bank for Reconstruction and Development estimates, at midyear 1995. See European Bank for Reconstruction and Development, *Transition Report: Investment and Enterprise Development* (London, 1995).

[2]National authorities; and IMF staff estimates. Figures reflect amounts transferred to budget, not total privatization receipts.

this area has been mixed. In most countries, the elimination of subsidies for many products was accompanied by increased expenditures on transfers for specific categories of beneficiaries. However, while such transfers need to be well targeted to contain costs and promote the social objectives for which they are intended, the requirement has generally not been met.[70]

Under central planning, the implicit guarantee by the state of lifetime employment and access to highly subsidized commodities rendered unemployment insurance and income support schemes superfluous. As part of the transformation process, most transition countries have introduced unemployment insurance schemes with benefits provided for a limited duration. The size of these benefits varies considerably. Among the countries more advanced in transition, Albania has unemployment benefits equal to about one half the average wage, while since 1992 Poland has limited benefits to about one third of the average wage.[71] Differences in unemployment benefits are even greater between countries less advanced in transition. In Uzbekistan, for example, unemployment benefits

were roughly 80 percent of the average wage in 1993, although the generosity of the scheme was matched by onerous administrative procedures, which ensured that few individuals qualified. In the Russian Federation, unemployment benefits were only 12 percent of the average wage in the same period.

In the more advanced transition countries, the costs of unemployment benefits increased as enterprises were restructured or closed. Unemployment rates in these countries have risen significantly and appear to have peaked at between 8 and 16 percent in most cases. To curb the deteriorating financial positions of their unemployment funds, some countries have adjusted eligibility criteria and reduced the duration of benefits. In Poland, for example, benefits were initially of unlimited duration and enforcement of eligibility criteria was lax, but benefits were subsequently limited to one year and eligibility was tightened. Similar measures were adopted by other countries.[72]

In most of the countries less advanced in transition, registered unemployment has remained low, suggesting that enterprise restructuring still has a long way to go. Enterprises have been able to avoid restructuring

---

[70]Kathie Krumm, Branko Milanovic, and Michael Walton, "Transfers and the Transition from Socialism: Key Tradeoffs," World Bank, Policy Research Working Paper 1380 (November 1994).

[71]See Expenditure Policy Division, Fiscal Affairs Department, "Social Safety Nets for Economic Transition: Options and Recent Experience," IMF Paper on Policy Analysis and Assessment 95/3 (February 1995).

[72]In some countries, however, spending on unemployment benefits has remained remarkably low because of tight eligibility requirements and modest benefits. These expenditures have been limited to about ½ of 1 percent of GDP in the Slovak Republic, and even less in the Czech Republic where unemployment has remained rather low.

Table 22. Pension Indicators for Central and Eastern European Countries, 1992
(In percent)

	Ratio of Public Expenditure on Pensions to GDP	Share of Population Aged 60 and Over[1]	Ratio of Average Old-Age Pension to Average Wage	Proportion of Pensioners With Pension Below 50 percent of Average Wage	Ratio of Minimum Pension to Average Wage
Albania	12.7[1]	8.2	45.5	...	...
Bulgaria	10.2	19.6	42.9	67.0	24.1
Czech Republic	8.3	17.9	48.9	62.9	37.7
Hungary	11.6	19.1	60.9	43.1	36.5
Poland	14.7	15.1	86.3[2]	40.4	35.2
Romania	5.8[1]	16.0	47.7	83.3	...
Russia	6.0	16.2	31.3	...	16.8
Slovak Republic	10.4	14.9	59.8	66.4	47.8
Ukraine	7.1	18.7	19.5	...	...

Source: UNICEF, *Crisis in Mortality, Health and Nutrition: Central and Eastern Europe in Transition—Public Policy and Social Conditions* (Florence, 1994).
[1]Refers to 1991.
[2]Polish data indicate a ratio of 72 percent.

and to retain workers partly because of dramatic declines in real wages, and the acceptance by workers of reduced hours of work and leave without pay. Workers have a strong interest in staying on the payrolls of enterprises despite the resulting hardship, because unemployment compensation is very low and because the immediate prospect of finding alternative employment is limited. Furthermore, even though wages are low, many nonwage benefits provided by enterprises are significant, including housing, medical care, education, and access to subsidized food provision.[73] The labor hoarding that results from these practices is "financed" through a variety of channels including tax arrears, interenterprise arrears, and bank loans that are unlikely to be repaid. Moreover, in many cases, workers are simply not paid, as illustrated by the recent strike by coal miners in Russia, who were owed wages for up to six months. The phenomenon of wage arrears seems to be common. As a result of such practices, many loss-making enterprises have continued to operate amid a general reluctance to enforce bankruptcy and liquidation legislation.

Pension and health insurance systems are also in need of reform. The high level of pension-related transfers in most transition countries reflects a combination of unfavorable demographics and poorly targeted benefits (Table 22). Both factors are acutely unfavorable in Poland, where the level of public expenditure on pensions in relation to GDP, at 15 percent, is the highest in Europe.[74] Poland began the transition process with higher mandatory retirement ages

than in other countries in transition—60 years of age for women, 65 for men. The average retirement age, however, is much lower and has fallen during the transition owing to an increase in early retirement, with the result that the number of eligible pensioners has increased sharply.[75] Poland also has relatively lenient eligibility criteria for disability pensions. The fiscal consequences of these factors have been compounded by the indexation of pensions to wages, starting when real wages were at their lowest point since the transition began. In 1993, the average pension was roughly two thirds the average wage. Moreover, many individuals remain eligible for special "occupational" pensions, which grant earlier retirement and higher pensions to designated groups. Finally, for individuals in the private sector, noncompliance with pension contribution requirements is a serious problem, the importance of which has been increasing as the private sector has expanded.

The costs of pensions are also very high in other transition countries. In Hungary, early retirement has increased significantly since 1989, and the frequency of disability pensions has doubled. The high payroll tax needed to finance pensions is increasingly being evaded. In Romania, workers were permitted in 1990 to retire with full retirement benefits as early as five years before their scheduled pension age. This con-

---

[73]Generous severance payments prescribed by legislation, which might be more costly than providing nonwage benefits, may provide enterprises with an incentive to keep workers on the payroll.

[74]See Louise Fox, "Old Age Security in Transition Economies," World Bank, Policy Research Department Working Paper 1257 (February 1994).

[75]The increase in early retirement is attributable to several factors, including the attractiveness of early retirement benefits relative to unemployment benefits, given that early retirement is widely perceived as an alternative to unemployment; liberal eligibility criteria that, initially, did not penalize pensioners who continue to work; limited supervision and enforcement capabilities to track working pensioners; and anticipation of restrictive pension reforms that would adversely affect later retirees. See Gerd Schwartz, "Social Impact of the Transition," in *Poland: The Path to a Market Economy*, IMF Occasional Paper 113 (October 1994).

tributed to a sharp deterioration in the financial position of the social security system. In contrast, Estonia and Lithuania have not used early retirement to facilitate the shedding of workers; instead they introduced earnings-related entitlement systems.

In transforming the role of the state, governments must also look ahead to defining the future role of government. Even in countries that have successfully contained the overall fiscal deficit, additional fiscal adjustment may be needed to improve the composition of expenditures. This would include reducing subsidies further to provide for the establishment and maintenance of the basic infrastructures needed to support economic activity and the provision of adequate health care and education services. Comprehensive public expenditure reviews conducted at an early stage in the transition can assist governments identify spending priorities and budget for them.

It is noteworthy in this context that health care has been a major casualty of the budgetary problems in most transition countries. In many countries, funding for health services has been squeezed, and both access to and the quality of health care have undoubtedly deteriorated. In some, health care has been integrated with social insurance, exacerbating the problems associated with unfunded pension transfers. Increasingly, insufficient budgetary funding has led poorly paid doctors to operate on a fee-for-services basis, which only a small share of the population can afford.

Challenges Remaining

Notwithstanding budgetary improvements in many transition countries, fiscal adjustment efforts must be sustained. Fiscal restraint has demonstrated governments' resolve to eschew inflationary finance and to implement fundamental reforms and is increasingly being rewarded by economic growth and rising living standards. As a result of these achievements, several countries have gained access to international capital markets and some have enjoyed large inflows of foreign direct investment.[76] In some countries, the magnitude of capital inflows has complicated macroeconomic management, posing new challenges both for fiscal and monetary policies.[77]

The lesson for countries less advanced in the transition process is straightforward. A credible commitment to sound public finances is a prerequisite for macroeconomic stabilization and sustained recovery of output. It is also necessary to proceed with the necessary fiscal adjustments without excessive delays: modest progress in reducing fiscal imbalances without much hope of a turnaround in output may increase public pressure for a relaxation of fiscal discipline, with risks of setbacks also to the process of structural reform.

Three challenges to sustained fiscal consolidation merit particular attention: the need to enhance revenue collection; the need to roll back both direct and indirect government support for unprofitable activities; and the continuing need to establish cost-effective social safety nets.

Revenue Collection

Weak tax revenues can be traced to several factors. High tax rates are often levied on modest tax bases, reduced not only by economic contraction but also by various exemptions, allowed in many instances on political grounds. Even the introduction of some new taxes—the VAT for instance—has led to pressures for exemptions and reduced rates,[78] which have distorted market-based restructuring. A broadening of tax bases and subsequent reduction of high marginal tax rates would help to enhance revenue mobilization and improve economic efficiency, and might also have the salutary effect of promoting greater horizontal equity in the tax system by raising compliance rates. Another major cause of poor tax revenues in many transition countries is dollarization and the continued use of barter, payment in kind, and arrears accumulation to facilitate transactions.[79] The use of such expedients means that a large share of transactions and income effectively escapes taxation.

The problem of weak tax administration—compounded in some cases by corruption—is common to most transition countries. The administrative structures implemented following the collapse of central planning have proven inadequate to administering the new taxes on the emerging private sector and in dealing with widespread tax arrears in the state-owned enterprise sector (see Box 8). Poor tax administration can frustrate efforts to generate additional revenue and result in higher collection costs. The introduction of various exemptions and different tax rates has complicated VAT systems, hindering effective enforcement

---

[76]The Czech Republic, Estonia, Hungary, Latvia, Lithuania, Poland, Romania, and the Slovak Republic have borrowed in international capital markets. The reform efforts of the Czech Republic, in particular, have been recognized with successive upgrading of its sovereign debt by international credit agencies.

[77]The policy challenges posed by large capital inflows were discussed in the context of the transition countries in the October 1995 *World Economic Outlook*, Chapter V, and in the context of the developing countries in the May 1995 *World Economic Outlook*, Chapter III.

---

[78]See Victoria P. Summers and Emil M. Sunley, "An Analysis of Value-Added Taxes in Russia and Other Countries of the Former Soviet Union," IMF Working Paper 95/1 (January 1995).

[79]See Ratna Sahay and Carlos A. Végh, "Dollarization in Transition Economies: Evidence and Policy Implications," IMF Working Paper 95/96 (September 1995).

Table 23. Subsidies to Enterprises in Selected Transition Countries

(As a percent of GDP)

	1991	1992	1993	1994	1995
Countries more advanced in transition					
Albania	17.9	4.5	—	0.2	—
Croatia	1.7	1.3	1.2	1.6	1.6
Czech Republic[1]	. . .	. . .	3.4	3.0	2.8
Hungary	2.4	1.8	1.7	2.3	1.7
Latvia	1.3	0.3	—	0.1	0.4
Poland	1.7	0.8	. . .	. . .	. . .
Slovak Republic[1]	. . .	4.9	4.7	4.3	3.9
Slovenia	4.2	4.4	3.9	3.6	3.3
Countries less advanced in transition					
Belarus[2]	. . .	11.4	15.3	8.3	5.4
Bulgaria	4.1	1.8	2.2	1.3	1.0
Georgia[3]	. . .	. . .	. . .	12.7	0.2
Kazakstan	. . .	3.3	2.3	1.7	1.0
Russian Federation	. . .	10.5	4.6	5.1	2.3

Sources: National authorities; and IMF staff estimates.

[1]Includes subsidies for residential heating and public transportation.

[2]Subsidies in budget and extrabudgetary accounts.

[3]For 1994, includes implicit energy subsidies.

by the tax administration. Weak tax administration also raises fundamental questions of equity and efficiency, since the effective tax burden on those who comply with the tax code is increased when large numbers of taxpayers successfully evade taxes.[80] Corruption and abuse of authority by poorly paid tax administrators are serious problems in some countries, one of the unfortunate consequences of the sharp decline in real public sector wages since the start of the transition process.

Direct and Indirect Government Subsidies

The second major challenge to sustained fiscal consolidation in many transition countries is the need to substantially reduce the continued efforts to shield sectors of the economy from the working of market forces. The rationale underlying such efforts is to sustain employment along with the various benefits attached to it, as well as to maintain the use of existing capital. However, this support perpetuates misallocation of resources by reducing incentives for enterprises to restructure and by permitting loss-making firms to remain in operation. In this respect, the outcome is sometimes not substantially different from that which prevailed under central planning. Without measures to force restructuring, these losses continue to accumulate, financed by wage, tax, and interenterprise arrears, and by increases in nonperforming loans in the bank-

ing sector. At the same time, these practices imply that the effective tax burden on productive firms will need to be greater than would otherwise be the case.

Although budgeted subsidies to state enterprises have fallen significantly, they remain an important component of total expenditures in some countries, including those more advanced in transition (Table 23). Subsidies to enterprises totaled more than 5 percent of GDP in 1995 in Belarus, 4 percent of GDP in the Slovak Republic, and 3 percent of GDP in the Czech Republic and Slovenia. Assessment of the scale of these subsidies in the Russian Federation is more difficult, as local social security and unemployment funds have provided various subsidies that are not recorded. Budgeted subsidies at the federal level have been reduced, however, from almost 11 percent of GDP in 1992 to about 2 percent of GDP in 1995. As noted above, these figures may be misleading, particularly with respect to countries less advanced in transition.

In many countries, government efforts to reduce direct credits and subsidies to the enterprise sector have led to enterprises using other routes to evade adjustment, including the nonpayment of tax obligations. This shows that while subsidies are relatively easy to cut, at least administratively, collecting taxes is more difficult. Moreover, because of the implications for unemployment, governments often prefer to postpone the necessary enterprise restructuring and inevitable layoffs. However, financial stabilization and long-term economic growth are undermined by the implicit budgetary subsidies to these enterprises and by the continuing misallocation of credit and other resources. This underscores the importance of deepening enterprise restructuring.

---

[80]In this sense, it has been argued that tax administration is tax policy. See Vito Tanzi and Anthony Pellechio, "The Reform of Tax Administration," IMF Working Paper 95/22 (February 1995).

Box 8. The Arrears Problem in Transition Countries

In many transition countries, interenterprise, tax, budgetary, and wage arrears, and increasing levels of nonperforming bank loans have raised concerns about the sustainability of fiscal consolidation and the transition process. Tax arrears undermine fiscal consolidation directly, while budgetary, wage, and interenterprise arrears contribute to the spread of dollarization, barter, and payment-in-kind, which all involve transactions outside the purview of the tax system. In addition to shrinking the revenue base, the arrears problem threatens the transition process by delaying restructuring and distorting the allocation of scarce resources.

It is difficult to assess the extent of *interenterprise arrears*, as comprehensive data are generally not available. To some extent, arrears between enterprises may be simply a reflection of underdeveloped payment systems, which result in unusually long delays in the settlement of invoices. Moreover, some arrears may reflect informal financing arrangements between suppliers and purchasers, which could be considered normal commercial credits. In many of the transition countries, however, large arrears between enterprises also seem to reflect a continuing reluctance to enforce stricter payments discipline. The accumulation of arrears can eventually lead to expectations that they will be monetized through government bailouts. The heavy resort to interenterprise arrears may also frustrate restructuring by permitting inefficient firms to divert resources from productive enterprises.[1] In those countries that have persevered with tight financial policies, the problem of interenterprise arrears has diminished considerably: firms have responded to recalcitrant customers by enforcing payment in advance, or simply by not shipping to enterprises with poor payment records.[2] Of course, the financial discipline of the market is not binding where enterprises have recourse to subsidies, directed credits, and other forms of financial assistance and where lax enforcement of the tax code has softened budget constraints.

Tax arrears seem to be a growing problem in many transition economies.[3] Estimates of the stock of tax arrears in selected countries indicate that they now range from roughly 2 percent to about 8 percent of GDP *(see*

Stock of Tax Arrears in Selected Transition Economies, End of 1994
(All figures in percent of GDP)

	Principal	Interest	Total
Countries more advanced in transition			
Albania	2.0	. . .	. . .
Czech Republic[1]	. . .	. . .	3–4
Estonia	3.3	. . .	. . .
Hungary	. . .	. . .	7.5
Latvia	. . .	. . .	7.0
Lithuania[1]	. . .	. . .	4.2
Poland	3.4	2–4	5–7
Slovak Republic	. . .	. . .	3.4
Countries less advanced in transition			
Armenia	1.1	. . .	. . .
Belarus	0.3	. . .	. . .
Georgia[2]	1.1	. . .	. . .
Kazakstan[3]	. . .	. . .	2.0[4]
Kyrgyz Republic	1.8	. . .	. . .
Moldova	5.9	. . .	. . .
Romania	. . .	. . .	4.6
Russia[5]	3.0	0.6	3.6
Turkmenistan	. . .	. . .	1.1[4]
Memorandum			
Market economy (New Zealand)	. . .	. . .	2.0

Sources: Mark E. Schaffer, "Tax Arrears in Transition Economies"; and IMF staff estimates.

[1]End of 1993.
[2]Mid-1995.
[3]First quarter 1994.
[4]Coverage unclear.
[5]End of 1995. Consolidated government, excluding payroll tax arrears.

table). Although tax arrears in most transition countries appear to be larger than in developed market economies, there is no apparent connection between their size and the progress of reforms. There are several reasons to believe, however, that the figures in the table may understate the extent of this problem. In most transition countries, tax arrears are often written off or rescheduled.[4] Also, in many countries less advanced in the transition, tax arrears often have not accrued interest or have done so at interest rates below the rate of inflation; if they had accrued interest at market rates, the stock of arrears as a percent of GDP would be considerably larger. The figures for coun-

---

[1]An aspect of the interenterprise arrears problem is that *all* enterprises may have an incentive to extend arrears if there is a possibility that the government will conduct a clearing or netting operation. If loss-making enterprises accumulate arrears, the best response of profitable firms may also be to accumulate arrears, to avoid the loss of prospective revenues from any bailout. This effect is exacerbated by the absence of a credible bankruptcy and liquidation threat.

[2]This does not apply to energy suppliers, which in many countries have been prevented from enforcing payments discipline.

[3]See Mark E. Schaffer, "Tax Arrears in Transition Economies," IMF Working Paper (forthcoming).

---

[4]The figures for both Lithuania and Poland are inclusive of rescheduled tax arrears.

Governments in transition countries have also supported some sectors through other off-balance-sheet and quasi-fiscal activities. These measures include the

use of directed credits, through either commercial banks or the central bank, the use of low interest rate loans to effect a quasi-fiscal transfer from households

tries less advanced in the transition in the table should therefore be considered as lower-bound estimates. In contrast, the countries more advanced in the transition have made more progress in containing inflation and strengthening tax administration. The data for these countries are probably a better indication of the extent of the problem.

Tax arrears exacerbate the problem of *budgetary arrears*, which arise as cash-strapped governments invoke sequestration to meet fiscal targets. Although there is often little else that governments can do to meet these targets in the short run, sequestration contributes to weak payments discipline and thereby undermines the principles of a market economy.

Governments in transition countries may tolerate tax arrears because the short-term benefits of the liquidation of distressed firms may be considered small in relation to the political costs. Indeed, tax arrears are a kind of subsidy to loss-making firms: in most cases, they can be thought of as wage subsidies, because wage taxes—notably social security contributions—are often the biggest single tax liability of distressed enterprises. Such practices entail a moral hazard, however, as the failure to take action against these firms perpetuates the accumulation of arrears and encourages the expectation of a generalized settlement on concessional terms of all arrears. In countries such as Romania and Russia, where the government has conducted a "clearing" of arrears through monetization or by assuming the remaining net balance, arrears accumulation did indeed subsequently resume.

Evidence of such moral hazard implications can be seen in the accumulation of *wage arrears* in many transition countries, particularly those of the former Soviet Union. An enterprise may frequently pay a low cash wage but record a higher accrued wage in the firm's accounts; the difference between the two is wage arrears. One explanation for this practice is that wage arrears are a useful lobbying tool that can help the firm obtain additional subsidies from the government.[5]

In accumulating large wage arrears, enterprises may be responding to the incentives created by government policies. This was likely the case in the Russian Federation where, in early 1994, the government introduced a scheme that allowed liquidity-constrained firms to set aside 30 percent of their income to pay wages and to defer tax payments to the extent that the remainder was inade-

quate to cover tax liabilities.[6] In practice, such deferrals were for an indefinite period, and the taxes deferred neither accrued interest nor were subject to late penalties. Wage arrears did fall after the introduction of the rule, but at the cost of a large increase in tax arrears. Moreover, the scheme provided a means by which enterprises could implicitly borrow funds at a negative real interest rate by not paying their tax liabilities and accumulating tax arrears on terms more favorable than could have been obtained through direct borrowing. All enterprises therefore had an incentive to run up wage arrears—irrespective of their financial situation.

Wage arrears pose a serious threat to the transition process because they may erode public support for stabilization. In addition, wage arrears lead to a deterioration in the financial position of social safety nets, resulting in pension and other benefit arrears. The result may be a weakening in the resolve of governments to persevere with financial stabilization and pursue structural reforms. Because wage arrears reflect weak payments discipline, their resolution will require a range of measures, including the establishment of effective bankruptcy and liquidation laws. Moreover, government agencies themselves need both to establish a record of prompt payment of wages and to adjust the size of the public sector labor force so as to ensure that the payroll can consistently be met in a timely fashion. For the enterprise sector, governments must eschew subsidies and other transfers that validate excessive wage claims and allow enterprises to avoid restructuring.

* * *

The nexus among the various types of arrears, which extends to the financial system through nonperforming bank loans, impairs efforts to sustain fiscal consolidation, impedes enterprise restructuring, and ultimately threatens to undermine the transition process. To break the cycle of arrears, governments must show more resolve in collecting outstanding tax arrears and eliminate incentives that firms have to accumulate additional tax, wage, and inter-enterprise arrears. A credible threat of bankruptcy is essential, yet the authorities in many transition countries have resisted the use of bankruptcy and liquidation sanctions. This underscores the need to accelerate the process of large-scale privatization because this would harden enterprises' budget constraints and facilitate the application of bankruptcy and liquidation sanctions. In addition, it remains essential to put in place affordable, well-targeted social safety nets to alleviate the social costs of the transitional rise in unemployment that is likely to be associated with enterprise restructuring.

---

[5]Strikes in 1995 and early 1996 by Russian and Ukrainian miners (as well as other workers) demanding payment of outstanding wage arrears may be viewed in this context. Implicit in this analysis is a conflict between enterprise managers and governments over the nature of the transition process. See James A. Haley, "A Strategy for Enterprise and Financial Reform in Transition Countries," IMF Working Paper (forthcoming).

---

[6]The scheme was eliminated in early 1996.

to ailing state enterprises, as well as the provision for sale of goods or services at below market prices. The nature of the problem is such that reliable data on the

potential costs of these measures are typically unavailable. To the extent that the banking system is used to implement these measures, however, the level of non-

Table 24. Nonperforming Bank Loans

(Percent of total loans)

	1991	1992	1993	1994	1995
Albania	. . .	. . .	14	27	31
Bulgaria	. . .	. . .	. . .	50	. . .
Czech Republic	. . .	19	24	38	38[1]
Georgia	. . .	. . .	. . .	25	38[2]
Hungary[3]	8	10	23	21	. . .
Kazakstan	. . .	. . .	. . .	. . .	40
Latvia	. . .	. . .	. . .	33	. . .
Poland	16	. . .	. . .	. . .	. . .
Russia	. . .	. . .	12	31	39

Sources: National authorities; IMF staff estimates; and Michael S. Borish, Millard F. Long, and Michel Noël, "Restructuring Banks and Enterprises: Recent Lessons from Transition Countries," World Bank Discussion Paper No. 275 (January 1995).

[1]September 1995.

[2]June 1995.

[3]In percent of domestic credit.

performing bank loans may give some indication of the scale and potential costs (Table 24).[81]

The available information suggests that the costs of such practices may be very large indeed. Bulgaria organized a debt write-off in December 1992, and in 1994 replaced nonperforming loans with government debt. The result has been a rising debt burden, with interest payments, equal to 14 percent of GDP in 1994. Moreover, where governments have monetized the costs of large quasi-fiscal deficits generated by loss-making, state-owned enterprises through a clearing of arrears, financial stabilization has been set back. In Romania, the government has on several occasions since 1991 engaged in netting out operations to reduce the level of arrears in the economy using central bank credits and government transfers; on one occasion, a scheme was introduced under which banks were required to extend credit to enterprises under government guarantee for the sole purpose of clearing arrears. The additional liquidity of these operations had a strong and sustained effect on inflation.[82] Similarly, the Russian authorities conducted a multilateral netting of arrears in August 1992. The net balance re-

maining, at about 3½ percent of GDP, was monetized with substantial inflationary consequences.[83]

Although difficult to monitor, loan guarantees provided to state enterprises that would not otherwise be able to borrow from commercial banks are a growing problem in many transition countries. Such guarantees distort the allocation of credit; in particular, they are likely to reduce the supply of funds to emerging private sector firms without access to guarantees. While production by inefficient state enterprises is maintained, the private sector is thus forced to scale back production or curtail investment plans. Of course, the loans guaranteed by the government eventually add to the budgetary problems if the guarantee is exercised.[84]

The failure of insolvent banks and the resulting demands for compensation from depositors, which are politically difficult to ignore, represent another potential threat to fiscal consolidation.[85] The possible fiscal consequences can be significant. In Latvia, the failure of one bank in early 1995 with negative net worth of around 8 percent of GDP led the government to promise compensation, which was subsequently revoked. Two banks failed in Lithuania late in 1995, with the government again promising to provide deposit compensation. In Estonia, concerns regarding the solvency of a large bank in which the state is a majority shareholder may necessitate a recapitalization by the government involving further budgetary costs.[86]

In many countries, governments have also resisted efforts by energy utilities to enforce payments discipline by disconnecting recalcitrant consumers. State-owned enterprises are frequently the largest debtors,

---

[81]Two caveats apply to these figures. First, they reflect a number of factors, including poor credit analysis, non-arm's-length lending to connected enterprises, and the reluctance of solvent enterprises to service their debts given prospective government bailouts, in addition to the direct effects of government policies. Second, increases in the level of nonperforming loans may be attributable to improved classification and reporting, as well as deteriorating loan quality. As a result of these factors, the figures in Table 24 are not comparable across countries and should be viewed as only indicative of the risks posed by banking sector problems in individual countries.

[82]See Eric V. Clifton and Mohsin S. Khan, "Interenterprise Arrears in Transforming Economies: The Case of Romania," *Staff Papers*, IMF, Vol. 40 (September 1993), pp. 680-96.

[83]Ashok K. Lahiri and Daniel A. Citrin, "Interenterprise Arrears," in *Policy Experiences in the Baltics, Russia, and Other Countries of the Former Soviet Union* ed. by Daniel A. Citrin and Ashok K. Lahiri, IMF Occasional Paper 133 (December 1995).

[84]The potential fiscal costs can be quite high. In Kazakstan, defaults on previously issued guaranteed loans resulted in additional outlays totaling almost 7½ percent of GDP in 1994. The experience there has been that only one third of external loans guaranteed by the government are serviced, while roughly three fourths of all domestic loans guaranteed by the government eventually go into default. To prevent further defaults from undermining the 1995 budget, the government made explicit provisions for the cost of meeting these loan guarantees.

[85]This is likely to be the case as many governments have extended explicit deposit insurance guarantees to the former state savings banks. Depositors in other banks would therefore demand equal treatment.

[86]The problem of bad loans is common to most transition countries, including several more advanced in transition: Bulgaria, Croatia, the Czech and Slovak Republics, and Hungary recapitalized banks using loan guarantees and government bonds to cover nonperforming loans, but loan losses continued in many cases. Poland recapitalized several banks prior to privatization, while Slovenia recapitalized its three largest banks in the context of a formal restructuring program. See Michael S. Borish, Millard F. Long, and Michel Noël, "Restructuring Banks and Enterprises: Recent Lessons from Transition Countries," World Bank Discussion Paper 279 (January 1995).

partly owing to distorted pricing policies in which enterprises subsidize household consumption. But households are also shielded from the effects of payments discipline in many countries. To some extent, this reflects genuine problems of monitoring consumption of communal services at the household level. It is also the result of efforts to protect poor households from the effects of higher energy prices. However, preventing utility companies from enforcing payments discipline ensures that all consumers benefit, regardless of genuine need. In this respect, the government is pursuing a social policy objective through poorly targeted quasi-fiscal means rather than through a transparent and properly targeted social safety net.[87] The provision of energy at below-market prices has a budgetary counterpart, as utility companies typically rely on government loan guarantees to purchase inputs from domestic or foreign suppliers. Because the utility companies are precluded from collecting on their bills, these guarantees are eventually exercised. The potential fiscal costs are large: in Belarus, ineffective domestic payments discipline resulted in external gas arrears of $510 million at the end of September 1995; in the first half of 1995, overdue obligations for domestic gas shipments in Ukraine totaled 8 percent of GDP, of which roughly half were incurred by enterprises. Severe collection problems on domestic gas debts have also been recorded in most other countries of the former Soviet Union.[88]

The use of off-balance-sheet and quasi-fiscal instruments reflects the lack of progress by transition governments in adequately redefining the role of the state in resource allocation. That this has been difficult to achieve in most transition countries is perhaps not surprising given the pervasive role played by the state under central planning. The poor revenue performance in most transition countries may also help explain this phenomenon, because it limits the pursuit of government objectives through direct budgetary means. For those governments that lack a commitment to market-based reforms, quasi-fiscal measures provide convenient means of continuing to intervene in the economy.[89]

The emergence and persistence of such practices are clearly of considerable concern. They reduce the transparency of the budget process as the means by which policy priorities are established and funded. The result is often large transfers between different sectors (usually from households to politically favored enterprises) without public scrutiny and parliamentary approval, which may lead to an erosion of public support for the transition process. Off-balance-sheet and quasi-fiscal instruments also undermine stabilization efforts by introducing additional uncertainties as regards the actual size of both current and future budget deficits, the associated financing requirements, and the eventual recourse to inflationary finance. Budgets that do not fully reflect government spending commitments associated with quasi-fiscal operations and unbudgeted spending commitments may also exacerbate currency substitution and capital flight and contribute to instability in foreign exchange markets. Finally, such practices delay needed restructuring efforts, thereby jeopardizing the prospects for sustained recovery of output and living standards.

There are many steps that transition governments need to take to contain quasi-fiscal subsidies and commitments. Existing loan guarantees should be budgeted as contingent liabilities; and the use of guarantees should be tightly controlled and used to support clearly defined budgetary objectives in the case of perceived market failures. Although important progress has been made to limit the practice of directed credits and minimize foreign exchange market distortions, the continued pursuit of financial sector liberalization is also critical. This will reduce both the scope for using nonmarket means to allocate credit and the quasi-fiscal deficits incurred by central banks. Enhanced prudential regulation and supervision of commercial banks, meanwhile, are necessary to reduce potential losses from bank failures. Several countries are contemplating the introduction of government-supported deposit insurance schemes. The motivation for these plans may be to correct a situation in which de facto insurance is provided, but premiums are not assessed. The establishment of explicit deposit insurance schemes should incorporate elements of depositor coinsurance with minimum (if any) support from the budget, and coverage limits to mitigate the moral hazard problems associated with insurance. High levels of nonperforming loans in many transition countries suggest that some form of bank restructuring is required. In many countries, the problem of nonperforming bank loans is exacerbated by the lack of, or inadequate, tax treatment for the provisioning of bad loans. In these countries, banks with the largest loan losses may well have to close. Other banks may be recapitalized to ensure that banks have an incentive to enforce bankruptcy threats on recalcitrant borrowers and that the cost of future loan losses is not transferred entirely to the bud-

---

[87]In several countries, governments have not only stopped energy companies from taking effective measures to collect outstanding debts but have maintained price controls that keep domestic energy costs below world levels and even below narrowly defined cost recovery levels.

[88]Some countries have taken decisive measures to contain this problem. In Lithuania, for example, the government has undertaken not to intervene in the enforcement of payments discipline. Needy households will be eligible for full compensation for energy outlays in excess of 20 percent of their incomes; the 1996 budget provides funding for this purpose.

[89]See Vito Tanzi, "Government Role and the Efficiency of Policy Instruments," IMF Working Paper 95/100 (October 1995), and Vito Tanzi, "The Budget Deficit in Transition," *Staff Papers*, IMF, Vol. 40 (September 1993), pp. 697–707.

get.[90] However, the experiences of many countries that have recapitalized banks clearly indicate that such efforts provide only a temporary solution if the banks are not privatized.

It is also necessary to establish regular payments practices and respect for contractual commitments in the enterprise sector, consistent with the needs of a market economy. At least for the state-owned sector, this is the government's responsibility. The first task must be to impose hard budget constraints. Early privatization would help in this regard by increasing incentives for enterprise managers to enforce payment. Enforcement of the tax code and of enterprises' obligation to pay their workers are minimum requirements. Of course, the government itself must meet its commitments, and stop making those it cannot honor. And the institutional and legal instruments to enforce bankruptcy and liquidation threats must be established.

Social Safety Nets

The third challenge to sustained fiscal consolidation, complementary to the process of industrial restructuring, is strengthening and redirecting affordable, well-targeted social safety nets. For countries less advanced in transition, which have not had much of an increase in unemployment owing to the slow pace of enterprise restructuring, existing unemployment insurance schemes should be strengthened to ensure adequate benefit levels and fair eligibility criteria. Funding of unemployment insurance schemes should also be assessed, and access to services of unemployment offices improved. In most countries, low rates of registered unemployment have permitted modest surpluses to accumulate, which would be depleted once the process of industrial restructuring begins in earnest. Budgetary funds will therefore need to be provided on an adequate scale and taken into account in the setting of budgetary priorities.

In most transition countries, proposals to reform social security have included the establishment of minimum retirement benefits, compulsory employment-related benefits, unification of treatment across occupations, increases in the retirement age, and steps to reduce access to benefits by younger working pensioners. Such proposals have met with vigorous political opposition in most countries, with the result that fundamental changes have generally been supplanted by ad hoc steps. Nevertheless, as in many of the industrial countries, pension reforms will clearly be needed to cope with existing and future public pension burdens. Particularly in those transition countries where benefits are low relative to the average wage, it is important that pension and social security reforms help to ensure adequate levels of protection without overburdening contributors to the system. This will require better collection of private sector contributions and improved targeting of benefits, including tying future eligibility for pension benefits to past contributions. Given the low level of administrative capacity in many countries, this may take time to achieve.

* * *

The progress made by most transition countries toward the establishment of growing, market-based economies is encouraging. Most have made substantial progress toward macroeconomic stabilization and have resumed growth. In some respects, the policy challenges facing the countries more advanced in transition now resemble those facing emerging market economies, particularly the policy dilemmas associated with sizable capital inflows. Countries less advanced in the transition typically have further to go toward stabilization. Additional fiscal consolidation is required in these countries to secure the conditions necessary to foster growth. In most transition countries, however, weak revenue performance, continuing state support of nonprofitable activities, and quasi-fiscal subsidies and contingent liabilities pose risks to sound public finances. These risks reflect the fundamental challenges that remain to be resolved by many transition countries: curtailing the role of the state in production and allocation decisions and establishing an effective and affordable social safety net.

One of the common lessons emerging from the experiences of a wide range of countries is that structural reforms that limit the role of the state in allocating resources are necessary to support fiscal adjustment, while sustained fiscal discipline is necessary to promote effective structural reform—especially enterprise restructuring. Although prices have been liberalized in most countries, the allocation of resources continues to be distorted by a plethora of direct and indirect measures that allow state enterprises to escape hard budget constraints. These measures undermine the financial stabilization that has been achieved thus far and threaten prospects for sustainable growth. Further progress in transition is dependent on the progressive disengagement of the state from production and allocation decisions.

---

[90]Measures to strengthen the banking system are especially urgent in most transition countries in view of the role of banks in screening and monitoring investment projects. Commercial banks in some countries may be unwilling to perform these functions, however, in the knowledge that calling nonperforming loans would eliminate their capital and result in closure. The outcome is continued financing of inefficient enterprises at the expense of more efficient firms in the nascent private sector. An additional complication in some countries is the absence, unenforceability, or weakness of laws needed to support a market economy, particularly collateral, property rights, and bankruptcy legislation.

Annex I

The Spillover Effects of Government Debt

Increasing capital market integration has expanded the markets in which governments can sell their debt. In principle, this provides greater scope for governments to smooth taxation and spending, and for countries to smooth consumption over time in the face of temporary shocks. But capital market integration also implies that the fiscal policies of one country will affect other countries. In a world with perfect capital market integration, a country that issues an amount of debt that is globally significant will thereby raise world real interest rates and crowd out private investment in all countries. An important policy implication is that countries with high levels of debt may not only jeopardize their own domestic macroeconomic stability and reduce their own living standards, but they may also impose significant spillovers on other countries.

For the industrial countries as a whole, government net financial liabilities increased by about 25 percentage points of GDP from the early 1980s to 1994.[1] Recent empirical evidence suggests that this massive buildup of government debt, which has been notably widespread across countries, has resulted in significantly higher global real interest rates and a lower world capital stock. For example, recent reduced-form evidence that links world government debt to real interest rates in individual industrial countries with integrated capital markets suggests that the growth in world government debt since the early 1980s has raised the average level of real interest rates by between 150 and 450 basis points.[2]

The recent empirical evidence that finds a strong link from world government debt to real interest rates is consistent with other empirical evidence that suggests that government deficits reduce national and world saving because consumers do not increase their saving by the full amount of the future increase in the tax burden that will be necessary to finance the higher level of debt. As a consequence, there will be a tendency to overconsume available resources, and this will result in higher real interest rates and a lower world capital stock. This tendency to overconsume available resources in the short run not only reduces the capital stock and labor productivity, but also lowers the sustainable level of consumption in the long run.

Recent estimates of the crowding-out effects of government debt from structural models also suggest that consumers would be significantly better off in the long run if aggregate government debt were reduced in the industrial countries. For example, in the May 1995 *World Economic Outlook*, which provided estimates of the long-run crowding-out effects of government debt from a structural model of the industrial economies, it was estimated that a 20 percentage point increase in the net debt-to-GDP ratio would result in an increase in world real interest rates of about 100 basis points.[3] These estimates are smaller than those obtained from recent reduced-form equations that provide direct links from world government debt to real interest rates, but they still suggest important crowding-out effects from government debt. For example, they imply that a permanent increase in the world real interest rate of 100 basis points would eventually reduce the world capital stock by 10½ percent. This lower capital stock would reduce labor productivity and real wages and lower the sustainable level of world output and consumption by 3¾ and 2¼ percent, respectively. While these aggregate estimates suggest that there could be very significant benefits for the world economy if governments were successful at reducing their debt, they tend to mask the spillover effects of one country's debt on other countries.

MULTIMOD, the Fund's multicountry model, is well designed to study such spillovers, because it captures the essential intertemporal aspects of govern-

---

This Annex was prepared by Douglas Laxton in the Economic Modeling and External Adjustment Division of the Research Department.

[1]There is clear evidence emerging that market participants demand significant risk premiums in cases where the government debt process has been explosive. See, for example, Tamim Bayoumi, Morris Goldstein, and Geoffrey Woglom, "Do Credit Markets Discipline Sovereign Borrowers? Evidence from States," *Journal of Money Credit and Banking*, Vol. 27 (November 1995), pp. 1046–59. This annex abstracts from these issues. For a discussion of the macroeconomic implications of debt-induced country risk premiums, see the October 1995 *World Economic Outlook*, pp. 73–81.

[2]In particular, Vito Tanzi and Domenico Fanizza, "Fiscal Deficit and Public Debt in Industrial Countries, 1970–1994," IMF Working Paper 95/49 (May 1995) suggest that a good estimate is around 150 basis points. Using a slightly different methodology, Robert Ford and Douglas Laxton, "World Public Debt and Real Interest Rates," IMF Working Paper 95/30 (March 1995) report a range of estimates between 250 and 450 basis points.

[3]See the May 1995 *World Economic Outlook*, Box 13, pp. 86–7.

ment debt and has well-defined short- and long-run properties.[4] As in any modern macro model that has well-defined properties, the extent of crowding out depends critically on (1) the degree to which consumers are assumed to count government bonds as net worth; (2) the relationship assumed between aggregate consumption and disposable income; and (3) the assumed sensitivity of aggregate consumption to changes in interest rates. If consumers are connected to all future generations by operative intergenerational transfers, increases in government debt will not crowd out private investment because consumers will change their saving rate today to prepare for tax liabilities in the future. In the economics literature, this is referred to as the Ricardian equivalence hypothesis. But empirical evidence on the response of private saving to changes in government deficits casts serious doubt on the Ricardian equivalence hypothesis.[5] This empirical evidence suggests that consumers save for only some fraction of the higher future tax burden that is associated with higher levels of government debt. In effect, this implies that they treat only some portion of their holdings of government bonds as net worth because they realize that they will have to pay higher taxes in the future to service the government's interest payments on this debt.

There seem to be two reasons why full Ricardian equivalence does not apply in practice, and both are embodied in MULTIMOD's properties. First, because a significant fraction of consumers cannot borrow against their future labor income, their expenditure is effectively constrained by their current disposable income. Second, consumers who are constrained by wealth rather than disposable income are assumed not to care about all of the tax burden that will be passed on to future generations. Thus, wealth-constrained consumers are assumed to adjust their saving rates in response to a higher expected future tax burden, but they also realize that future generations will help share

the tax burden associated with higher levels of government debt. Both imperfect capital markets and the disconnectedness of today's generation from future generations imply that higher levels of government debt will be associated with a tendency to overconsume available resources. And this tendency to overconsume will result in higher real interest rates and eventually in less capital and lower sustainable levels of real income and consumption.

The increase in interest rates needed to eliminate the tendency to overconsume available resources will depend critically on the interest sensitivity of consumption. If consumption were highly sensitive to changes in real interest rates, then it would take only a small rise in interest rates to induce consumers to adjust their saving rates in response to an increase in government debt. However, the empirical literature suggests that the interest sensitivity of consumption and saving is low.[6] Thus, this evidence also implies significant long-run crowding-out effects of government debt.

Three MULTIMOD-based fiscal scenarios were constructed to illustrate the domestic and external effects of changing government debt. In the first scenario, government debt in the United States is reduced by 5 percent of baseline nominal GDP, through reductions in government expenditures.[7] The second scenario is similar except that the 5 percent debt reduction is now assumed for all industrial countries except the United States. A third simulation considers the case in which debt reduction in the United States is achieved by raising taxes instead of reducing government expenditures.

Scenario 1. Debt Reduction in the United States Through Lower Expenditures

In this scenario (see Table 25), the reduction in government debt is achieved by reducing government expenditures by 1 percent of GDP forever and then allowing taxes to fall once the desired reduction in government debt has been achieved. Lower government expenditures in this simulation result in smaller government deficits of about 1 percent of nominal GDP for the first five years of the simulation and then

---

[4]This section is a brief summary of Hamid Faruqee, Peter Isard, and Douglas Laxton, "Reducing Government Debt: Short-Run Pain Versus Long-Run Gain," IMF Working Paper (forthcoming). A simple closed economy prototype version of the model can be found in Hamid Faruqee, Douglas Laxton, and Steven Symansky, "Government Debt, Life-Cycle Income, and Liquidity Constraints: Beyond Approximate Ricardian Evidence" (unpublished, IMF, 1995).

[5]There is an active debate in the academic literature about the empirical relevance of Ricardian equivalence. For two recent survey papers that reach opposite conclusions, see John J. Seater, "Ricardian Equivalence," *Journal of Economic Literature*, No. 31, (1993), pp. 142–90, and B. Douglas Bernheim, "Ricardian Equivalence: An Evaluation of Theory and Evidence," in *NBER Macroeconomics Annual 1987*, ed. by Stanley Fischer (Cambridge, Massachusetts: MIT Press, 1987), pp. 263–304. For policymakers, it may be best to err on the side of caution and assume that government debt reduces world saving and raises real interest rates. The reason for this is that a failure to recognize a link between government debt and real interest rates could result in extreme instabilities in the debt process—see Box 6.

[6]The intertemporal elasticity of substitution is 0.3 in MULTIMOD. Blundell provides a survey paper on empirical estimates of this elasticity and concludes that it is likely to be less than 0.5. None of the qualitative conclusions in this annex would be affected if it was set at 0.5. See Richard Blundell, "Consumer Behaviour: Theory and Empirical Evidence: A Survey," *The Economic Journal*, Vol. 98 (March 1988), pp. 16–65.

[7]Specifically, the cuts in government expenditures are assumed to fall on government consumption goods and not on productive investment goods. Consequently, the expenditure reductions are assumed not to have any direct deleterious effects on the capital stock and potential output.

Table 25. Effects of Debt Reduction in the United States Through Lower Government Expenditures

(Percentage deviation from baseline unless otherwise noted)

	1996	1997	1998	1999	2000	2001	2002	Long Run
United States								
Real GDP	−1.1	−0.2	0.4	0.6	0.5	0.4	0.3	0.6
Consumption	−0.9	—	0.6	1.0	1.2	1.2	1.2	2.1
Investment	1.1	2.6	3.1	3.0	2.5	2.0	1.8	2.2
Capital stock	0.1	0.3	0.6	0.8	0.9	1.0	1.1	2.2
Inflation (GDP deflator)[1]	−0.6	−0.6	−0.2	0.1	0.2	0.2	0.1	—
Real long-term interest rate[1]	−0.7	−0.8	−0.7	−0.5	−0.3	−0.1	−0.1	−0.2
General government deficit/GDP[1]	−1.1	−1.1	−1.1	−1.0	−0.8	−0.5	−0.2	−0.2
Net government debt/GDP[1]	−0.1	−1.4	−2.6	−3.7	−4.4	−4.6	−4.7	−4.8
Industrial countries excluding the United States								
Real GDP	−0.4	—	0.2	0.2	0.2	0.2	0.2	0.4
Real long-term interest rate[1]	−0.3	−0.4	−0.3	−0.2	−0.2	−0.1	−0.1	−0.2
Developing countries								
Real GDP (creditor countries)	−0.5	—	0.2	0.3	0.3	0.2	0.1	0.3
Real GDP (debtor countries)	−0.3	−0.1	0.1	0.1	0.1	0.1	0.1	0.3

[1]In percentage points.

gradually declining percentages of GDP after the desired debt reduction has been achieved.[8]

The short-run effects of lower government expenditures are contractionary; real GDP in the United States declines by 1.1 percent in the first year and this induces a 0.4 percent reduction in real GDP in the other industrial countries. The short-run effects on aggregate demand and output will, however, depend critically on the response of the monetary authorities. In this simulation, a monetary policy rule is employed whereby the money stock is held constant. In the short run, this results in a decline in short-term interest rates, but this is not sufficient to completely offset the contractionary effects of the fiscal contraction on real GDP. Consequently, there is a temporary decline in inflation in the first three years of the simulation and thus a lower price level in the long run. If the monetary authorities were to provide some monetary accommodation by reducing interest rates more in the short run and allowing the money stock to expand, this would result in even smaller contractionary effects in the short run. However, even without monetary accommodation the contractionary effects are short-lived as lower real interest rates stimulate investment demand.

In the first year, real long-term interest rates decline by 70 basis points in the United States and by 30 basis points in the other industrial countries.[9] In the long

run, the lower level of world government debt reduces world real interest rates by 20 basis points. This will lower the financial cost of capital in all countries and provide an incentive for firms to invest. There will, however, be an additional effect on the capital stock in the United States. Because capital taxes are distortionary in MULTIMOD, the permanent reduction in government expenditures combined with lower financing requirements on the debt will imply a permanent reduction in the tax burden.[10] In the United States, the combined effects of lower interest rates and less distortionary taxation of capital raise the capital stock in the long run by 2.2 percent, which in turn raises the long-run sustainable level of real income by 0.6 percent and the sustainable level of real consumption by 2.1 percent. In this simulation, the effects on consumption and investment are greater than those on output because the U.S. government is assumed to absorb a smaller share of output and because the reduction in U.S. government debt improves the net foreign liability position of the United States. In the long run, this raises permanent income in the United States because it results in lower net interest payments to the rest of the world and higher net imports of goods and services.

As argued above, the international integration of capital markets implies that the long-term benefits of debt reduction in the United States will not be limited to the U.S. economy. Because a reduction in U.S. government debt will reduce the cost of capital in other

---

[8]The actual change in the debt-to-GDP ratio is slightly less than 5 percentage points because of the endogenous reaction of nominal GDP.

[9]This simulation is meant to be illustrative. If the bond market has already anticipated future fiscal consolidation in the United States, real long-term interest rates will decline by less when the fiscal consolidation actually takes place.

---

[10]The composition of capital and labor taxes is held fixed in this simulation so both tax rates are assumed to adjust by equal amounts.

Table 26. Effects of Debt Reduction in All Industrial Countries Except the United States
(Percentage deviation from baseline unless otherwise noted)

	1996	1997	1998	1999	2000	2001	2002	Long Run
United States								
Real GDP	−0.7	—	0.4	0.5	0.4	0.3	0.3	0.7
Consumption	−0.7	—	0.4	0.5	0.5	0.4	0.4	0.9
Investment	1.4	3.1	3.5	3.4	2.9	2.5	2.4	2.8
Capital stock	0.1	0.4	0.7	0.9	1.1	1.2	1.3	2.8
Inflation (GDP deflator)[1]	−0.7	−0.6	−0.2	—	0.1	—	−0.1	—
Real long-term interest rate[1]	−0.7	−0.9	−0.8	−0.6	−0.4	−0.3	−0.3	−0.4
Industrial countries excluding the United States								
Real GDP	−1.6	−0.2	0.5	0.8	0.7	0.6	0.5	1.2
Real long-term interest rate[1]	−0.8	−1.0	−1.0	−0.8	−0.5	−0.3	−0.2	−0.4
General government deficit/GDP[1]	−1.0	−1.1	−1.1	−1.0	−0.7	−0.4	−0.2	−0.2
Net government debt/GDP[1]	0.2	−1.0	−2.2	−3.1	−3.8	−4.0	−4.0	−4.6
Developing countries								
Real GDP (creditor countries)	−0.8	0.2	0.6	0.8	0.8	0.6	0.5	0.7
Real GDP (debtor countries)	−0.4	—	0.2	0.3	0.3	0.3	0.3	0.8

[1]In percentage points.

countries, consumers in other industrial countries and the developing countries will also experience a rise in their real incomes. In fact, real GDP in the long run increases almost as much in the rest of the world as it does in the United States. In aggregate, there are permanent increases in real GDP of 0.4 percent in the other industrial countries and 0.3 percent in the developing countries as both debtor and creditor countries benefit from the increase in world saving.

Scenario 2. Debt Reduction in the Other Industrial Countries

The second scenario considers the effects of debt reduction in all countries except the United States (Table 26). Because these countries, in aggregate, are larger than the United States, the same reduction in debt-to-GDP ratios in all of these countries would be expected to produce larger changes in world saving and real interest rates. Indeed, in this case, real interest rates decline by 40 basis points in the long run, and this results in even larger permanent gains in real income. In fact, in this scenario consumers in the United States are even better off because there are smaller contractionary effects in the short run and significantly greater gains in permanent income in the long run. Very similar long-run gains in real income are realized in the developing countries. However, the reduction in real long-term interest rates in the short run implies that there are smaller short-run contractionary effects for net debtor countries than for net creditors.

Scenario 3. Debt Reduction in the United States Through Higher Taxes

The third simulation illustrates the effects of debt reduction in the United States through tax increases rather than reductions in expenditures (Table 27). Again, once the desired effect on government debt has been achieved, taxes are allowed to decline to stabilize the debt-to-GDP ratio. However, because government expenditures are unchanged in the scenario, taxes decline less in the long run than they did in the first scenario.

In the third scenario, private sector demand and economic activity are stimulated significantly less than in the first scenario for two reasons. First, although the lower level of government debt implies lower taxes in the long run, because lower debt results in a smaller interest burden from government securities, the reduction in taxes is smaller because of higher government expenditures. Second, since taxes on capital are distortionary in MULTIMOD, higher taxes imply a smaller capital stock. As a consequence, a reduction in government debt achieved through higher taxes in the short run will be less beneficial in the long run than if the same debt reduction is achieved through a permanent reduction in government expenditures.

* * *

This annex has focused mainly on the spillover effects of a significant but small reduction in government debt. For countries that have very high levels of government debt, debt reduction may lead to changes in market participants' views about the riskiness of

Table 27. Effects of Debt Reduction in the United States Through Higher Taxes

(Percentage deviation from baseline unless otherwise noted)

	1996	1997	1998	1999	2000	2001	2002	Long Run
United States								
Real GDP	−0.7	−0.2	0.2	0.3	0.3	0.2	0.1	0.2
Consumption	−1.5	−1.0	−0.6	−0.4	−0.3	−0.2	−0.2	0.4
Investment	0.5	1.2	1.6	1.6	1.4	1.1	0.9	0.9
Capital stock	—	0.2	0.3	0.4	0.5	0.5	0.6	0.9
Inflation (GDP deflator)[1]	−0.4	−0.4	−0.2	—	0.1	0.1	—	—
Real long-term interest rate[1]	−0.5	−0.6	−0.5	−0.4	−0.3	−0.2	−0.2	−0.1
General government deficit/GDP[1]	−0.8	−0.9	−1.0	−1.0	−0.9	−0.7	−0.5	−0.2
Net government debt/GDP[1]	−0.2	−1.2	−2.3	−3.3	−4.0	−4.5	−4.7	−4.9
Industrial countries excluding the United States								
Real GDP	−0.3	—	0.1	0.2	0.1	0.1	0.1	0.2
Real long-term interest rate[1]	−0.2	−0.3	−0.2	−0.2	−0.1	−0.1	−0.1	−0.1
Developing countries:								
Real GDP (creditor countries)	−0.4	−0.1	0.1	0.2	0.2	0.2	0.1	0.2
Real GDP (debtor countries)	−0.2	−0.1	—	0.1	0.1	—	—	0.2

[1] In percentage points.

government securities and may consequently result in even larger benefits through lower risk premiums in interest rates. Moreover, in the scenarios it is assumed that the private sector views the permanence of the debt reduction as perfectly credible. Some recent evidence suggests that fiscal consolidation achieved through higher taxes may be less credible than the same debt reduction achieved through lower government expenditures (see Chapter III). This suggests that the short-term contractionary effects of higher taxes in the short run may be larger than those estimated in the third scenario. Finally, the three scenarios assume that monetary policy is such as to allow inflation to fall in the short run. But, if the debt-reduction policy is viewed as being credible, there may be a case, depending on the initial rate of inflation and inflationary pressures, for the monetary authorities to ease monetary conditions further in the short run to offset more of the short-run contractionary effects on both output and inflation.

Annex II

Macroeconomic and Structural Adjustment in the Middle East and North Africa

The economies of the Middle East and North Africa (MENA) region offer striking contrasts with considerable variations in per capita incomes and underlying economic structures.[1] Most countries in the region are classified as middle-income economies with per capita incomes ranging from $1,000 to $7,000. However, Israel, Kuwait, Qatar, and the United Arab Emirates are classified as high-income economies with an average per capita income of about $15,000, while Egypt and the Republic of Yemen—with per capita incomes below $1,000—are classified as low-income countries. Israel, Jordan, Lebanon, Morocco, and Tunisia have a more diversified economic structure than most countries of the region, which are characterized by a narrow production and export base, particularly the major fuel exporters—Algeria, the Islamic Republic of Iran, and the countries belonging to the Gulf Cooperation Council for Arab States (GCC).[2]

Because of their high dependence on mineral resources, most countries of the MENA region remain particularly vulnerable to adverse developments in their external environment (Table 28). For example, the terms of trade of all the major fuel producers have deteriorated by more than 50 percent since the reverse oil shock of 1986, which has complicated macroeconomic management and hampered economic performance. Furthermore, the reverse oil shock had important consequences for most of the other countries of the region, particularly Egypt, Jordan, Lebanon, the Republic of Yemen, and the Syrian Arab Republic, because a large share of their foreign exchange earnings derives from the GCC countries in the form of workers' remittances. Also, the regional crisis of the early

Table 28. Middle East and North Africa: Revenue from Mineral Resources
(In percent of total revenue)

Country	Government Revenue[1]	Export Revenue[1,2]
Algeria	58.6	78.9
Bahrain	63.2	29.3[3]
Egypt	29.5[4]	10.4
Iran, Islamic Rep. of	58.3	73.4
Israel	—	—
Jordan	0.3	6.8[5]
Kuwait	68.1[6]	53.2[6]
Lebanon	—	—
Morocco	0.8	9.8[6]
Oman	72.9	87.8[6]
Qatar	69.6	75.3[6]
Saudi Arabia	74.8	74.5
Syria	15.9	34.6
Tunisia	5.4	7.9
United Arab Emirates	79.1	52.7[6]
Yemen, Rep. of	28.2	43.4

[1]Averages for 1993/94, unless otherwise indicated.
[2]Exports of goods and services plus workers' remittances
[3]Average for 1992.
[4]Including Suez Canal receipts.
[5]Average for 1992/94.
[6]Average for 1992/93.

1990s triggered by Iraq's invasion of Kuwait resulted in a marked deterioration in the fiscal positions of several GCC countries while having a major impact on the flows of aid and workers' remittances to other countries of the MENA region.

Overall economic performance over the last decade and a half has been disappointing, in particular among fuel exporting countries where real per capita GDP fell by 20 percent on average from 1981 to 1995 (Chart 30). The fall in per capita GDP coincided with weak oil market conditions, the widening of fiscal and current account imbalances, and the accumulation of external debt (Charts 31 and 32). However, a number of countries have achieved important progress, particularly the more diversified exporters, in strengthening growth performance since the mid-1980s. In addition, most MENA countries have reassessed their economic policy strategy and initiated reforms aimed at reducing internal and external imbalances while addressing structural weaknesses. The main challenge faced by most MENA countries in the period ahead is the in-

---

This annex was prepared by Alain Jean-Pierre Féler and Oussama T. Kanaan in the Middle East Department.

[1]The coverage of MENA in this annex includes the economies of the Middle East country grouping used in *International Financial Statistics* plus the three North African countries of Algeria, Morocco, and Tunisia. Iraq and the Libyan Jamahiriya, however, are excluded from the analysis because of data limitations.

[2]Fuel exporters are defined as countries whose fuel exports account for over 50 percent of total exports of goods and services plus workers' remittances. The GCC includes Bahrain, Kuwait, Oman, Qatar, Saudi Arabia, and the United Arab Emirates. Although Bahrain does not technically meet the above definition of fuel exporters, it is closely interconnected and has many similarities with other GCC countries and is therefore included among the group of fuel exporters for the present analysis.

tensification and sustained implementation of these reforms with a view to reaping the benefits of globalization and favorable regional developments.[3]

The Adjustment Experience

Most of the economies of the MENA region have suffered adverse exogenous shocks since 1986 onward, including a terms of trade deterioration, several episodes of war and civil strife, and, in the North African countries and the Republic of Yemen, recurrent droughts. The nature, intensity, and timing of these shocks, and the associated policy responses, have differed significantly among countries. The fuel exporters have faced a major adjustment challenge as a result of the erosion of real oil prices since the early 1980s. The associated terms of trade deterioration and resulting macroeconomic instability were much more severe than those experienced over the same period by the other MENA countries with a more diversified economic and export base (Chart 33).

Fuel Exporting Economies

MENA's fuel exporting countries are heavily dependent on hydrocarbon export proceeds as a source of both foreign exchange and budgetary revenue, making these countries particularly vulnerable to fluctuations in world oil prices. Because of the relatively limited scope of the nonhydrocarbon sector and the narrow domestic tax base in most of these countries, budgetary revenue fell sharply from about 39 percent of GDP in 1981–85, to about 29 percent of GDP during 1986–90. Partly offsetting this revenue contraction, government spending declined by only about 2 to 3 percentage points of GDP over the same periods, mainly as a result of cuts in capital expenditure.[4] The average fiscal deficit widened markedly from 1½ percent of GDP in 1981–85 to 8 percent of GDP in 1986–90. In the early 1990s, the regional crisis resulted in a marked increase in public expenditure in some GCC countries. Because of a subsequent decline in budgetary revenue associated with falling oil prices,

---

[3]Recent analyses of macroeconomic and structural issues in the MENA region are also provided in Mohamed El-Erian and Shamsuddin Tareq, "Economic Reform in the Arab Countries: A Review of Structural Issues," in *Economic Development of the Arab Countries: Selected Issues*, ed. by Said El-Naggar (Washington: IMF, 1993), pp. 26–50; International Monetary Fund, *Macroeconomics of the Middle East and North Africa: Exploiting Potential for Growth and Financial Stability* (Washington, 1995); and The World Bank, *Claiming the Future: Choosing Prosperity in the Middle East and North Africa* (Washington, 1995).

[4]The decline in expenditure was more pronounced in the case of the Islamic Republic of Iran, largely as a result of the cessation of the war with Iraq in 1988.

Chart 30. Middle East and North Africa: Economic Performance

(In percent change unless otherwise noted)

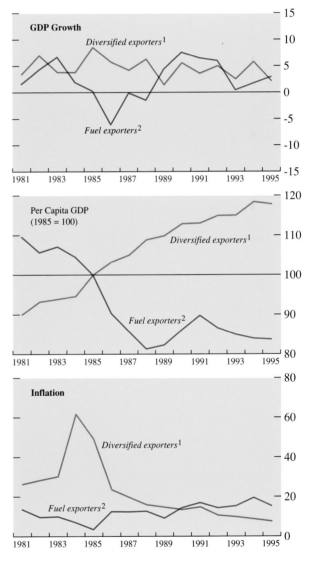

[1]Egypt, Israel, Jordan, Morocco, Syria, and Tunisia.
[2]Algeria, Bahrain, Islamic Republic of Iran, Kuwait, Oman, Qatar, Saudi Arabia, and the United Arab Emirates.

Chart 31. Middle East and North Africa: Fiscal Balances

(In percent of GDP)

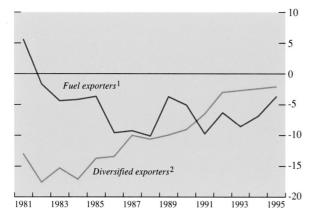

¹Algeria, Bahrain, Islamic Republic of Iran, Kuwait, Oman, Qatar, Saudi Arabia, and the United Arab Emirates.
²Egypt, Israel, Jordan, Morocco, Syria, and Tunisia.

and notwithstanding a curtailment in public spending, budget deficits have remained excessive and averaged 9 percent of GDP for the group of fuel exporters in 1991–95. The economic implications of these fiscal imbalances have differed significantly between the GCC countries on the one hand, and Algeria and the Islamic Republic of Iran on the other, mainly because of the differing degrees of outward orientation and levels of foreign exchange reserves of these countries.

The *GCC countries* have traditionally pegged their currencies to the U.S. dollar and maintained their trade and payment systems free of current and capital account restrictions. As a result, inflation in these countries was not affected by aggregate demand pressures stemming from the expansionary fiscal stance in the second half of the 1980s. These pressures, however, contributed to a substantial deterioration of the countries' external current account position, which shrunk from a surplus of 7 percent of GDP on average in 1981–85 to near balance in 1986–90.

In the first half of the 1990s, most of the GCC countries stepped up their efforts at expenditure restraint. For instance, government spending in Saudi Arabia was reduced from 54 percent of GDP in 1986–90 to 44 percent of GDP in 1991–95, and this spending restraint was supplemented by steps in 1995 to increase non-oil revenues significantly. The expenditure cuts were broad-based, including in services and supplies, operations and maintenance, and subsidies.[5] Efforts in GCC countries, however, proved insufficient to bring down fiscal deficits to the low levels that had prevailed in the mid-1980s. The persistence of large fiscal imbalances contributed to a shift of the external current account balance from a surplus to a deficit of about 10 percent of GDP on average in 1991–95 which led to a drawdown of official foreign assets and of the foreign asset positions of the domestic private sector. There was also a rapid buildup of domestic public debt as a ratio to GDP, which, in the case of Saudi Arabia, had risen from about 50 percent to more than 80 percent over the last three years. A strengthening of efforts to reduce primary deficits and improve growth performance through structural reforms will be needed to reverse this trend.

In contrast to the GCC countries, the nonhydrocarbon sector has played a much more important role in the economies of *Algeria* and the *Islamic Republic of Iran*. This has reflected in part the import-substitution strategy originally pursued by these two countries whose populations and domestic markets are much larger than those of the GCC countries. The import-substitution policy also favored less open trade and payment systems than other MENA fuel exporters,

---

[5]Kuwait, however, sharply increased its government expenditure from 55 percent of GDP in 1986–90 to about 100 percent of GDP in 1991–95, mainly for reconstruction following the regional crisis.

which allowed Algeria and the Islamic Republic of Iran to avoid a significant deterioration in their current account positions despite the widening of their fiscal imbalances in the second half of the 1980s. On the other hand, demand pressures stemming from fiscal imbalances gave rise to substantial inflationary pressures that, despite pervasive price controls, translated into an increase in the rate of inflation from an average of 14 percent in 1981–85 to an average of 19 percent in 1986–90. The persistence of internal and external imbalances and the associated buildup of external debt prompted these two countries in the early 1990s to initiate some steps toward tighter demand-management policies and to implement key structural reforms, including unifying exchange rates and liberalizing external current transactions. These efforts were undertaken in the context of an IMF-supported adjustment program in Algeria in 1991. They were undermined, however, by wage policies and, mainly as result of insufficient commitment to reform, could not be sustained for long.

The reimposition of an array of trade and exchange restrictions and a significant relaxation of fiscal and monetary policies in Algeria in 1992–93, as well as in the Islamic Republic of Iran in 1993–94 in the context of a difficult external environment, had a detrimental effect on economic performance. Per capita income levels continued to decline, while inflation increased further to 25 percent on average in 1991–95. The deterioration compelled Algeria to formulate, in 1994, a more comprehensive program of macroeconomic stabilization and structural reform. This program, which has been supported by the Fund, has been predicated upon tight demand-management policies and wage restraint, as well as realigning relative prices, removing trade and payments restrictions, and establishing market mechanisms with a view to giving the private sector a greater role in the economy. As a result, the decline in economic activity has been arrested and the fiscal deficit has shrunk from about 9 percent of GDP in 1993 to about 1 percent in 1995. The Islamic Republic of Iran has also been able to reduce substantially its budget deficit in the last two years, which has contributed to a decline in inflation, but has maintained trade and payments restrictions in the face of continued tight external constraints.

Diversified Exporters

The more diversified exporters form a rather heterogeneous group of countries that differ significantly with regard to the comprehensiveness and consistency of their adjustment efforts. Israel, Jordan, Morocco, and Tunisia launched early on comprehensive programs of macroeconomic stabilization and structural reforms in the 1980s. These policies have been sustained over time, contributing to a reduction of both internal and external imbalances, as well as to a sub-

Chart 32. Middle East and North Africa: External Balances
(In percent of GDP)

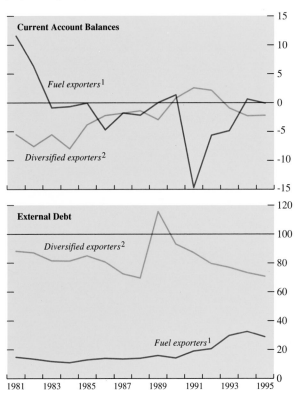

[1]Algeria, Bahrain, Islamic Republic of Iran, Kuwait, Oman, Qatar, Saudi Arabia, and the United Arab Emirates.
[2]Egypt, Israel, Jordan, Morocco, Syria, and Tunisia.

101

Chart 33. Middle East and North Africa: External Conditions
(1985 = 100)

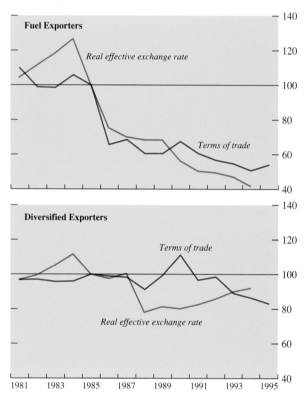

stantial overall improvement in economic performance. Egypt and the Syrian Arab Republic have also undertaken reforms, although later (early 1990s) and more gradually. Lebanon and the Republic of Yemen have only recently been in a position to start tackling their macroeconomic imbalances and structural weaknesses, following the ending of protracted periods of civil strife and political instability that severely impaired economic policy formulation and disrupted economic activity.

During the 1970s, *Israel, Jordan, Morocco,* and *Tunisia* pursued an inward-oriented development strategy characterized by pervasive government controls and lax financial policies. The strategy proved unsustainable in the early 1980s and both internal and external imbalances widened. Failure to restrain public expenditure in the face of declining revenues resulted in a significant widening of their fiscal deficits, which averaged over 14 percent of GDP during 1980–85. Growing fiscal imbalances contributed to both rising inflation and a worsening in their external positions: external debt burdens reached more than 90 percent of GDP on average during the first half of the 1980s.

In the second half of the 1980s, Morocco, Tunisia, and Israel, and later Jordan, reassessed their policy strategy and tried to redress their fiscal positions and reduce government absorption, first by restraining both current and capital expenditure, and in a second stage, by reforming their tax systems. The tax reforms entailed a widening of the tax base, improving the elasticity of tax systems, and introducing less distortionary taxes, including the value-added tax (Israel, Morocco, and Tunisia) or a general sales tax (Jordan). The tightening of fiscal policy led to a steep decline in budget deficits from an average of 14 percent of GDP in 1981–85 to about 5 percent of GDP in 1986–90 and 3 percent of GDP in 1991–95. At the same time, the introduction of market-oriented treasury debt instruments allowed for an increased reliance on noninflationary sources of deficit financing. The improvement in fiscal positions has been supported by nonaccommodating monetary policies and has allowed a shift in credit to support private sector activity.

These policies contributed to a substantial decline in inflation, especially in Israel where the rate of inflation fell from an average of over 200 percent a year during 1981–85 to under 25 percent during 1986–90 and 13 percent in 1991–95. In Jordan, Morocco, and Tunisia, average inflation fell from 9 percent in 1981–85 to about 6 percent in 1986–95. In addition to their anti-inflationary fiscal and monetary policies, broadly flexible exchange rate policies enabled these countries to respond to a deterioration of their average terms of trade of about 12 percent from 1986 to 1995 and avoid any significant misalignment of real exchange rates.

On the supply side, all four countries have taken wide-ranging actions to liberalize the incentive structure and reform the regulatory framework. Important steps have been taken to liberalize foreign trade, which was critical for promoting exports and enhancing domestic competition, in particular by virtually abolishing quantitative restrictions and reducing effective protection. They have also made considerable progress in decontrolling domestic prices. Ambitious privatization programs have been launched (Jordan, Morocco, Tunisia) to widen the scope for private sector activity and help reduce the burden of public enterprises on governments' finances. Financial sector reforms have facilitated the financing of private sector investment. Interest rates have been largely deregulated and compulsory credit allocation schemes eliminated, while banking legislation has been modernized and prudential standards brought closer to international norms.

The substantial reduction of internal imbalances and the liberalization of the incentive structure have enabled these countries to attain external current account convertibility while at the same time allowing for the accumulation of foreign exchange reserves. In addition, some progress with the phasing out of restrictions on longer-term capital account transactions has helped to attract private foreign investment.

As a result of the reforms, the share of saving and investment in GDP increased. There was also a substantial increase in the efficiency of investment. Consequently, economic activity accelerated significantly, with real GDP growth increasing from 3½ percent a year in the first half of the 1980s to almost 5 percent in 1991–95. This translated into a more limited, albeit substantial, increase in the growth of per capita income from 1.1 percent a year in 1981–85 to 1.7 percent in 1991–95, reflecting in part the impact of the large number of Palestinian workers who returned from the GCC countries to Jordan following the Persian Gulf crisis of 1990–91 and of emigrants from the former Soviet Union who moved to Israel.

Egypt and the *Syrian Arab Republic* undertook steps to liberalize their economies in the early 1990s, following several decades of extensive public ownership in most areas of economic activity and inward-oriented trade policies. Nevertheless, the public sector still plays a pervasive role in both countries, not only in the hydrocarbon sector but also in industry where public enterprises account for more than two thirds of output.

In the second half of the 1980s, *Egypt* faced large macroeconomic imbalances, including an average budget deficit of 18 percent of GDP, an average inflation rate of about 20 percent, and an external debt of more than 90 percent of GDP. Following several attempts at tackling these imbalances and liberalizing the economy, Egypt embarked, in 1991, on a program of macroeconomic stabilization and structural reform supported by the IMF. Under this program substantial progress in fiscal adjustment was achieved, coupled

with a strengthening of the budget through the introduction of a general sales tax and a global income tax reform, and significant efforts at expenditure restraint. Reflecting these measures, as well as higher oil revenues and Suez Canal receipts, the fiscal deficit declined steadily from 17 percent of GDP in 1990/91 to less than 2 percent of GDP in 1994/95, contributing to a decline in the rate of inflation to about 9 percent in 1994/95. The intensified adjustment efforts from 1991 onward, combined with debt relief and a surge in capital inflows, have also resulted in substantial accumulation of external reserves. Egypt has also undertaken a number of structural reforms toward liberalizing the trade system, eliminating input and consumer goods subsidies, and privatizing public sector companies. The continued pursuit of appropriate macroeconomic and structural reform policies will be needed to provide the basis for growth in real per capita GDP.

Since the early 1990s, the *Syrian Arab Republic*'s ongoing transition from a tightly regulated economy dominated by the public sector to a market based economy driven by the private sector has centered on promoting private investment, foreign trade, a more realistic pricing of foreign exchange, and increased price flexibility. The realignment of relative prices has induced a strong supply response and a marked improvement in growth performance, with output growing on average at 7 percent a year during 1991–95. The Syrian Arab Republic's liberalization efforts, however, have not been backed by sufficient fiscal adjustment. High public expenditure resulted in budgetary pressures that were intensified by the drying up of external financing following the 1990–91 regional crisis and the weakening of oil prices. Thus, the fiscal balance shifted from a surplus of about 2 percent of GDP in 1992 to a deficit of about 4 percent in 1995. The associated aggregate demand pressures have contributed to a deterioration of the external current account position from a surplus of 8 percent of GDP in 1991–92 to a deficit of 3½ percent of GDP in 1993–95.

In recent years, economic difficulties in the *Republic of Yemen* have been exacerbated by a sharp decline in external assistance and workers' remittances following the breakup of the former Soviet Union and the Persian Gulf war and also by a terms of trade deterioration. Civil strife, in the wake of the country's unification, limited the government's capacity to respond to these external factors and burdened the economy with rehabilitation costs. The resolution of the political conflict in late 1994 was quickly followed, in 1995, by determined actions to adjust the course of demand-management policies and initiate structural reforms. These initial measures were reinforced by the formulation, for 1996, of a comprehensive adjustment program incorporating forceful stabilization policies and a broad set of far-reaching structural reforms. This program aims at achieving higher growth in the nonhydrocarbon sector while quickly reducing inflation and progressing toward the restoration of external sector viability. The core policy actions recently initiated emphasize a further realignment and liberalization of relative prices, including the exchange rate and interest rates, a substantial tightening of the fiscal stance, a major liberalization of the trade and payments system, and an aggressive privatization program.

Lebanon's civil war, which spanned 15 years (1975–90), exacted a heavy toll in human and economic terms. Per capita income is estimated to have fallen by more than 50 percent during that period. The end of the hostilities in 1990 and the restoration of political stability allowed for concerted economic policies to ensure a sustainable recovery of the economy. In addition to a pickup in real GDP growth, stabilization efforts centered on a nominal exchange rate anchor that resulted in a sharp decline in inflation and an accumulation of foreign exchange reserves to comfortable levels. Notwithstanding the need to finance a large reconstruction program, further reduction in the budget deficit will be necessary to reach the authorities' stabilization objectives.

Challenges for the Period Ahead

The MENA region has considerable natural, human, and financial resources; it is strategically located, has long-standing economic and financial links with industrial countries, and has considerable trading skills. To realize more fully this potential, there has been a broad reassessment by all MENA countries of their economic strategy toward attaining high and sustainable growth. Consequently, the focus has turned to achieving both a more stable macroeconomic environment and more efficient resource allocation.

So far, the progress toward these objectives has varied substantially among countries with regard to the timeliness, depth, and consistency of adjustment policies. The challenges for the period ahead are bound to vary considerably among countries in accordance with these differences and the results of past adjustment efforts. In addition, they will also depend, to an important degree, on future developments in the external environment, including, in particular (1) the prospects for Arab-Israeli peace;[6] (2) the opportunities for a closer integration with the European Union under the Mediterranean Basin Initiative;[7] (3) the economic out-

look in industrial countries; and (4) the evolution of world hydrocarbon prices, which could be subject to strong downward pressures as a result of developments in the countries of the former Soviet Union and Iraq's possible return to the oil market.

Current projections indicate the continuation of a relatively moderate expansion of economic activity in industrial countries and point to a rather subdued outlook for oil prices over the next two years. Nevertheless, the short-term outlook for the MENA region is expected to improve. Real GDP growth should average about 3½ percent in 1996–97, allowing for gains in per capita incomes of 1 percent a year. Concurrently, average inflation is expected to slow down to 6½ percent while the external current account should narrow to 1½ percent of GDP by 1997. To realize these projections and strengthen their potential for achieving sustainable economic growth, all MENA countries will need to act forcefully to address macroeconomic imbalances and structural weaknesses that have limited saving and investment.

First, large fiscal imbalances remain in many countries, especially among the GCC members where they have contributed to both large external account deficits and mounting public debt in recent years. Fuel exporting countries need to broaden their domestic tax base by adopting broad-based domestic taxes to reduce the dependence of budgetary revenues on hydrocarbon earnings. Similarly, among the more diversified exporters, Lebanon, the Syrian Arab Republic, and the Republic of Yemen would benefit from adopting broader-based domestic taxes, while Jordan, Morocco, and Tunisia would need to strengthen alternative revenue sources with a view to compensating for the losses in trade taxes expected to result from the implementation of the agreements with the European Union. On the expenditure side, certain MENA countries should aim at targeting better the remaining generalized subsidies to the most vulnerable population groups and at strengthening public education to reduce poverty and facilitate these countries' integration in the world economy. This should be accompanied by civil service reform to reduce the government wage bill and improve the efficiency of government operations. The prospects for broadening the peace process between the Arab countries and Israel should also increase the scope for significant reductions in defense spending over time.

Second, MENA countries will need to intensify privatization programs to revitalize their manufacturing sectors and limit government operations to the efficient provision of public goods. While tangible progress has already been achieved in some countries, such as Morocco, the need for promoting the role of the private sector is particularly pressing for Algeria, Egypt, the Islamic Republic of Iran, and the Syrian Arab Republic where industrial sectors remain largely dominated by public enterprises.

---

[6]See Said El-Naggar and Mohamed El-Erian, "The Economic Implications of a Comprehensive Peace in the Middle East," in *The Economics of the Middle East Peace: Views from the Region*, ed. by Stanley Fischer, Dani Rodrik, and Elias Tuma (Cambridge, Massachusetts: MIT Press, 1993).

[7]For more details see Saleh Nsouli, Amer Bisat, Oussama T. Kanaan, "The European Union's New Mediterranean Strategy," *Finance & Development* (forthcoming).

Third, stepped-up efforts are also needed to scale back regulations and remove distortions in both goods and factor markets to improve the efficiency of resource allocation. The external trade and payments systems of several MENA countries are still saddled with restrictions, including excessive tariffs and pervasive quantitative restrictions. While the economies of the GCC are relatively open, trade reform is needed in several other countries, such as Egypt, the Islamic Republic of Iran, and the Syrian Arab Republic. For Israel, Jordan, Morocco, and Tunisia, which have already committed to join a free-trade area with the European Union, dismantling trade barriers with third countries will help to minimize the risk of trade diversion. Regarding factor markets, measures must be adopted to facilitate labor mobility within certain countries and within the region to maximize the creation of employment opportunities for a rapidly growing labor force in most MENA countries. Moreover, further steps should be taken to strengthen financial intermediation in most non-GCC countries, through

the removal of controls on rates of return and credit allocation—particularly in the Islamic Republic of Iran and the Syrian Arab Republic—the promotion of greater competition among financial institutions and the strengthening of prudential regulations.

Fourth, there is a need for greater diversification of the nonhydrocarbon export base to reduce the excessive vulnerability of most MENA countries to adverse terms of trade movements. The need is particularly acute for countries such as Algeria, Egypt, the Islamic Republic of Iran, and the Syrian Arab Republic, which have the capacity to develop strong export driven growth strategies.[8] The latter two countries would also benefit from further liberalization of their foreign exchange markets. Beyond these structural measures, sustaining reform programs will require a stable macroeconomic environment with consistent fiscal, monetary, and exchange rate policies.

---

[8]For an analysis of the sources of comparative advantage in these countries, see The World Bank, *Claiming the Future*, pp. 65–7.

Statistical Appendix

Assumptions

The statistical tables in this appendix have been compiled on the basis of information available through April 3, 1996. The estimates and projections for 1996 and 1997, as well as the 1998–2001 medium-term scenarios, are based on the following assumptions.

- For the industrial countries, real effective exchange rates are assumed to remain constant at their average four-week level, February 16–March 14, 1996, except for the bilateral exchange rates among the ERM currencies, which are assumed to remain constant in nominal terms. For 1996 and 1997, these assumptions imply average U.S. dollar/SDR conversion rates of 1.466 and 1.465, respectively.

- Established policies of national authorities will be maintained. The more specific policy assumptions underlying the projections for industrial countries are described in Box 1.

- The price of oil will average $17.39 a barrel in 1996 and $16.12 a barrel in 1997. In the medium term, the oil price is assumed to remain unchanged in real terms.

- Interest rates, as represented by the London interbank offered rate (LIBOR) on six-month U.S. dollar deposits, will average 5.4 percent in 1996 and 5.6 percent in 1997; the three-month certificate of deposit rate in Japan will average 0.6 percent in 1996 and 1.7 percent in 1997; and the three-month interbank deposit rate in Germany will average 3.3 percent in 1996 and 4.3 percent in 1997.

Data and Conventions

Data and projections for more than 180 countries form the statistical basis for the *World Economic Outlook* (the World Economic Outlook data base). The data are maintained jointly by the IMF's Research Department and area departments, with the latter regularly updating country projections based on consistent global assumptions.

Although national statistical agencies are the ultimate providers of historical data and definitions, international organizations are also involved in statistical

issues, with the objective of harmonizing differences among national statistical systems, of setting international standards with respect to definitions, and of providing conceptual frameworks for measurement and presentation of economic statistics. The World Economic Outlook data base reflects information from both national source agencies and international organizations.

The completion of the comprehensive revision of the United Nations' standardized *System of National Accounts (SNA)* and the IMF's fifth edition of the *Balance of Payments Manual (BPM)* is an important improvement in the standards of economic statistics and analysis.[1] The IMF was actively involved in both projects, particularly the *Manual*, which is central to the IMF's interest in countries' external positions. Key changes introduced with the revised *Manual* were summarized in Box 13 of the May 1994 *World Economic Outlook*. The process of adapting country balance of payments data to the definitions of the revised *Balance of Payments Manual* began with the May 1995 *World Economic Outlook*; however, full concordance is ultimately dependent on national statistical compilers providing revised country data, and hence the *World Economic Outlook* estimates are still only partly adapted to the *Manual*.

Composite data for country groups in the *World Economic Outlook* are either sums or weighted averages of data for individual countries. Arithmetic weighted averages are used for all data except inflation and money growth for nonindustrial country groups, for which geometric averages are used. The following conventions are used.

- Country group composites for interest rates, exchange rates, and the growth of monetary aggregates are weighted by GDP converted to U.S. dollars at market exchange rates (averaged over the preceding three years) as a share of world or group GDP.

- Composites for other data relating to the domestic economy, whether growth rates or ratios, are weighted by GDP valued at purchasing power

---

[1]Commission of the European Communities, IMF, OECD, UN, and World Bank, *System of National Accounts 1993* (Brussels/Luxembourg, New York, Paris, and Washington, 1993); and IMF, *Balance of Payments Manual* (5th ed., 1993).

Table A. Industrial Countries: Classification by Standard *World Economic Outlook* Groups, and Their Shares in Aggregate GDP and Exports of Goods and Services, 1995[1]

	Number of Countries Included in Group	Percentage of			
		Total GDP of		Total exports of goods and services of	
		Industrial countries	World	Industrial countries	World
Industrial countries	**23**	**100.0**	**53.9**	**100.0**	**69.0**
United States		39.5	21.3	18.3	12.6
Japan		14.8	8.0	11.6	8.0
Germany		8.7	4.7	13.6	9.4
France		6.7	3.6	9.1	6.3
Italy		6.3	3.4	7.9	5.4
United Kingdom		6.2	3.4	7.3	5.0
Canada		3.5	1.9	4.9	3.4
Other industrial countries	16	14.2	7.7	27.3	18.9
Industrial country groups					
Seven major industrial countries	7	85.8	46.3	72.7	50.1
European Union	15	38.4	20.7	59.2	40.8
Industrial countries except the United States, Japan, and Germany	20	37.5	20.2	56.5	39.0
Industrial countries except the United States, the European Union, and Japan	6	9.7	5.2	16.0	11.1
Major European industrial countries	4	28.0	15.1	37.9	26.1

[1]The GDP shares are based on the purchasing power parity (PPP) valuation of country GDPs.

parities (PPPs) as a share of total world or group GDP.[2]

- Composite unemployment rates and employment growth are weighted by labor force as a share of group labor force.

- Composites for data relating to the external economy are sums of individual country data after conversion to U.S. dollars at the average exchange rates in the years indicated for balance of payments, and at end-of-period exchange rates for debt denominated in currencies other than U.S. dollars. Composites of foreign trade volumes and prices, however, are arithmetic averages of percentage changes for individual countries weighted by the U.S. dollar value of exports or imports as a share of total world or group exports or imports (in the preceding year).

For central and eastern European countries in existence before 1991, external transactions in nonconvertible currencies (through 1990) are converted to U.S. dollars at the implicit U.S. dollar/ruble conversion rates obtained from each country's national currency exchange rate for the U.S. dollar and for the ruble.

Unless otherwise indicated, multiyear averages of growth rates are expressed as compound annual rates of change.

Classification of Countries

Summary of the Country Classification

The country classification in the *World Economic Outlook* divides the world into three major groups: industrial countries, developing countries, and countries in transition.[3] Rather than being based on strict criteria, economic or otherwise, this classification has evolved over time with the objective of facilitating the analysis by providing a reasonably meaningful organization of data. Each of the three main country groups is further divided into a number of subgroups. Tables A and B provide an overview of these standard groups in the *World Economic Outlook*, showing the number of countries in each group and the average 1995 shares of groups in aggregate PPP-valued GDP, total exports of goods and services, and total debt outstanding.

---

[2]See Annex IV, May 1993 *World Economic Outlook* and Anne Marie Gulde and Marianne Schulze-Ghattas, "Purchasing Power Parity Based Weights for the *World Economic Outlook*," in *Staff Studies for the World Economic Outlook* (IMF, December 1993), pp. 106–23.

[3]As used here, the term "country" does not in all cases refer to a territorial entity that is a state as understood by international law and practice. It also covers some territorial entities that are not states, but for which economic policies are formulated, and statistical data are maintained, on a separate and independent basis.

Table B. Developing Countries and Countries in Transition: Classification by Standard *World Economic Outlook* Groups and Their Shares in Aggregate GDP, Exports of Goods and Services, and Total Debt Outstanding, 1995[1]

		Percentage of				
		Total GDP of		Total exports of goods and services of		Total debt of
	Number of Countries Included in Group	Developing countries	World	Developing countries	World	Developing countries
Developing countries	**132**	**100.0**	**41.2**	**100.0**	**27.0**	**100.0**
By region						
Africa	50	7.9	3.2	6.4	1.7	15.1
Asia	30	59.1	24.4	65.5	17.7	35.5
Middle East and Europe	18	11.5	4.8	13.5	3.6	16.1
Western Hemisphere	34	21.5	8.8	14.6	3.9	33.2
Sub-Saharan Africa	45	3.3	1.4	2.3	0.6	8.6
Four newly industrializing Asian economies	4	7.9	3.2	38.3	10.3	6.8
By predominant export						
Fuel	15	9.1	3.7	10.2	2.7	11.9
Nonfuel exports	117	90.9	37.5	89.7	24.2	88.1
Manufactures	7	33.8	13.9	49.1	13.3	13.2
Primary products	43	7.0	2.9	5.6	1.5	16.0
Agricultural products	29	4.7	1.9	3.5	0.9	10.9
Minerals	14	2.2	0.9	2.2	0.6	5.1
Services, income, and private transfers	37	3.6	1.5	3.4	0.9	5.2
Diversified export base	30	46.6	19.2	31.7	8.6	53.6
By financial criteria						
Net creditor countries	7	5.1	2.1	13.9	3.8	1.9
Net debtor countries	125	94.9	39.1	86.0	23.2	98.1
Market borrowers	23	58.0	23.9	64.7	17.5	49.2
Diversified borrowers	33	25.3	10.4	14.9	4.0	30.8
Official borrowers	69	11.6	4.8	6.5	1.8	18.2
Countries with recent debt-servicing difficulties	72	29.9	12.3	21.3	5.8	55.1
Countries without debt-servicing difficulties	53	64.9	26.8	64.7	17.5	43.0
Other groups						
Small low-income economies	50	10.6	4.4	5.0	1.4	17.0
Least developed countries	46	4.2	1.7	1.6	0.4	8.0
Countries in transition	**28**	...	**4.9**	...	**4.0**	...
Central and eastern Europe	18	...	2.5	...	2.3	...
Excluding Belarus and Ukraine	16	...	1.9	...	2.0	...
Russia		...	1.9	...	1.5	...
Transcaucasus and central Asia	9	...	0.4	...	0.2	...

[1]The GDP shares are based on the purchasing power parity (PPP) valuation of country GDPs.

The general features and the compositions of groups in the *World Economic Outlook* classification are as follows.[4]

[4]A few countries are presently not included in the country groups listed, either because they are not IMF members, and their economies are not monitored by the IMF, or because data bases have not yet been compiled. Cuba and the Democratic People's Republic of Korea are examples of countries that are not IMF members, whereas San Marino, among the industrial countries, and Eritrea, among the developing countries, are examples of economies for which data bases have not been completed. It should also be noted that, owing to lack of data, only three of the former republics of the dissolved Socialist Federal Republic of Yugoslavia (Croatia, the for-

The group of *industrial countries* (23 countries) comprises

Australia	Greece	Norway
Austria	Iceland	Portugal
Belgium	Ireland	Spain
Canada	Italy	Sweden
Denmark	Japan	Switzerland
Finland	Luxembourg	United Kingdom
France	Netherlands	United States
Germany	New Zealand	

mer Yugoslav Republic of Macedonia, and Slovenia) are included in the group composites for countries in transition.

The seven largest countries in this group in terms of GDP—the United States, Japan, Germany, France, Italy, the United Kingdom, and Canada—are collectively referred to as the *major industrial countries.*

The current members of the *European Union* (15 countries) are also distinguished as a subgroup. They are

Austria	Germany	Netherlands
Belgium	Greece	Portugal
Denmark	Ireland	Spain
Finland	Italy	Sweden
France	Luxembourg	United Kingdom

Composite data shown in the tables under the heading "European Union" cover the current 15 members of the European Union for all years, even though the membership has changed over time.

In 1991 and subsequent years, data for *Germany* refer to west Germany *and* the eastern Länder (i.e., the former German Democratic Republic). Before 1991, economic data are not available on a unified basis or in a consistent manner. Hence, in tables featuring data expressed as annual percent change, these apply to west Germany in 1991 as well. In general, data on national accounts and domestic economic and financial activity through 1990 cover west Germany only, whereas data for the central government and balance of payments apply to west Germany through June 1990 and to unified Germany thereafter.

The group of *developing countries* (132 countries) includes all countries that are not classified as industrial countries or as countries in transition, together with a few dependent territories for which adequate statistics are available.

The *regional breakdowns* of developing countries in the *World Economic Outlook* conform to the IMF's *International Financial Statistics (IFS)* classification, with one important exception. Because all of the developing countries in Europe except Cyprus, Malta, and Turkey are included in the group of countries in transition, the *World Economic Outlook* classification places these three countries in a combined Middle East and Europe region. It should also be noted that in both classifications, Egypt and the Libyan Arab Jamahiriya are included in this region, not in Africa. Two additional regional groupings are included in the *World Economic Outlook* because of their analytical significance. These are sub-Saharan Africa[5] and four newly industrializing Asian economies.[6]

The developing countries are also grouped according to *analytical criteria*: predominant export, financial, and other groups. The first analytical criterion, by *predominant export*, distinguishes among five groups: fuel (Standard International Trade Classification— SITC 3); manufactures (SITC 5 to 9, less 68); nonfuel

primary products (SITC 0, 1, 2, 4, and 68); services, factor income, and private transfers (factor and non-factor service receipts plus workers' remittances); and diversified export base. A further distinction is made among the exporters of nonfuel primary products on the basis of whether countries' exports of primary commodities consist primarily of agricultural commodities (SITC 0, 1, 2 except 27, 28, and 4) or minerals (SITC 27, 28, and 68). The export criteria, which in the October 1995 *World Economic Outlook* were updated to correspond more closely to the World Bank classification, are based on countries' export composition in 1988–92.

The *financial* criterion first distinguishes between net creditor and net debtor countries. Countries in the latter, much larger group are then differentiated on the basis of two additional financial criteria: by predominant type of creditor and by experience with debt servicing. The financial criteria reflect net creditor and debtor positions as of 1987, sources of borrowing as of the end of 1989, and experience with debt servicing during 1986–90.

The country groups shown under *other groups* constitute the small low-income economies and the least developed countries.

The group of *countries in transition* (28 countries) comprises central and eastern European countries, Russia, non-European states of the former Soviet Union, and Mongolia. A common characteristic of these countries is the transitional state of their economies from a centrally administered system to one based on market principles. The group of countries in transition comprises

Albania	Hungary	Romania
Armenia	Kazakstan	Russia
Azerbaijan	Kyrgyz Republic	Slovak Republic
Belarus	Latvia	Slovenia
Bosnia and	Lithuania	Tajikistan
Herzegovina[7]	Macedonia, former	Turkmenistan
Bulgaria	Yugoslav Rep. of	Ukraine
Croatia	Moldova	Uzbekistan
Czech Republic	Mongolia	Yugoslavia, Fed. Rep. of
Estonia	Poland	(Serbia/Montenegro)[7]
Georgia		

The countries in transition are classified in three subgroups: *central and eastern Europe, Russia,* and *Transcaucasus and central Asia.* The Transcaucasian and central Asian countries include Kazakstan for purposes of the *World Economic Outlook.* The countries in central and eastern Europe (18 countries) are

Albania	Estonia	Poland
Belarus	Hungary	Romania
Bosnia and	Latvia	Slovak Republic
Herzegovina[7]	Lithuania	Slovenia
Bulgaria	Macedonia, former	Ukraine
Croatia	Yugoslav Rep. of	Yugoslavia, Fed. Rep. of
Czech Republic	Moldova	(Serbia/Montenegro)[7]

---

[5]Excluding Nigeria and South Africa.

[6]Hong Kong, Korea, Singapore, and Taiwan Province of China.

[7]Not included in the World Economic Outlook data base.

The countries in the Transcaucasian and central Asian group (9 countries) are

Armenia	Kazakstan	Tajikistan
Azerbaijan	Kyrgyz Republic	Turkmenistan
Georgia	Mongolia	Uzbekistan

Detailed Description of the Developing Country Classification by Analytical Group

Countries Classified by Predominant Export

Fuel exporters (15 countries) are countries whose ratio of fuel exports to total export earnings in 1988–92 exceeded 50 percent. The group comprises

Angola	Iran, Islamic Rep. of	Qatar
Algeria	Iraq	Saudi Arabia
Bahrain	Libya	Trinidad and Tobago
Congo	Nigeria	United Arab Emirates
Gabon	Oman	Venezuela

Nonfuel exporters (117 countries) are countries with total exports of goods and services including a substantial share of (a) manufactures, (b) primary products, or (c) services, factor income, and private transfers. However, those countries whose export structure is so diversified that they do not fall clearly into any one of these three groups are assigned to a fourth group, (d) diversified export base.

(a) Economies whose exports of manufactures accounted for 50 percent or more of their total export earnings in 1988–92 are included in the group of *exporters of manufactures* (7 countries). This group includes

China	Korea	Singapore
Hong Kong	Lebanon	Taiwan Province of China
Israel		

(b) The group of *exporters of primary products* (43 countries) consists of those countries whose exports of agricultural and mineral primary products (SITC 0, 1, 2, 4, and 68) accounted for at least half of their total export earnings in 1988–92. These countries are

Afghanistan,	Guyana	São Tomé and Principe
Islamic State of	Honduras	Solomon Islands
Argentina	Liberia	Somalia
Bolivia	Madagascar	St. Vincent and
Botswana	Malawi	the Grenadines
Burundi	Mali	Sudan
Chad	Mauritania	Suriname
Chile	Myanmar	Swaziland
Côte d'Ivoire	Namibia	Tanzania
Equatorial Guinea	Nicaragua	Togo
Ethiopia	Niger	Uganda
Ghana	Papua New Guinea	Vietnam
Guatemala	Paraguay	Zaïre
Guinea	Peru	Zambia
Guinea-Bissau	Rwanda	Zimbabwe

Among exporters of primary products, a further distinction is made between exporters of agricultural products and minerals. The group of *mineral exporters* (14 countries) comprises

Bolivia	Liberia	Suriname
Botswana	Mauritania	Togo
Chile	Namibia	Zaïre
Guinea	Niger	Zambia
Guyana	Peru	

All other exporters of primary products are classified as *agricultural exporters* (29 countries).

(c) The *exporters of services and recipients of factor income and private transfers* (37 countries) are defined as those countries whose average income from services, factor income, and workers' remittances accounted for half or more of total export earnings in 1988–92. This group comprises

Antigua and Barbuda	Egypt	Marshall Islands
Aruba	El Salvador	Micronesia, The
Bahamas, The	Fiji	Federated States of
Barbados	Gambia, The	Nepal
Belize	Grenada	Panama
Benin	Haiti	Seychelles
Bhutan	Jamaica	St. Kitts and Nevis
Burkina Faso	Jordan	St. Lucia
Cambodia	Kiribati	Tonga
Cape Verde	Kuwait	Vanuatu
Cyprus	Lesotho	Western Samoa
Djibouti	Maldives	Yemen, Rep. of
Dominican Rep.	Malta	

(d) *Countries with a diversified export base* (30 countries) are those whose export earnings in 1988–92 were not dominated by any one of the categories mentioned under (a) through (c) above. This group comprises

Bangladesh	Indonesia	Philippines
Brazil	Kenya	Senegal
Cameroon	Lao People's Dem. Rep.	Sierra Leone
Central African Rep.	Malaysia	South Africa
Colombia	Mauritius	Sri Lanka
Comoros	Mexico	Syrian Arab Rep.
Costa Rica	Morocco	Thailand
Dominica	Mozambique, Rep. of	Tunisia
Ecuador	Netherlands Antilles	Turkey
India	Pakistan	Uruguay

Countries Classified by Financial Criteria

Net creditor countries (7 countries) are defined as developing countries that were net external creditors in 1987 or that experienced substantial cumulated current account surpluses (excluding official transfers) between 1967 (the beginning of most balance of payments series in the World Economic Outlook data base) and 1987. The net creditor group consists of the following economies:

Kuwait	Qatar	Taiwan Province of China
Libya	Saudi Arabia	United Arab Emirates
Oman		

Net debtor countries (125 countries) are disaggregated according to two criteria: (a) predominant type of creditor and (b) experience with debt servicing.

(a) Within the classification *predominant type of creditor* (sources of borrowing), three subgroups are identified: market borrowers, official borrowers, and diversified borrowers. *Market borrowers* (23 countries) are defined as net debtor countries with more than two thirds of their total liabilities outstanding at the end of 1989 owed to commercial creditors. This group comprises

Algeria	Iran, Islamic Rep. of	Peru
Antigua and Barbuda	Israel	Singapore
Argentina	Kiribati	Suriname
Bahamas, The	Korea	Thailand
Brazil	Malaysia	Trinidad and Tobago
Chile	Mexico	Uruguay
China	Panama	Venezuela
Hong Kong	Papua New Guinea	

Official borrowers (69 countries) are defined as net debtor countries with more than two thirds of their total liabilities outstanding at the end of 1989 owed to official creditors. This group comprises

Afghanistan, Islamic State of	Ghana	Nicaragua
Aruba	Grenada	Niger
Bangladesh	Guinea	Nigeria
Belize	Guinea-Bissau	Pakistan
Bhutan	Guyana	Rwanda
Bolivia	Haiti	São Tomé and Principe
Botswana	Honduras	Somalia
Burkina Faso	Jamaica	St. Kitts and Nevis
Burundi	Lao People's Dem. Rep.	St. Lucia
Cambodia	Lesotho	St. Vincent and the Grenadines
Cameroon	Madagascar	Sudan
Cape Verde	Malawi	Swaziland
Central African Rep.	Maldives	Tanzania
Chad	Mali	Togo
Comoros	Malta	Tonga
Djibouti	Mauritania	Tunisia
Dominica	Mauritius	Uganda
Dominican Rep.	Morocco	Vietnam
Egypt	Mozambique, Rep. of	Western Samoa
El Salvador	Myanmar	Yemen, Rep. of
Equatorial Guinea	Namibia	Zaïre
Ethiopia	Nepal	Zambia
Gabon	Netherlands Antilles	
Gambia, The		

Diversified borrowers (33 countries) consist of those net debtor developing countries that are classified neither as market nor as official borrowers.

(b) Within the classification *experience with debt servicing*, a further distinction is made. *Countries with recent debt-servicing* difficulties (71 countries) are defined as those countries that incurred external pay-

ments arrears or entered into official or commercial bank debt-rescheduling agreements during 1986–90. Information on these developments is taken from relevant issues of the IMF's *Annual Report on Exchange Arrangements and Exchange Restrictions*.

All other net debtor countries are classified as *countries without debt-servicing difficulties* (54 countries).

Other Groups

The countries classified by the World Bank as *small low-income economies* (50 countries) are those whose GNP per capita (as estimated by the World Bank) did not exceed the equivalent of $695 in 1993. This group comprises

Afghanistan, Islamic State of	Guinea-Bissau	Nigeria
Bangladesh	Guyana	Pakistan
Benin	Haiti	Rwanda
Bhutan	Honduras	São Tomé and Principe
Burkina Faso	Kenya	Sierra Leone
Burundi	Lao People's Dem. Rep.	Somalia
Cambodia	Lesotho	Sri Lanka
Central African Rep.	Liberia	Sudan
Chad	Madagascar	Tanzania
Comoros	Malawi	Togo
Côte d'Ivoire	Mali	Uganda
Egypt	Mauritania	Vietnam
Equatorial Guinea	Mozambique, Rep. of	Yemen, Rep. of
Ethiopia	Myanmar	Zaïre
Gambia, The	Nepal	Zambia
Ghana	Nicaragua	Zimbabwe
Guinea	Niger	

The countries currently classified by the United Nations as the *least developed countries* (46 countries) are[8]

Afghanistan, Islamic State of	Gambia, The	Niger
Bangladesh	Guinea	Rwanda
Benin	Guinea-Bissau	São Tomé and Principe
Bhutan	Haiti	Sierra Leone
Botswana	Kiribati	Solomon Islands
Burkina Faso	Lao People's Dem. Rep.	Somalia
Burundi	Lesotho	Sudan
Cambodia	Liberia	Tanzania
Cape Verde	Madagascar	Togo
Central African Rep.	Malawi	Uganda
Chad	Maldives	Vanuatu
Comoros	Mali	Western Samoa
Djibouti	Mauritania	Yemen, Rep. of
Equatorial Guinea	Mozambique, Rep. of	Zaïre
Ethiopia	Myanmar	Zambia
	Nepal	

---

[8]The United Nations classification also covers Tuvalu, which is not included in the *World Economic Outlook* classification.

List of Tables

Balance of Payments and External Financing

External Debt and Debt Service

Flow of Funds

Medium-Term Baseline Scenario

Table A1. Summary of World Output[1]

(Annual percent change)

	Average 1978–87	1988	1989	1990	1991	1992	1993	1994	1995	1996	1997
World	**3.3**	**4.6**	**3.7**	**2.6**	**1.5**	**2.4**	**2.4**	**3.7**	**3.5**	**3.8**	**4.3**
Industrial countries	**2.7**	**4.3**	**3.6**	**2.5**	**0.8**	**1.7**	**0.8**	**2.8**	**2.1**	**2.0**	**2.6**
United States	2.7	3.8	3.4	1.3	−1.0	2.7	2.2	3.5	2.0	1.8	2.2
European Union	2.1	4.2	3.5	3.0	1.6	1.1	−0.5	2.8	2.6	1.8	2.7
Japan	3.7	6.2	4.8	5.1	4.0	1.1	0.1	0.5	0.9	2.7	3.1
Other industrial countries	2.9	3.9	3.1	1.0	−1.1	0.7	1.4	4.1	2.6	2.3	2.6
Developing countries	**4.5**	**5.3**	**4.3**	**4.3**	**5.2**	**6.3**	**6.2**	**6.4**	**5.9**	**6.3**	**6.4**
By region											
Africa	2.1	3.6	3.4	2.1	1.7	0.7	0.7	2.4	3.2	5.3	4.5
Asia	6.8	9.1	6.1	5.9	7.1	8.7	8.9	8.8	8.4	8.2	7.7
Middle East and Europe	2.4	—	3.2	5.3	3.2	6.2	3.7	0.7	3.7	3.1	3.8
Western Hemisphere	3.1	1.1	1.6	1.1	3.3	2.9	3.1	4.7	0.9	3.1	4.8
By analytical criteria											
Fuel exporters	0.8	−0.2	3.3	5.5	4.7	4.5	0.5	0.2	2.2	2.4	3.5
Nonfuel exporters	5.2	6.0	4.5	4.1	5.2	6.6	6.9	7.0	6.2	6.7	6.7
Net creditor countries	2.4	4.8	6.8	5.6	6.6	7.5	4.4	2.9	3.0	3.1	3.7
Net debtor countries	4.6	5.3	4.2	4.2	5.1	6.3	6.3	6.6	6.0	6.5	6.6
Market borrowers	5.2	5.5	3.7	3.9	6.6	8.1	7.8	8.1	6.3	7.0	7.2
Official borrowers	3.5	3.7	3.7	3.5	3.9	2.8	2.3	3.4	4.2	5.5	5.1
Countries with recent debt-servicing difficulties	3.0	1.9	2.1	0.8	2.4	2.3	2.5	4.3	1.6	3.7	4.9
Countries without debt-servicing difficulties	5.9	7.5	5.5	6.1	6.5	8.3	8.2	7.7	8.0	7.7	7.3
Countries in transition	**3.0**	**4.2**	**2.1**	**−3.7**	**−11.5**	**−14.7**	**−8.5**	**−8.8**	**−1.3**	**2.5**	**3.8**
Central and eastern Europe	...	...	...	...	−10.8	−10.0	−5.0	−2.9	1.4	3.0	4.2
Excluding Belarus and Ukraine	...	...	...	...	−11.6	−7.0	−0.1	3.4	5.2	4.5	4.6
Russia, Transcaucasus, and central Asia	...	...	...	...	−12.0	−18.7	−11.7	−14.8	−4.3	1.9	3.3
Memorandum											
Median growth rate											
Industrial countries	2.6	4.1	3.8	2.1	1.3	1.1	0.2	2.9	2.4	2.3	2.7
Developing countries	3.5	3.6	4.0	3.2	3.0	3.5	3.4	3.6	4.1	4.5	4.7
Countries in transition	3.4	5.3	3.0	−2.3	−12.1	−13.9	−8.4	1.1	1.6	3.9	4.5
Output per capita											
Industrial countries	2.0	3.7	2.9	1.7	—	1.0	0.2	2.2	1.5	1.4	2.0
Developing countries	2.0	3.1	2.2	2.4	3.2	3.9	4.3	4.3	4.1	4.6	4.7
Countries in transition	2.3	3.6	1.6	−4.3	−11.5	−14.9	−8.6	−8.8	−1.3	2.5	3.7
Value of world output in billions of U.S. dollars											
At market exchange rates	12,396	19,155	20,020	22,223	23,318	23,542	24,193	26,058	28,872	29,852	31,668
At purchasing power parities	15,020	22,019	23,847	25,542	26,941	28,313	29,572	31,207	32,910	34,929	37,530

[1]Real GDP.

Table A2. Industrial Countries: Real GDP and Total Domestic Demand
(Annual percent change)

	Average 1978–87	1988	1989	1990	1991	1992	1993	1994	1995	1996	1997	Fourth Quarter[1] 1995	1996	1997
Real GDP														
Industrial countries	**2.7**	**4.3**	**3.6**	**2.5**	**0.8**	**1.7**	**0.8**	**2.8**	**2.1**	**2.0**	**2.6**	...	...	...
Major industrial countries	2.7	4.4	3.6	2.5	0.8	1.8	1.0	2.8	2.0	1.9	2.6	1.5	2.3	2.6
United States	2.7	3.8	3.4	1.3	−1.0	2.7	2.2	3.5	2.0	1.8	2.2	1.3	2.0	2.2
Japan	3.7	6.2	4.8	5.1	4.0	1.1	0.1	0.5	0.9	2.7	3.1	2.2	2.7	3.4
Germany[2]	1.8	3.7	3.6	5.7	5.0	2.2	−1.2	2.9	1.9	1.0	2.9	1.0	2.0	2.7
France	2.1	4.4	4.3	2.5	0.8	1.3	−1.5	2.9	2.4	1.3	2.8	0.7	2.3	3.0
Italy	2.7	4.1	2.9	2.1	1.2	0.7	−1.2	2.2	3.2	2.4	2.7	2.1	3.0	2.3
United Kingdom[3]	2.3	5.0	2.2	0.4	−2.0	−0.5	2.3	3.8	2.4	2.2	2.7	1.9	2.5	2.7
Canada	3.2	5.0	2.4	−0.2	−1.8	0.8	2.2	4.6	2.2	1.9	2.9	0.6	2.8	2.8
Other industrial countries	2.3	3.8	3.9	2.7	1.0	1.1	0.1	3.0	2.8	2.4	2.6	...	...	...
Spain	1.9	5.2	4.7	3.6	2.2	0.9	−1.2	2.0	3.0	2.7	2.9	...	...	...
Netherlands	1.6	2.6	4.7	4.1	2.3	2.0	0.2	2.7	2.4	1.7	2.7	...	...	...
Belgium	1.3	4.9	3.4	3.4	2.2	1.8	−1.6	2.2	1.9	1.4	2.5	...	...	...
Sweden	2.2	2.1	2.5	1.1	−1.4	−1.4	−2.6	2.2	3.2	2.2	2.0	...	...	...
Austria	1.7	4.1	3.8	4.2	2.9	2.0	0.4	3.0	2.1	1.3	1.4	...	...	...
Denmark	2.2	1.2	0.6	1.4	1.3	0.2	1.5	4.4	2.9	1.9	2.2	...	...	...
Finland	3.6	4.9	5.7	—	−7.1	−3.6	−1.2	4.4	4.2	2.8	2.5	...	...	...
Greece[4]	1.9	4.5	4.0	−1.0	3.2	0.8	−0.5	1.5	2.0	2.3	2.5	...	...	...
Portugal	2.8	4.0	5.7	4.1	2.3	1.7	−1.2	1.0	2.4	2.6	2.8	...	...	...
Ireland	3.4	4.3	6.1	7.8	2.2	3.9	3.1	6.7	7.4	5.9	4.3	...	...	...
Luxembourg	3.7	10.2	9.9	3.4	5.4	5.8	8.5	4.1	3.5	3.0	3.5	...	...	...
Switzerland	1.9	2.9	3.9	2.3	—	−0.3	−0.8	1.2	0.7	0.9	2.0	...	...	...
Norway	3.7	−0.5	0.3	1.6	2.9	3.3	2.1	5.7	3.7	4.3	2.0	...	...	...
Iceland	4.2	−0.1	0.3	1.1	1.3	−3.3	1.1	2.8	2.6	3.2	2.6	...	...	...
Australia	3.3	4.1	4.4	1.3	−1.2	2.2	3.3	5.5	3.5	3.4	3.1	...	...	...
New Zealand	2.0	3.9	−1.4	0.1	−3.7	0.3	5.5	3.8	3.2	3.5	4.4	...	...	...
Memorandum														
European Union	2.1	4.2	3.5	3.0	1.6	1.1	−0.5	2.8	2.6	1.8	2.7	...	...	...
Real total domestic demand														
Industrial countries	**2.6**	**4.5**	**3.7**	**2.3**	**0.3**	**1.6**	**0.6**	**3.0**	**2.1**	**2.0**	**2.5**	...	...	...
Major industrial countries	2.8	4.5	3.4	2.2	0.2	1.8	0.9	3.0	1.9	1.9	2.5	1.3	2.3	2.6
United States	2.8	2.9	2.7	0.9	−1.6	2.8	2.9	3.9	2.1	1.6	2.2	1.1	2.1	2.2
Japan	3.5	7.4	5.6	5.2	2.9	0.4	0.1	0.8	1.6	3.5	2.9	3.6	2.7	3.3
Germany	1.6	3.6	2.9	5.2	4.8	2.8	−1.3	2.8	1.7	0.5	2.9	−0.1	2.0	3.0
France	2.1	4.6	3.9	2.8	0.6	0.4	−2.3	3.2	2.0	1.8	2.8	0.6	2.5	3.2
Italy	2.8	4.4	2.8	2.5	1.9	0.8	−5.5	1.9	2.2	2.1	2.7	0.7	2.4	2.0
United Kingdom	2.6	7.9	2.9	−0.6	−3.1	0.2	2.1	3.1	1.5	2.1	2.3	1.2	1.8	2.5
Canada	3.1	5.5	4.3	−0.5	−1.2	0.4	2.0	3.2	1.1	1.1	2.6	−0.2	2.6	2.6
Other industrial countries	2.0	4.5	5.0	2.5	0.6	0.9	−1.4	3.1	3.2	2.5	2.7	...	...	...
Memorandum														
European Union	2.1	5.0	3.7	2.9	1.4	1.1	−1.9	2.6	2.1	1.8	2.7	...	...	...

[1]From fourth quarter of preceding year.
[2]Data through 1991 apply to west Germany only.
[3]Average of expenditure, income, and output estimates of GDP at market prices.
[4]Based on revised national accounts for 1988 onward.

Table A3. Industrial Countries: Components of Real GDP

(Annual percent change)

	Average 1978–87	1988	1989	1990	1991	1992	1993	1994	1995	1996	1997
Private consumer expenditure											
Industrial countries	**2.8**	**4.1**	**3.2**	**2.6**	**1.0**	**2.1**	**1.4**	**2.3**	**2.1**	**2.0**	**2.5**
Major industrial countries	3.0	4.3	3.1	2.6	0.9	2.1	1.6	2.3	2.0	2.0	2.5
United States	3.1	3.9	2.3	1.7	−0.6	2.8	2.8	3.0	2.4	2.0	2.3
Japan	3.6	5.3	4.8	4.4	2.5	2.1	1.2	1.8	1.6	2.3	2.8
Germany[1]	1.8	2.7	2.8	5.4	5.6	2.8	0.5	0.9	1.7	1.8	2.8
France	2.5	3.3	3.0	2.7	1.4	1.4	0.2	1.5	2.0	1.1	2.7
Italy	3.2	4.2	3.5	2.5	2.7	1.1	−2.5	1.6	1.3	1.9	2.9
United Kingdom	3.3	7.5	3.2	0.6	−2.2	−0.1	2.6	2.8	2.3	2.6	2.5
Canada	3.0	4.5	3.4	1.0	−1.6	1.3	1.6	3.0	1.4	1.7	2.5
Other industrial countries	1.9	3.2	3.8	2.6	2.0	1.8	−0.2	2.2	2.3	2.4	2.5
Memorandum											
European Union	2.4	4.1	3.3	3.0	2.3	1.5	−0.1	1.6	1.9	1.9	2.6
Public consumption											
Industrial countries	**2.5**	**2.2**	**2.0**	**2.3**	**1.7**	**1.3**	**0.7**	**0.8**	**0.6**	**0.5**	**0.9**
Major industrial countries	2.5	2.2	1.8	2.1	1.5	1.2	0.7	0.7	0.6	0.4	1.0
United States	2.5	2.0	2.7	2.3	1.0	−0.1	−0.1	0.2	−0.3	−0.3	0.6
Japan	3.2	2.3	2.0	1.5	2.0	2.0	2.4	2.2	2.0	0.9	2.4
Germany[1]	1.9	2.1	−1.6	2.2	0.5	5.0	−0.5	0.7	2.1	2.0	1.8
France	2.7	3.5	0.4	2.1	2.8	3.4	3.3	1.1	2.2	1.7	1.0
Italy	2.9	2.8	0.8	1.2	1.6	1.0	0.7	—	−0.8	1.2	−0.9
United Kingdom	1.2	0.7	1.4	2.5	2.6	−0.1	0.3	1.9	0.6	0.6	0.4
Canada	1.9	4.1	4.0	3.2	2.7	1.0	0.5	−1.7	−0.9	−2.0	0.6
Other industrial countries	2.9	2.1	3.3	3.1	3.0	1.7	0.7	1.4	0.8	1.1	0.7
Memorandum											
European Union	2.4	2.1	1.1	2.2	2.1	2.4	0.9	0.9	1.0	1.4	0.7
Gross fixed capital formation											
Industrial countries	**2.7**	**6.3**	**5.2**	**2.0**	**−2.5**	**1.2**	**−0.7**	**4.5**	**3.8**	**3.8**	**3.8**
Major industrial countries	2.8	5.9	4.6	1.9	−2.5	1.9	—	4.5	3.4	3.5	3.7
United States	3.0	1.5	2.0	−1.4	−6.6	5.2	5.1	7.9	5.3	3.3	3.3
Japan	3.7	11.5	8.2	8.5	3.3	−1.5	−2.0	−1.0	0.8	6.6	3.2
Germany[1]	1.0	4.4	6.3	8.5	6.0	3.5	−5.6	4.3	1.5	−0.6	3.5
France	1.1	9.6	7.9	2.8	—	−3.1	−5.8	1.7	2.5	2.5	4.6
Italy	1.8	6.9	4.3	3.8	0.6	−1.7	−13.1	−0.1	6.8	3.5	5.0
United Kingdom	2.6	14.0	6.0	−3.5	−9.5	−1.5	0.6	3.2	−0.8	3.3	4.1
Canada	4.8	10.3	6.1	−3.5	−2.9	−1.5	0.6	7.2	0.2	5.6	5.7
Other industrial countries	1.8	8.7	8.7	2.5	−2.8	−2.5	−5.1	4.3	6.5	5.5	4.7
Memorandum											
European Union	1.5	8.8	7.1	3.8	−0.4	−1.1	−6.5	2.3	3.7	3.0	4.4

117

Table A3 (concluded)

	Average 1978–87	1988	1989	1990	1991	1992	1993	1994	1995	1996	1997
Final domestic demand											
Industrial countries	**2.7**	**4.4**	**3.5**	**2.5**	**0.5**	**1.7**	**0.7**	**2.4**	**2.1**	**2.2**	**2.5**
Major industrial countries	2.8	4.4	3.3	2.5	0.4	1.8	1.0	2.3	2.0	2.1	2.5
United States	3.0	3.2	2.4	1.3	−1.4	2.7	2.7	3.3	2.5	1.9	2.2
Japan	3.6	6.8	5.5	5.4	2.7	0.9	0.3	1.0	1.4	3.5	2.9
Germany[1]	1.7	3.0	2.6	5.4	4.7	3.4	−1.1	1.6	1.7	1.3	2.8
France	2.2	4.6	3.6	2.6	1.3	0.8	−0.5	1.5	2.2	1.5	2.8
Italy	2.9	4.5	3.3	2.6	2.1	0.5	−4.2	1.0	2.0	2.1	2.7
United Kingdom	2.7	7.2	3.4	0.2	−2.6	−0.3	1.8	2.7	1.4	2.3	2.4
Canada	3.1	5.6	4.1	0.4	−1.0	0.6	1.1	2.9	0.7	1.8	2.9
Other industrial countries	2.0	4.2	4.8	2.6	1.1	0.8	−1.1	2.5	2.9	2.8	2.6
Memorandum											
European Union	2.1	4.6	3.7	3.0	1.7	1.1	−1.3	1.6	2.1	2.0	2.6
Stock building[2]											
Industrial countries	**−0.1**	**0.1**	**0.2**	**−0.3**	**−0.2**	**—**	**−0.2**	**0.6**	**−0.1**	**−0.2**	**—**
Major industrial countries	−0.1	0.1	0.2	−0.3	−0.2	—	−0.1	0.6	−0.1	−0.2	—
United States	−0.1	−0.2	0.4	−0.4	−0.2	0.2	0.2	0.6	−0.4	−0.3	—
Japan	—	0.6	0.1	−0.2	0.2	−0.4	−0.1	−0.2	0.2	—	—
Germany[1]	−0.1	0.6	0.3	−0.1	0.1	−0.6	−0.2	1.2	—	−0.7	0.1
France	—	—	0.4	0.2	−0.7	−0.4	−1.8	1.7	−0.2	0.3	0.1
Italy	−0.1	—	−0.4	—	−0.1	0.3	−1.4	0.8	0.2	—	—
United Kingdom	−0.1	0.7	−0.4	−0.8	−0.5	0.5	0.4	0.4	0.2	−0.2	—
Canada	—	−0.1	0.2	−1.0	−0.1	−0.2	0.9	0.3	0.4	−0.7	−0.3
Other industrial countries	—	0.3	0.3	−0.1	−0.5	0.1	−0.3	0.6	0.3	−0.3	—
Memorandum											
European Union	−0.1	0.4	—	−0.1	−0.3	—	−0.7	0.9	0.1	−0.2	—
Foreign balance[2]											
Industrial countries	**—**	**−0.2**	**−0.2**	**0.2**	**0.5**	**0.1**	**0.3**	**−0.2**	**—**	**—**	**0.1**
Major industrial countries	−0.1	−0.2	—	0.2	0.5	—	0.1	−0.2	0.1	—	0.1
United States	−0.2	0.7	0.5	0.3	0.7	−0.1	−0.7	−0.5	−0.1	0.2	—
Japan	0.3	−1.0	−0.7	—	1.0	0.6	—	−0.3	−0.7	−0.8	0.2
Germany[1]	0.2	0.3	0.9	0.7	0.5	−0.6	0.2	0.1	0.3	0.4	—
France	−0.1	−0.3	0.3	−0.3	0.2	1.0	0.8	−0.3	0.4	−0.5	−0.1
Italy	−0.3	−0.5	—	−0.5	−0.8	−0.1	4.6	0.3	1.0	0.4	0.1
United Kingdom	−0.3	−2.9	−0.8	1.0	1.3	−0.7	0.1	0.9	0.7	0.1	0.3
Canada	—	−1.2	−1.6	0.6	−0.6	0.5	0.3	1.1	1.0	0.9	0.3
Other industrial countries	0.2	−0.6	−1.3	0.2	0.5	0.2	1.5	−0.1	−0.4	—	0.1
Memorandum											
European Union	—	−0.8	−0.3	—	—	−0.1	1.4	0.3	0.4	—	0.1

[1]Data through 1991 apply to west Germany only.
[2]Changes expressed as percent of GDP in the preceding period.

Table A4. Industrial Countries: Unemployment, Employment, and Real Per Capita GDP

(In percent)

	Average[1] 1978–87	1988	1989	1990	1991	1992	1993	1994	1995	1996	1997
Unemployment rate											
Industrial countries	**6.9**	**6.9**	**6.3**	**6.2**	**6.9**	**7.8**	**8.2**	**8.1**	**7.7**	**7.8**	**7.6**
Major industrial countries	6.6	6.3	5.8	5.7	6.5	7.2	7.3	7.2	6.9	7.0	6.9
United States[2]	7.4	5.5	5.3	5.6	6.9	7.5	6.9	6.1	5.6	5.8	5.9
Japan	2.4	2.5	2.3	2.1	2.1	2.2	2.5	2.9	3.1	3.3	3.2
Germany[3]	6.2	7.8	6.8	6.2	5.5	7.7	8.9	9.6	9.4	10.5	10.1
France	8.2	10.0	9.4	8.9	9.4	10.3	11.6	12.4	11.6	11.7	11.2
Italy[4]	8.8	12.0	12.0	11.0	10.9	10.7	10.2	11.3	12.0	11.5	10.8
United Kingdom	8.4	8.0	6.2	5.8	8.0	9.7	10.3	9.3	8.2	7.9	7.7
Canada	9.4	7.8	7.5	8.1	10.4	11.3	11.2	10.4	9.5	9.6	9.2
Other industrial countries	8.5	9.5	8.5	8.2	9.0	10.3	12.3	12.7	11.9	11.4	11.0
Spain	16.0	19.5	17.3	16.3	16.3	18.4	22.7	24.2	22.9	22.0	21.2
Netherlands	6.9	8.4	7.7	7.0	6.6	6.6	7.7	8.7	8.4	8.2	7.9
Belgium	10.5	10.3	9.3	8.7	9.3	10.3	12.0	13.0	13.0	13.1	12.8
Sweden	2.6	1.6	1.4	1.5	2.9	5.3	8.2	8.0	7.5	6.4	6.2
Austria	3.6	5.3	3.1	3.2	3.5	3.6	4.2	4.4	4.6	4.7	5.5
Denmark	8.5	8.6	9.3	9.6	10.5	11.2	12.3	12.1	10.0	9.5	9.5
Finland	5.4	4.5	3.5	3.5	7.6	13.1	17.9	18.4	17.2	16.0	15.0
Greece	6.8	7.7	7.5	7.0	7.7	8.7	9.7	9.6	9.5	9.4	9.2
Portugal	8.2	7.0	5.8	4.7	4.1	4.1	5.5	6.8	7.2	6.9	6.5
Ireland	12.4	16.7	15.6	13.4	15.5	16.2	16.6	15.3	13.2	12.6	12.0
Luxembourg	1.3	1.5	1.4	1.3	1.4	1.6	2.1	2.7	2.8	2.8	2.8
Switzerland	0.6	0.6	0.5	0.5	1.1	2.5	4.5	4.7	4.2	4.3	4.2
Norway	2.3	3.2	4.9	5.2	5.5	5.9	5.9	5.4	5.0	4.5	4.3
Iceland	0.6	0.6	1.7	1.8	1.5	3.0	4.4	4.8	5.0	4.4	4.2
Australia	7.5	7.2	6.2	7.0	9.6	10.8	10.9	9.7	8.5	7.8	7.5
New Zealand	4.4	6.8	7.3	9.2	10.3	10.3	9.5	8.1	6.4	6.1	5.4
Memorandum											
European Union	8.4	9.8	8.8	8.2	8.7	9.9	11.1	11.6	11.2	11.2	10.8
Growth in employment											
Industrial countries	**1.1**	**2.0**	**1.9**	**1.5**	**−0.2**	**−0.2**	**−0.2**	**0.8**	**1.0**	**0.5**	**1.0**
Major industrial countries	1.2	2.0	1.8	1.4	−0.1	−0.1	0.2	0.9	0.8	0.3	0.9
United States	2.0	2.3	2.0	1.3	−0.9	0.7	1.5	2.3	1.5	0.6	1.1
Japan	1.0	1.7	1.9	2.0	1.9	1.1	0.2	0.1	0.1	0.3	1.0
Germany[3]	0.4	0.8	1.4	2.6	1.7	−1.9	−1.8	−0.7	−0.3	−1.5	—
France	−0.1	0.9	1.5	1.1	0.2	−0.6	−1.0	0.1	1.5	0.5	1.1
Italy	0.4	0.5	−0.1	1.2	0.8	−0.9	−2.5	−1.7	−0.5	0.7	1.0
United Kingdom	0.1	4.2	2.7	0.4	−3.1	−2.4	−0.8	0.7	0.6	0.5	0.7
Canada	2.2	3.2	2.1	0.6	−1.9	−0.6	1.4	2.1	1.6	1.3	1.9
Other industrial countries	0.4	1.8	2.2	1.8	−0.4	−0.8	−1.7	0.4	1.9	1.5	1.4
Memorandum											
European Union	0.2	1.7	1.7	1.5	−0.1	−1.3	−1.8	−0.3	0.7	0.3	0.8

Table A4 *(concluded)*

	Average[1] 1978–87	1988	1989	1990	1991	1992	1993	1994	1995	1996	1997
Growth in real per capita GDP											
Industrial countries	**2.0**	**3.7**	**2.9**	**1.7**	**—**	**1.0**	**0.2**	**2.2**	**1.5**	**1.4**	**2.0**
Major industrial countries	2.1	3.7	2.8	1.6	—	1.1	0.3	2.2	1.3	1.3	2.0
United States	1.7	2.9	2.4	0.3	−2.0	1.6	1.1	2.4	1.0	0.8	1.3
Japan	3.0	5.7	4.4	4.7	3.6	0.7	−0.1	0.3	0.6	2.5	2.8
Germany[3]	1.8	3.1	2.6	3.8	4.2	1.4	−1.8	2.6	1.6	0.7	2.9
France	1.6	4.0	3.8	2.0	0.4	0.9	−1.9	2.4	2.0	0.9	2.4
Italy	2.6	3.9	2.8	2.0	0.9	1.1	0.2	2.0	3.2	2.4	2.7
United Kingdom	2.2	4.8	1.9	0.1	−2.6	−0.9	2.0	3.5	2.1	1.9	2.4
Canada	2.1	3.6	0.7	−1.7	−3.0	−0.4	1.1	3.5	1.1	0.8	1.8
Other industrial countries	1.7	3.4	3.4	2.1	0.3	0.7	−0.5	2.6	2.3	1.9	2.1
Memorandum											
European Union	1.9	3.9	3.1	2.3	1.0	0.8	−0.7	2.5	2.2	1.5	2.5

[1]Compound annual rate of change for employment and per capita GDP; arithmetic average for unemployment rate.

[2]The projections for unemployment have been adjusted to reflect the new survey techniques adopted by the U.S. Bureau of Labor Statistics in January 1994.

[3]Data through 1991 apply to west Germany only.

[4]New series starting in 1993, reflecting revisions in the labor force surveys and the definition of unemployment to bring data in line with those of other industrial countries.

Table A5. Developing Countries: Real GDP

(Annual percent change)

	Average 1978–87	1988	1989	1990	1991	1992	1993	1994	1995	1996	1997
Developing countries	**4.5**	**5.3**	**4.3**	**4.3**	**5.2**	**6.3**	**6.2**	**6.4**	**5.9**	**6.3**	**6.4**
By region											
Africa	2.1	3.6	3.4	2.1	1.7	0.7	0.7	2.4	3.2	5.3	4.5
Asia	6.8	9.1	6.1	5.9	7.1	8.7	8.9	8.8	8.4	8.2	7.7
Middle East and Europe	2.4	—	3.2	5.3	3.2	6.2	3.7	0.7	3.7	3.1	3.8
Western Hemisphere	3.1	1.1	1.6	1.1	3.3	2.9	3.1	4.7	0.9	3.1	4.8
Sub-Saharan Africa	2.9	2.7	2.4	1.2	1.5	1.0	1.2	1.7	4.8	5.4	5.2
Four newly industrializing Asian economies	8.1	9.5	6.3	7.1	8.4	5.7	6.3	7.4	7.6	6.8	6.7
By predominant export											
Fuel	0.8	−0.2	3.3	5.5	4.7	4.5	0.5	0.2	2.2	2.4	3.5
Nonfuel exports	5.2	6.0	4.5	4.1	5.2	6.6	6.9	7.0	6.2	6.7	6.7
Manufactures	8.8	10.5	4.5	4.7	9.1	11.8	11.5	10.6	9.5	9.2	8.4
Primary products	1.8	0.3	−0.1	0.7	4.6	5.0	4.0	5.0	3.8	4.6	5.5
Agricultural products	1.4	0.2	−0.4	1.0	4.8	5.5	3.9	4.3	2.3	4.4	5.4
Minerals	2.7	0.5	0.6	0.1	4.0	3.9	4.3	6.3	6.7	5.0	5.6
Services, income, and private transfers	4.2	1.9	4.9	0.1	0.5	7.3	5.1	2.8	3.4	4.1	4.5
Diversified export base	4.3	4.8	5.1	4.6	3.5	3.5	4.4	5.2	4.4	5.4	5.7
By financial criteria											
Net creditor countries	2.4	4.8	6.8	5.6	6.6	7.5	4.4	2.9	3.0	3.1	3.7
Net debtor countries	4.6	5.3	4.2	4.2	5.1	6.3	6.3	6.6	6.0	6.5	6.6
Market borrowers	5.2	5.5	3.7	3.9	6.6	8.1	7.8	8.1	6.3	7.0	7.2
Diversified borrowers	4.1	5.7	5.5	5.0	2.5	4.1	5.0	4.7	6.2	5.7	5.8
Official borrowers	3.5	3.7	3.7	3.5	3.9	2.8	2.3	3.4	4.2	5.5	5.1
Countries with recent debt-servicing difficulties	3.0	1.9	2.1	0.8	2.4	2.3	2.5	4.3	1.6	3.7	4.9
Countries without debt-servicing difficulties	5.9	7.5	5.5	6.1	6.5	8.3	8.2	7.7	8.0	7.7	7.3
Other groups											
Small low-income economies	3.5	3.9	3.8	3.7	3.8	2.8	2.7	3.0	4.9	5.3	5.3
Least developed countries	2.8	2.2	3.1	2.4	2.3	3.1	3.0	2.5	6.0	5.2	5.2
Memorandum											
Real per capita GDP											
Developing countries	2.0	3.1	2.2	2.4	3.2	3.9	4.3	4.3	4.1	4.6	4.7
By region											
Africa	−0.7	0.9	0.6	−0.7	−1.0	−1.9	−1.9	−0.2	0.6	2.7	1.9
Asia	4.7	7.2	4.3	4.2	5.3	7.0	7.2	6.9	7.0	6.7	6.3
Middle East and Europe	−1.1	−3.3	0.9	3.3	1.2	−0.2	1.2	−2.1	1.0	0.5	1.3
Western Hemisphere	0.8	−0.7	−0.8	−0.9	1.3	0.9	1.2	2.9	−0.8	1.4	3.0

Table A6. Developing Countries—by Country: Real GDP[1]

(Annual percent change)

	Average 1978–87	1988	1989	1990	1991	1992	1993	1994	1995
Africa	**2.1**	**3.6**	**3.4**	**2.1**	**1.7**	**0.7**	**0.7**	**2.4**	**3.2**
Algeria	1.7	−1.9	4.8	—	−1.3	1.6	−2.2	−0.9	3.9
Angola	. . .	−8.4	4.4	−5.3	−1.6	1.3	−23.8	2.7	9.2
Benin	3.2	3.5	−2.5	3.1	4.7	4.1	3.2	3.6	5.8
Botswana	11.0	14.1	9.2	7.3	7.6	2.3	0.4	2.8	4.4
Burkina Faso	3.6	6.6	0.9	−1.5	10.0	2.5	−0.8	1.2	4.5
Burundi	3.0	5.0	1.3	3.5	5.0	2.7	−5.7	−6.7	6.6
Cameroon	7.4	−12.9	−3.5	−4.5	−6.4	−3.3	−3.3	−3.7	3.1
Cape Verde	5.9	7.6	6.9	2.4	1.0	2.9	4.3	4.5	4.7
Central African Republic	0.9	1.3	3.4	−1.0	−0.6	−2.5	−2.2	7.4	3.5
Chad	0.6	13.8	5.8	−2.3	13.2	8.1	−12.0	4.1	5.4
Comoros	4.3	2.7	−3.2	2.5	2.1	1.6	1.3	0.8	2.2
Congo	7.7	1.8	2.9	0.7	2.2	2.4	−1.2	−6.7	0.9
Côte d'Ivoire	2.4	1.1	3.0	−1.1	—	−0.2	−0.2	1.8	6.5
Djibouti	1.8	1.2	−2.6	−0.6	1.3	2.4	−2.3	−4.5	−1.0
Equatorial Guinea	1.2	2.7	−1.2	3.3	−1.1	14.0	7.1	6.8	10.7
Ethiopia	2.5	2.4	1.2	−2.2	−1.0	−3.2	−12.3	1.3	5.5
Gabon	−3.9	3.5	5.0	5.4	5.0	0.7	3.2	1.7	2.8
Gambia, The	2.5	1.7	4.3	5.7	2.2	4.4	1.8	1.3	−4.0
Ghana	1.4	5.6	5.1	3.3	5.3	3.9	5.0	3.8	4.5
Guinea	2.4	6.3	4.0	4.3	2.4	3.0	4.7	4.0	4.6
Guinea-Bissau	7.9	6.9	4.5	3.2	3.0	2.8	2.7	5.9	3.6
Kenya	4.7	6.0	4.6	4.8	1.2	−0.8	0.3	3.9	5.0
Lesotho	3.8	8.8	11.7	5.3	1.9	3.3	8.5	13.5	7.4
Liberia	0.7	3.1	−10.8	0.3	2.9	1.9	2.2	2.2	2.7
Madagascar	0.2	3.4	4.1	3.1	−6.3	1.1	2.1	0.2	3.4
Malawi	2.6	3.3	4.1	4.8	7.8	−7.9	10.8	−12.4	9.9
Mali	1.6	−0.2	11.8	0.4	−0.9	8.4	−2.4	2.3	6.0
Mauritania	4.9	3.1	4.8	−1.8	2.6	1.7	4.9	4.6	4.3
Mauritius	4.1	8.7	5.7	4.7	6.3	4.7	6.7	4.7	4.1
Morocco	3.3	10.4	2.5	3.9	6.9	−4.1	−1.1	11.5	−6.0
Mozambique, Rep. of	−0.9	8.2	6.5	0.9	4.9	−0.8	19.3	5.4	4.3
Namibia	. . .	0.2	2.1	0.3	6.6	7.5	−1.9	5.4	1.7
Niger	1.4	6.9	0.9	−1.3	2.5	−6.5	1.4	4.0	3.0
Nigeria	−0.6	9.9	7.2	8.2	4.8	2.9	2.3	1.3	2.9
Rwanda	4.3	0.3	−5.7	0.4	0.3	0.4	−10.9	−56.0	46.2
São Tomé and Principe	−1.8	2.0	3.1	−2.2	1.5	1.5	1.3	1.5	2.5
Senegal	2.3	5.1	−1.4	4.5	−0.7	2.8	−2.1	2.0	4.5
Seychelles	3.2	5.3	10.3	7.5	2.7	6.9	5.8	−1.1	2.5
Sierra Leone	—	2.1	5.0	1.6	−8.0	−9.6	0.1	3.5	−10.0
Somalia	1.9	−5.0	2.4	−0.2	−18.6	2.5	5.0	5.2	5.4
South Africa	2.2	4.2	2.4	−0.3	−1.0	−2.2	1.3	2.7	3.4
Sudan	0.9	1.4	1.5	—	6.1	8.6	5.0	2.2	4.2
Swaziland	5.0	10.0	3.5	7.9	−0.1	1.2	2.5	2.6	3.1
Tanzania	2.0	4.2	4.0	4.8	5.7	3.5	3.7	3.1	4.5
Togo	1.3	6.2	3.9	−0.4	−0.9	−6.3	−15.5	13.9	8.3
Tunisia	4.6	0.1	2.6	7.1	3.9	7.8	2.3	3.4	3.5
Uganda	1.9	6.0	5.7	5.1	3.1	8.4	5.5	10.0	6.5
Zaïre	1.3	0.6	−1.4	−6.6	−8.4	−10.5	−14.5	−7.2	−0.7
Zambia	1.1	1.9	1.0	−0.5	—	−2.5	6.5	−5.1	—
Zimbabwe	3.0	7.6	4.2	1.2	3.6	−6.8	4.2	5.2	−1.1

Table A6 *(continued)*

	Average 1978–87	1988	1989	1990	1991	1992	1993	1994	1995
Asia	**6.8**	**9.1**	**6.1**	**5.9**	**7.1**	**8.7**	**8.9**	**8.8**	**8.4**
Afghanistan, Islamic State of	−0.1	−8.3	−7.1	−2.6	0.8	1.0	−3.1	−3.0	26.2
Bangladesh	4.1	3.5	5.0	5.1	4.1	4.8	4.8	4.4	4.7
Bhutan	7.8	1.1	4.7	6.6	3.5	4.1	5.7	6.0	7.0
Cambodia	. . .	9.9	3.5	1.2	7.6	7.0	4.1	4.0	7.6
China	9.5	11.3	4.1	3.8	9.3	14.2	13.5	11.8	10.2
Fiji	1.7	3.5	13.9	3.2	1.5	4.8	3.5	4.2	2.4
Hong Kong	8.3	8.0	2.6	3.4	5.1	6.3	6.4	5.4	5.0
India	4.5	8.7	7.4	5.9	1.7	3.6	4.5	5.9	6.2
Indonesia	5.2	5.8	9.1	9.0	8.9	7.2	7.3	7.5	8.1
Kiribati	−5.8	10.6	−2.2	−3.2	2.8	−1.6	0.9	1.8	2.5
Korea	7.7	11.3	6.4	9.5	9.1	5.1	5.8	8.4	9.0
Lao P.D. Republic	5.0	−2.1	9.9	6.7	4.0	7.0	5.9	8.1	7.1
Malaysia	5.5	8.9	9.2	9.7	8.6	7.8	8.3	9.2	9.6
Maldives	9.5	8.7	9.3	16.2	7.6	6.3	6.2	6.6	5.8
Marshall Islands	. . .	5.1	−1.7	3.2	0.1	0.1	2.5	2.0	−2.0
Micronesia, Fed. States of	. . .	12.4	−1.7	−2.7	4.3	−1.2	5.2	−0.4	2.8
Myanmar	3.8	−11.4	3.7	2.8	−0.7	9.7	5.9	6.8	7.2
Nepal	3.2	4.3	4.6	6.4	4.1	3.4	7.1	3.0	5.8
Pakistan	6.5	4.8	4.7	5.6	8.2	5.0	3.1	4.2	5.3
Papua New Guinea	2.2	2.9	−1.4	−3.0	9.5	11.8	16.6	3.0	−4.6
Philippines	1.8	6.8	6.2	3.0	0.6	—	2.1	4.4	4.8
Singapore	6.9	11.1	9.6	8.8	6.7	6.0	10.1	10.1	8.9
Solomon Islands	2.6	1.3	4.3	1.0	1.7	10.5	0.5	3.7	0.2
Sri Lanka	5.0	2.7	2.3	6.2	4.6	4.3	6.9	5.6	5.5
Taiwan Province of China	8.6	7.3	7.5	4.9	9.2	6.5	6.3	6.4	6.4
Thailand	6.4	13.3	12.2	11.6	8.4	7.9	8.4	8.6	8.6
Vanuatu	2.9	0.6	4.5	5.2	6.5	0.6	4.4	2.0	2.0
Vietnam	4.5	5.1	7.8	4.9	6.0	8.6	8.1	8.9	9.5
Western Samoa	2.4	−1.5	6.4	−9.4	−2.1	−0.9	6.3	−7.8	6.7
Middle East and Europe	**2.4**	**—**	**3.2**	**5.3**	**3.2**	**6.2**	**3.7**	**0.7**	**3.7**
Bahrain	3.3	10.9	1.2	1.3	4.6	7.8	8.2	2.3	1.6
Cyprus	6.2	8.7	8.0	7.3	0.4	9.7	1.8	5.6	4.5
Egypt	5.9	3.9	3.0	2.4	2.1	0.3	0.5	2.7	3.2
Iran, Islamic Republic of	−1.4	−9.7	4.5	11.2	8.6	8.1	2.3	1.8	3.0
Iraq	3.2	−10.2	12.0	−26.0	−61.3	—	—	1.0	2.0
Israel	3.6	3.6	1.2	6.1	6.3	6.8	3.4	6.5	6.9
Jordan	6.9	−1.9	−13.4	1.0	1.8	16.1	5.9	5.9	6.4
Kuwait	−1.8	−10.0	25.9	−26.2	−41.0	69.9	34.2	1.1	−0.3
Lebanon	4.4	−28.2	−42.2	−13.4	38.2	4.5	7.0	8.0	9.0
Libya	−2.8	−5.0	7.2	5.6	3.6	−3.0	−6.1	−3.0	1.2
Malta	3.6	8.4	8.2	6.2	6.3	4.7	4.5	5.0	6.2
Oman	7.6	6.1	3.3	7.1	9.2	6.0	6.4	3.5	2.0
Qatar	—	4.7	5.3	2.7	−0.8	9.7	−0.6	0.2	1.1
Saudi Arabia	1.0	8.4	−0.2	8.9	9.7	3.1	−0.5	−0.1	−0.8
Syrian Arab Republic	3.5	13.3	−9.0	7.6	7.1	10.5	3.9	5.5	5.0
Turkey	4.1	2.3	0.3	9.2	0.8	5.0	7.7	−4.7	7.4
United Arab Emirates	−2.2	−2.6	13.3	17.5	0.2	2.8	−1.5	1.1	3.0
Yemen Arab Republic, former	7.8	6.7	3.4	1.7	. . .	. . .	. . .	. . .	. . .
Yemen, former P.D. Republic of	0.4	1.0	2.5	3.0	. . .	. . .	. . .	. . .	. . .
Yemen, Republic of	. . .	. . .	. . .	. . .	—	4.2	5.9	—	3.6

Table A6 *(concluded)*

	Average 1978–87	1988	1989	1990	1991	1992	1993	1994	1995
Western Hemisphere	**3.1**	**1.1**	**1.6**	**1.1**	**3.3**	**2.9**	**3.1**	**4.7**	**0.9**
Antigua and Barbuda	7.3	7.7	6.3	3.5	4.4	1.1	3.4	4.2	3.4
Argentina	0.3	−1.9	−6.2	0.1	8.9	8.7	5.9	7.4	−4.4
Aruba	. . .	16.7	9.1	11.7	3.8	3.8	3.8	3.8	3.8
Bahamas, The	5.1	2.3	2.3	1.2	−3.1	0.1	2.0	2.3	2.5
Barbados	2.3	3.5	3.6	−3.3	−3.9	−5.7	0.8	4.0	2.3
Belize	3.4	9.0	13.0	9.3	4.6	9.0	4.2	1.5	−0.1
Bolivia	−0.6	3.0	3.6	4.4	4.6	2.8	4.1	4.2	3.8
Brazil	3.7	0.3	3.3	−3.1	0.3	−0.8	4.2	5.7	4.2
Chile	3.4	7.3	9.9	3.3	7.3	11.0	6.3	4.2	8.5
Colombia	4.1	4.1	3.4	4.3	2.0	4.0	5.2	5.7	5.3
Costa Rica	2.7	3.4	5.6	3.6	2.2	7.3	6.0	3.5	3.5
Dominica	4.0	7.4	−1.1	6.3	2.3	2.9	2.1	1.0	−1.5
Dominican Republic	3.6	2.2	4.8	−5.8	1.0	8.0	3.0	4.3	4.8
Ecuador	2.4	10.4	0.3	3.0	5.0	3.6	2.0	4.0	2.5
El Salvador	−1.1	1.6	1.0	3.4	3.5	5.0	5.3	5.8	6.5
Grenada	4.7	6.8	5.0	6.8	2.1	—	1.0	1.4	−0.5
Guatemala	1.1	4.0	3.9	3.1	3.7	4.8	3.9	4.0	5.0
Guyana	−2.0	−2.6	−3.3	−2.5	6.1	7.8	8.2	8.5	5.5
Haiti	1.3	0.8	1.1	−0.1	−3.0	−14.8	−2.6	−10.6	4.4
Honduras	3.0	4.5	4.3	0.1	3.3	5.6	6.0	−1.5	4.5
Jamaica	2.4	−4.0	4.7	4.1	0.8	1.8	1.0	0.5	0.5
Mexico	3.7	1.2	3.3	4.4	3.6	3.4	0.1	3.7	−6.9
Netherlands Antilles	0.7	2.6	3.1	0.6	5.8	5.2	−1.8	3.0	3.0
Nicaragua	−3.2	−12.5	−1.7	−0.1	−0.2	0.4	−0.2	3.2	3.0
Panama	4.9	−15.6	−0.4	4.6	9.5	8.6	5.6	4.7	3.0
Paraguay	4.8	6.4	5.8	3.1	2.5	1.8	4.1	3.5	3.5
Peru	2.7	−8.8	−11.6	−3.8	2.9	−1.8	5.9	12.8	6.9
St. Kitts and Nevis	4.9	9.8	6.7	3.0	3.9	3.0	4.5	3.2	4.9
St. Lucia	5.9	12.2	9.1	4.1	2.3	7.1	2.3	2.2	3.0
St. Vincent and the Grenadines	6.2	8.9	6.5	5.4	3.1	4.9	2.1	0.2	4.4
Suriname	−1.6	8.5	4.0	0.1	2.4	3.9	−5.7	−2.3	4.0
Trinidad and Tobago	−2.1	−4.0	−0.7	1.5	2.7	−1.7	−1.6	4.2	3.5
Uruguay	2.0	—	1.3	0.9	3.2	7.9	2.5	5.1	−2.5
Venezuela	0.7	5.8	−8.6	6.5	9.7	6.1	0.3	−2.8	2.2

[1]For many countries, figures for recent years are IMF staff estimates. Data for some countries are for fiscal years.

Table A7. Countries in Transition: Real GDP[1]

(Annual percent change)

	Average 1978–87	1988	1989	1990	1991	1992	1993	1994	1995
Central and eastern Europe	...	...	...	...	**−10.8**	**−10.0**	**−5.0**	**−2.9**	**1.4**
Albania	2.2	−1.4	9.8	−10.0	−28.0	−7.2	9.6	9.4	8.6
Belarus	...	...	...	...	−1.2	−9.7	−10.6	−12.6	−10.2
Bulgaria	4.7	2.4	−0.5	−9.1	−11.7	−7.3	−2.4	1.4	2.5
Croatia	...	...	...	...	...	...	−3.7	0.8	5.0
Czech Republic	...	...	...	...	...	...	−0.9	2.6	5.0
Czechoslovakia, former	2.5	2.5	4.5	−0.4	−15.9	−8.5	...	...	...
Estonia	...	...	...	...	−7.9	−21.6	−8.4	3.0	4.0
Hungary	2.2	−0.1	0.7	−3.5	−11.9	−3.0	−0.8	2.9	1.9
Latvia	...	...	...	...	−11.1	−35.2	−16.1	2.2	0.4
Lithuania	...	...	...	...	−13.1	−56.6	−24.2	1.7	5.3
Macedonia, former Yugoslav Rep. of	...	...	...	...	...	...	−8.4	−8.2	−3.0
Moldova	...	...	...	...	−17.5	−29.1	−1.2	−31.2	−3.0
Poland	0.9	4.1	0.2	−11.6	−7.0	2.6	3.8	6.0	6.5
Romania	3.6	−0.5	−5.8	−5.6	−12.9	−8.8	1.3	3.9	6.9
Slovak Republic	...	...	...	...	...	...	−3.7	4.9	7.4
Slovenia	...	...	...	...	...	...	1.3	5.3	4.8
Ukraine	...	...	...	...	−11.9	−17.0	−16.8	−23.7	−11.4
Yugoslavia, former	2.2	−2.0	0.8	−7.5	−17.0	−34.0	...	...	...
Russia	...	...	...	...	**−13.0**	**−19.0**	**−12.0**	**−15.0**	**−4.0**
Transcaucasus and central Asia	...	...	...	...	**−7.7**	**−17.4**	**−10.5**	**−14.2**	**−5.7**
Armenia	...	...	...	...	−12.4	−52.6	−14.1	5.4	5.0
Azerbaijan	...	...	...	...	−0.7	−22.1	−23.1	−20.8	−13.2
Georgia	...	...	...	...	−20.6	−44.8	−25.4	−11.4	−5.0
Kazakstan	...	...	...	...	−13.0	−14.0	−12.0	−25.0	−11.0
Kyrgyz Republic	...	...	...	...	−7.9	−13.9	−15.5	−20.1	1.3
Mongolia	6.5	8.5	4.2	−5.6	−9.2	−9.5	−3.0	2.3	6.3
Tajikistan	...	...	...	...	−7.1	−28.9	−11.1	−21.4	−12.5
Turkmenistan	...	...	...	...	−4.7	−5.3	−10.0	−20.0	−13.9
Uzbekistan	...	...	...	...	−0.5	−11.1	−2.3	−4.2	−1.2

[1]Data for some countries refer to real net material product (NMP) or are estimates based on NMP. For many countries, figures for recent years are IMF staff estimates. The figures should be interpreted only as indicative of broad orders of magnitude because reliable, comparable data are not generally available. In particular, the growth of output of new private enterprises or of the informal economy is not fully reflected in the recent figures.

Table A8. Summary of Inflation
(In percent)

	Average 1978–87	1988	1989	1990	1991	1992	1993	1994	1995	1996	1997
GDP deflators											
Industrial countries	**6.5**	**3.6**	**4.3**	**4.3**	**4.3**	**3.1**	**2.6**	**2.0**	**2.2**	**2.1**	**2.2**
United States	5.9	3.7	4.2	4.3	4.0	2.7	2.6	2.3	2.5	2.1	2.4
European Union	8.4	4.3	4.9	5.3	5.4	4.4	3.6	2.6	3.0	2.8	2.6
Japan	2.7	0.7	2.0	2.3	2.7	1.7	0.6	0.3	−0.5	0.2	0.6
Other industrial countries	7.1	5.3	5.7	4.6	3.6	1.6	1.7	1.4	2.2	2.3	2.2
Consumer prices											
Industrial countries	**6.7**	**3.4**	**4.4**	**5.0**	**4.5**	**3.3**	**2.9**	**2.3**	**2.4**	**2.3**	**2.5**
United States	6.5	4.1	4.8	5.4	4.2	3.0	3.0	2.6	2.8	2.6	3.0
European Union	8.0	3.5	4.7	5.3	5.1	4.5	3.7	3.0	3.0	2.6	2.5
Japan	3.0	0.7	2.3	2.8	3.3	1.7	1.3	0.7	−0.1	0.4	1.3
Other industrial countries	7.0	4.8	4.9	5.6	5.2	2.4	2.5	1.3	2.2	2.1	2.2
Developing countries	**27.4**	**50.9**	**59.7**	**62.5**	**33.3**	**35.3**	**42.5**	**48.0**	**19.9**	**12.6**	**9.8**
By region											
Africa	15.5	17.0	19.3	20.1	24.4	27.9	27.4	33.8	25.8	13.7	8.6
Asia	7.6	11.6	11.0	6.6	7.8	6.9	9.5	13.5	10.9	8.4	7.7
Middle East and Europe	20.9	25.6	21.4	21.9	25.1	25.6	24.0	32.0	33.1	23.8	20.9
Western Hemisphere	76.9	233.2	340.0	438.6	128.8	151.5	209.5	223.7	37.9	19.0	11.2
By analytical criteria											
Fuel exporters	12.2	17.0	22.0	18.4	18.9	20.7	24.5	31.5	35.3	23.0	12.7
Nonfuel exporters	30.3	55.8	65.0	69.0	35.2	37.1	44.7	49.8	18.4	11.7	9.6
Market borrowers	40.4	87.3	110.0	115.7	45.9	51.8	67.3	74.7	22.1	12.5	9.1
Official borrowers	17.2	21.6	23.3	20.6	26.2	23.0	20.1	23.9	21.5	12.7	8.9
Countries with recent debt-servicing difficulties	54.5	143.7	195.9	240.7	91.4	106.1	138.3	149.8	33.6	17.1	10.2
Countries without debt-servicing difficulties	11.6	15.3	13.7	10.0	11.4	11.0	13.2	18.0	15.2	11.3	10.2
Countries in transition	**5.6**	**10.1**	**27.0**	**34.6**	**94.2**	**674.4**	**614.3**	**264.8**	**128.2**	**38.2**	**13.6**
Central and eastern Europe	...	...	...	...	95.4	300.9	364.5	152.9	75.3	27.1	13.0
Excluding Belarus and Ukraine	...	...	...	...	98.9	114.8	79.2	46.2	25.7	17.3	11.8
Russia	...	...	...	...	92.7	1,353.0	896.0	302.0	190.2	51.2	13.3
Transcaucasus and central Asia	...	...	...	...	95.7	913.6	1,243.3	1,610.6	263.5	52.2	19.3
Memorandum											
Median inflation rate											
Industrial countries	7.4	4.6	4.8	5.4	3.9	3.1	3.0	2.2	2.3	2.3	2.3
Developing countries	10.3	8.3	9.4	10.0	11.9	9.9	8.9	11.3	8.9	6.0	5.0
Countries in transition	1.1	0.6	2.0	6.7	101.4	871.0	472.3	129.7	39.6	21.4	13.3

Table A9. Industrial Countries: GDP Deflators and Consumer Prices

(Annual percent change)

	Average 1978–87	1988	1989	1990	1991	1992	1993	1994	1995	1996	1997	Fourth Quarter[1] 1995	1996	1997
GDP deflators														
Industrial countries	**6.5**	**3.6**	**4.3**	**4.3**	**4.3**	**3.1**	**2.6**	**2.0**	**2.2**	**2.1**	**2.2**	...	...	...
Major industrial countries	6.1	3.3	4.0	4.1	4.1	3.0	2.5	1.9	2.1	2.0	2.1	...	...	...
United States	5.9	3.7	4.2	4.3	4.0	2.7	2.6	2.3	2.5	2.1	2.4	2.4	2.2	2.5
Japan	2.7	0.7	2.0	2.3	2.7	1.7	0.6	0.3	−0.5	0.2	0.6	−0.5	0.7	0.7
Germany[2]	3.4	1.5	2.4	3.2	3.9	5.5	3.8	2.3	2.2	1.7	1.7	2.2	1.7	1.7
France	8.5	2.8	3.0	3.1	3.3	2.1	2.5	1.3	2.1	1.9	1.8	2.4	1.8	1.8
Italy	13.2	6.6	6.2	7.6	7.7	4.5	4.3	3.6	5.2	3.8	3.9	5.7	3.5	4.0
United Kingdom	8.7	6.0	7.1	6.4	6.5	4.4	3.3	2.1	2.6	3.9	3.3	2.1	4.7	3.3
Canada	6.4	4.6	4.8	3.1	2.9	1.2	1.0	0.6	1.7	2.0	1.9	1.9	2.2	1.8
Other industrial countries	8.8	5.3	6.2	6.0	5.3	4.1	3.4	2.9	3.0	2.8	2.7	...	...	...
Spain	12.5	5.7	7.0	7.4	7.0	6.7	4.5	4.1	4.0	3.7	3.4	...	...	...
Netherlands	3.0	1.2	1.2	2.3	2.7	2.3	2.1	2.3	2.0	2.2	1.9	...	...	...
Belgium	4.8	1.8	4.8	3.0	2.7	3.5	4.1	2.6	1.9	2.0	2.0	...	...	...
Sweden	8.2	6.7	7.9	9.1	7.9	1.0	2.7	3.0	3.5	3.2	3.3	...	...	...
Austria	4.6	1.7	2.9	3.4	3.9	4.1	3.4	3.4	2.1	2.4	1.5	...	...	...
Denmark	7.3	3.4	4.2	2.7	2.2	3.2	0.7	1.7	1.8	2.1	1.7	...	...	...
Finland	7.7	7.0	6.1	5.7	2.6	0.7	2.4	1.1	3.7	2.0	2.0	...	...	...
Greece	18.2	13.8	14.5	21.1	18.4	14.2	13.6	10.9	9.0	7.2	5.5	...	...	...
Portugal	20.2	13.3	12.0	12.9	14.7	13.1	6.9	5.1	3.8	3.5	3.3	...	...	...
Ireland	10.1	3.4	5.4	−0.8	1.7	2.0	4.1	1.2	2.2	2.0	2.6	...	...	...
Luxembourg	5.0	−1.6	−0.4	1.7	3.0	2.0	2.2	4.6	2.9	1.9	2.0	...	...	...
Switzerland	3.7	2.4	4.2	5.7	5.5	2.6	2.0	1.4	1.3	1.0	1.0	...	...	...
Norway	7.4	4.4	6.4	4.2	2.7	−0.5	2.6	0.3	2.9	2.1	2.3	...	...	...
Iceland	41.0	22.8	19.8	16.8	7.6	3.7	2.1	2.6	2.4	3.7	3.5	...	...	...
Australia	8.3	8.4	7.5	4.6	1.9	1.6	1.4	1.2	2.4	3.1	3.3	...	...	...
New Zealand	15.5	4.9	8.0	3.0	4.4	1.2	1.1	2.5	2.3	1.7	1.5	...	...	...
Memorandum														
European Union	8.4	4.3	4.9	5.3	5.4	4.4	3.6	2.6	3.0	2.8	2.6	...	...	...
Consumer prices														
Industrial countries	**6.7**	**3.4**	**4.4**	**5.0**	**4.5**	**3.3**	**2.9**	**2.3**	**2.4**	**2.3**	**2.5**	...	...	...
Major industrial countries	6.4	3.2	4.2	4.8	4.3	3.2	2.8	2.2	2.3	2.2	2.5	2.2	2.2	2.5
United States	6.5	4.1	4.8	5.4	4.2	3.0	3.0	2.6	2.8	2.6	3.0	2.7	2.8	3.0
Japan	3.0	0.7	2.3	2.8	3.3	1.7	1.3	0.7	−0.1	0.4	1.3	−0.5	0.7	1.7
Germany[2,3]	3.1	1.3	2.8	2.7	3.5	5.1	4.4	2.8	1.8	1.5	1.5	1.7	1.3	1.5
France	8.6	2.7	3.5	3.4	3.2	2.4	2.1	1.7	1.8	1.8	1.8	1.9	1.8	1.8
Italy	12.8	5.1	6.3	6.5	6.3	5.2	4.5	4.0	5.4	4.4	4.0	5.8	4.1	4.0
United Kingdom[4]	8.0	4.6	5.9	8.1	6.8	4.7	3.0	2.4	2.8	2.8	2.6	2.9	2.8	2.4
Canada	7.1	4.0	5.0	4.8	5.6	1.5	1.8	0.2	1.9	1.3	1.9	1.9	1.5	1.8
Other industrial countries	8.2	4.7	5.4	6.3	5.5	4.3	3.7	3.1	3.1	2.9	2.6	...	...	...
Memorandum														
European Union	8.0	3.5	4.7	5.3	5.1	4.5	3.7	3.0	3.0	2.6	2.5	...	...	...

[1]From fourth quarter of preceding year.
[2]Data through 1991 apply to west Germany only.
[3]Based on the revised consumer price index for united Germany introduced in September 1995.
[4]Retail price index excluding mortgage interest.

Table A10. Industrial Countries: Hourly Earnings, Productivity, and Unit Labor Costs in Manufacturing
(Annual percent change)

	Average 1978–87	1988	1989	1990	1991	1992	1993	1994	1995	1996	1997
Hourly earnings											
Industrial countries	**7.9**	**4.7**	**5.3**	**6.0**	**6.3**	**5.2**	**3.3**	**2.9**	**3.3**	**3.4**	**3.7**
Major industrial countries	7.6	4.4	5.1	5.7	6.1	5.0	3.1	2.8	3.2	3.3	3.6
United States	6.8	3.9	3.3	4.6	5.4	4.4	2.5	2.9	3.0	3.1	3.3
Japan	4.2	3.2	6.7	6.5	5.9	4.6	2.6	2.7	2.4	1.9	3.4
Germany[1]	5.6	4.0	4.2	5.7	7.3	7.1	6.1	1.6	4.8	4.0	4.2
France	10.8	3.9	4.8	4.8	5.4	5.2	2.0	2.3	2.8	2.1	3.4
Italy	15.4	7.5	9.7	8.5	9.3	7.3	4.6	3.9	4.5	6.5	5.5
United Kingdom	11.6	8.6	9.0	9.0	8.0	5.1	4.5	4.4	4.8	4.8	4.9
Canada	6.8	3.9	5.3	5.2	4.7	3.5	2.1	1.6	1.5	3.5	1.6
Other industrial countries	9.9	6.1	6.2	7.6	7.4	6.3	4.3	3.8	3.6	4.2	4.2
Memorandum											
European Union	10.3	5.9	6.6	7.2	7.6	6.5	4.6	3.3	4.2	4.3	4.4
Productivity											
Industrial countries	**2.8**	**3.6**	**2.8**	**1.9**	**2.1**	**2.3**	**1.8**	**5.2**	**3.6**	**2.5**	**2.7**
Major industrial countries	2.7	3.7	2.9	2.1	2.2	2.2	1.6	5.0	3.8	2.6	2.7
United States	2.0	1.3	1.8	1.6	2.6	3.4	2.2	4.2	3.6	3.2	2.6
Japan	3.2	7.4	4.5	2.8	1.5	−3.7	−1.6	3.5	4.6	1.3	3.3
Germany[1]	2.7	4.1	3.1	3.5	2.9	1.3	2.4	8.2	5.2	4.2	3.5
France	3.9	7.3	5.1	1.5	1.3	5.0	—	8.9	2.9	2.0	2.0
Italy	4.4	5.7	2.9	1.6	1.8	4.3	1.9	6.8	6.6	1.7	1.7
United Kingdom	3.3	5.1	4.4	2.2	2.1	4.3	4.7	4.4	1.4	2.4	3.6
Canada	1.7	0.4	0.5	3.4	0.9	4.3	3.1	3.2	−0.3	−0.3	0.5
Other industrial countries	3.7	3.2	2.5	0.5	1.8	2.6	3.4	6.1	2.3	2.3	2.5
Memorandum											
European Union	3.7	5.1	3.6	1.9	2.0	3.3	2.8	7.2	3.8	2.6	2.8
Unit labor costs											
Industrial countries	**5.0**	**1.1**	**2.4**	**4.0**	**4.1**	**3.0**	**1.5**	**−2.1**	**−0.2**	**0.9**	**1.0**
Major industrial countries	4.8	0.8	2.2	3.5	3.9	2.8	1.5	−2.1	−0.5	0.7	0.9
United States	4.7	2.6	1.5	3.0	2.7	0.9	0.2	−1.3	−0.6	−0.1	0.7
Japan	0.9	−3.9	2.0	3.5	4.3	8.6	4.3	−0.7	−2.1	0.6	0.1
Germany[1]	2.8	−0.1	1.0	2.1	4.2	5.7	3.6	−6.1	−0.4	−0.2	0.7
France	6.6	−3.2	−0.3	3.3	4.0	0.1	2.1	−6.1	−0.2	0.1	0.8
Italy	10.5	1.7	6.6	6.8	7.4	2.9	2.6	−2.7	−1.9	4.7	3.7
United Kingdom	8.0	3.3	4.4	6.7	5.7	0.8	−0.2	—	3.3	2.4	1.2
Canada	5.0	3.4	4.8	1.7	3.8	−0.8	−1.0	−1.5	1.7	3.8	1.1
Other industrial countries	6.0	2.8	3.6	7.1	5.5	3.7	1.0	−2.0	1.4	1.9	1.6
Memorandum											
European Union	6.4	0.9	2.9	5.2	5.5	3.1	1.8	−3.6	0.4	1.6	1.5

[1]Data through 1991 apply to west Germany only.

Table A11. Developing Countries: Consumer Prices

(Annual percent change)

	Average 1978–87	1988	1989	1990	1991	1992	1993	1994	1995	1996	1997
Developing countries	**27.4**	**50.9**	**59.7**	**62.5**	**33.3**	**35.3**	**42.5**	**48.0**	**19.9**	**12.6**	**9.8**
By region											
Africa	15.5	17.0	19.3	20.1	24.4	27.9	27.4	33.8	25.8	13.7	8.6
Asia	7.6	11.6	11.0	6.6	7.8	6.9	9.5	13.5	10.9	8.4	7.7
Middle East and Europe	20.9	25.6	21.4	21.9	25.1	25.6	24.0	32.0	33.1	23.8	20.9
Western Hemisphere	76.9	233.2	340.0	438.6	128.8	151.5	209.5	223.7	37.9	19.0	11.2
Sub-Saharan Africa	20.2	23.1	21.9	22.0	35.5	39.7	33.2	50.9	29.5	16.3	10.2
Four newly industrializing Asian economies	7.9	5.2	5.8	7.0	7.5	5.9	4.6	5.6	4.7	4.5	4.1
By predominant export											
Fuel	12.2	17.0	22.0	18.4	18.9	20.7	24.5	31.5	35.3	23.0	12.7
Nonfuel exports	30.3	55.8	65.0	69.0	35.2	37.1	44.7	49.8	18.4	11.6	9.6
Manufactures	8.2	15.2	14.6	3.9	4.5	5.8	10.9	17.4	12.2	8.7	7.8
Primary products	70.0	129.1	298.1	305.4	97.9	36.2	25.8	26.1	17.3	10.9	7.7
Agricultural products	78.5	125.6	314.5	285.9	85.6	25.9	18.8	18.1	17.0	11.0	8.2
Minerals	53.3	136.4	266.1	349.8	126.7	61.5	42.6	45.0	18.1	10.8	6.6
Services, income, and private transfers	12.3	12.0	16.5	19.2	20.9	16.7	11.6	12.2	10.5	7.3	6.1
Diversified export base	35.8	77.2	80.6	98.7	49.0	62.7	79.3	85.7	24.0	14.3	11.5
By financial criteria											
Net creditor countries	4.6	1.6	2.8	3.6	5.1	3.4	3.2	4.4	5.8	4.2	3.6
Net debtor countries	28.9	54.3	63.7	66.8	35.2	37.4	45.2	50.9	20.7	13.1	10.2
Market borrowers	40.4	87.3	110.0	115.7	45.9	51.8	67.3	74.7	22.1	12.5	9.1
Diversified borrowers	15.4	17.7	15.0	17.9	19.6	17.5	16.6	18.8	17.0	14.6	13.5
Official borrowers	17.2	21.6	23.3	20.6	26.2	23.0	20.1	23.9	21.5	12.7	8.9
Countries with recent debt-servicing difficulties	54.5	143.7	195.9	240.7	91.4	106.1	138.3	149.8	33.6	17.1	10.2
Countries without debt-servicing difficulties	11.6	15.3	13.7	10.0	11.4	11.0	13.2	18.0	15.2	11.3	10.2
Other groups											
Small low-income economies	16.4	23.2	24.7	21.9	27.8	25.9	23.1	26.8	22.5	14.0	9.3
Least developed countries	17.5	23.1	24.9	25.1	38.6	35.9	29.0	39.0	24.5	15.4	11.8
Memorandum											
Median											
Developing countries	10.3	8.3	9.4	10.0	11.9	9.9	8.9	11.3	8.9	6.0	5.0
By region											
Africa	11.0	8.0	9.6	10.0	9.1	10.1	8.9	24.7	12.4	6.3	5.0
Asia	8.0	8.4	7.4	8.6	11.7	8.8	6.9	7.9	7.9	6.0	5.3
Middle East and Europe	8.2	5.8	6.9	9.5	10.4	8.9	7.9	6.5	6.4	5.9	5.2
Western Hemisphere	12.8	12.1	14.3	21.8	22.7	12.1	10.7	8.5	8.6	5.0	5.0

129

Table A12. Developing Countries—by Country: Consumer Prices[1]

(Annual percent change)

	Average 1978–87	1988	1989	1990	1991	1992	1993	1994	1995
Africa	**15.5**	**17.0**	**19.3**	**20.1**	**24.4**	**27.9**	**27.4**	**33.8**	**25.8**
Algeria	10.3	5.9	9.2	46.9	31.7	20.5	29.0	30.5	16.3
Angola	...	...	...	...	80.1	299.0	1,379.0	950.0	43.0
Benin	8.3	4.3	0.5	1.1	2.1	5.9	0.5	38.6	15.1
Botswana	11.5	8.0	11.6	11.4	12.6	15.0	14.2	11.1	9.1
Burkina Faso	5.2	4.2	−0.3	−0.8	2.5	−2.0	0.6	24.7	7.8
Burundi	10.0	4.5	11.5	7.1	8.7	5.0	9.7	14.7	14.9
Cameroon	9.8	1.7	1.6	1.5	−0.6	1.9	−3.7	12.7	26.9
Cape Verde	13.4	3.7	6.9	6.6	7.0	5.2	4.4	4.6	5.4
Central African Republic	9.4	−3.9	0.6	−0.2	−2.8	−0.8	−2.9	24.5	19.2
Chad	5.5	14.9	−4.9	0.5	4.0	−3.8	−7.0	41.3	5.6
Comoros	6.9	1.1	5.7	1.6	1.7	−1.4	1.9	25.0	4.8
Congo	8.2	4.4	4.0	2.6	1.5	2.0	0.3	56.9	8.9
Côte d'Ivoire	9.1	6.9	1.0	−0.7	1.6	4.2	2.1	26.0	14.2
Djibouti	6.5	6.4	3.0	7.8	6.8	5.0	5.8	4.0	3.5
Equatorial Guinea	15.7	−3.4	5.2	2.7	−0.9	0.9	1.6	38.9	6.3
Ethiopia	6.7	2.2	9.6	5.2	20.9	21.0	10.0	1.5	11.4
Gabon	8.5	−9.8	6.6	6.0	3.3	−10.8	0.6	36.1	10.9
Gambia, The	16.0	12.4	10.8	10.2	9.1	12.0	6.0	4.0	5.0
Ghana	51.5	31.4	25.2	37.2	18.0	10.1	25.0	24.9	58.1
Guinea	29.1	27.4	28.3	19.4	19.6	16.6	7.1	4.1	4.0
Guinea-Bissau	38.2	60.3	80.8	33.0	57.6	69.4	48.2	15.2	45.4
Kenya	11.4	8.3	9.9	15.7	19.6	27.3	46.0	28.8	1.7
Lesotho	13.8	14.9	14.4	12.1	16.6	13.0	7.0	9.5	7.7
Liberia	5.8	9.7	25.3	10.0	10.0	10.0	10.0	10.0	10.0
Madagascar	17.0	26.3	9.0	11.8	8.5	15.3	9.2	39.1	33.0
Malawi	14.2	28.0	7.5	14.0	8.3	23.0	22.8	34.6	56.5
Mali	7.4	8.5	−0.2	1.6	1.5	−5.9	−0.6	24.7	12.4
Mauritania	4.2	6.3	13.0	6.4	5.6	10.1	9.3	4.1	3.5
Mauritius	11.3	1.5	16.0	10.7	12.8	2.9	8.9	9.4	6.1
Morocco	8.8	2.4	3.1	7.0	8.0	5.7	5.2	5.1	6.6
Mozambique, Rep. of	26.5	58.5	42.1	43.7	33.3	45.1	42.3	63.1	44.3
Namibia	...	12.5	15.5	12.0	11.9	17.7	8.5	10.8	9.3
Niger	5.7	0.6	−0.8	−2.0	−1.9	−1.7	−0.4	35.6	10.5
Nigeria	15.4	34.5	50.5	7.4	13.0	44.6	57.2	57.0	73.5
Rwanda	7.1	3.0	1.0	4.2	4.2	19.5	12.5	64.0	22.0
São Tomé and Principe	7.3	41.2	44.8	40.4	52.7	33.7	25.5	26.6	34.3
Senegal	8.2	−1.8	0.4	0.3	−1.8	−0.1	−0.6	32.1	8.0
Seychelles	6.0	1.8	1.6	3.9	2.0	3.2	1.3	1.0	1.0
Sierra Leone	50.5	32.7	62.8	111.0	102.7	65.5	17.6	18.4	29.1
Somalia	37.5	82.0	111.0	216.8	17.2	36.3	24.3	18.9	16.3
South Africa	14.5	12.7	14.7	14.4	15.3	13.9	9.7	9.0	8.9
Sudan	28.3	62.9	65.3	56.0	111.0	110.0	103.0	120.0	85.0
Swaziland	14.7	12.2	6.2	11.0	11.0	8.2	11.2	13.8	12.8
Tanzania	26.6	31.2	25.8	19.7	22.3	22.2	26.1	29.0	22.0
Togo	5.8	0.2	−1.2	1.1	0.4	1.7	−0.1	40.6	14.7
Tunisia	8.5	7.2	7.7	6.5	8.2	5.8	4.0	4.7	6.2
Uganda	97.9	130.8	45.4	32.9	42.2	30.0	6.5	6.1	5.0
Zaïre	54.3	82.7	104.1	81.3	2,154.4	4,129.2	1,893.1	23,760.5	533.3
Zambia	24.7	54.0	128.3	109.6	93.4	191.3	187.3	35.2	30.0
Zimbabwe	12.7	7.1	11.6	15.5	23.3	42.1	27.6	22.3	23.0

Table A12 *(continued)*

	Average 1978–87	1988	1989	1990	1991	1992	1993	1994	1995
Asia	**7.6**	**11.6**	**11.0**	**6.6**	**7.8**	**6.9**	**9.5**	**13.5**	**10.9**
Afghanistan, Islamic State of	11.9	29.2	89.8	157.8	166.0	58.2	34.0	20.0	14.0
Bangladesh	12.5	9.6	8.7	6.0	6.3	3.5	3.1	6.3	8.9
Bhutan	6.0	10.1	8.7	10.0	12.3	12.7	8.9	8.2	8.0
Cambodia	...	...	55.3	141.8	197.0	75.0	114.5	−0.5	7.8
China	3.9	18.5	17.8	2.1	2.7	5.4	13.0	21.7	14.8
Fiji	6.9	11.9	6.1	8.2	6.5	4.9	5.2	0.6	2.0
Hong Kong	8.6	7.5	10.1	9.7	11.6	9.3	8.5	8.1	9.0
India	8.4	8.9	6.5	9.9	13.0	10.0	8.7	10.0	10.2
Indonesia	11.1	8.1	6.4	7.8	9.4	7.5	9.7	8.5	9.4
Kiribati	7.3	3.1	5.3	3.8	5.7	4.0	6.1	5.1	6.5
Korea	10.0	7.6	5.7	8.6	9.3	6.2	4.8	6.3	4.5
Lao P.D. Republic	47.0	14.8	59.7	35.7	13.4	9.8	6.3	6.8	19.7
Malaysia	4.0	2.5	2.8	3.1	4.4	4.7	3.6	3.7	3.4
Maldives	11.8	6.5	7.2	3.6	14.7	16.8	20.2	16.5	7.7
Marshall Islands	...	2.6	2.2	0.7	4.0	10.3	5.0	2.8	3.0
Micronesia, Fed. States of	...	3.7	4.5	3.5	4.0	5.0	6.0	5.0	4.7
Myanmar	5.6	24.0	23.8	21.9	29.1	22.3	33.6	22.4	28.9
Nepal	8.4	6.3	11.5	9.8	21.0	8.9	8.9	7.6	7.0
Pakistan	7.1	3.3	7.2	9.7	11.8	9.5	9.4	12.5	12.3
Papua New Guinea	6.5	5.4	4.5	7.0	7.0	4.3	5.0	2.9	15.9
Philippines	14.8	9.1	10.6	12.7	18.7	8.9	7.6	9.1	8.1
Singapore	3.3	1.6	2.3	3.5	3.4	2.3	2.2	3.1	1.7
Solomon Islands	10.6	16.8	14.9	8.6	15.2	10.7	9.2	13.7	7.9
Sri Lanka	12.1	14.0	11.6	21.5	12.2	11.4	11.7	8.4	7.7
Taiwan Province of China	5.4	1.3	4.4	4.1	3.6	4.5	2.9	4.1	3.7
Thailand	6.5	3.9	5.5	6.0	5.7	4.1	3.3	5.0	5.8
Vanuatu	8.1	8.4	7.5	5.0	6.4	5.1	1.7	3.5	7.0
Vietnam	86.9	394.0	35.0	67.0	68.1	17.5	5.2	14.5	13.1
Western Samoa	13.0	8.5	6.4	15.2	−1.3	8.5	1.7	18.4	−0.3
Middle East and Europe	**20.9**	**25.6**	**21.4**	**21.9**	**25.1**	**25.6**	**24.0**	**32.0**	**33.1**
Bahrain	3.6	0.2	1.2	1.3	0.8	−0.2	2.5	0.9	1.0
Cyprus	6.7	3.4	3.8	4.5	5.0	6.5	4.8	4.7	3.1
Egypt	16.0	14.2	20.2	21.2	19.5	21.1	11.2	9.0	9.4
Iran, Islamic Republic of	17.2	28.9	17.4	9.0	20.7	24.4	22.9	35.2	48.8
Iraq	16.9	15.0	15.0	50.0	50.0	50.0	75.0	60.0	50.0
Israel	118.5	16.3	20.2	17.2	19.0	11.9	10.9	12.3	10.0
Jordan	5.8	6.7	25.6	16.2	8.2	4.0	4.7	3.5	3.0
Kuwait	4.0	1.5	3.3	1.8	16.9	−1.0	−1.2	4.7	5.4
Lebanon	50.2	155.0	72.2	68.8	51.5	120.0	29.1	8.3	6.0
Libya	10.8	3.1	1.3	8.6	11.7	15.0	20.0	30.0	30.0
Malta	4.4	0.9	0.8	3.0	2.5	1.6	4.1	4.1	4.0
Oman	3.0	1.6	1.6	10.0	4.6	1.0	1.2	−0.7	1.5
Qatar	4.8	4.6	3.3	3.0	4.4	3.0	3.1	3.0	3.0
Saudi Arabia	1.4	0.9	1.0	2.1	4.6	−0.4	0.8	0.6	5.0
Syrian Arab Republic	18.0	34.6	10.0	11.1	9.0	11.0	13.2	15.0	8.0
Turkey	47.6	73.7	63.3	60.3	66.0	70.1	66.1	106.3	93.6
United Arab Emirates	6.7	5.0	3.3	0.6	5.5	6.8	4.7	4.6	3.6
Yemen Arab Republic, former	14.1	13.9	19.4	14.0	...	...	...	...	...
Yemen, former P.D. Republic of	6.0	0.5	—	2.1	...	...	...	...	...
Yemen, Republic of	...	...	...	...	44.9	50.6	62.3	71.8	48.0

Table A12 (concluded)

	Average 1978–87	1988	1989	1990	1991	1992	1993	1994	1995
Western Hemisphere	**76.9**	**233.2**	**340.0**	**438.6**	**128.8**	**151.5**	**209.5**	**223.7**	**37.9**
Antigua and Barbuda	6.7	6.8	3.7	7.0	5.7	3.0	3.1	3.5	3.4
Argentina	210.9	343.0	3,080.5	2,314.7	171.7	24.9	10.6	4.3	3.4
Aruba	. . .	3.1	4.0	5.8	5.6	3.9	5.2	5.2	5.2
Bahamas, The	6.8	4.1	5.4	4.6	7.3	5.7	2.7	3.2	2.8
Barbados	8.4	4.7	6.3	3.0	6.3	6.1	1.1	0.1	1.9
Belize	3.2	3.2	2.1	3.0	5.6	2.8	1.6	2.3	3.0
Bolivia	229.8	16.0	15.2	17.1	21.4	12.1	8.5	7.9	10.2
Brazil[2]	127.1	684.6	1,319.9	2,740.0	413.3	991.4	2,103.3	2,407.6	67.4
Chile	25.2	14.7	17.0	26.0	21.8	15.4	12.7	11.4	8.2
Colombia	22.7	28.1	25.9	29.1	30.5	27.0	22.4	22.8	20.9
Costa Rica	23.0	20.8	16.5	19.0	28.7	21.8	9.8	13.5	18.0
Dominica	9.2	2.2	6.9	2.0	6.2	5.3	1.4	1.6	1.4
Dominican Republic	13.2	43.9	40.7	50.5	47.1	4.3	5.2	8.3	12.5
Ecuador	22.1	58.2	75.7	48.4	48.8	54.6	45.0	27.3	23.0
El Salvador	17.2	19.9	17.6	24.0	14.4	11.2	18.5	10.8	9.4
Grenada	9.7	4.0	5.6	2.8	2.6	3.8	2.8	2.6	3.5
Guatemala	12.1	10.8	13.0	41.0	35.1	10.2	13.4	12.5	8.6
Guyana	18.1	39.9	89.7	63.6	101.5	28.2	11.3	14.0	7.8
Haiti	6.8	2.9	11.0	20.4	19.5	17.7	20.2	42.6	15.0
Honduras	7.7	6.6	7.0	21.2	26.0	9.1	10.7	22.5	18.5
Jamaica	20.7	8.2	14.3	21.9	51.0	77.3	22.1	35.1	19.9
Mexico	55.2	114.2	20.0	26.7	22.7	15.5	9.8	7.1	35.0
Netherlands Antilles	6.2	2.6	3.8	3.7	3.9	1.5	1.9	3.5	3.5
Nicaragua	110.7	14,315.8	4,709.3	3,127.5	7,755.3	40.5	20.4	7.7	8.4
Panama	4.0	1.0	0.2	0.8	1.4	1.8	0.5	1.3	1.0
Paraguay	19.2	23.0	26.0	38.2	24.3	15.1	18.3	20.6	8.0
Peru	84.9	667.0	3,398.7	7,481.6	409.2	73.2	48.5	23.7	11.2
St. Kitts and Nevis	7.6	0.2	5.1	4.2	4.2	2.9	1.8	2.6	2.9
St. Lucia	6.9	0.8	4.4	3.8	6.1	5.7	0.8	2.7	5.4
St. Vincent and the Grenadines	8.1	0.3	2.7	7.3	5.9	3.8	4.3	0.4	2.0
Suriname	13.7	7.3	0.8	21.8	26.0	43.7	143.4	368.5	235.9
Trinidad and Tobago	12.7	12.1	4.6	11.0	3.8	6.5	11.1	8.5	5.3
Uruguay	53.7	62.2	80.4	112.5	101.8	68.5	54.1	44.7	42.7
Venezuela	13.5	29.4	84.5	40.7	34.2	31.4	38.1	60.8	60.0

[1]For many countries, figures for recent years are IMF staff estimates. Data for some countries are for fiscal years.

[2]From December 1994 to December 1995, consumer prices increased by about 15 percent. The figure differs from the year-on-year changes reported in the table.

Table A13. Countries in Transition: Consumer Prices[1]

(Annual percent change)

	Average 1978–87	1988	1989	1990	1991	1992	1993	1994	1995
Central and eastern Europe	...	...	...	...	**95.4**	**300.9**	**364.5**	**152.9**	**75.3**
Albania	—	—	—	—	35.8	225.2	85.0	22.6	7.8
Belarus	...	...	...	...	83.5	969.0	1,188.0	2,220.0	709.0
Bulgaria	1.7	2.5	6.4	23.9	333.5	82.0	72.8	96.0	62.1
Croatia	...	...	...	...	...	...	1,516.0	97.5	2.1
Czech Republic	...	...	...	...	...	...	20.8	10.0	9.1
Czechoslovakia, former	...	0.2	1.4	10.8	59.0	11.0	...	...	...
Estonia	...	...	...	...	210.6	1,069.0	89.0	47.8	28.9
Hungary	7.0	15.7	16.9	29.0	34.2	23.0	22.5	18.8	28.2
Latvia	...	...	...	...	124.4	951.3	109.0	35.0	25.0
Lithuania	...	...	...	...	224.7	1,020.5	410.4	72.1	36.5
Macedonia, former Yugoslav Rep. of	...	...	...	...	...	...	334.5	122.6	16.1
Moldova	...	...	...	...	162.0	1,276.0	788.5	329.6	30.2
Poland	22.2	60.2	251.1	585.8	70.3	43.0	35.3	32.2	27.8
Romania	3.0	2.6	0.9	4.7	161.1	210.3	256.0	136.8	32.3
Slovak Republic	...	...	...	...	...	...	23.0	13.4	9.9
Slovenia	...	...	...	...	...	...	32.3	19.8	12.1
Ukraine	...	...	...	...	91.2	1,209.7	4,734.9	891.0	376.0
Yugoslavia, former	48.4	194.1	1,239.9	583.1	117.4	6,146.6	...	...	...
Russia	...	...	...	...	**92.7**	**1,353.0**	**896.0**	**302.0**	**190.2**
Transcaucasus and central Asia	...	...	...	...	**95.7**	**913.6**	**1,243.3**	**1,610.6**	**263.5**
Armenia	...	...	...	...	100.3	824.5	3,731.8	5,273.4	175.6
Azerbaijan	...	...	...	...	105.6	912.6	1,129.7	1,664.4	411.7
Georgia	...	...	...	...	78.5	887.4	3,125.4	17,271.5	169.3
Kazakstan	...	...	...	...	91.0	1,381.0	1,662.3	1,879.9	176.0
Kyrgyz Republic	...	...	...	...	85.0	854.6	1,208.8	278.1	42.8
Mongolia	0.2	—	—	—	20.2	202.6	268.4	87.6	56.8
Tajikistan	...	...	...	...	111.6	1,156.7	2,194.9	350.4	635.4
Turkmenistan	...	...	...	...	102.5	492.9	3,102.4	1,748.0	1,261.5
Uzbekistan	...	...	...	...	105.0	644.7	534.2	1,568.0	305.0

[1]For many countries, inflation for the earlier years is measured based on a retail price index. Consumer price indices with a broader and more up-to-date coverage are typically used for more recent years.

Table A14. Summary Financial Indicators

(In percent)

	1988	1989	1990	1991	1992	1993	1994	1995	1996	1997
Industrial countries										
Central government fiscal balance[1]										
Industrial countries	−2.6	−2.3	−2.7	−3.1	−.1	−4.5	−3.9	−3.3	−3.0	−2.5
United States	−2.7	−2.4	−3.0	-3.5	.7	−3.9	−2.7	−2.1	−1.9	−1.9
European Union	−3.2	−2.9	−3.5	−3.8	−4.8	−6.0	−5.3	−4.3	−3.8	−3.2
Japan	−1.3	−1.2	−0.5	−0.2	−1.6	−2.7	−3.7	−4.4	−4.7	−3.8
Other industrial countries	−0.8	−0.5	−1.2	−2.9	−4.2	−5.5	−4.3	−3.4	−1.8	−1.2
General government fiscal balance[1]										
Industrial countries	−1.9	−1.3	−2.1	−2.8	−3.9	−4.5	−3.7	−3.4	−3.1	−2.4
United States	−2.1	−1.7	−2.7	−3.3	−4.4	−3.6	−2.3	−2.0	−1.7	−1.6
European Union	−3.2	−2.4	−3.6	−4.4	−5.3	−6.5	−5.8	−5.1	−4.6	−3.6
Japan	1.5	2.5	2.9	2.9	1.4	−1.6	−2.1	−3.1	−4.1	−2.4
Other industrial countries	−0.1	0.1	−0.7	−3.5	−5.5	−6.1	−4.5	−3.3	−1.7	−0.9
Growth of broad money										
Industrial countries	9.0	9.2	7.8	5.8	3.3	4.1	2.0	4.4	. . .	. . .
United States	5.8	5.5	3.7	3.1	1.6	1.6	0.4	4.3	. . .	. . .
European Union	9.9	10.9	12.3	10.1	5.6	6.7	2.3	4.9	. . .	. . .
Japan	10.2	12.0	7.4	2.3	−0.2	2.2	2.8	3.3	. . .	. . .
Other industrial countries	16.0	11.6	7.9	19.0	6.7	6.2	5.0	5.1	. . .	. . .
Short-term interest rates[2]										
United States	6.7	8.1	7.5	5.4	3.4	3.0	4.2	5.5	5.1	5.2
Japan	4.0	4.7	6.9	7.0	4.1	2.7	1.9	1.0	0.6	1.7
Germany	4.3	7.1	8.4	9.2	9.5	7.2	5.3	4.5	3.3	4.3
LIBOR	8.1	9.3	8.4	6.1	3.9	3.4	5.1	6.1	5.4	5.6
Developing countries										
Central government fiscal balance[1]										
Weighted average	−5.3	−4.1	−2.9	−3.2	−2.8	−3.0	−2.4	−2.1	−2.1	−1.5
Median	−4.9	−4.6	−4.1	−4.0	−3.7	−3.8	−4.0	−3.0	−2.6	−2.0
Growth of broad money										
Weighted average	76.8	89.3	82.0	60.8	68.1	71.1	58.0	23.0	17.9	16.5
Median	17.3	16.5	17.6	18.7	16.6	16.0	17.3	12.9	10.9	10.1
Countries in transition										
Central government fiscal balance[1,3]	−2.3	−2.2	−5.1	−10.0	−12.9	−7.1	−8.0	−3.7	−3.1	−2.4
Growth of broad money	17.5	19.0	20.2	113.0	537.4	442.8	221.4	53.4	28.2	16.8

[1]In percent of GDP.

[2]For the United States, three-month treasury bills; for Japan, three-month certificates of deposit; for Germany, three-month interbank deposits; for LIBOR, London interbank offered rate on six-month U.S. dollar deposits.

[3]For many transition countries, the fiscal balance reflects a broader definition of goverment. Because of these country differences in definition and coverage, the estimates should be interpreted only as indicative of broad orders of magnitude.

Table A15. Industrial Countries: General and Central Government Fiscal Balances and Balances Excluding Social Security Transactions[1]

(In percent of GDP)

	1988	1989	1990	1991	1992	1993	1994	1995	1996	1997
General government fiscal balance										
Industrial countries	**−1.9**	**−1.3**	**−2.1**	**−2.8**	**−3.9**	**−4.5**	**−3.7**	**−3.4**	**−3.1**	**−2.4**
Major industrial countries	−1.9	−1.2	−2.1	−2.7	−3.8	−4.3	−3.5	−3.3	−3.1	−2.5
United States	−2.1	−1.7	−2.7	−3.3	−4.4	−3.6	−2.3	−2.0	−1.7	−1.6
Japan	1.5	2.5	2.9	2.9	1.4	−1.6	−2.1	−3.1	−4.1	−2.4
Germany[2]	−2.1	0.1	−2.0	−3.3	−2.9	−3.5	−2.6	−3.5	−3.9	−3.4
France[3]	−1.5	−1.1	−1.4	−2.0	−3.9	−6.0	−5.8	−5.0	−4.2	−3.6
Italy[4]	−10.7	−9.9	−10.9	−10.2	−9.5	−9.6	−9.0	−7.2	−7.3	−5.9
United Kingdom[5]	1.0	0.9	−1.2	−2.5	−6.3	−7.8	−6.8	−5.1	−3.8	−2.5
Canada	−2.5	−2.9	−4.1	−6.6	−7.4	−7.3	−5.3	−4.2	−2.4	−1.3
Other industrial countries	−1.9	−1.6	−2.2	−3.6	−4.6	−5.9	−5.0	−4.0	−2.9	−2.2
Spain	−3.3	−2.8	−3.9	−5.0	−4.4	−7.5	−6.7	−5.9	−4.7	−3.9
Netherlands	−4.6	−4.7	−4.6	−2.9	−3.9	−3.2	−3.6	−3.8	−3.5	−2.5
Belgium	−6.8	−6.5	−5.8	−6.7	−7.1	−6.7	−5.3	−4.5	−3.4	−3.7
Sweden	3.5	5.4	4.2	−1.1	−7.8	−13.4	−10.4	−6.8	−4.5	−2.5
Austria	−3.0	−2.8	−2.2	−2.4	−2.0	−4.3	−4.4	−6.1	−5.1	−4.0
Denmark	0.6	−0.5	−1.5	−2.1	−2.9	−3.9	−3.5	−1.7	−1.0	−0.6
Finland	4.1	6.3	5.3	−1.5	−5.9	−8.0	−6.3	−5.6	−3.0	−0.5
Greece	−11.9	−14.7	−14.0	−11.4	−11.7	−12.1	−11.4	−9.0	−7.9	−6.5
Portugal	−3.6	−2.3	−5.4	−6.5	−3.3	−7.0	−5.8	−5.2	−4.5	−4.2
Ireland	−4.4	−1.7	−2.2	−2.1	−2.3	−2.3	−2.3	−2.1	−2.6	−2.5
Luxembourg	1.6	4.6	5.0	−0.4	−0.8	0.5	0.9	0.4	—	—
Switzerland	1.0	0.8	—	−2.1	−3.5	−3.7	−3.0	−2.5	−2.1	−2.0
Norway	4.8	3.6	4.2	2.1	−2.4	−3.3	−1.2	0.5	1.9	2.4
Iceland	−2.0	−4.6	−3.3	−2.9	−2.8	−4.5	−4.8	−3.3	−2.3	−1.3
Australia	1.0	1.5	0.4	−2.6	−4.6	−3.9	−2.7	−0.7	0.9	1.0
New Zealand	−1.4	−1.8	−2.3	−2.2	−2.1	—	1.4	2.7	3.4	3.6
Memorandum										
European Union	−3.2	−2.4	−3.6	−4.4	−5.3	−6.5	−5.8	−5.1	−4.6	−3.6
Fiscal balance excluding social security transactions										
United States	−4.2	−4.0	−4.9	−5.2	−6.0	−5.1	−4.1	−3.9	−3.7	−3.6
Japan	−1.6	−0.7	−0.6	−0.8	−2.0	−4.8	−5.2	−6.2	−7.0	−5.2
Germany[2]	−2.2	−0.6	−2.9	−4.0	−2.9	−3.8	−2.9	−3.1	−3.6	−3.4
France	−1.8	−1.4	−1.5	−1.7	−3.2	−4.6	−4.8	−4.0	−3.6	−3.5
Italy[4]	−5.8	−4.9	−5.3	−5.1	−4.0	−4.5	−3.7	−3.0	−3.4	−3.1
Canada	−0.9	−1.3	−2.4	−4.8	−5.3	−5.0	−3.0	−2.0	−0.1	1.0

135

Table A15 (concluded)

	1988	1989	1990	1991	1992	1993	1994	1995	1996	1997
Central government fiscal balance										
Industrial countries	**−2.6**	**−2.3**	**−2.7**	**−3.1**	**−4.1**	**−4.5**	**−3.9**	**−3.3**	**−3.0**	**−2.5**
Major industrial countries	−2.6	−2.3	−2.8	−3.0	−4.2	−4.3	−3.7	−3.2	−3.0	−2.5
United States[6]	−2.7	−2.4	−3.0	−3.5	−4.7	−3.9	−2.7	−2.1	−1.9	−1.9
Japan[7]	−1.3	−1.2	−0.5	−0.2	−1.6	−2.7	−3.7	−4.4	−4.7	−3.8
Germany[8,9]	−1.7	−0.9	−2.0	−1.9	−1.3	−2.1	−1.5	−1.5	−1.9	−1.7
France[9]	−1.6	−1.3	−1.4	−1.5	−2.8	−4.3	−4.7	−3.8	−3.4	−3.4
Italy[10]	−11.0	−10.7	−10.1	−10.3	−10.4	−10.0	−9.5	−7.3	−6.8	−5.4
United Kingdom	1.1	1.2	−1.1	−2.2	−7.0	−8.0	−6.5	−4.8	−3.6	−2.3
Canada	−3.2	−3.2	−3.9	−4.5	−4.2	−4.9	−3.8	−3.5	−1.7	−0.7
Other industrial countries	−2.3	−2.0	−2.3	−3.2	−3.9	−5.7	−4.8	−3.8	−2.9	−2.5
Memorandum										
European Union	−3.2	−2.9	−3.5	−3.8	−4.8	−6.0	−5.3	−4.3	−3.8	−3.2

[1]On a national income accounts basis except as indicated in footnotes. The projections are based on "unchanged fiscal policies" which may differ from countries' stated fiscal objectives. For a summary of medium-term fiscal objectives, see the May 1995 *World Economic Outlook*, Table 5, p. 28.

[2]Data through 1990 apply to west Germany only.

[3]Adjusted for valuation changes of the foreign exchange stabilization fund.

[4]Includes interest accruing on zero coupon bonds.

[5]Excludes asset sales.

[6]Data are on a budget basis.

[7]Data are on a national income basis and exclude social security transactions.

[8]Data through June 1990 apply to west Germany only.

[9]Data are on an administrative basis and exclude social security transactions.

[10]Data refer to the state sector and cover the transactions of the state budget as well as those of several autonomous entities operating at the same level; data do not include the gross transactions of social security institutions, only their deficits. Includes interest accruing on zero coupon bonds.

Table A16. Industrial Countries: General Government Structural Balances and Fiscal Impulses[1]

(In percent of GDP)

	1988	1989	1990	1991	1992	1993	1994	1995	1996	1997
Structural balance[2]										
Major industrial countries	**-2.7**	**-2.5**	**-3.3**	**-3.0**	**-3.5**	**-3.3**	**-2.7**	**-2.5**	**-2.1**	**-1.6**
United States	-3.1	-3.0	-3.8	-3.1	-4.1	-3.4	-2.5	-2.2	-1.7	-1.6
Japan	1.0	1.7	1.7	1.8	1.1	-1.0	-0.8	-1.2	-2.2	-0.9
Germany[3]	-1.7	—	-3.2	-5.6	-4.0	-2.4	-1.3	-2.1	-1.6	-1.4
France	-1.6	-2.1	-2.6	-2.3	-3.5	-3.4	-3.6	-3.1	-1.8	-1.7
Italy[4]	-11.6	-11.3	-12.3	-11.1	-9.6	-7.9	-7.3	-6.0	-6.2	-5.1
United Kingdom	-0.8	-2.0	-3.7	-2.7	-3.8	-4.4	-4.1	-3.2	-2.3	-1.4
Canada	-4.7	-5.1	-4.9	-4.9	-4.8	-4.6	-3.8	-2.9	-0.9	-0.2
Other industrial countries	...	**-3.2**	**-4.2**	**-4.6**	**-4.6**	**-4.3**	**-3.6**	**-3.1**	**-2.1**	**-1.5**
Spain	-4.1	-5.0	-6.8	-7.6	-5.7	-5.9	-4.6	-4.3	-3.4	-2.8
Netherlands	-3.0	-4.6	-5.6	-3.9	-4.6	-2.2	-2.7	-3.0	-2.4	-1.7
Belgium	-6.9	-7.4	-7.5	-8.4	-8.6	-5.9	-4.7	-3.9	-2.5	-3.1
Sweden	-0.4	1.5	0.7	-1.9	-6.2	-8.1	-7.3	-5.7	-4.2	-2.2
Austria	-2.8	-3.9	-3.6	-3.6	-2.6	-3.5	-3.9	-5.4	-3.9	-2.2
Denmark	-0.3	-0.5	-0.6	-0.3	-0.4	-0.4	-0.9	-0.8	-0.3	-0.2
Finland	2.6	3.3	2.3	0.1	-1.1	-1.4	-1.3	-2.4	-0.6	1.3
Greece	-11.7	-15.5	-13.6	-11.4	-11.3	-10.5	-9.6	-7.4	-6.5	-5.3
Portugal	-3.8	-3.4	-7.1	-7.8	-4.2	-6.2	-4.3	-3.7	-3.1	-3.0
Ireland	-3.4	-1.6	-3.6	-2.0	-1.4	-0.4	-1.2	-2.1	-2.8	-2.7
Norway	...	3.6	4.5	3.1	-1.3	-1.8	-0.7	0.6	1.9	2.5
Australia	0.3	0.2	-0.4	-1.6	-2.9	-2.3	-2.1	-0.5	0.9	1.0
New Zealand[5]	-5.5	-4.8	-7.5	-4.4	-0.2	-0.7	1.3	2.8	3.8	3.6
Memorandum										
European Union[6]	-3.7	-3.7	-5.2	-5.4	-5.1	-4.5	-3.9	-3.6	-2.9	-2.3
Fiscal impulse[7]										
Major industrial countries	**—**	**-0.3**	**0.8**	**-0.1**	**0.4**	**-0.1**	**-0.5**	**-0.3**	**-0.3**	**-0.5**
United States[8]	—	—	0.8	—	—	-0.7	-0.7	-0.4	-0.4	—
Japan[8]	—	-0.7	—	—	1.0	2.2	—	0.6	1.0	-1.4
Germany[3,8]	0.7	-1.7	3.2	1.1	-0.8	-1.5	-0.9	0.8	-0.5	—
France[8]	0.6	0.4	—	—	1.0	—	0.4	-0.5	-1.2	—
Italy	0.5	—	0.8	-1.3	-1.6	-1.9	-0.6	-1.3	—	-1.1
United Kingdom	-1.0	—	1.1	-0.5	2.2	1.5	—	-1.2	-1.0	-0.9
Canada	—	—	—	—	—	—	-0.7	-0.8	-1.9	-0.7

[1]On a national income accounts basis.

[2]The structural budget position is defined as the actual budget deficit (or surplus) less the effects of cyclical deviations of output from potential output. Because of the margin of uncertainty that attaches to estimates of cyclical gaps and to tax and expenditure elasticities with respect to national income, indicators of structural budget positions should be interpreted as broad orders of magnitude. Moreover, it is important to note that changes in structural budget balances are not necessarily attributable to policy changes but may reflect the built-in momentum of existing expenditure programs. In the period beyond that for which specific consolidation programs exist, it is assumed that the structural deficit remains unchanged.

[3]Data through 1990 apply to west Germany only. The estimate of the fiscal impulse for 1995 is affected by the assumption by the federal government of the debt of the Treuhandanstalt and various other agencies, which were formerly held outside the general government sector. At the public sector level, there would be an estimated withdrawal of fiscal impulse amounting to just over 1 percent of GDP.

[4]Includes interest accruing on zero coupon bonds.

[5]Excludes privatization proceeds.

[6]Excludes Luxembourg.

[7]For a definition of the fiscal impulse measure, see *The New Palgrave Dictionary of Money and Finance*, edited by Peter Newman, Murray Milgate, and John Eatwell (London: Macmillan, 1992; New York: Stockton, 1992). Impulse estimates equal to or less than ±0.3 percent of GDP are indicated by "—."

[8]For relevant years, the fiscal impulse is calculated on the basis of data adjusted for net international financial transfers related to the 1990–91 regional conflict in the Middle East.

Table A17. Industrial Countries: Monetary Aggregates

(Annual percent change)[1]

	1988	1989	1990	1991	1992	1993	1994	1995
Narrow money[2]								
Industrial countries	**6.9**	**4.3**	**7.8**	**6.7**	**7.5**	**8.1**	**3.7**	**4.7**
Major industrial countries	6.6	3.3	6.5	6.8	8.2	8.2	3.5	4.4
United States	4.9	0.9	4.0	8.6	14.2	10.2	1.8	−2.1
Japan	8.6	2.4	4.5	9.5	3.9	7.0	4.2	13.1
Germany[3]	10.9	5.6	29.6	3.4	10.8	8.5	5.2	6.8
France	4.1	7.7	3.9	−4.7	−0.2	1.5	3.0	5.6
Italy	7.3	10.3	6.6	10.5	0.7	7.6	3.2	1.6
United Kingdom	7.7	5.7	2.7	3.0	2.8	6.0	6.7	5.7
Canada	7.4	3.3	−0.9	5.5	5.7	14.6	7.0	6.3
Other industrial countries	10.0	12.6	17.7	6.1	2.3	7.3	5.1	7.0
Memorandum								
European Union	8.7	7.4	11.9	4.0	3.7	6.6	4.5	5.6
Broad money[4]								
Industrial countries	**9.0**	**9.2**	**7.8**	**5.8**	**3.3**	**4.1**	**2.0**	**4.4**
Major industrial countries	8.3	8.9	7.7	3.8	2.6	3.3	1.6	4.2
United States	5.8	5.5	3.7	3.1	1.6	1.6	0.4	4.3
Japan	10.2	12.0	7.4	2.3	−0.2	2.2	2.8	3.3
Germany[3]	6.9	5.5	19.7	6.3	7.6	10.9	1.6	3.6
France	8.2	10.0	9.3	2.3	5.5	−3.1	1.8	4.0
Italy	9.5	10.7	9.4	9.1	4.7	8.1	1.7	2.6
United Kingdom	17.7	19.0	12.3	5.6	2.7	5.1	4.2	10.1
Canada	12.9	14.4	8.2	4.6	3.1	3.1	2.7	4.0
Other industrial countries	13.9	11.3	8.6	17.5	7.5	9.3	4.2	5.5
Memorandum								
European Union	9.9	10.9	12.3	10.1	5.6	6.7	2.3	4.9

[1]Based on end-of-period data.

[2]M1 except for the United Kingdom, where M0 is used here as a measure of narrow money; it comprises notes in circulation plus bankers' operational deposits. M1 is generally currency in circulation plus private demand deposits. In addition, the United States includes traveler's checks of nonbank issues and other checkable deposits and excludes private sector float and demand deposits of banks. Japan includes government demand deposits and excludes float. Germany includes demand deposits at fixed interest rates. Canada excludes private sector float.

[3]Data through 1989 apply to west Germany only. The growth rates for the monetary aggregates in 1990 are affected by the extension of the currency area.

[4]M2, defined as M1 plus quasi-money, except for Japan, Germany, and the United Kingdom, for which the data are based on M2 plus certificates of deposit (CDs), M3, and M4, respectively. Quasi-money is essentially private term deposits and other notice deposits. The United States also includes money market mutual fund balances, money market deposit accounts, overnight repurchase agreements, and overnight Eurodollars issued to U.S. residents by foreign branches of U.S. banks. For Japan, M2 plus CDs is currency in circulation plus total private and public sector deposits and installments of Sogo Banks plus CDs. For Germany, M3 is M1 plus private time deposits with maturities of less than four years plus savings deposits at statutory notice. For the United Kingdom, M4 is composed of non-interest-bearing M1, private sector interest-bearing sterling sight bank deposits, private sector sterling time bank deposits, private sector holdings of sterling bank CDs, private sector holdings of building society shares and deposits, and sterling CDs less building society holdings of bank deposits and bank CDs, and notes and coins.

Table A18. Industrial Countries: Interest Rates

(In percent a year)

	1988	1989	1990	1991	1992	1993	1994	1995	March 1996
Policy-related interest rate[1]									
Major industrial countries	7.1	8.9	9.1	7.7	6.3	4.7	4.5	5.4	4.5
United States	7.6	9.2	8.1	5.7	3.5	3.0	4.2	5.9	5.3
Japan	3.6	4.9	7.2	7.5	4.6	3.0	2.1	1.2	0.4
Germany	3.8	6.5	7.9	8.8	9.4	7.4	5.3	4.4	3.3
France	7.6	9.4	10.0	9.5	10.7	8.6	5.6	6.3	4.0
Italy	11.2	12.7	12.3	12.7	14.5	10.5	8.8	10.7	9.9
United Kingdom	10.3	13.9	14.8	11.5	9.4	5.9	5.5	6.7	6.0
Canada	9.2	11.9	12.9	9.0	6.6	4.6	5.1	6.9	4.9
Short-term interest rate[2]									
Industrial countries	**7.5**	**9.2**	**9.5**	**8.2**	**6.9**	**5.2**	**5.0**	**5.6**	**4.8**
Major industrial countries	7.4	9.0	9.3	7.8	6.3	4.8	4.8	5.5	4.6
United States	7.7	9.1	8.2	5.8	3.7	3.2	4.6	5.9	5.3
Japan	4.4	5.3	7.6	7.2	4.3	2.8	2.1	1.1	0.5
Germany	4.3	7.1	8.4	9.2	9.5	7.2	5.3	4.5	3.3
France	7.9	9.3	10.3	9.7	10.4	8.4	5.8	6.8	4.2
Italy	11.2	12.7	12.3	12.7	14.5	10.5	8.8	10.7	9.9
United Kingdom	10.3	13.9	14.8	11.5	9.6	5.9	5.5	6.7	6.1
Canada	9.6	12.2	13.0	9.0	6.7	5.0	5.6	7.1	5.2
Other industrial countries	8.5	10.2	10.8	10.7	10.3	8.3	6.4	6.8	6.3
Memorandum									
European Union	8.0	10.1	11.0	10.8	11.0	8.3	6.4	6.9	5.8
Long-term interest rate[3]									
Industrial countries	**8.5**	**8.6**	**9.4**	**8.6**	**7.8**	**6.5**	**7.1**	**6.9**	**6.2**
Major industrial countries	8.3	8.3	9.1	8.4	7.6	6.3	7.0	6.7	6.3
United States	8.8	8.5	8.6	7.9	7.0	5.9	7.1	6.6	6.3
Japan	4.8	5.1	7.0	6.3	5.1	4.0	4.2	3.3	3.2
Germany	6.5	7.0	8.7	8.5	7.9	6.5	6.9	6.9	6.5
France	9.1	8.8	10.0	9.0	8.6	6.9	7.4	7.6	6.7
Italy[4]	12.0	13.3	13.6	13.1	13.1	11.3	10.3	11.9	10.4
United Kingdom	9.7	10.2	11.8	10.1	9.1	7.5	8.2	8.2	8.1
Canada	10.2	9.9	10.8	9.8	8.8	7.9	8.6	8.4	7.9
Other industrial countries	9.6	10.4	11.3	9.9	9.4	7.6	8.0	8.4	7.5
Memorandum									
European Union	9.2	9.8	11.0	10.0	9.6	7.9	8.1	8.5	7.7

[1]For the United States, federal funds rate; for Japan, overnight call rate; for Germany, repurchase rate; for France, day-to-day money rate; for Italy, three-month treasury bill rate; for the United Kingdom, base lending rate; and for Canada, overnight money market financing rate.

[2]For the United States, three-month certificates of deposit (CDs) in secondary markets; for Japan, three-month CDs; for Germany, France, and the United Kingdom, three-month interbank deposits; for Italy, three-month treasury bills; and for Canada, three-month prime corporate paper.

[3]For the United States, yield on ten-year treasury bonds; for Japan, over-the-counter sales yield on ten-year government bonds with longest residual maturity; for Germany, yield on government bonds with maturities of nine to ten years; for France, long-term (seven- to ten-year) government bond yield (Emprunts d'Etat à long terme TME); for Italy, secondary market yield on fixed-coupon (BTP) government bonds with two to four years' residual maturity; for the United Kingdom, yield on medium-dated (ten-year) government stock; and for Canada, average yield on government bonds with residual maturities of over ten years.

[4]March 1996 data refer to yield on ten-year government bonds.

Table A19. Industrial Countries: Exchange Rates

	1988	1989	1990	1991	1992	1993	1994	1995	March[1] 1996
	National currency units per U.S. dollar								
U.S. dollar nominal exchange rates									
Japanese yen	128.2	138.0	144.8	134.7	126.7	111.2	102.2	94.1	105.2
Deutsche mark	1.76	1.88	1.62	1.66	1.56	1.65	1.62	1.43	1.47
French franc	5.96	6.38	5.45	5.64	5.29	5.66	5.55	4.99	5.03
Pound sterling[2]	1.78	1.64	1.78	1.76	1.76	1.50	1.53	1.58	1.53
Italian lira	1302	1372	1198	1241	1232	1574	1612	1630	1564
Canadian dollar	1.23	1.18	1.17	1.15	1.21	1.29	1.37	1.37	1.37
Spanish peseta	116.5	118.4	101.9	103.9	102.4	127.3	134.0	124.7	123.6
Dutch guilder	1.98	2.12	1.82	1.87	1.76	1.86	1.82	1.61	1.64
Belgian franc	36.8	39.4	33.4	34.1	32.1	34.6	33.5	29.5	30.2
Swedish krona	6.13	6.45	5.92	6.05	5.82	7.78	7.72	7.13	6.80
Austrian schilling	12.3	13.2	11.4	11.7	11.0	11.6	11.4	10.1	10.3
Danish krone	6.73	7.31	6.19	6.40	6.04	6.48	6.36	5.60	5.67
Finnish markka	4.18	4.29	3.82	4.04	4.48	5.71	5.22	4.37	4.56
Greek drachma	141.9	162.4	158.5	182.3	190.6	229.2	242.6	231.6	241.2
Portuguese escudo	144.0	157.5	142.6	144.5	135.0	160.8	166.0	150.0	152.3
Irish pound	0.66	0.71	0.60	0.62	0.59	0.68	0.67	0.62	0.63
Swiss franc	1.46	1.64	1.39	1.43	1.41	1.48	1.37	1.18	1.19
Norwegian krone	6.52	6.90	6.26	6.48	6.21	7.09	7.06	6.34	6.39
Icelandic krona	43.0	57.0	58.3	59.0	57.5	67.6	69.9	64.7	66.2
Australian dollar	1.28	1.26	1.28	1.28	1.36	1.47	1.37	1.35	1.31
New Zealand dollar	1.53	1.67	1.68	1.73	1.86	1.85	1.69	1.52	1.48
	Annual percent change								
Real effective exchange rates[3]									
United States	−6.3	3.3	−4.8	−2.0	−1.9	2.7	−2.2	−4.3	...
Japan	5.0	−6.1	−10.5	6.2	3.3	20.4	6.8	3.6	...
Germany	−0.3	−1.9	5.3	−1.0	3.3	7.9	2.3	7.5	...
France	−3.1	−2.3	3.0	−3.9	0.8	2.1	—	2.0	...
United Kingdom	7.3	−0.1	−5.9	3.7	—	−6.5	0.8	−4.1	...
Italy	−1.0	4.1	3.6	0.6	−1.8	−17.5	−5.3	−11.0	...
Canada	9.4	6.4	1.4	3.1	−6.3	−8.5	−5.5	−6.6	...
Spain	4.5	8.1	6.1	2.2	0.8	−9.7	−8.0	−1.6	...
Netherlands	−4.2	−4.9	1.0	−1.8	2.7	2.8	−1.6	1.7	...
Belgium	−2.9	−0.9	4.0	−0.7	1.0	−0.9	−0.4	1.8	...
Sweden	3.6	7.1	0.8	−0.1	1.0	−23.6	−1.7	−1.3	...
Austria	−3.8	−3.3	−1.4	−3.1	0.6	−0.2	−2.1	0.2	...
Denmark	0.2	−2.1	5.8	−2.7	1.8	3.1	−0.3	4.3	...
Finland	2.4	4.9	3.0	−8.3	−18.3	−16.0	3.3	9.2	...
Ireland	−5.7	−6.9	1.6	−6.3	−2.0	−7.8	−4.2	−1.6	...
Switzerland	1.8	−4.3	7.1	2.9	−4.3	0.9	9.6	7.2	...
Norway	2.1	−1.0	0.4	−0.5	−0.6	−2.0	0.6	4.8	...

[1]March data refer to the average for February 16–March 14, 1996, the reference period for the exchange rate assumptions. See "Assumptions" in the introduction to this Statistical Appendix.

[2]Expressed in U.S. dollars per pound.

[3]Defined as the ratio, in common currency, of the normalized unit labor costs in the manufacturing sector to the weighted average of those of its industrial country trading partners, using 1989–91 trade weights.

Table A20. Developing Countries: Central Government Fiscal Balances

(In percent of GDP)

	1988	1989	1990	1991	1992	1993	1994	1995	1996	1997
Developing countries	**−5.3**	**−4.1**	**−2.9**	**−3.2**	**−2.8**	**−3.0**	**−2.4**	**−2.1**	**−2.1**	**−1.5**
By region										
Africa	−6.3	−4.5	−3.1	−4.2	−6.1	−8.6	−6.1	−3.9	−3.6	−2.5
Asia	−3.3	−2.9	−2.6	−2.6	−2.6	−2.4	−1.9	−1.9	−2.0	−1.6
Middle East and Europe	−12.6	−9.0	−8.9	−10.9	−6.1	−7.2	−5.9	−4.1	−4.0	−3.5
Western Hemisphere	−4.9	−4.1	−0.3	−0.2	−0.3	−0.1	−0.3	−0.9	−0.8	—
Sub-Saharan Africa	−7.2	−6.6	−6.5	−6.1	−8.0	−8.3	−6.8	−5.0	−4.9	−4.0
Four newly industrializing Asian economies	1.9	1.3	1.0	—	−0.1	1.0	1.4	0.9	0.7	1.1
By predominant export										
Fuel	−13.6	−7.7	−5.1	−5.8	−4.6	−8.8	−7.2	−3.6	−2.5	−1.5
Nonfuel exports	−4.2	−3.7	−2.7	−2.9	−2.6	−2.3	−1.9	−1.9	−2.0	−1.5
Manufactures	−1.4	−1.4	−1.3	−1.8	−1.8	−1.2	−1.0	−1.2	−1.3	−0.6
Primary products	−5.4	−6.4	−3.9	−3.4	−3.3	−3.3	−2.9	−2.4	−2.5	−1.9
Agricultural products	−7.0	−8.7	−4.5	−3.9	−4.2	−4.0	−3.8	−3.5	−3.4	−2.8
Minerals	−2.1	−1.5	−2.7	−2.3	−1.5	−1.9	−1.1	−0.2	−0.6	—
Services, income, and private transfers	−11.4	−9.6	−13.7	−18.5	−9.8	−5.6	−4.4	−2.9	−2.5	−2.5
Diversified export base	−5.0	−4.0	−2.3	−2.3	−2.4	−2.7	−2.1	−2.3	−2.5	−2.1
By financial criteria										
Net creditor countries	−7.2	−2.3	−6.0	−11.9	−8.0	−6.2	−4.9	−3.5	−2.6	−2.7
Net debtor countries	−5.2	−4.2	−2.8	−2.7	−2.5	−2.8	−2.2	−2.0	−2.1	−1.5
Market borrowers	−3.4	−2.5	−0.5	−0.7	−0.8	−1.0	−0.8	−0.9	−0.8	−0.3
Diversified borrowers	−6.5	−5.7	−4.9	−4.3	−4.1	−4.7	−4.0	−3.6	−4.0	−3.6
Official borrowers	−9.7	−8.4	−7.5	−7.8	−6.4	−7.0	−5.5	−4.1	−3.9	−3.2
Countries with recent debt-servicing difficulties	−7.4	−6.1	−3.1	−2.8	−2.3	−2.6	−2.1	−1.9	−1.7	−1.0
Countries without debt-servicing difficulties	−3.7	−3.1	−2.6	−2.7	−2.6	−2.9	−2.3	−2.0	−2.2	−1.7
Other groups										
Small low-income economies	−11.0	−9.4	−8.7	−9.0	−7.3	−8.0	−6.1	−4.6	−4.5	−3.5
Least developed countries	−9.3	−8.3	−8.1	−7.0	−7.8	−7.5	−7.4	−6.1	−6.3	−5.5
Memorandum										
Median										
Developing countries	−4.9	−4.6	−4.1	−4.0	−3.7	−3.8	−4.0	−3.0	−2.6	−2.0
By region										
Africa	−6.8	−5.0	−4.5	−4.9	−5.8	−7.0	−6.3	−3.7	−3.2	−3.0
Asia	−2.2	−3.3	−4.6	−4.7	−3.6	−2.6	−2.3	−3.3	−2.9	−2.4
Middle East and Europe	−11.7	−5.3	−5.4	−6.6	−4.4	−5.3	−5.3	−4.7	−3.4	−3.3
Western Hemisphere	−3.5	−3.7	−1.7	−2.1	−1.9	−1.8	−2.1	−1.6	−0.9	−0.7

Table A21. Developing Countries: Broad Money Aggregates

(Annual percent change)

	1988	1989	1990	1991	1992	1993	1994	1995	1996	1997
Developing countries	**76.8**	**89.3**	**82.0**	**60.8**	**68.1**	**71.1**	**58.0**	**23.0**	**17.9**	**16.5**
By region										
Africa	24.9	15.2	18.1	27.4	29.4	23.8	36.1	20.5	13.1	12.6
Asia	25.3	23.3	21.5	22.0	20.4	20.8	21.7	19.2	17.4	16.0
Middle East and Europe	17.2	21.5	18.7	26.1	25.9	26.1	36.7	31.4	24.9	20.5
Western Hemisphere	351.4	505.0	435.0	213.7	266.4	292.6	171.5	24.8	15.9	16.0
Sub-Saharan Africa	24.5	19.8	21.5	46.9	54.7	41.8	78.3	32.3	18.7	13.6
Four newly industrializing										
Asian economies	20.0	18.8	15.9	19.2	15.3	15.5	16.5	12.8	12.1	12.7
By predominant export										
Fuel	13.9	14.8	18.3	17.5	16.2	19.1	21.6	23.9	17.2	15.2
Nonfuel exports	94.5	107.9	95.7	69.0	77.9	80.9	64.2	22.8	18.0	16.7
Manufactures	20.8	18.9	21.1	22.4	22.3	22.0	24.2	20.3	17.1	15.5
Primary products	232.4	453.1	339.3	90.8	45.5	51.8	33.5	11.4	8.8	14.1
Agricultural products	254.7	516.9	308.4	84.3	45.4	36.5	20.5	9.9	10.6	12.5
Minerals	165.2	282.9	442.8	109.7	45.8	112.3	89.4	16.9	2.6	20.1
Services, income, and										
private transfers	8.3	12.6	17.0	19.2	15.0	15.6	13.6	11.9	10.3	9.2
Diversified export base	128.8	133.6	125.4	104.3	137.4	146.5	113.3	28.9	22.0	19.0
By financial criteria										
Net creditor countries	8.0	8.4	7.1	12.1	9.8	8.4	8.5	7.8	6.9	8.5
Net debtor countries	85.7	99.9	92.0	67.0	76.1	80.1	64.7	24.7	19.1	17.3
Market borrowers	135.8	171.4	153.2	95.6	113.3	122.6	83.8	23.2	16.5	15.8
Diversified borrowers	26.0	27.5	22.1	27.2	25.4	25.1	37.8	30.0	25.9	21.8
Official borrowers	57.7	40.9	40.3	37.4	36.3	29.8	33.1	21.1	17.9	15.8
Countries with recent debt-										
servicing difficulties	194.0	250.9	228.9	137.6	169.5	181.2	118.8	25.5	17.1	16.0
Countries without debt-										
servicing difficulties	22.4	22.2	22.5	25.4	24.7	24.7	29.6	24.0	20.9	18.6
Other groups										
Small low-income economies	61.9	44.0	44.3	40.2	42.1	35.0	38.9	23.9	19.1	16.9
Least developed countries	25.5	28.3	30.6	56.0	59.4	47.6	53.0	30.0	21.9	19.2
Memorandum										
Median										
Developing countries	17.3	16.5	17.6	18.7	16.6	16.0	17.3	12.9	10.9	10.1
By region										
Africa	14.6	12.3	12.8	16.7	12.9	11.9	26.6	13.8	10.7	10.1
Asia	18.4	18.5	19.0	20.5	17.2	16.8	17.2	15.4	14.1	14.2
Middle East and Europe	7.8	13.0	10.7	14.5	10.7	8.6	8.2	10.6	9.3	9.2
Western Hemisphere	22.9	18.6	27.5	30.9	19.7	17.0	16.9	11.2	9.5	7.7

Table A22. Summary of World Trade Volumes and Prices

(Annual percent change)

	Average 1978–87	1988	1989	1990	1991	1992	1993	1994	1995	1996	1997
Trade in goods and services											
World trade[1]											
Volume	4.0	8.1	7.4	5.5	3.9	4.8	3.8	9.0	8.7	6.4	7.0
Price deflator											
In U.S. dollars	4.6	5.5	0.8	8.9	−0.6	2.4	−4.0	2.4	8.3	0.2	0.6
In SDRs	3.5	1.5	5.7	2.9	−1.4	−0.5	−3.2	−0.2	2.2	3.6	0.7
Volume of trade											
Exports											
Industrial countries	4.2	7.5	8.1	6.8	5.1	4.3	2.4	8.2	7.1	4.8	5.4
Developing countries	3.0	11.0	6.1	6.2	6.6	9.9	7.5	12.0	12.2	10.2	11.2
Imports											
Industrial countries	4.4	8.3	8.2	5.0	2.0	3.7	0.8	9.1	7.3	4.8	5.0
Developing countries	3.7	9.6	7.1	7.9	11.2	9.9	8.9	9.0	11.8	10.1	11.6
Terms of trade											
Industrial countries	0.5	1.0	−0.8	−0.5	0.5	0.5	1.0	0.3	0.3	0.1	−0.1
Developing countries	0.8	−3.8	1.5	2.2	−2.5	−1.2	−0.6	—	0.1	−0.5	−0.1
Trade in goods											
World trade[1]											
Volume	4.2	8.6	6.9	4.8	4.0	6.0	4.0	9.2	8.8	6.2	7.0
Price deflator											
In U.S. dollars	4.3	5.2	1.3	8.5	−1.1	1.5	−4.5	3.0	9.3	0.7	0.7
In SDRs	3.2	1.2	6.2	2.5	−1.9	−1.4	−3.6	0.5	3.1	4.2	0.8
World trade prices in U.S. dollars[2]											
Manufactures	5.4	6.6	−0.6	9.8	−0.4	3.7	−5.8	3.2	10.2	−1.4	1.0
Oil	...	−18.9	21.2	28.7	−15.8	−1.6	−11.6	−6.8	9.5	1.3	−7.3
Nonfuel primary commodities	0.6	24.2	−1.6	−6.4	−5.7	0.1	1.8	13.6	8.5	−1.4	−1.7
World trade prices in SDRs[2]											
Manufactures	4.4	2.5	4.2	3.7	−1.2	0.7	−5.0	0.7	4.0	2.0	1.1
Oil	...	−22.0	27.1	21.6	−16.5	−4.4	−10.9	−9.1	3.3	4.8	−7.2
Nonfuel primary commodities	−0.4	19.5	3.2	−11.6	−6.5	−2.8	2.7	10.8	2.4	2.0	−1.6

Table A22 *(concluded)*

	Average 1978–87	1988	1989	1990	1991	1992	1993	1994	1995	1996	1997
Trade in goods											
Volume of trade											
Exports											
Industrial countries	4.4	7.9	7.5	6.3	5.0	4.0	1.9	8.6	7.5	4.7	5.4
Developing countries	2.5	12.7	7.9	5.4	5.9	9.6	6.2	10.6	11.3	9.8	10.5
Fuel exporters	−5.0	10.3	11.4	10.9	−0.4	2.8	−2.8	1.2	2.9	2.8	12.4
Nonfuel exporters	7.2	13.3	7.3	4.2	7.5	11.2	8.0	12.2	12.5	10.7	10.2
Imports											
Industrial countries	4.9	8.1	7.4	4.6	3.1	4.0	1.0	10.1	7.7	4.5	5.2
Developing countries	4.1	11.9	6.8	6.4	8.7	13.6	9.4	8.4	11.6	9.5	11.0
Fuel exporters	−1.6	5.1	1.6	2.4	−1.1	15.5	−3.2	−11.8	−1.6	1.8	21.0
Nonfuel exporters	5.8	13.2	7.7	7.1	10.3	13.4	11.3	10.9	12.9	10.2	10.2
Price deflators in SDRs											
Exports											
Industrial countries	3.5	2.6	4.5	2.8	−2.2	−0.3	−4.4	0.5	3.8	3.2	0.4
Developing countries	3.7	−2.1	9.8	2.3	−1.6	−1.9	0.8	1.3	1.4	5.5	1.3
Fuel exporters	2.4	−16.1	18.2	14.8	−9.4	−3.4	−5.4	−3.6	0.1	5.8	0.7
Nonfuel exporters	3.0	1.1	8.2	−0.5	0.4	−1.6	2.1	2.1	1.6	5.5	1.3
Imports											
Industrial countries	2.8	1.2	6.1	3.6	−3.6	−2.0	−6.5	−0.3	3.6	3.7	0.5
Developing countries	2.8	2.5	9.1	1.1	2.1	−2.0	1.3	0.9	1.4	6.5	1.6
Fuel exporters	1.5	3.4	7.0	2.4	8.4	−6.5	−2.1	−3.9	7.2	5.1	0.7
Nonfuel exporters	3.3	2.3	9.5	0.9	1.1	−1.4	1.8	1.5	0.9	6.6	1.7
Terms of trade											
Industrial countries	0.8	1.4	−1.4	−0.7	1.5	1.7	2.2	0.8	0.2	−0.4	—
Developing countries	0.8	−4.5	0.6	1.2	−3.6	0.1	−0.4	0.3	−0.1	−0.9	−0.3
Fuel exporters	0.9	−18.9	10.4	12.2	−16.4	3.3	−3.3	0.3	−6.7	0.6	−0.1
Nonfuel exporters	−0.3	−1.2	−1.2	−1.3	−0.7	−0.2	0.3	0.6	0.7	−1.1	−0.3
Memorandum											
World exports in billions of U.S. dollars											
Goods and services	2,139	3,476	3,747	4,293	4,406	4,736	4,735	5,282	6,201	6,640	7,148
Goods	1,716	2,777	2,988	3,381	3,460	3,691	3,673	4,132	4,908	5,241	5,639

[1]Average of annual percent change for world exports and imports. The estimates of world trade comprise, in addition to trade of industrial and developing countries (which is summarized in the table), trade of countries in transition.

[2]As represented, respectively, by the export unit value index for the manufactures of the industrial countries the average of U.K. Brent, Dubai, and West Texas Intermediate crude oil spot prices; and the average of world market prices for nonfuel primary commodities weighted by their 1987–89 shares in world commodity exports.

Table A23. Industrial Countries: Export Volumes, Import Volumes, and Terms of Trade

(Annual percent change)

	Average 1978–87	1988	1989	1990	1991	1992	1993	1994	1995	1996	1997
Trade in goods and services											
Export volume											
Industrial countries	**4.2**	**7.5**	**8.1**	**6.8**	**5.1**	**4.3**	**2.4**	**8.2**	**7.1**	**4.8**	**5.4**
Major industrial countries	4.1	8.0	9.0	7.5	5.6	4.4	2.0	8.0	7.2	4.6	5.3
United States	4.6	15.9	11.7	8.5	6.3	6.6	3.3	8.3	8.3	6.8	5.2
Japan	5.1	5.9	9.1	6.9	5.4	4.9	1.3	4.6	5.0	3.6	6.2
Germany[1]	3.8	5.5	10.2	10.4	12.8	−0.3	−4.7	7.5	3.8	3.6	4.3
France	3.2	7.9	10.3	5.4	4.1	4.9	−0.4	5.8	6.0	2.0	5.6
Italy	3.4	5.4	8.8	7.0	0.5	5.0	9.4	10.9	13.6	6.2	6.0
United Kingdom	3.0	0.5	4.7	5.0	−0.7	4.0	3.3	9.0	5.7	2.6	5.5
Canada	6.0	9.5	0.8	4.1	1.4	7.6	10.4	14.2	11.8	6.0	4.1
Other industrial countries	4.5	6.4	5.7	5.1	4.0	4.0	3.1	8.7	6.8	5.3	5.6
Memorandum											
European Union	3.9	5.7	7.7	6.7	5.2	3.2	1.5	8.6	7.2	4.1	5.4
Import volume											
Industrial countries	**4.4**	**8.3**	**8.2**	**5.0**	**2.0**	**3.7**	**0.8**	**9.1**	**7.3**	**4.8**	**5.0**
Major industrial countries	4.6	8.5	8.0	5.5	2.0	4.0	1.4	9.1	7.2	4.6	4.8
United States	6.2	4.0	3.9	3.9	−0.7	7.5	9.9	12.0	8.0	4.3	5.0
Japan	2.5	20.9	18.6	7.9	−4.7	−1.1	1.7	9.0	13.5	10.9	4.8
Germany[1]	3.1	5.1	8.4	9.4	13.7	2.2	−5.2	7.1	2.7	1.9	4.2
France	3.5	8.3	8.3	6.1	3.0	1.1	−3.4	6.9	4.4	3.8	5.7
Italy	4.4	6.8	7.6	8.0	3.4	4.6	−7.8	9.8	10.2	5.3	6.0
United Kingdom	4.5	12.6	7.4	0.5	−5.3	6.5	2.8	5.1	3.2	2.3	4.2
Canada	6.3	13.8	6.3	2.0	3.3	5.6	8.8	10.5	9.0	3.8	3.4
Other industrial countries	3.7	7.7	8.9	3.9	2.1	2.7	−0.7	9.2	7.8	5.4	5.5
Memorandum											
European Union	3.8	8.1	8.3	5.8	4.3	3.3	−3.0	7.7	5.9	4.0	5.1
Terms of trade											
Industrial countries	**0.5**	**1.0**	**−0.8**	**−0.5**	**0.5**	**0.5**	**1.0**	**0.3**	**0.3**	**0.1**	**−0.1**
Major industrial countries	0.4	0.9	−1.5	−1.0	0.9	0.8	1.2	0.3	0.1	0.1	−0.1
United States	−0.4	0.7	−0.6	−1.7	1.9	−0.3	1.3	0.3	0.2	0.1	0.1
Japan	−0.2	2.4	−3.0	−6.1	2.6	1.7	1.7	1.4	−0.5	0.7	−0.5
Germany[1]	0.3	0.1	−2.3	0.7	−1.0	2.5	1.7	0.1	1.1	—	0.2
France	0.3	—	−1.6	0.1	0.7	0.9	1.2	0.2	−0.4	−0.1	—
Italy	0.5	−0.7	−3.0	−0.2	1.7	−1.2	−2.4	0.8	−2.6	0.2	0.3
United Kingdom	0.8	1.1	1.6	1.0	1.3	1.7	0.3	−2.3	−1.2	0.8	−0.2
Canada	0.6	2.3	2.1	−2.1	−1.5	−0.5	0.3	0.5	2.2	−0.1	−0.8
Other industrial countries	0.4	1.2	1.0	0.6	−0.5	−0.1	0.4	0.3	0.7	—	−0.1
Memorandum											
European Union	0.5	0.4	−0.8	0.4	0.1	1.0	0.4	−0.3	−0.1	0.1	0.1
Memorandum											
Trade in goods											
Industrial countries											
Export volume	4.4	7.9	7.5	6.3	5.0	4.0	1.9	8.6	7.5	4.7	5.4
Import volume	4.9	8.1	7.4	4.6	3.1	4.0	1.0	10.1	7.7	4.5	5.2
Terms of trade	0.8	1.4	−1.4	−0.7	1.5	1.7	2.2	0.8	0.2	−0.4	—

[1]Data through 1991 apply to west Germany only.

Table A24. Developing Countries—by Region: Total Trade in Goods

(Annual percent change)

	Average 1978–87	1988	1989	1990	1991	1992	1993	1994	1995	1996	1997
Developing countries											
Value in U.S. dollars											
Exports	6.5	14.4	12.6	13.6	5.0	9.9	6.1	14.9	19.4	11.9	11.6
Imports	7.4	18.7	10.3	13.3	11.6	13.3	9.5	12.1	19.7	12.6	12.4
Volume											
Exports	2.5	12.7	7.9	5.4	5.9	9.6	6.2	10.6	11.3	9.8	10.5
Imports	4.1	11.9	6.8	6.4	8.7	13.6	9.4	8.4	11.6	9.5	11.0
Unit value in U.S. dollars											
Exports	4.7	1.7	4.7	8.2	−0.8	1.0	—	3.8	7.4	2.0	1.2
Imports	3.9	6.5	4.1	7.0	2.9	0.9	0.4	3.5	7.5	3.0	1.5
Terms of trade	0.8	−4.5	0.6	1.2	−3.6	0.1	−0.4	0.3	−0.1	−0.9	−0.3
Memorandum											
Real GDP growth in developing country trading partners	4.1	5.5	4.2	3.7	2.8	3.8	3.3	4.4	3.7	3.8	4.1
Market prices of nonfuel commodities exported by developing countries	−1.1	17.8	−2.7	−5.4	−3.4	−2.4	2.5	18.0	8.1	−5.6	−1.7
By region											
Africa											
Value in U.S. dollars											
Exports	3.9	−0.6	7.8	17.0	−3.6	−1.4	−3.6	1.1	13.1	8.6	6.1
Imports	2.9	13.9	4.5	9.0	−1.2	5.5	−3.7	5.6	17.3	6.0	6.5
Volume											
Exports	0.1	5.0	5.3	5.3	2.6	−1.6	2.6	−1.2	5.4	7.0	4.4
Imports	−0.6	6.3	2.6	1.3	−2.0	1.0	−0.6	3.4	10.7	4.2	5.6
Unit value in U.S. dollars											
Exports	5.4	−4.2	2.9	11.6	−5.6	0.7	−5.7	2.7	7.5	1.9	1.7
Imports	4.7	9.7	3.9	10.3	1.7	5.3	−2.1	3.5	6.6	1.9	1.0
Terms of trade	0.7	−12.7	−1.0	1.2	−7.2	−4.4	−3.7	−0.8	0.9	—	0.7
Asia											
Value in U.S. dollars											
Exports	13.8	23.4	11.4	11.3	13.9	13.4	10.5	19.0	22.1	14.0	12.7
Imports	13.0	27.2	13.4	13.6	14.5	13.6	13.4	17.2	23.8	15.3	13.2
Volume											
Exports	10.1	17.1	8.6	6.0	11.6	11.7	8.7	14.1	13.6	11.7	11.2
Imports	9.2	19.6	10.4	6.9	12.3	12.8	12.3	12.5	15.2	12.1	11.0
Unit value in U.S. dollars											
Exports	3.8	5.4	2.6	5.3	2.3	2.0	1.8	4.1	7.6	2.2	1.5
Imports	3.8	6.5	3.1	6.6	2.2	0.9	1.1	4.3	7.5	3.1	2.2
Terms of trade	—	−1.0	−0.5	−1.2	0.1	1.1	0.7	−0.1	0.1	−0.9	−0.7

Table A24 *(concluded)*

	Average 1978–87	1988	1989	1990	1991	1992	1993	1994	1995	1996	1997
Middle East and Europe											
Value in U.S. dollars											
Exports	−1.0	1.8	21.6	21.8	−9.6	8.5	−3.8	4.8	8.3	5.5	13.1
Imports	3.9	5.2	6.9	14.8	5.9	10.0	3.3	−8.6	13.4	6.6	16.2
Volume											
Exports	−5.0	10.0	13.0	2.5	−5.7	11.6	−1.7	4.1	3.7	2.2	11.9
Imports	1.1	1.6	3.0	6.0	−1.6	20.2	4.5	−9.1	4.9	3.7	14.9
Unit value in U.S. dollars											
Exports	4.7	−6.7	8.2	19.5	−3.5	—	−1.9	1.0	4.6	3.4	1.2
Imports	3.1	4.1	4.6	8.5	7.7	−4.0	0.1	0.6	9.7	2.8	1.2
Terms of trade	1.6	−10.4	3.4	10.1	−10.3	4.2	−1.9	0.4	−4.6	0.6	0.1
Western Hemisphere											
Value in U.S. dollars											
Exports	6.3	12.7	10.1	9.6	−1.3	4.9	5.2	15.3	21.4	9.4	7.4
Imports	3.9	11.6	7.2	13.0	16.2	21.0	8.3	16.9	9.3	8.1	7.7
Volume											
Exports	4.9	8.1	2.0	6.7	3.8	6.4	7.5	8.5	11.3	9.4	8.4
Imports	0.2	3.7	1.0	8.9	15.6	16.6	9.0	13.0	3.0	5.1	10.0
Unit value in U.S. dollars											
Exports	2.3	4.4	8.9	2.9	−4.9	−1.4	−2.0	6.3	9.2	—	−0.9
Imports	4.6	7.4	7.1	3.9	0.3	4.1	−0.5	3.4	5.8	3.1	−1.4
Terms of trade	−2.3	−2.8	1.7	−1.0	−5.2	−5.3	−1.5	2.9	3.2	−3.0	0.5
Sub-Saharan Africa											
Value in U.S. dollars											
Exports	3.6	2.4	5.7	7.4	−3.0	−2.8	−2.3	8.9	14.0	7.9	6.1
Imports	5.6	4.9	0.8	9.2	0.7	0.2	−3.7	1.1	12.7	6.0	7.4
Volume											
Exports	0.3	0.2	6.5	3.8	−0.3	−2.3	1.1	2.4	5.3	5.8	4.6
Imports	0.1	−0.7	−2.7	4.7	0.4	−1.4	−3.9	−2.6	5.5	2.4	4.7
Unit value in U.S. dollars											
Exports	7.3	3.5	1.7	5.7	−1.8	1.0	−2.0	8.2	8.7	2.6	1.9
Imports	8.6	7.2	8.7	11.1	2.5	3.7	2.7	6.9	7.9	3.8	2.9
Terms of trade	−1.2	−3.5	−6.4	−4.8	−4.2	−2.6	−4.5	1.2	0.7	−1.2	−0.9
Four newly industrializing Asian economies											
Value in U.S. dollars											
Exports	17.0	26.4	10.0	8.4	14.3	12.3	10.4	15.2	21.9	13.3	10.7
Imports	14.4	32.6	12.7	13.9	16.5	13.1	10.1	17.4	24.6	13.4	11.0
Volume											
Exports	13.2	18.3	6.8	3.1	10.3	11.8	7.4	10.4	12.7	11.1	9.8
Imports	10.0	23.6	8.7	7.5	13.1	13.5	7.9	11.6	14.9	10.4	8.9
Unit value in U.S. dollars											
Exports	3.6	6.8	3.1	5.5	3.9	0.6	2.9	4.2	8.4	2.3	0.8
Imports	4.4	7.6	3.8	6.5	3.5	−0.1	2.0	5.4	8.6	2.9	2.0
Terms of trade	−0.8	−0.8	−0.7	−0.9	0.4	0.7	0.8	−1.1	−0.1	−0.6	−1.1

Table A25. Developing Countries—by Predominant Export: Total Trade in Goods

(Annual percent change)

	Average 1978–87	1988	1989	1990	1991	1992	1993	1994	1995	1996	1997
Fuel											
Value in U.S. dollars											
Exports	−2.1	−4.4	25.2	33.4	−8.7	1.9	−9.2	−0.4	9.0	4.9	12.7
Imports	0.6	11.5	3.4	10.5	8.4	9.2	−5.9	−12.7	9.6	3.3	22.1
Volume											
Exports	−5.0	10.3	11.4	10.9	−0.4	2.8	−2.8	1.2	2.9	2.8	12.4
Imports	−1.6	5.1	1.6	2.4	−1.1	15.5	−3.2	−11.8	−1.6	1.8	21.0
Unit value in U.S. dollars											
Exports	3.5	−12.8	12.7	21.6	−8.6	−0.5	−6.2	−1.1	6.0	2.3	0.6
Imports	2.6	7.5	2.0	8.4	9.3	−3.7	−3.0	−1.4	13.6	1.6	0.6
Terms of trade	0.9	−18.9	10.4	12.2	−16.4	3.3	−3.3	0.3	−6.7	0.6	−0.1
Nonfuel exports											
Value in U.S. dollars											
Exports	10.5	18.9	10.2	9.3	8.5	11.6	9.2	17.4	20.9	12.8	11.5
Imports	9.5	20.1	11.6	13.7	12.1	13.9	11.8	15.2	20.7	13.4	11.6
Volume											
Exports	7.2	13.3	7.3	4.2	7.5	11.2	8.0	12.2	12.5	10.7	10.2
Imports	5.8	13.2	7.7	7.1	10.3	13.4	11.3	10.9	12.9	10.2	10.2
Unit value in U.S. dollars											
Exports	4.1	5.1	3.2	5.4	1.3	1.3	1.3	4.7	7.6	2.0	1.2
Imports	4.3	6.3	4.4	6.8	1.9	1.5	0.9	4.1	6.9	3.1	1.6
Terms of trade	−0.3	−1.2	−1.2	−1.3	−0.7	−0.2	0.3	0.6	0.7	−1.1	−0.3
Manufactures											
Value in U.S. dollars											
Exports	16.4	24.4	9.1	10.0	13.6	13.1	9.7	18.9	21.7	13.1	11.7
Imports	14.5	29.3	10.7	9.5	16.6	14.9	13.8	16.0	22.3	14.5	12.3
Volume											
Exports	12.5	16.0	6.2	4.8	10.0	12.2	7.6	13.8	13.2	10.9	10.8
Imports	9.8	20.8	6.8	3.5	13.5	14.6	12.4	10.9	13.8	11.8	10.6
Unit value in U.S. dollars											
Exports	3.8	7.2	2.8	5.4	3.5	1.0	2.0	4.3	7.8	2.2	1.0
Imports	4.7	7.4	3.7	6.3	3.1	0.4	1.4	4.7	7.5	2.6	1.8
Terms of trade	−0.9	−0.1	−0.8	−0.9	0.4	0.5	0.6	−0.4	0.3	−0.4	−0.8
Primary products											
Value in U.S. dollars											
Exports	3.3	9.2	9.0	7.9	−1.1	4.1	2.9	18.0	24.2	6.9	7.6
Imports	5.0	−4.0	2.0	8.7	14.5	20.6	5.6	14.3	13.0	9.1	7.9
Volume											
Exports	2.9	−0.8	−0.1	11.1	2.2	5.5	5.9	9.7	11.6	7.6	8.4
Imports	0.7	−8.7	0.3	2.1	12.7	18.2	5.5	10.2	5.4	6.3	5.4
Unit value in U.S. dollars											
Exports	3.2	10.8	12.2	−1.4	−2.5	−0.3	−2.2	8.0	11.5	−0.5	−0.5
Imports	6.2	6.2	11.2	10.6	3.1	3.8	1.4	4.5	6.8	2.7	2.4
Terms of trade	−2.8	4.3	0.8	−10.8	−5.5	−4.0	−3.5	3.4	4.4	−3.1	−2.9

Table A25 (concluded)

	Average 1978–87	1988	1989	1990	1991	1992	1993	1994	1995	1996	1997
Agricultural products											
Value in U.S. dollars											
Exports	1.6	4.4	4.9	16.2	−1.1	3.2	9.1	17.4	24.6	9.0	7.8
Imports	5.2	−10.6	−3.2	6.4	23.9	26.5	8.5	16.4	5.9	9.8	9.1
Volume											
Exports	2.5	−2.9	−7.3	21.4	1.8	5.2	7.3	11.2	13.9	7.8	8.8
Imports	1.0	−14.8	−5.6	1.4	19.4	22.6	6.9	12.4	−0.7	6.3	5.7
Unit value in U.S. dollars											
Exports	2.9	8.7	17.8	−2.2	−1.5	−0.8	2.6	6.2	9.9	1.1	−0.9
Imports	6.7	6.2	17.9	11.0	6.3	6.4	3.6	4.8	6.8	3.1	3.0
Terms of trade	−3.6	2.4	−0.1	−11.9	−7.3	−6.7	−1.0	1.3	2.9	−1.9	−3.8
Minerals											
Value in U.S. dollars											
Exports	6.3	16.3	14.3	−1.9	−1.2	5.4	−5.5	19.1	23.5	3.6	7.4
Imports	4.5	8.5	10.1	11.9	2.1	11.2	0.3	10.2	27.6	7.8	5.8
Volume											
Exports	3.4	2.3	9.1	−1.1	2.7	6.1	3.8	7.4	7.9	7.3	7.6
Imports	0.1	3.0	9.6	3.1	3.7	11.1	3.0	6.0	18.6	6.5	4.8
Unit value in U.S. dollars											
Exports	3.7	13.9	4.9	−0.4	−4.0	0.2	−8.7	10.9	14.2	−3.1	—
Imports	5.2	6.3	0.7	9.9	−1.0	−0.4	−2.6	3.9	6.8	2.0	1.3
Terms of trade	−1.4	7.1	4.2	−9.4	−2.9	0.6	−6.3	6.7	6.9	−5.1	−1.2
Services, income, and private transfers											
Value in U.S. dollars											
Exports	1.0	2.9	22.7	−11.8	−28.5	38.5	19.1	13.2	6.6	3.1	2.0
Imports	5.6	7.8	2.9	4.7	3.1	14.5	3.2	1.6	8.1	9.6	5.2
Volume											
Exports	−3.3	2.6	27.0	−20.8	−25.3	74.1	−2.3	4.0	7.4	0.7	1.3
Imports	1.9	6.0	−0.6	−3.7	−1.0	28.0	−5.4	−2.5	7.4	2.6	3.2
Unit value in U.S. dollars											
Exports	5.7	2.0	−0.7	12.9	5.4	−0.8	20.3	10.1	−0.3	2.9	2.4
Imports	4.3	2.3	5.4	8.4	4.8	3.2	12.1	5.6	0.8	6.4	2.5
Terms of trade	1.4	−0.3	−5.8	4.1	0.5	−3.9	7.3	4.3	−1.0	−3.3	−0.1
Diversified export base											
Value in U.S. dollars											
Exports	9.0	15.6	10.7	10.8	6.7	9.4	9.0	15.5	20.1	14.0	12.3
Imports	7.2	16.8	16.5	22.0	7.4	11.3	11.4	16.0	21.2	12.9	11.9
Volume											
Exports	5.6	14.1	8.4	4.6	8.2	7.1	9.7	10.7	12.0	11.8	10.4
Imports	4.2	10.6	12.2	14.8	7.5	8.8	13.3	12.8	13.5	9.3	11.1
Unit value in U.S. dollars											
Exports	4.0	1.4	2.0	6.0	−1.4	2.3	−0.6	4.3	7.2	2.0	1.8
Imports	3.6	5.8	3.8	6.4	−0.2	2.4	−1.4	2.9	6.8	3.5	1.0
Terms of trade	0.3	−4.2	−1.7	−0.4	−1.2	−0.1	0.8	1.3	0.4	−1.4	0.8

Table A26. Nonfuel Commodity Prices[1]

(Annual percent change; U.S. dollar terms)

	Average 1978–87	1988	1989	1990	1991	1992	1993	1994	1995	1996	1997
Nonfuel primary commodities	**0.6**	**24.2**	**−1.6**	**−6.4**	**−5.7**	**0.1**	**1.8**	**13.6**	**8.5**	**−1.4**	**−1.7**
By commodity group											
Food	−0.3	28.8	1.8	−9.6	−0.9	2.3	−1.3	5.1	8.1	4.3	−7.6
Beverages	−6.9	2.8	−17.2	−12.7	−6.5	−13.9	6.3	74.9	0.9	−24.7	−1.4
Agricultural raw materials	5.2	7.9	3.3	2.8	−3.6	2.7	16.2	10.1	4.6	0.1	2.5
Metals	2.5	49.5	−5.7	−10.7	−14.3	−2.3	−14.2	16.6	19.5	−3.3	0.1
Fertilizers	1.6	15.4	2.1	−4.5	3.2	−5.0	−15.4	8.0	10.6	5.9	2.0
Developing countries	**−1.1**	**17.8**	**−2.7**	**−5.4**	**−3.4**	**−2.4**	**2.5**	**18.0**	**8.1**	**−5.6**	**−1.7**
By region											
Africa	−2.3	10.3	−3.9	−3.4	−5.3	−6.5	2.7	21.9	5.9	−9.1	0.1
Asia	0.1	15.4	−0.7	−5.1	−0.9	2.7	8.3	14.2	9.2	−3.5	−1.3
Middle East and Europe	1.8	14.6	4.5	−3.2	−6.1	−5.3	−9.2	16.6	11.7	−3.0	−1.7
Western Hemisphere	−1.8	24.8	−4.8	−6.9	−4.9	−5.8	−3.5	21.4	7.6	−6.9	−3.1
Sub-Saharan Africa	−2.9	8.0	−5.4	−3.5	−5.3	−7.2	6.8	24.6	4.4	−11.3	0.2
Four newly industrializing Asian economies	0.5	16.9	−3.9	−6.2	−4.5	4.3	1.9	21.2	15.0	−3.4	−0.9
By predominant export											
Fuel	1.2	29.1	−12.3	−10.0	−10.5	0.1	11.6	10.4	8.1	−3.7	0.6
Nonfuel exports	−1.2	17.5	−2.3	−5.3	−3.2	−2.4	2.2	18.3	8.1	−5.7	−1.8
Manufactures	−0.2	15.8	0.2	−5.0	−4.9	−1.0	0.6	14.8	11.7	−1.2	−2.4
Primary products	−1.6	20.2	−2.5	−5.4	−6.0	−4.6	−2.5	20.0	10.1	−8.1	−2.5
Agricultural products	−2.8	11.0	−4.6	−6.0	−4.2	−6.3	4.7	21.7	4.4	−7.1	−2.3
Minerals	0.8	36.0	0.3	−4.7	−8.4	−2.1	−12.0	17.4	19.3	−9.4	−2.9
Services, income, and private transfers	0.3	20.1	−1.3	−2.5	−7.7	−7.0	−2.4	18.8	10.2	−6.1	−0.3
Diversified export base	−1.2	16.3	−2.7	−5.3	−1.3	−1.5	4.8	18.1	6.7	−5.3	−1.4
By financial criteria											
Net creditor countries	2.2	39.5	−2.7	−14.7	−11.2	6.1	−6.8	14.0	17.4	−1.1	−6.3
Net debtor countries	−1.1	17.7	−2.7	−5.3	−3.4	−2.4	2.5	18.1	8.1	−5.7	−1.6
Market borrowers	−0.6	21.5	−3.4	−6.5	−3.1	−0.6	3.0	14.0	9.7	−3.8	−2.7
Diversified borrowers	−1.8	13.5	−1.5	−3.9	−2.4	−2.6	2.3	22.4	5.0	−6.8	−0.3
Official borrowers	−1.6	13.0	−2.5	−4.0	−6.2	−8.5	1.3	24.6	8.7	−10.1	−0.6
Countries with recent debt-servicing difficulties	−1.5	19.8	−3.5	−5.5	−4.7	−4.8	−2.0	18.2	7.8	−6.0	−2.0
Countries without debt-servicing difficulties	−0.6	15.3	−1.7	−5.2	−1.8	0.2	7.4	17.9	8.3	−5.3	−1.3
Other groups											
Small low-income economies	−2.9	6.7	−3.8	−3.4	−5.3	−8.7	1.6	28.1	7.1	−11.2	−0.3
Least developed countries	−1.6	16.8	−1.7	−4.1	−6.3	−9.1	−1.6	29.4	9.7	−14.0	−1.4
Memorandum											
Average oil spot price[2]	. . .	−18.9	21.2	28.7	−15.8	−1.6	−11.6	−5.5	8.0	1.3	−7.3
In U.S. dollars a barrel	. . .	14.72	17.84	22.97	19.33	19.03	16.82	15.89	17.17	17.39	16.12
Export unit value of manufactures[3]	5.4	6.6	−0.6	9.8	−0.4	3.7	−5.8	3.2	10.2	−1.4	1.0

[1]Averages of world market prices weighted by 1987–89 exports as a share of world or group commodity estimates.
[2]Average of U.K. Brent, Dubai, and West Texas Intermediate crude oil spot prices.
[3]For the manufactures exported by the industrial countries.

Table A27. Summary of Payments Balances on Current Account

(In billions of U.S. dollars)

	1988	1989	1990	1991	1992	1993	1994	1995	1996	1997
Industrial countries	**−65.7**	**−92.5**	**−113.0**	**−36.5**	**−37.0**	**32.5**	**−2.2**	**20.2**	**11.6**	**21.3**
United States	−127.1	−103.8	−92.7	−7.4	−61.5	−99.9	−151.2	−152.9	−149.7	−160.8
European Union	4.5	−11.3	−30.9	−78.7	−74.7	11.0	30.0	67.0	71.1	81.7
Japan	79.6	57.2	35.8	68.4	112.3	132.0	130.6	111.2	87.9	98.1
Other industrial countries	−26.4	−43.4	−37.5	−28.7	−26.0	−16.4	−11.4	—	10.5	13.0
Developing countries	**−15.9**	**−10.6**	**−4.9**	**−83.0**	**−67.4**	**−101.9**	**−67.3**	**−79.0**	**−93.3**	**−106.2**
By region										
Africa	−9.5	−7.4	−2.9	−4.4	−8.5	−8.0	−10.2	−15.5	−14.8	−14.9
Asia	13.7	5.1	2.4	3.3	3.3	−12.0	0.2	−16.0	−28.5	−37.3
Middle East and Europe	−11.9	−2.5	−1.8	−64.1	−27.1	−37.0	−10.3	−14.7	−15.2	−16.5
Western Hemisphere	−8.1	−5.7	−2.6	−17.8	−35.1	−44.9	−47.1	−32.8	−34.8	−37.5
By analytical criteria										
Fuel exporters	−24.7	−11.1	8.8	−34.0	−27.4	−29.6	−7.3	−7.4	−3.8	−5.0
Nonfuel exporters	9.1	0.7	−13.4	−48.8	−39.8	−72.1	−60.0	−71.4	−89.4	−101.1
Net creditor countries	8.0	16.8	19.5	−39.4	−7.6	−12.8	−3.1	−1.1	3.1	−0.2
Net debtor countries	−23.6	−27.3	−24.1	−43.4	−59.5	−88.9	−64.2	−77.6	−96.3	−105.8
Countries with recent debt-servicing difficulties	−24.2	−19.2	−14.0	−24.8	−43.8	−55.7	−57.0	−44.6	−49.0	−49.2
Countries without debt-servicing difficulties	0.6	−8.1	−10.1	−18.6	−15.7	−33.2	−7.2	−33.0	−47.3	−56.7
Countries in transition	**1.2**	**−7.7**	**−22.2**	**1.5**	**−3.2**	**−3.5**	**−2.7**	**−2.2**	**−13.6**	**−21.8**
Central and eastern Europe	...	...	...	−7.0	−0.3	−8.1	−4.3	−4.9	−8.3	−9.8
Excluding Belarus and Ukraine	...	...	...	1.3	0.1	−6.1	−2.2	−3.4	−6.8	−8.2
Russia	...	...	...	4.1	−1.2	5.4	3.4	4.7	−2.4	−8.7
Transcaucasus and central Asia	...	...	...	4.4	−1.7	−0.8	−1.8	−1.9	−2.9	−3.3
Total[1]	**−80.4**	**−110.7**	**−140.1**	**−118.1**	**−107.6**	**−72.9**	**−72.3**	**−60.9**	**−95.3**	**−106.7**
In percent of sum of world exports and imports of goods and services	−1.2	−1.5	−1.6	−1.3	−1.1	−0.8	−0.7	−0.5	−0.7	−0.8

[1]Reflects errors, omissions, and asymmetries in balance of payments statistics on current account, as well as the exclusion of data for international organizations and a limited number of countries. See "Classification of Countries" in the introduction to this Statistical Appendix.

Table A28. Industrial Countries: Balance of Payments on Current Account

	1988	1989	1990	1991	1992	1993	1994	1995	1996	1997
					In billions of U.S. dollars					
Balance on current account										
Industrial countries	**−65.7**	**−92.5**	**−113.0**	**−36.5**	**−37.0**	**32.5**	**−2.2**	**20.2**	**11.6**	**21.3**
Major industrial countries	−55.6	−65.4	−90.7	−26.5	−32.9	−1.3	−34.4	−32.5	−38.1	−33.2
United States	−127.1	−103.8	−92.7	−7.4	−61.5	−99.9	−151.2	−152.9	−149.7	−160.8
Japan	79.6	57.2	35.8	68.4	112.3	132.0	130.6	111.2	87.9	98.1
Germany[1]	49.5	57.2	48.9	−19.2	−21.6	−16.3	−21.4	−17.4	−11.2	−11.4
France	−4.8	−4.6	−9.7	−5.9	3.9	10.5	9.7	18.6	12.7	12.8
Italy	−6.3	−11.8	−17.0	−23.6	−27.8	11.3	17.1	26.2	29.4	32.0
United Kingdom	−29.3	−36.7	−34.4	−15.1	−16.7	−16.6	−2.8	−8.7	−3.3	−0.1
Canada	−17.2	−22.8	−21.6	−23.6	−21.4	−22.3	−16.3	−9.6	−3.8	−3.8
Other industrial countries	−10.1	−27.1	−22.3	−10.0	−4.1	33.8	32.1	52.7	49.7	54.5
Spain	−3.7	−11.5	−16.9	−16.7	−18.4	−4.0	−3.7	7.3	3.1	1.5
Netherlands	5.3	8.3	10.5	7.9	7.5	12.6	13.6	17.5	13.7	16.0
Belgium-Luxembourg	3.7	3.6	3.6	4.9	6.6	11.2	12.7	16.1	16.5	17.7
Sweden	−0.7	−3.4	−6.5	−3.4	−7.9	−4.0	0.7	4.9	7.9	9.2
Austria	−0.2	0.2	1.2	0.1	−0.1	−0.7	−1.8	−4.2	−3.4	−1.9
Denmark	−1.3	−1.1	1.4	2.0	4.2	4.7	2.7	2.5	2.2	2.4
Finland	−2.7	−5.7	−6.9	−6.6	−4.9	−1.1	1.3	4.4	3.7	3.4
Greece	−3.0	−4.6	−4.9	−3.7	−2.0	−0.7	−0.1	−2.6	−2.5	−2.5
Portugal	−1.9	−0.6	−0.2	−0.7	—	0.8	−1.1	−2.0	−1.9	−1.6
Ireland	0.1	−0.5	0.1	1.5	2.5	3.1	3.1	4.3	4.1	4.2
Switzerland	8.9	6.8	8.5	10.6	15.1	19.4	18.4	19.8	18.3	17.7
Norway	−3.9	0.2	3.9	5.1	4.7	3.5	3.0	5.1	7.6	8.4
Iceland	−0.2	−0.1	−0.1	−0.3	−0.2	—	0.1	—	−0.1	−0.1
Australia	−9.9	−17.2	−14.6	−9.5	−10.1	−10.4	−15.6	−18.4	−17.1	−17.4
New Zealand	−0.5	−1.6	−1.2	−1.0	−1.2	−0.8	−1.1	−2.1	−2.5	−2.6
Memorandum										
European Union	4.5	−11.3	−30.9	−78.7	−74.7	11.0	30.0	67.0	71.1	81.7
					In percent of GDP					
Balance on current account										
United States	−2.5	−1.9	−1.6	−0.1	−1.0	−1.5	−2.2	−2.1	−2.0	−2.0
Japan	2.7	2.0	1.2	2.0	3.0	3.1	2.8	2.2	1.9	2.0
Germany[1]	4.1	4.8	3.3	−1.1	−1.1	−0.9	−1.0	−0.7	−0.5	−0.5
France	−0.5	−0.5	−0.8	−0.5	0.3	0.8	0.7	1.2	0.8	0.8
Italy	−0.8	−1.4	−1.6	−2.1	−2.3	1.1	1.7	2.4	2.4	2.6
United Kingdom	−3.5	−4.3	−3.5	−1.5	−1.6	−1.8	−0.3	−0.8	−0.3	—
Canada	−3.5	−4.1	−3.8	−4.0	−3.8	−4.0	−3.0	−1.7	−0.6	−0.6
Spain	−1.1	−3.0	−3.4	−3.2	−3.2	−0.8	−0.8	1.3	0.5	0.2
Netherlands	2.3	3.6	3.7	2.7	2.3	4.0	4.1	4.4	3.4	3.8
Belgium-Luxembourg	2.4	2.3	1.9	2.5	3.0	5.4	5.6	6.0	6.1	6.3
Sweden	−0.4	−1.8	−2.8	−1.4	−3.2	−2.2	0.4	2.2	3.2	3.5
Austria	−0.2	0.2	0.8	—	−0.1	−0.4	−0.9	−1.8	−1.4	−0.8
Denmark	−1.2	−1.1	1.1	1.5	3.0	3.5	1.8	1.5	1.2	1.3
Finland	−2.6	−5.1	−5.1	−5.4	−4.6	−1.3	1.3	3.5	2.9	2.6
Greece	−4.7	−7.0	−5.9	−4.3	−2.1	−0.7	−0.1	−2.3	−2.1	−2.0
Portugal	−4.0	−1.1	−0.3	−0.9	—	1.0	−1.2	−1.9	−1.7	−1.4
Ireland	0.3	−1.4	0.1	3.3	4.8	6.6	5.9	7.0	6.4	6.1
Switzerland	4.8	3.8	3.7	4.6	6.3	8.4	7.1	6.5	5.9	5.5
Norway	−3.9	0.2	3.3	4.3	3.7	3.1	2.4	3.5	4.9	5.3
Iceland	−3.5	−1.4	−2.1	−4.6	−3.1	—	1.8	0.4	−1.5	−1.4
Australia	−4.0	−6.1	−4.9	−3.2	−3.5	−3.7	−4.8	−5.3	−4.6	−4.5
New Zealand	−1.1	−3.7	−2.8	−2.3	−2.9	−1.8	−2.3	−3.6	−4.2	−4.0

[1]Data through June 1990 apply to west Germany only.

Table A29. Industrial Countries: Current Account Transactions

(In billions of U.S. dollars)

	1988	1989	1990	1991	1992	1993	1994	1995	1996	1997
Exports	1,959.2	2,097.6	2,411.0	2,454.9	2,616.2	2,524.7	2,817.2	3,333.0	3,484.6	3,686.4
Imports	1,974.6	2,141.4	2,457.2	2,464.8	2,588.2	2,433.3	2,733.2	3,221.5	3,372.0	3,562.3
Trade balance	−15.4	−43.8	−46.2	−9.9	28.0	91.4	84.0	111.5	112.5	124.1
Services, credits	529.6	570.7	698.6	732.9	813.2	802.8	856.3	945.5	1,011.6	1,072.8
Services, debits	527.4	567.4	698.7	714.5	796.8	781.8	834.0	932.5	977.7	1,028.2
Balance on services	2.3	3.2	−0.2	18.4	16.4	21.0	22.3	13.0	33.8	44.6
Balance on goods and services	−7.2	−30.4	−37.4	13.4	49.0	118.7	97.4	109.4	121.1	137.3
Factor income, net	6.0	10.2	8.9	4.9	4.7	6.2	−9.0	−15.1	−25.3	−31.4
Current transfers, net	−58.5	−62.1	−75.6	−49.9	−86.0	−86.2	−99.6	−89.2	−109.6	−116.1
Current account balance	**−65.7**	**−92.5**	**−113.0**	**−36.5**	**−37.0**	**32.5**	**−2.2**	**20.2**	**11.6**	**21.3**
Balance on goods and services										
Industrial countries	**−13.2**	**−40.6**	**−46.3**	**8.5**	**44.3**	**112.4**	**106.3**	**124.5**	**146.4**	**168.7**
Major industrial countries	−17.5	−30.3	−47.8	−4.3	20.9	58.1	46.8	54.1	72.8	90.2
United States	−115.3	−91.4	−80.0	−29.4	−39.5	−74.8	−106.2	−111.4	−89.7	−87.2
Japan	62.7	37.9	18.0	54.3	80.7	96.5	96.4	74.6	50.0	54.0
Germany[1]	65.4	65.7	56.1	0.6	−0.8	8.2	11.4	24.5	36.4	39.5
France	3.4	3.5	1.7	6.5	21.8	25.5	27.6	30.3	26.5	27.3
Italy	−4.9	−9.2	−14.7	−17.7	−22.2	16.7	22.9	29.0	34.3	37.3
United Kingdom	−31.2	−35.0	−27.0	−11.6	−14.2	−11.6	−9.3	−6.8	−3.5	−0.3
Canada	2.4	−1.8	−2.0	−6.9	−5.0	−2.5	4.1	14.1	18.8	19.5
Other industrial countries	4.3	−10.3	1.5	12.8	23.4	54.4	59.5	70.3	73.6	78.5
Memorandum										
European Union	37.3	17.7	10.0	−26.2	−10.8	72.3	93.6	129.4	144.4	159.0
Factor income, net										
Industrial countries	**6.0**	**10.2**	**8.9**	**4.9**	**4.7**	**6.2**	**−9.0**	**−15.1**	**−25.3**	**−31.4**
Major industrial countries	26.6	33.9	40.6	37.4	42.0	34.8	22.3	14.6	5.0	−1.4
United States	13.3	13.7	20.7	15.1	10.1	9.0	−9.3	−11.4	−24.4	−36.4
Japan	21.0	23.4	23.2	25.9	35.4	40.6	40.3	44.4	46.5	54.1
Germany[1]	3.7	11.1	16.8	17.9	14.4	10.8	5.1	−1.4	−3.3	−5.2
France	−1.5	−0.6	−3.2	−5.1	−9.1	−8.9	−9.5	−6.7	−8.4	−8.7
Italy	1.7	1.7	1.4	1.3	1.2	0.7	2.2	3.9	6.0	6.4
United Kingdom	8.1	5.7	1.3	−1.0	6.5	2.8	14.7	9.9	11.4	12.1
Canada	−19.8	−21.2	−19.6	−16.7	−16.5	−20.2	−21.2	−24.0	−22.9	−23.6
Other industrial countries	−20.7	−23.7	−31.7	−32.5	−37.3	−28.6	−31.3	−29.7	−30.2	−30.0
Memorandum										
European Union	−4.7	2.1	−6.1	−9.4	−16.4	−17.2	−9.2	−14.4	−11.9	−12.6

[1]Data through June 1990 apply to west Germany only.

Table A30. Developing Countries: Payments Balances on Current Account

	1988	1989	1990	1991	1992	1993	1994	1995	1996	1997
	In billions of U.S. dollars									
Developing countries	**−15.9**	**−10.6**	**−4.9**	**−83.0**	**−67.4**	**−101.9**	**−67.3**	**−79.0**	**−93.3**	**−106.2**
By region										
Africa	−9.5	−7.4	−2.9	−4.4	−8.5	−8.0	−10.2	−15.5	−14.8	−14.9
Asia	13.7	5.1	2.4	3.3	3.3	−12.0	0.2	−16.0	−28.5	−37.3
Middle East and Europe	−11.9	−2.5	−1.8	−64.1	−27.1	−37.0	−10.3	−14.7	−15.2	−16.5
Western Hemisphere	−8.1	−5.7	−2.6	−17.8	−35.1	−44.9	−47.1	−32.8	−34.8	−37.5
Sub-Saharan Africa	−7.6	−7.0	−8.5	−8.5	−9.0	−8.1	−5.7	−7.1	−7.0	−7.1
Four newly industrializing Asian economies	31.7	27.4	18.4	14.0	15.6	20.7	16.9	9.2	11.0	11.1
By predominant export										
Fuel	−24.7	−11.1	8.8	−34.0	−27.4	−29.6	−7.3	−7.4	−3.8	−5.0
Nonfuel exports	9.1	0.7	−13.4	−48.8	−39.8	−72.1	−60.0	−71.4	−89.4	−101.1
Manufactures	27.6	23.9	30.1	24.6	19.3	4.1	18.0	15.0	9.6	3.9
Primary products	−11.0	−6.8	−5.9	−11.8	−19.1	−20.8	−20.7	−16.5	−20.7	−22.3
Agricultural products	−7.5	−4.5	−1.8	−7.6	−14.3	−14.7	−16.0	−10.3	−13.1	−15.0
Minerals	−3.5	−2.4	−4.1	−4.2	−4.9	−6.0	−4.7	−6.2	−7.6	−7.3
Services, income, and private transfers	1.5	5.6	1.5	−25.9	−1.6	0.1	1.8	1.7	0.1	−0.2
Diversified export base	−9.3	−22.1	−39.3	−35.9	−38.6	−55.7	−59.2	−71.9	−78.4	−82.6
By financial criteria										
Net creditor countries	8.0	16.8	19.5	−39.4	−7.6	−12.8	−3.1	−1.1	3.1	−0.2
Net debtor countries	−23.6	−27.3	−24.1	−43.4	−59.5	−88.9	−64.2	−77.6	−96.3	−105.8
Market borrowers	8.2	4.1	10.8	−22.7	−32.7	−51.1	−33.5	−28.0	−36.8	−48.3
Diversified borrowers	−16.5	−17.8	−25.5	−11.8	−15.0	−22.8	−18.1	−34.6	−40.9	−37.9
Official borrowers	−15.6	−13.8	−9.6	−9.2	−12.1	−15.3	−12.7	−15.3	−18.7	−19.8
Countries with recent debt-servicing difficulties	−24.2	−19.2	−14.0	−24.8	−43.8	−55.7	−57.0	−44.6	−49.0	−49.2
Countries without debt-servicing difficulties	0.6	−8.1	−10.1	−18.6	−15.7	−33.2	−7.2	−33.0	−47.3	−56.7
Other groups										
Small low-income economies	−15.6	−12.6	−9.1	−9.4	−10.7	−13.2	−11.8	−13.5	−17.4	−18.4
Least developed countries	−5.9	−5.5	−6.5	−7.7	−7.7	−7.3	−5.8	−7.6	−9.0	−9.1

Table A30 (concluded)

	Average 1978–87	1988	1989	1990	1991	1992	1993	1994	1995	1996	1997
	In percent of exports of goods and services										
Developing countries	**−4.1**	**−2.1**	**−1.2**	**−0.5**	**−8.0**	**−5.9**	**−8.3**	**−4.8**	**−4.7**	**−5.0**	**−5.1**
By region											
Africa	−12.6	−12.0	−8.7	−2.9	−4.6	−8.8	−8.5	−10.7	−14.4	−12.7	−12.1
Asia	−4.5	3.3	1.1	0.5	0.6	0.5	−1.6	—	−1.5	−2.3	−2.6
Middle East and Europe	3.5	−8.1	−1.5	−0.9	−33.9	−13.3	−18.6	−5.0	−6.5	−6.4	−6.1
Western Hemisphere	−17.8	−6.2	−3.9	−1.6	−11.0	−20.5	−24.6	−22.7	−13.4	−13.1	−13.2
Sub-Saharan Africa	−26.2	−25.4	−22.0	−24.6	−25.3	−27.1	−24.8	−16.4	−18.2	−16.6	−15.9
Four newly industrializing Asian economies	2.3	12.1	9.4	5.8	3.9	3.8	4.6	3.2	1.4	1.5	1.4
By predominant export											
Fuel	−1.0	−20.7	−7.6	4.7	−19.8	−15.7	−18.5	−4.6	−4.3	−2.1	−2.4
Nonfuel exports	−7.9	1.4	0.1	−1.7	−5.6	−4.1	−6.8	−4.8	−4.8	−5.3	−5.4
Manufactures	2.9	8.5	6.7	7.6	5.4	3.8	0.7	2.7	1.8	1.0	0.4
Primary products	−28.1	−21.7	−12.2	−9.8	−19.5	−30.0	−31.6	−26.9	−17.5	−20.6	−20.5
Agricultural products	−29.8	−25.9	−14.4	−5.2	−21.1	−37.8	−36.2	−33.7	−17.8	−20.7	−21.9
Minerals	−25.9	−16.2	−9.6	−16.5	−17.0	−18.7	−24.1	−16.0	−17.1	−20.3	−18.0
Services, income, and private transfers	12.8	4.3	14.3	3.7	−73.7	−3.8	0.1	3.5	3.0	0.1	−0.4
Diversified export base	−17.9	−3.9	−8.3	−12.9	−11.1	−10.9	−14.4	−13.3	−13.5	−13.1	−12.3
By financial criteria											
Net creditor countries	14.5	5.9	10.7	10.8	−21.3	−3.8	−6.4	−1.5	−0.5	1.2	−0.1
Net debtor countries	2.3	−3.7	−3.8	−3.0	−5.1	−6.3	−8.7	−5.4	−5.4	−5.9	−5.8
Market borrowers	−7.2	1.9	0.9	1.9	−3.7	−4.8	−6.8	−3.7	−2.6	−3.0	−3.5
Diversified borrowers	−14.5	−11.7	−11.3	−15.1	−7.3	−8.5	−12.1	−8.6	−13.9	−15.0	−11.7
Official borrowers	−24.5	−24.0	−19.5	−11.6	−10.8	−13.8	−17.3	−13.4	−14.0	−15.8	−15.7
Countries with recent debt-servicing difficulties	−17.7	−11.3	−8.0	−5.3	−10.0	−16.7	−20.4	−18.8	−12.5	−12.5	−11.1
Countries without debt-servicing difficulties	−29.8	0.1	−1.7	−1.9	−3.1	−2.3	−4.4	−0.8	−3.0	−3.9	−4.1
Other groups											
Small low-income economies	−25.9	−32.1	−23.7	−14.4	−14.7	−16.2	−19.9	−16.4	−16.0	−18.9	−18.7
Least developed countries	−40.0	−32.8	−28.9	−32.3	−39.8	−40.0	−35.7	−25.1	−29.2	−31.6	−29.8
Memorandum											
Median											
Developing countries	−18.0	−13.2	−13.0	−13.8	−13.1	−15.4	−16.0	−10.8	−11.5	−12.1	−11.3

Table A31. Developing Countries—by Region: Current Account Transactions

(In billions of U.S. dollars)

	1988	1989	1990	1991	1992	1993	1994	1995	1996	1997
Developing countries										
Exports	636.5	716.5	813.7	854.1	938.5	995.9	1,143.9	1,365.9	1,528.2	1,705.4
Imports	604.1	666.4	754.9	842.4	954.4	1,045.3	1,172.2	1,403.6	1,580.2	1,776.0
Trade balance	32.4	50.1	58.8	11.8	−15.9	−49.3	−28.3	−37.7	−52.0	−70.6
Services, net	−14.1	−23.6	−25.6	−42.0	−35.6	−29.1	−21.0	−12.9	−12.7	−9.1
Balance on goods and services	18.3	26.5	33.2	−30.3	−51.5	−78.4	−49.3	−50.6	−64.7	−79.8
Factor income, net	−54.7	−59.3	−56.6	−55.6	−50.7	−54.2	−52.9	−65.0	−65.4	−64.1
Current transfers, net	20.5	22.3	18.4	2.8	34.8	30.7	34.8	36.6	36.7	37.7
Current account balance	**−15.9**	**−10.6**	**−4.9**	**−83.0**	**−67.4**	**−101.9**	**−67.3**	**−79.0**	**−93.3**	**−106.2**
Memorandum										
Exports of goods and services	771.5	868.7	988.4	1,041.2	1,149.8	1,227.5	1,408.0	1,673.8	1,870.9	2,093.3
Interest payments	79.8	88.2	92.2	86.3	86.2	87.9	95.8	110.8	115.3	121.8
Oil trade balance	78.6	104.2	135.8	113.0	116.0	99.4	94.1	98.7	117.9	120.3
By region										
Africa										
Exports	67.4	72.6	85.0	82.0	80.8	77.9	78.7	89.1	96.8	102.6
Imports	65.8	68.8	75.0	74.1	78.2	75.2	79.5	93.2	98.8	105.2
Trade balance	1.6	3.9	10.0	7.9	2.7	2.6	−0.7	−4.1	−2.0	−2.6
Services, net	−7.3	−8.0	−9.8	−9.3	−8.7	−8.5	−7.6	−9.1	−10.0	−10.3
Balance on goods and services	−5.7	−4.1	0.3	−1.4	−6.1	−5.9	−8.3	−13.2	−12.0	−12.8
Factor income, net	−13.3	−14.2	−15.2	−15.0	−14.6	−13.7	−13.0	−13.9	−14.3	−13.9
Current transfers, net	9.4	10.8	12.0	12.0	12.3	11.6	11.2	11.6	11.5	11.8
Current account balance	**−9.5**	**−7.4**	**−2.9**	**−4.4**	**−8.5**	**−8.0**	**−10.2**	**−15.5**	**−14.8**	**−14.9**
Memorandum										
Exports of goods and services	79.4	85.0	98.2	96.0	96.4	93.5	95.2	107.4	116.5	123.8
Interest payments	14.2	14.7	16.0	15.8	15.4	14.2	14.0	15.7	16.3	16.2
Oil trade balance	10.5	15.5	24.4	22.0	21.4	19.2	15.8	17.7	18.8	19.3
Asia										
Exports	352.3	392.5	436.7	497.5	564.4	623.9	742.2	906.0	1,032.7	1,163.9
Imports	339.9	385.4	437.7	501.3	569.6	646.1	757.2	937.4	1,080.8	1,223.6
Trade balance	12.4	7.1	−1.0	−3.8	−5.2	−22.2	−15.0	−31.5	−48.2	−59.7
Services, net	3.3	2.2	4.9	4.5	1.7	1.7	6.4	6.1	6.4	8.3
Balance on goods and services	15.6	9.4	3.9	0.8	−3.5	−20.5	−8.7	−25.3	−41.8	−51.4
Factor income, net	−8.4	−8.6	−6.8	−8.3	−5.3	−3.5	−6.2	−4.9	−1.6	−2.3
Current transfers, net	6.5	4.3	5.4	10.9	12.0	12.1	15.1	14.3	14.9	16.5
Current account balance	**13.7**	**5.1**	**2.4**	**3.3**	**3.3**	**−12.0**	**0.2**	**−16.0**	**−28.5**	**−37.3**
Memorandum										
Exports of goods and services	414.1	464.1	522.3	594.4	677.6	753.0	899.7	1,095.9	1,250.9	1,415.8
Interest payments	19.9	20.8	21.7	22.9	24.8	25.6	30.9	37.3	38.3	41.9
Oil trade balance	−5.7	−8.1	−12.0	−14.0	−17.9	−18.1	−19.5	−22.9	−25.0	−27.1

Table A31 (concluded)

	1988	1989	1990	1991	1992	1993	1994	1995	1996	1997
Middle East and Europe										
Exports	111.0	134.9	164.3	148.6	161.2	155.1	162.6	176.1	185.7	210.1
Imports	114.4	122.3	140.4	148.7	163.6	169.0	154.5	175.2	186.8	217.0
Trade balance	−3.4	12.6	23.9	−0.1	−2.4	−13.9	8.1	0.9	−1.0	−6.9
Services, net	−12.9	−20.6	−22.5	−37.6	−29.3	−23.6	−22.9	−17.0	−15.0	−12.7
Balance on goods and services	−16.3	−7.9	1.4	−37.7	−31.7	−37.5	−14.8	−16.1	−16.1	−19.5
Factor income, net	4.1	5.4	5.6	4.4	6.2	4.6	8.7	5.5	4.2	7.6
Current transfers, net	0.3	—	−8.9	−30.8	−1.6	−4.2	−4.2	−4.1	−3.4	−4.6
Current account balance	**−11.9**	**−2.5**	**−1.8**	**−64.1**	**−27.1**	**−37.0**	**−10.3**	**−14.7**	**−15.2**	**−16.5**
Memorandum										
Exports of goods and services	147.1	172.8	205.2	189.1	204.8	198.6	205.3	225.7	237.3	268.6
Interest payments	10.9	11.9	12.7	10.1	9.6	9.6	10.9	12.7	13.6	14.0
Oil trade balance	63.2	82.8	103.9	89.5	98.0	85.7	83.7	88.9	108.9	112.6
Western Hemisphere										
Exports	105.8	116.5	127.7	126.0	132.1	139.1	160.4	194.8	213.0	228.7
Imports	84.0	90.1	101.8	118.3	143.1	154.9	181.0	197.8	213.8	230.2
Trade balance	21.8	26.4	25.9	7.7	−11.0	−15.9	−20.7	−3.0	−0.8	−1.5
Services, net	2.9	2.7	1.8	0.3	0.7	1.3	3.1	7.1	6.0	5.6
Balance on goods and services	24.6	29.1	27.6	8.0	−10.2	−14.6	−17.5	4.1	5.2	4.1
Factor income, net	−37.1	−41.9	−40.2	−36.6	−36.9	−41.6	−42.3	−51.7	−53.7	−55.6
Current transfers, net	4.4	7.1	9.9	10.7	12.1	11.3	12.8	14.8	13.7	14.0
Current account balance	**−8.1**	**−5.7**	**−2.6**	**−17.8**	**−35.1**	**−44.9**	**−47.1**	**−32.8**	**−34.8**	**−37.5**
Memorandum										
Exports of goods and services	130.9	146.8	162.8	161.7	171.0	182.4	207.7	244.8	266.1	285.1
Interest payments	34.8	40.8	41.8	37.4	36.4	38.4	39.9	45.1	47.1	49.6
Oil trade balance	10.7	14.0	19.6	15.5	14.5	12.6	14.1	15.0	15.2	15.6
Four newly industrializing Asian economies										
Exports	223.8	246.1	266.9	304.9	342.5	378.3	436.0	531.4	602.2	666.4
Imports	199.3	224.6	255.9	298.0	337.0	371.1	435.5	542.6	615.5	683.2
Trade balance	24.6	21.5	11.0	6.9	5.5	7.3	0.5	−11.3	−13.3	−16.8
Services, net	6.4	5.2	4.3	3.9	6.3	11.1	16.0	20.0	22.4	25.2
Balance on goods and services	31.0	26.7	15.4	10.8	11.8	18.3	16.5	8.7	9.1	8.4
Factor income, net	1.4	3.0	4.0	4.1	4.4	3.5	1.9	3.5	4.9	5.0
Current transfers, net	−0.8	−2.2	−0.9	−0.9	−0.6	−1.1	−1.5	−3.1	−3.0	−2.3
Current account balance	**31.7**	**27.4**	**18.4**	**14.0**	**15.6**	**20.7**	**16.9**	**9.2**	**11.0**	**11.1**
Memorandum										
Exports of goods and services	261.7	290.4	317.0	361.0	406.7	454.4	525.6	641.5	730.5	816.0
Interest payments	4.4	4.8	5.2	4.9	4.3	4.3	5.0	5.0	5.5	5.7
Oil trade balance	−7.2	−9.0	−11.7	−12.2	−14.7	−13.5	−14.4	−16.0	−16.9	−17.2

Table A32. Developing Countries—by Analytical Criteria: Current Account Transactions

(In billions of U.S. dollars)

	1988	1989	1990	1991	1992	1993	1994	1995	1996	1997
By predominant export										
Fuel										
Exports	101.5	127.1	169.5	154.8	157.7	143.2	142.7	155.6	163.3	184.0
Imports	90.1	93.2	102.9	111.5	121.8	114.6	100.0	109.6	113.2	138.2
Trade balance	11.4	33.9	66.6	43.2	35.9	28.7	42.8	46.0	50.1	45.8
Services, net	−19.3	−25.3	−32.9	−45.4	−40.7	−32.8	−27.4	−26.3	−26.3	−26.2
Balance on goods and services	−7.9	8.6	33.7	−2.1	−4.7	−4.1	15.4	19.7	23.8	19.7
Factor income, net	−6.0	−7.4	−4.3	−5.7	−4.7	−5.7	−4.9	−8.6	−8.9	−5.6
Current transfers, net	−10.9	−12.3	−20.6	−26.2	−18.0	−19.8	−17.8	−18.4	−18.6	−19.0
Current account balance	**−24.7**	**−11.1**	**8.8**	**−34.0**	**−27.4**	**−29.6**	**−7.3**	**−7.4**	**−3.8**	**−5.0**
Memorandum										
Exports of goods and services	119.8	146.7	187.2	172.0	174.2	159.9	157.2	170.4	179.6	205.5
Interest payments	11.2	11.7	12.3	9.4	9.6	8.7	9.1	10.8	11.0	11.9
Oil trade balance	81.1	103.2	143.7	129.5	131.5	114.2	107.6	114.6	135.6	138.2
Nonfuel exports										
Exports	533.8	588.3	643.2	698.1	779.5	851.4	999.9	1,209.1	1,363.6	1,519.9
Imports	512.9	572.2	650.9	729.7	831.4	929.5	1,071.1	1,292.9	1,465.7	1,636.5
Trade balance	20.9	16.1	−7.7	−31.6	−51.9	−78.1	−71.2	−83.8	−102.2	−116.6
Services, net	5.5	1.9	7.6	3.7	5.4	4.0	6.6	13.7	13.8	17.3
Balance on goods and services	26.4	18.0	−0.2	−27.9	−46.5	−74.1	−64.6	−70.0	−88.3	−99.3
Factor income, net	−48.7	−51.9	−52.3	−49.8	−46.0	−48.5	−47.9	−56.4	−56.4	−58.5
Current transfers, net	31.4	34.6	39.1	29.0	52.8	50.5	52.6	55.0	55.4	56.7
Current account balance	**9.1**	**0.7**	**−13.4**	**−48.8**	**−39.8**	**−72.1**	**−60.0**	**−71.4**	**−89.4**	**−101.1**
Memorandum										
Exports of goods and services	650.5	720.7	800.1	867.9	974.2	1,066.1	1,249.3	1,501.9	1,689.6	1,886.0
Interest payments	68.6	76.5	79.9	76.8	76.5	79.1	86.6	100.0	104.2	109.9
Oil trade balance	−2.5	1.0	−7.9	−16.6	−15.4	−14.8	−13.5	−15.9	−17.7	−17.9
Manufactures										
Exports	276.1	301.3	331.6	376.7	426.2	467.4	555.5	676.3	765.0	854.4
Imports	260.8	288.6	316.1	368.4	423.3	481.8	558.7	683.5	782.3	878.8
Trade balance	15.3	12.7	15.5	8.3	2.9	−14.4	−3.2	−7.2	−17.4	−24.4
Services, net	6.2	5.0	5.3	6.0	5.0	6.6	8.1	11.3	13.5	14.7
Balance on goods and services	21.5	17.7	20.9	14.3	7.9	−7.8	4.9	4.1	−3.9	−9.8
Factor income, net	1.7	2.9	3.9	3.7	4.0	5.2	6.3	5.3	6.7	6.9
Current transfers, net	4.5	3.3	5.4	6.5	7.4	6.8	6.9	5.6	6.7	6.7
Current account balance	**27.6**	**23.9**	**30.1**	**24.6**	**19.3**	**4.1**	**18.0**	**15.0**	**9.6**	**3.9**
Memorandum										
Exports of goods and services	326.5	358.8	397.9	451.3	513.9	567.4	676.3	822.0	931.5	1,046.1
Interest payments	8.6	9.0	10.0	10.8	12.7	12.9	16.8	20.8	21.2	23.2
Oil trade balance	−5.7	−7.4	−9.9	−10.7	−13.7	−12.8	−13.9	−15.1	−15.5	−13.7

Table A32 (continued)

	1988	1989	1990	1991	1992	1993	1994	1995	1996	1997
Primary products										
Exports	42.6	46.4	50.1	49.5	51.6	53.1	62.7	77.8	83.2	89.6
Imports	39.9	40.7	44.3	50.7	61.1	64.5	73.8	83.4	90.9	98.2
Trade balance	2.6	5.7	5.8	−1.1	−9.6	−11.5	−11.1	−5.5	−7.7	−8.6
Services, net	−5.2	−4.9	−5.1	−5.4	−5.5	−5.8	−5.1	−5.4	−5.9	−6.0
Balance on goods and services	−2.6	0.8	0.7	−6.6	−15.0	−17.2	−16.2	−10.9	−13.6	−14.6
Factor income, net	−13.7	−13.8	−13.4	−12.9	−12.8	−11.6	−12.6	−14.3	−15.7	−16.5
Current transfers, net	5.3	6.3	6.7	7.6	8.8	8.1	8.1	8.8	8.6	8.8
Current account balance	**−11.0**	**−6.8**	**−5.9**	**−11.8**	**−19.1**	**−20.8**	**−20.7**	**−16.5**	**−20.7**	**−22.3**
Memorandum										
Exports of goods and services	50.6	55.7	60.3	60.6	63.8	65.8	76.9	94.1	100.7	108.7
Interest payments	13.1	15.4	14.5	13.6	12.8	12.0	12.9	13.7	14.8	15.6
Oil trade balance	−3.1	−3.0	−3.2	−3.6	−2.8	−2.0	−2.2	−2.5	−2.5	−2.5
Services, income, and **private transfers**										
Exports	18.8	23.1	20.4	14.6	20.2	24.0	27.2	29.0	29.9	30.5
Imports	32.9	33.9	35.5	36.6	41.9	43.2	43.9	47.5	52.0	54.7
Trade balance	−14.1	−10.7	−15.1	−22.0	−21.7	−19.2	−16.7	−18.5	−22.1	−24.2
Services, net	4.0	3.0	6.2	4.0	6.2	6.3	7.3	9.3	11.5	12.7
Balance on goods and services	−10.1	−7.7	−8.9	−18.0	−15.5	−12.9	−9.4	−9.1	−10.6	−11.5
Factor income, net	3.6	5.0	4.4	3.9	3.9	2.7	2.4	2.0	1.7	2.3
Current transfers, net	8.0	8.4	6.0	−11.9	10.0	10.2	8.9	8.8	8.9	9.1
Current account balance	**1.5**	**5.6**	**1.5**	**−25.9**	**−1.6**	**0.1**	**1.8**	**1.7**	**0.1**	**−0.2**
Memorandum										
Exports of goods and services	35.3	39.4	39.7	35.2	43.1	48.0	52.5	56.8	60.5	62.7
Interest payments	5.1	5.8	6.7	5.7	4.3	4.2	4.4	4.5	4.5	4.0
Oil trade balance	6.3	10.4	6.3	1.0	6.0	8.4	10.8	11.4	11.2	10.9
Diversified export base										
Exports	197.4	218.6	242.1	258.5	282.8	308.2	355.8	427.2	486.8	546.9
Imports	180.3	210.0	256.1	275.1	306.3	341.1	395.8	479.7	541.7	606.1
Trade balance	17.1	8.5	−14.0	−16.6	−23.5	−32.9	−40.0	−52.5	−54.8	−59.3
Services, net	0.2	−1.4	0.8	−1.3	−0.7	−3.4	−3.9	−1.7	−5.6	−4.3
Balance on goods and services	17.3	7.1	−13.2	−17.9	−24.1	−36.3	−44.0	−54.2	−60.5	−63.6
Factor income, net	−40.3	−45.9	−47.1	−44.6	−41.0	−44.8	−44.0	−49.5	−49.2	−51.2
Current transfers, net	13.7	16.7	21.0	26.7	26.6	25.5	28.7	31.9	31.2	32.1
Current account balance	**−9.3**	**−22.1**	**−39.3**	**−35.9**	**−38.6**	**−55.7**	**−59.2**	**−71.9**	**−78.4**	**−82.6**
Memorandum										
Exports of goods and services	239.3	268.0	303.3	322.2	354.9	386.4	445.1	530.4	598.6	670.3
Interest payments	41.8	46.3	48.8	46.8	46.8	50.0	52.4	61.0	63.7	67.2
Oil trade balance	—	1.0	−1.1	−3.3	−5.1	−8.4	−8.2	−9.7	−11.0	−12.7

Table A32 *(continued)*

	1988	1989	1990	1991	1992	1993	1994	1995	1996	1997
By financial criteria										
Net debtor countries										
Exports	520.0	580.2	652.6	689.1	758.8	819.3	958.1	1,156.2	1,302.8	1,470.6
Imports	513.7	571.6	653.2	724.2	816.5	903.2	1,027.0	1,237.0	1,400.9	1,584.8
Trade balance	6.3	8.6	−0.7	−35.1	−57.6	−83.9	−68.9	−80.9	−98.1	−114.1
Services, net	0.8	−3.2	0.9	3.5	4.1	3.9	8.7	19.3	20.1	24.9
Balance on goods and services	7.1	5.4	0.2	−31.7	−53.5	−80.0	−60.2	−61.6	−78.0	−89.2
Factor income, net	−66.6	−72.6	−70.7	−66.6	−63.0	−64.5	−62.5	−77.4	−79.1	−78.6
Current transfers, net	35.9	39.9	46.4	54.9	57.0	55.6	58.5	61.3	60.8	62.0
Current account balance	**−23.6**	**−27.3**	**−24.1**	**−43.4**	**−59.5**	**−88.9**	**−64.2**	**−77.6**	**−96.3**	**−105.8**
Memorandum										
Exports of goods and services	634.9	710.1	806.0	854.4	946.8	1,026.1	1,198.9	1,439.4	1,618.3	1,828.1
Interest payments	77.8	85.4	89.5	83.9	83.7	85.6	92.9	108.1	112.9	119.5
Oil trade balance	36.7	50.3	60.2	41.6	36.7	28.8	25.8	26.4	42.3	48.2
Market borrowers										
Exports	361.5	402.0	457.0	501.4	562.5	614.2	730.6	891.5	1,011.2	1,132.3
Imports	329.8	373.3	428.7	506.1	578.0	645.1	751.4	903.4	1,031.9	1,165.9
Trade balance	31.7	28.7	28.3	−4.7	−15.5	−30.9	−20.8	−12.0	−20.7	−33.7
Services, net	5.7	5.5	5.8	3.6	2.1	2.8	6.9	16.7	17.6	20.8
Balance on goods and services	37.4	34.3	34.1	−1.1	−13.3	−28.1	−13.9	4.8	−3.1	−12.9
Factor income, net	−38.3	−41.6	−37.1	−36.4	−37.0	−40.7	−39.6	−53.4	−54.2	−55.9
Current transfers, net	9.0	11.5	13.7	14.8	17.6	17.8	20.0	20.6	20.5	20.4
Current account balance	**8.2**	**4.1**	**10.8**	**−22.7**	**−32.7**	**−51.1**	**−33.5**	**−28.0**	**−36.8**	**−48.3**
Memorandum										
Exports of goods and services	430.5	483.4	554.6	608.3	685.5	751.2	893.9	1,083.5	1,228.6	1,380.7
Interest payments	42.9	48.3	50.5	47.4	48.7	51.0	56.5	67.5	70.0	75.7
Oil trade balance	22.2	27.5	42.4	35.3	31.4	27.2	26.2	26.1	26.8	26.8
Official borrowers										
Exports	45.8	52.0	61.3	60.7	61.1	60.4	65.0	74.7	80.6	85.6
Imports	69.0	71.7	80.9	83.3	88.1	89.4	92.5	105.7	115.6	123.5
Trade balance	−23.2	−19.7	−19.7	−22.5	−27.0	−29.0	−27.6	−30.9	−35.0	−37.9
Services, net	—	−2.7	−1.1	−1.7	—	−0.1	1.8	2.0	3.7	4.7
Balance on goods and services	−23.2	−22.4	−20.7	−24.3	−27.0	−29.1	−25.8	−28.9	−31.3	−33.3
Factor income, net	−9.0	−8.8	−9.6	−10.6	−10.1	−10.0	−10.1	−10.3	−10.8	−10.4
Current transfers, net	16.6	17.4	20.7	25.7	24.9	23.9	23.1	23.9	23.4	23.9
Current account balance	**−15.6**	**−13.8**	**−9.6**	**−9.2**	**−12.1**	**−15.3**	**−12.7**	**−15.3**	**−18.7**	**−19.8**
Memorandum										
Exports of goods and services	64.7	70.5	83.5	84.9	87.8	88.2	94.9	108.7	118.2	125.7
Interest payments	13.7	14.6	16.1	15.2	14.1	13.7	13.7	14.4	14.8	14.1
Oil trade balance	2.9	6.8	9.9	8.1	8.2	7.1	5.5	6.8	6.0	5.4

Table A32 *(concluded)*

	1988	1989	1990	1991	1992	1993	1994	1995	1996	1997
Countries with recent debt-servicing difficulties										
Exports	177.1	197.4	212.1	197.5	204.6	212.2	236.9	284.0	311.8	354.6
Imports	160.9	170.0	185.7	195.7	225.4	238.4	269.4	301.9	330.3	375.2
Trade balance	16.2	27.4	26.3	1.9	−20.8	−26.2	−32.6	−17.9	−18.5	−20.5
Services, net	−9.1	−12.9	−12.2	−8.2	−7.0	−8.9	−6.4	−4.2	−5.3	−5.7
Balance on goods and services	7.1	14.5	14.2	−6.4	−27.8	−35.1	−39.0	−22.1	−23.8	−26.3
Factor income, net	−49.3	−55.2	−54.9	−46.6	−45.1	−48.5	−46.4	−53.2	−54.4	−52.9
Current transfers, net	18.0	21.4	26.7	28.1	29.1	27.9	28.4	30.7	29.2	30.0
Current account balance	**−24.2**	**−19.2**	**−14.0**	**−24.8**	**−43.8**	**−55.7**	**−57.0**	**−44.6**	**−49.0**	**−49.2**
Memorandum										
Exports of goods and services	215.3	241.3	262.8	249.2	261.9	272.9	303.5	356.9	391.3	442.5
Interest payments	51.7	59.1	61.1	54.0	51.4	52.6	53.4	59.3	61.9	65.0
Oil trade balance	28.6	40.4	43.5	28.2	27.4	24.4	24.4	25.8	41.3	45.7
Countries without debt-servicing difficulties										
Exports	342.9	382.8	440.5	491.6	554.2	607.1	721.3	872.2	991.0	1,116.0
Imports	352.7	401.6	467.5	528.6	591.0	664.8	757.6	935.2	1,070.5	1,209.6
Trade balance	−9.9	−18.8	−27.0	−37.0	−36.8	−57.7	−36.3	−63.0	−79.6	−93.6
Services, net	9.9	9.7	13.1	11.7	11.1	12.8	15.2	23.5	25.4	30.6
Balance on goods and services	—	−9.1	−13.9	−25.3	−25.8	−44.9	−21.2	−39.4	−54.2	−62.9
Factor income, net	−17.3	−17.4	−15.8	−20.1	−17.9	−16.0	−16.0	−24.2	−24.7	−25.7
Current transfers, net	17.9	18.4	19.7	26.8	28.0	27.8	30.0	30.6	31.6	32.0
Current account balance	**0.6**	**−8.1**	**−10.1**	**−18.6**	**−15.7**	**−33.2**	**−7.2**	**−33.0**	**−47.3**	**−56.7**
Memorandum										
Exports of goods and services	419.6	468.8	543.2	605.3	684.9	753.2	895.4	1,082.4	1,227.0	1,385.6
Interest payments	26.1	26.3	28.5	29.9	32.3	32.9	39.4	48.8	51.0	54.5
Oil trade balance	8.1	10.0	16.7	13.3	9.3	4.4	1.3	0.6	1.0	2.5
Other groups										
Least developed countries										
Exports	14.1	15.1	15.5	14.9	14.5	15.3	17.8	19.9	21.7	23.1
Imports	22.7	23.0	24.9	25.2	25.5	26.3	27.9	31.8	34.8	37.1
Trade balance	−8.5	−7.9	−9.3	−10.4	−11.0	−11.0	−10.1	−11.9	−13.0	−14.0
Services, net	−2.5	−3.4	−2.7	−2.8	−2.8	−2.7	−2.2	−2.5	−2.4	−2.1
Balance on goods and services	−11.0	−11.3	−12.0	−13.2	−13.8	−13.7	−12.3	−14.4	−15.5	−16.2
Factor income, net	−3.0	−2.5	−2.0	−2.5	−2.6	−2.3	−2.6	−2.8	−2.7	−2.1
Current transfers, net	8.1	8.3	7.5	8.0	8.7	8.7	9.0	9.6	9.2	9.2
Current account balance	**−5.9**	**−5.5**	**−6.5**	**−7.7**	**−7.7**	**−7.3**	**−5.8**	**−7.6**	**−9.0**	**−9.1**
Memorandum										
Exports of goods and services	18.1	18.9	20.0	19.4	19.2	20.4	23.3	26.0	28.5	30.4
Interest payments	3.4	4.1	3.5	3.6	3.6	3.5	3.7	3.9	4.0	3.6
Oil trade balance	−2.6	−1.6	−2.7	−3.0	−3.1	−3.2	−2.9	−2.6	−3.0	−3.2

Table A33. Summary of Balance of Payments and External Financing

(In billions of U.S. dollars)

	1988	1989	1990	1991	1992	1993	1994	1995	1996	1997
Developing countries										
Balance of payments										
Balance on current account	−15.9	−10.6	−4.9	−83.0	−67.4	−101.9	−67.3	−79.0	−93.3	−106.2
Balance on capital and financial account	15.9	10.6	4.9	83.0	67.4	101.9	67.3	79.0	93.3	106.2
By balance of payments component										
Capital transfers[1]	2.0	1.9	13.8	3.5	0.9	5.7	2.7	3.9	4.4	4.8
Net financial flows	24.2	35.3	43.5	154.9	130.1	172.9	151.6	193.3	147.4	185.0
Errors and omissions, net	−9.0	−2.0	−3.0	−2.9	−6.5	−16.6	−29.1	−42.5	−1.6	−1.1
Change in reserves (− = increase)	−1.3	−24.7	−49.5	−72.5	−57.1	−60.1	−57.9	−75.7	−56.8	−82.6
By type of financing flow										
Nonexceptional financing flows	−8.6	−2.6	3.9	121.3	97.0	129.6	106.7	136.3	134.4	172.6
Exceptional financing flows	25.8	37.9	50.5	34.2	27.4	32.4	18.5	18.4	15.7	16.2
Arrears on debt service	11.5	13.6	18.5	12.9	4.1	15.8	−5.5	−7.9	. . .	. . .
Debt forgiveness	0.3	3.0	13.6	1.9	0.6	2.2	1.7	5.3	. . .	. . .
Rescheduling of debt service	20.9	17.2	13.3	13.8	14.8	20.6	13.7	14.3	. . .	. . .
Change in reserves (− = increase)	−1.3	−24.7	−49.5	−72.5	−57.1	−60.1	−57.9	−75.7	−56.8	−82.6
External financing										
Balance on current account	−15.9	−10.6	−4.9	−83.0	−67.4	−101.9	−67.3	−79.0	−93.3	−106.2
Change in reserves (− = increase)[2]	−1.3	−24.7	−49.5	−72.5	−57.1	−60.1	−57.9	−75.7	−56.8	−82.6
Asset transactions, including net errors and omissions[3]	−15.2	−28.1	−41.8	34.5	−16.6	−41.7	−46.5	−55.7	−44.0	−46.1
Total, net external financing[4]	**32.3**	**63.3**	**96.2**	**121.0**	**141.0**	**203.7**	**171.8**	**210.3**	**194.1**	**234.8**
Non-debt-creating flows, net	20.1	19.5	31.9	36.2	55.7	85.1	79.0	89.9	95.6	123.7
Capital transfers[1]	2.0	1.9	13.8	3.5	0.9	5.7	2.7	3.9	4.4	4.8
Direct investment and other equity flows	18.1	17.6	18.0	32.7	54.8	79.4	76.3	86.0	91.2	118.9
Net credit and loans from IMF[5]	−4.1	−1.5	−1.9	1.1	−0.2	−0.1	−0.8	12.5	. . .	. . .
Net external borrowing[6]	16.3	45.4	66.3	83.6	85.5	118.8	93.5	108.2	99.6	113.7
Borrowing from official creditors[7]	17.5	20.8	7.9	20.2	4.3	20.0	4.3	32.6	3.6	−7.1
Borrowing from banks[8]	−4.4	5.6	4.2	21.5	21.0	25.1	−17.8	40.9	26.9	36.6
Other borrowing[9]	3.2	19.0	54.2	41.9	60.3	73.7	107.1	34.8	69.1	84.2
Memorandum										
Balance on goods and services in percent of GDP[10]	0.6	0.8	0.9	−0.8	−1.2	−1.6	−1.0	−0.9	−1.0	−1.1
Scheduled amortization of external debt	95.7	87.8	94.0	95.6	115.0	118.8	129.8	157.0	137.8	139.4
Gross external financing[11]	128.0	151.1	190.2	216.5	256.0	322.5	301.5	367.4	331.9	374.3
Gross external borrowing[11]	112.0	133.2	160.3	179.2	200.5	237.5	223.3	265.3	237.3	253.2
Countries in transition										
Balance of payments										
Balance on current account	1.2	−7.7	−22.2	1.5	−3.2	−3.5	−2.7	−2.2	−13.6	−21.8
Balance on capital and financial account	−1.2	7.7	22.2	−1.5	3.2	3.5	2.7	2.2	13.6	21.8
By balance of payments component										
Capital transfers[1]	—	0.4	—	0.9	2.4	2.1	0.2	0.1	—	—
Net financial flows	2.8	9.9	11.9	−0.5	5.0	10.9	13.6	34.4	26.5	34.8
Errors and omissions, net	1.6	3.8	3.6	−2.3	0.6	4.1	−3.0	−0.8	0.3	0.6
Change in reserves (− = increase)	−5.6	−6.4	6.6	0.5	−4.9	−13.6	−8.1	−31.6	−13.2	−13.6

Table A33 (concluded)

	1988	1989	1990	1991	1992	1993	1994	1995	1996	1997
By type of financing flow										
Nonexceptional financing flows	−2.3	11.4	−1.8	−16.4	−12.5	−6.1	−8.8	20.1	18.7	27.5
Exceptional financing flows	6.7	2.7	17.3	14.5	20.6	23.2	19.5	13.7	8.1	7.9
Arrears on debt service	0.1	0.8	9.0	6.1	8.5	4.6	3.0	−14.9	...	...
Debt forgiveness	—	0.4	—	0.9	2.4	2.1	0.1	—	...	...
Rescheduling of debt service	6.5	1.5	8.3	7.2	9.0	16.6	16.2	29.3	...	...
Change in reserves (− = increase)	−5.6	−6.4	6.6	0.5	−4.9	−13.6	−8.1	−31.6	−13.2	−13.6
External financing										
Balance on current account	1.2	−7.7	−22.2	1.5	−3.2	−3.5	−2.7	−2.2	−13.6	−21.8
Change in reserves (− = increase)[2]	−5.6	−6.4	6.6	0.5	−4.9	−13.6	−8.1	−31.6	−13.2	−13.6
Asset transactions, including net errors and omissions[3]	−7.4	0.9	−1.2	−0.7	0.9	12.2	−0.8	0.8	0.1	0.9
Total, net external financing[4]	**11.7**	**13.1**	**16.8**	**−1.3**	**7.1**	**4.9**	**11.5**	**33.0**	**26.7**	**34.4**
Non-debt-creating flows, net	0.5	0.6	—	3.2	6.6	7.9	5.4	11.3	8.1	10.0
Capital transfers[1]	—	0.4	—	0.9	2.4	2.1	0.2	0.1	—	—
Direct investment and other equity flows	0.5	0.2	—	2.3	4.1	5.8	5.3	11.2	8.1	10.1
Net credit and loans from IMF[5]	−0.5	−0.3	0.3	2.4	1.6	3.7	2.4	4.7	...	...
Net external borrowing[6]	11.7	12.8	16.4	−6.9	−1.0	−6.8	3.7	17.0	14.7	22.0
Borrowing from official creditors[7]	−3.1	−0.9	10.9	23.7	15.9	3.4	1.0	9.8	8.1	15.6
Borrowing from banks[8]	6.0	12.4	−0.6	−4.5	−0.3	4.2	2.3	−0.9	0.1	0.4
Other borrowing[9]	8.8	1.3	6.1	−26.1	−16.6	−14.4	0.5	8.1	6.5	6.0
Memorandum										
Balance on goods and services in percent of GDP[10]	0.3	−0.2	−0.9	—	−0.2	−0.6	0.1	0.4	−0.4	−1.2
Scheduled amortization of external debt	22.9	17.1	29.1	28.0	27.4	24.4	26.4	24.2	19.3	18.4
Gross external financing[11]	34.6	30.3	45.8	26.7	34.5	29.2	37.9	57.2	46.0	52.8
Gross external borrowing[11]	34.6	29.9	45.5	21.1	26.4	17.6	30.1	41.2	34.0	40.5

[1]Comprise debt forgiveness as well as all other identified transactions on capital account as defined in the 5th edition of the IMF's *Balance of Payments Manual*.

[2]Positioned here to reflect the discretionary nature of many countries' transactions in reserves.

[3]Include changes in recorded private external assets (mainly portfolio investment), export credit, the collateral for debt-reduction operations, and the net change in unrecorded balance of payments flows (net errors and omissions).

[4]Equals, with opposite sign, the sum of transactions listed above. It is the amount required to finance the deficit on goods and services, factor income, and current transfers; the increase in the official reserve level; the net asset transactions; and the transactions underlying net errors and omissions.

[5]Comprise use of IMF resources under the General Resources Account, Trust Fund, structural adjustment facility (SAF), and enhanced structural adjustment facility (ESAF). For further detail, see Table A37.

[6]Net disbursement of long- and short-term credits (including exceptional financing) by both official and private creditors.

[7]Net disbursements by official creditors (other than monetary authorities) based on directly reported flows, and flows derived from statistics on debt stocks. The estimates include the increase in official claims caused by the transfer of officially guaranteed claims to the guarantor agency in the creditor country, usually in the context of debt rescheduling.

[8]Net disbursements by commercial banks based on directly reported flows and on cross-border claims and liabilities reported in the International Banking section of the IMF's *International Financial Statistics*.

[9]Includes primary bond issues and loans on the international capital markets. Since the estimates are residually derived, they also reflect any underrecording or misclassification of official and commercial bank credits above.

[10]This is often referred to as the "resource balance" and, with opposite sign, the "net resource transfer."

[11]Net external financing/borrowing (see footnotes 4 and 6, respectively) plus amortization due on external debt.

Table A34. Developing Countries—by Region: Balance of Payments and External Financing[1]

(In billions of U.S. dollars)

	1988	1989	1990	1991	1992	1993	1994	1995	1996	1997
Africa										
Balance on current account	−9.5	−7.4	−2.9	−4.4	−8.5	−8.0	−10.2	−15.5	−14.8	−14.9
Change in reserves (− = increase)	0.5	−2.4	−4.3	−5.6	5.6	−1.2	−5.1	−1.4	−2.6	−3.0
Asset transactions, including net errors and omissions	2.5	0.9	0.9	4.3	−1.9	−0.2	0.2	2.3	1.3	0.4
Total, net external financing	**6.8**	**9.0**	**6.6**	**5.9**	**5.0**	**9.6**	**15.2**	**14.8**	**16.2**	**17.6**
Non-debt-creating flows, net	1.5	4.8	5.0	2.8	3.7	2.5	3.4	3.0	4.1	4.6
Net credit and loans from IMF	−0.3	0.1	−0.6	0.2	−0.2	0.2	0.9	0.8	. . .	. . .
Net external borrowing	5.6	4.2	2.2	3.0	1.6	6.8	10.8	10.9	11.5	13.7
From official creditors	4.8	3.5	1.8	4.2	−0.1	4.8	2.4	3.3	0.9	−7.5
From banks	−1.6	−3.4	−2.0	−0.9	−4.1	3.5	−2.9	1.9	1.8	0.8
Other	2.4	4.1	2.4	−0.3	5.9	−1.5	11.3	5.8	8.8	20.4
Memorandum										
Net financial flows	5.6	6.8	2.0	3.5	2.7	7.2	13.4	12.6	14.8	16.2
Exceptional financing	5.9	15.0	12.7	9.9	7.8	7.4	12.5	11.9	10.2	8.2
Asia										
Balance on current account	13.7	5.1	2.4	3.3	3.3	−12.0	0.2	−16.0	−28.5	−37.3
Change in reserves (− = increase)	−12.9	−12.6	−25.1	−43.8	−32.6	−46.3	−61.6	−50.0	−44.4	−66.0
Asset transactions, including net errors and omissions	−19.7	−18.4	−17.0	−21.9	−19.0	−28.0	−47.7	−66.4	−52.6	−51.8
Total, net external financing	**18.9**	**26.0**	**39.7**	**62.4**	**48.3**	**86.3**	**109.1**	**132.4**	**125.5**	**155.1**
Non-debt-creating flows, net	9.2	6.2	10.0	15.1	14.4	32.8	42.0	52.5	50.4	71.9
Net credit and loans from IMF	−2.4	−1.1	−2.4	1.9	1.3	0.6	−0.8	−1.5	. . .	. . .
Net external borrowing	12.1	20.9	32.1	45.3	32.6	52.9	67.9	81.7	76.4	84.4
From official creditors	6.6	6.3	3.2	11.8	9.7	8.0	6.0	7.5	8.5	7.0
From banks	4.6	8.7	7.5	13.4	14.5	17.8	15.1	46.0	28.5	31.3
Other	0.9	5.9	21.4	20.1	8.4	27.1	46.9	28.2	39.4	46.0
Memorandum										
Net financial flows	8.2	9.5	23.1	49.8	32.1	70.5	81.1	104.1	76.8	105.9
Exceptional financing	1.9	1.8	2.3	2.4	2.2	1.7	1.7	0.1	0.2	0.2
Middle East and Europe										
Balance on current account	−11.9	−2.5	−1.8	−64.1	−27.1	−37.0	−10.3	−14.7	−15.2	−16.5
Change in reserves (− = increase)	9.7	−11.0	−5.4	−7.6	−10.1	6.1	−0.2	−2.6	2.2	−1.3
Asset transactions, including net errors and omissions	−7.1	−1.6	−7.0	56.2	13.7	1.8	16.1	15.0	6.0	5.1
Total, net external financing	**9.3**	**15.2**	**14.3**	**15.5**	**23.6**	**29.1**	**−5.6**	**2.3**	**7.0**	**12.7**
Non-debt-creating flows, net	2.0	1.7	10.8	1.9	1.2	4.6	0.7	1.5	4.2	5.9
Net credit and loans from IMF	−0.5	−0.2	−0.1	—	0.4	—	0.4	0.3	. . .	. . .
Net external borrowing	7.8	13.7	3.6	13.6	22.0	24.6	−6.7	0.5	2.8	6.7
From official creditors	2.0	3.2	−6.2	1.0	−2.5	5.7	−1.2	−1.8	−3.0	−3.7
From banks	7.6	−0.2	2.1	4.3	12.8	−1.7	−0.4	−4.7	−1.6	2.6
Other	−1.9	10.6	7.7	8.3	11.7	20.5	−5.1	7.0	7.4	7.8
Memorandum										
Net financial flows	1.7	12.0	−0.1	78.6	42.2	31.9	9.9	14.8	9.6	14.0
Exceptional financing	—	1.1	14.2	7.2	6.3	14.5	−5.5	0.2	−0.2	0.8

Table A34 *(concluded)*

	1988	1989	1990	1991	1992	1993	1994	1995	1996	1997
Western Hemisphere										
Balance on current account	−8.1	−5.7	−2.6	−17.8	−35.1	−44.9	−47.1	−32.8	−34.8	−37.5
Change in reserves (− = increase)	1.4	1.3	−14.7	−15.5	−19.9	−18.7	9.0	−21.7	−12.1	−12.3
Asset transactions, including net errors and omissions	9.2	−8.9	−18.7	−4.1	−9.5	−15.3	−15.0	−6.5	1.4	0.2
Total, net external financing	**−2.4**	**13.3**	**36.0**	**37.4**	**64.4**	**78.9**	**53.1**	**61.0**	**45.5**	**49.6**
Non-debt-creating flows, net	9.0	7.2	6.7	12.1	13.2	14.7	17.9	18.5	22.4	24.2
Net credit and loans from IMF	−0.9	−0.2	1.2	−1.0	−1.6	−0.9	−1.3	12.9	...	...
Net external borrowing	−10.5	6.3	28.1	26.3	52.8	65.1	36.5	29.6	23.5	26.3
From official creditors	4.1	7.8	9.1	3.2	−2.8	1.4	−2.9	23.6	−2.8	−2.9
From banks	−15.0	0.4	−3.4	4.8	−2.2	5.5	−29.7	−2.2	−1.8	1.9
Other	0.4	−1.9	22.4	18.3	57.8	58.2	69.1	8.3	28.1	27.3
Memorandum										
Net financial flows	8.7	6.9	18.5	23.0	53.1	63.4	47.2	61.8	46.1	48.9
Exceptional financing	17.9	20.0	21.3	14.8	11.1	8.8	9.7	6.2	5.5	7.0
Sub-Saharan Africa										
Balance on current account	−7.6	−7.0	−8.5	−8.5	−9.0	−8.1	−5.7	−7.1	−7.0	−7.1
Change in reserves (− = increase)	−0.2	−1.2	−0.4	−4.2	2.7	−0.7	−3.4	−1.6	−1.2	−0.6
Asset transactions, including net errors and omissions	0.2	1.0	2.5	5.7	−0.8	2.2	0.9	1.7	0.7	0.5
Total, net external financing	**7.8**	**7.3**	**6.7**	**7.3**	**7.4**	**6.7**	**8.2**	**7.2**	**7.6**	**7.4**
Non-debt-creating flows, net	1.2	1.9	1.7	1.8	1.8	1.5	2.0	1.0	1.7	2.0
Net credit and loans from IMF	−0.2	−0.4	−0.3	—	—	−0.2	0.5	0.6	...	...
Net external borrowing	6.8	5.8	5.3	5.5	5.6	5.3	5.7	5.6	5.6	6.2
From official creditors	4.1	3.2	5.7	6.3	1.2	3.8	4.8	4.8	2.9	−5.7
From banks	0.3	−0.1	0.8	−0.1	0.2	0.2	−0.4	0.2	—	0.1
Other	2.3	2.6	−1.2	−0.8	4.3	1.3	1.3	0.5	2.7	11.8
Memorandum										
Net financial flows	6.5	5.1	5.2	5.2	5.5	4.4	6.4	5.5	6.3	6.0
Exceptional financing	5.0	6.0	6.9	6.5	7.9	7.4	6.8	6.2	5.4	4.7
Four newly industrializing Asian economies										
Balance on current account	31.7	27.4	18.4	14.0	15.6	20.7	16.9	9.2	11.0	11.1
Change in reserves (− = increase)	−11.4	−7.9	−5.9	−16.9	−17.8	−19.8	−20.3	−22.1	−17.9	−36.3
Asset transactions, including net errors and omissions	−15.9	−20.4	−19.5	−14.0	−12.2	−21.2	−33.3	−32.1	−24.4	−26.3
Total, net external financing	**−4.4**	**0.9**	**7.0**	**16.9**	**14.4**	**20.3**	**36.7**	**45.1**	**31.3**	**51.5**
Non-debt-creating flows, net	1.1	−2.9	−0.5	3.0	−0.5	1.2	1.0	1.1	2.9	21.7
Net credit and loans from IMF	−0.5	—	—	—	—	—	—	—	...	...
Net external borrowing	−5.0	3.8	7.4	13.9	14.9	19.2	35.7	44.0	28.4	29.7
From official creditors	−2.1	−1.7	−0.8	0.2	−0.6	−1.9	−0.3	−0.6	−0.5	−0.5
From banks	−4.1	4.3	−3.5	0.9	5.6	5.4	2.7	10.1	7.9	7.6
Other	1.2	1.2	11.7	12.7	9.8	15.6	33.3	34.4	21.0	22.6
Memorandum										
Net financial flows	−14.7	−14.3	−7.5	5.3	−0.9	4.2	10.7	20.3	9.9	28.2
Exceptional financing	—	—	—	—	—	—	—	—	—	—

[1]For definitions, see footnotes to Table A33.

Table A35. Developing Countries—by Analytical Criteria: Balance of Payments and External Financing[1]

(In billions of U.S. dollars)

	1988	1989	1990	1991	1992	1993	1994	1995	1996	1997
By predominant export										
Fuel										
Balance on current account	−24.7	−11.1	8.8	−34.0	−27.4	−29.6	−7.3	−7.4	−3.8	−5.0
Change in reserves (− = increase)	12.6	−6.7	−9.2	−3.2	3.9	9.5	—	2.8	−1.1	−5.3
Asset transactions, including										
net errors and omissions	3.0	8.4	−7.2	20.9	16.4	10.4	10.3	9.6	5.5	8.0
Total, net external financing	**9.1**	**9.4**	**7.7**	**16.3**	**7.0**	**9.7**	**−3.0**	**−5.0**	**−0.6**	**2.2**
Non-debt-creating flows, net	0.8	3.0	0.6	2.6	1.4	1.0	1.5	1.6	2.1	2.6
Net credit and loans from IMF	0.2	1.7	1.9	0.5	−0.5	−0.8	0.4	−0.2	. . .	. . .
Net external borrowing	8.2	4.8	5.1	13.1	6.1	9.5	−4.9	−6.4	−3.6	−1.3
From official creditors	3.3	1.9	1.1	−1.0	−2.7	1.0	−3.4	−1.9	−2.1	−1.3
From banks	−0.6	—	−20.9	8.7	1.5	4.8	−5.0	−0.9	0.8	2.2
Other	5.4	2.9	24.9	5.5	7.3	3.6	3.4	−3.6	−2.3	−2.2
Memorandum										
Net financial flows	9.2	16.8	2.2	39.1	23.9	19.6	8.4	5.3	5.3	10.6
Exceptional financing	0.7	10.7	4.4	3.9	2.5	11.0	−0.7	3.5	4.6	4.1
Nonfuel exports										
Balance on current account	9.1	0.7	−13.4	−48.8	−39.8	−72.1	−60.0	−71.4	−89.4	−101.1
Change in reserves (− = increase)	−13.9	−18.0	−40.3	−69.3	−60.9	−69.5	−57.8	−78.4	−55.5	−77.1
Asset transactions, including										
net errors and omissions	−18.4	−36.6	−34.9	13.3	−33.3	−52.3	−56.9	−65.6	−49.8	−54.4
Total, net external financing	**23.2**	**53.9**	**88.6**	**104.7**	**134.0**	**194.0**	**174.8**	**215.4**	**194.7**	**232.6**
Non-debt-creating flows, net	20.9	16.9	31.8	29.3	31.1	53.5	62.6	74.0	79.0	103.9
Net credit and loans from IMF	−4.3	−3.2	−3.8	0.6	0.3	0.6	−1.2	12.7	. . .	. . .
Net external borrowing	6.6	40.2	60.6	74.8	102.6	139.8	113.4	129.0	117.7	132.2
From official creditors	14.2	18.9	6.7	21.3	6.9	19.0	7.7	34.5	5.7	−5.8
From banks	−3.8	5.6	25.2	12.9	19.6	20.3	−12.9	41.7	26.0	34.4
Other	−3.8	15.7	28.7	40.7	76.2	100.6	118.6	52.8	85.9	103.6
Memorandum										
Net financial flows	15.0	18.6	41.3	115.9	106.2	153.4	143.2	188.0	142.1	174.5
Exceptional financing	25.0	27.2	46.1	30.3	24.9	21.4	19.2	14.9	11.2	12.1
By financial criteria										
Net creditor countries										
Balance on current account	8.0	16.8	19.5	−39.4	−7.6	−12.8	−3.1	−1.1	3.1	−0.2
Change in reserves (− = increase)	10.5	−0.3	5.0	−12.9	−5.0	9.1	−3.6	−4.4	−5.7	−5.0
Asset transactions, including										
net errors and omissions	−12.0	−8.7	−21.8	48.5	5.8	−2.2	0.4	10.2	2.1	0.8
Total, net external financing	**−6.4**	**−7.8**	**−2.6**	**3.8**	**6.8**	**5.9**	**6.3**	**−4.7**	**0.4**	**4.4**
Non-debt-creating flows, net	−3.5	−6.1	−4.0	−0.7	−2.0	−2.2	−2.1	−5.6	−2.9	−3.3
Net credit and loans from IMF	—	—	—	—	—	—	—	—	. . .	. . .
Net external borrowing	−2.9	−1.7	1.4	4.5	8.8	8.1	8.4	1.0	3.4	7.7
From official creditors	−0.2	—	—	—	—	—	—	—	—	—
From banks	−2.2	0.1	−1.2	4.8	7.6	2.2	3.1	—	−0.2	2.6
Other	−0.5	−1.8	2.5	−0.3	1.2	5.9	5.4	1.0	3.5	5.1
Memorandum										
Net financial flows	−18.3	−15.6	−19.1	64.7	21.4	4.9	11.8	10.5	2.8	5.4
Exceptional financing	—	—	—	—	—	—	—	—	—	—

Table A35 *(continued)*

	1988	1989	1990	1991	1992	1993	1994	1995	1996	1997
Net debtor countries										
Balance on current account	−23.6	−27.3	−24.1	−43.4	−59.5	−88.9	−64.2	−77.6	−96.3	−105.8
Change in reserves (− = increase)	−11.7	−24.4	−54.5	−59.6	−52.1	−69.2	−54.3	−71.2	−51.0	−77.4
Asset transactions, including										
net errors and omissions	−3.4	−19.5	−20.3	−14.2	−22.7	−39.7	−47.0	−66.1	−46.4	−47.2
Total, net external financing	**38.7**	**71.1**	**98.9**	**117.2**	**134.2**	**197.8**	**165.4**	**215.0**	**193.7**	**230.4**
Non-debt-creating flows, net	25.2	26.0	36.4	32.6	34.5	56.8	66.2	81.2	84.0	109.9
Net credit and loans from IMF	−4.1	−1.5	−1.9	1.1	−0.2	−0.1	−0.8	12.5	. . .	. . .
Net external borrowing	17.6	46.6	64.3	83.4	100.0	141.2	100.1	121.6	110.7	123.2
From official creditors	17.7	20.8	7.9	20.3	4.3	20.0	4.3	32.6	3.6	−7.1
From banks	−2.2	5.4	5.4	16.8	13.4	22.9	−20.9	40.8	27.0	34.0
Other	2.1	20.4	51.1	46.4	82.3	98.3	116.7	48.2	80.1	96.3
Memorandum										
Net financial flows	42.4	51.0	62.7	90.2	108.7	168.0	139.8	182.8	144.6	179.7
Exceptional financing	25.8	37.9	50.5	34.2	27.4	32.4	18.5	18.4	15.7	16.2
Market borrowers										
Balance on current account	8.2	4.1	10.8	−22.7	−32.7	−51.1	−33.5	−28.0	−36.8	−48.3
Change in reserves (− = increase)	−12.5	−16.5	−41.2	−36.6	−40.4	−53.3	−42.0	−67.7	−42.4	−60.5
Asset transactions, including										
net errors and omissions	−3.6	−22.2	−28.7	−22.0	−27.0	−37.4	−50.6	−63.6	−51.3	−51.5
Total, net external financing	**7.9**	**34.6**	**59.0**	**81.4**	**100.1**	**141.8**	**126.1**	**159.3**	**130.6**	**160.3**
Non-debt-creating flows, net	18.4	12.4	14.6	21.5	22.3	44.4	52.8	60.4	61.0	84.2
Net credit and loans from IMF	−1.4	0.2	0.7	−1.2	−1.6	−1.2	−0.7	13.4	. . .	. . .
Net external borrowing	−9.1	22.0	43.7	61.1	79.4	98.6	74.1	85.5	69.4	76.5
From official creditors	2.8	6.4	4.8	5.2	0.3	6.4	−2.5	26.1	−0.4	−1.7
From banks	−9.5	8.1	−1.6	13.4	14.9	20.7	−24.3	38.8	21.6	24.9
Other	−2.5	7.6	40.4	42.5	64.3	71.4	100.8	20.5	48.3	53.3
Memorandum										
Net financial flows	13.6	20.0	38.9	61.2	77.8	115.5	95.1	128.3	79.7	108.7
Exceptional financing	14.4	15.9	18.1	11.5	10.0	15.4	5.0	8.7	9.7	9.8
Diversified borrowers										
Balance on current account	−16.5	−17.8	−25.5	−11.8	−15.0	−22.8	−18.1	−34.6	−40.9	−37.9
Change in reserves (− = increase)	0.9	−6.6	−7.1	−13.8	−10.1	−11.9	−6.5	−3.3	−8.2	−15.4
Asset transactions, including										
net errors and omissions	−1.0	6.1	6.3	—	−0.5	−5.8	4.2	−3.7	4.2	2.0
Total, net external financing	**16.6**	**18.3**	**26.3**	**25.6**	**25.5**	**40.4**	**20.4**	**41.6**	**45.0**	**51.3**
Non-debt-creating flows, net	3.9	4.7	4.5	5.0	5.8	5.2	7.2	13.0	15.9	17.8
Net credit and loans from IMF	−1.9	−1.5	−1.5	2.0	1.1	1.4	−0.5	−1.0	. . .	. . .
Net external borrowing	14.6	15.0	23.4	18.7	18.6	33.9	13.7	30.0	30.4	34.8
From official creditors	3.6	5.4	6.5	10.9	5.5	9.4	2.8	3.2	1.1	−0.6
From banks	8.4	−1.0	8.1	3.3	1.6	5.0	4.3	2.0	5.4	9.0
Other	2.7	10.6	8.9	4.4	11.4	19.5	6.6	24.8	23.9	26.4
Memorandum										
Net financial flows	15.7	19.2	27.2	24.5	22.7	39.9	27.3	43.3	47.0	51.9
Exceptional financing	4.6	5.7	6.4	6.0	4.9	4.5	4.6	1.8	1.8	1.4

Table A35 *(continued)*

	1988	1989	1990	1991	1992	1993	1994	1995	1996	1997
Official borrowers										
Balance on current account	−15.6	−13.8	−9.6	−9.2	−12.1	−15.3	−12.7	−15.3	−18.7	−19.8
Change in reserves (− = increase)	−0.2	−1.3	−6.2	−9.1	−1.6	−4.1	−5.7	−0.4	−0.5	−1.7
Asset transactions, including										
net errors and omissions	1.5	−3.2	2.3	8.1	5.1	3.7	−0.5	1.5	1.1	2.6
Total, net external financing	**14.5**	**18.4**	**13.8**	**10.5**	**8.9**	**15.8**	**19.0**	**14.3**	**18.3**	**19.0**
Non-debt-creating flows, net	2.9	8.9	17.4	6.1	6.4	7.2	6.2	7.7	7.1	7.9
Net credit and loans from IMF	−0.8	−0.2	−1.1	0.3	0.3	−0.3	0.5	0.2	...	...
Net external borrowing	12.4	9.7	−2.5	4.0	2.2	8.9	12.4	6.4	11.0	12.0
From official creditors	11.3	9.0	−3.4	4.2	−1.5	4.2	4.0	3.3	2.9	−4.8
From banks	−1.0	−1.7	−1.1	0.1	−3.2	−2.9	−0.9	—	—	0.1
Other	2.1	2.4	2.1	−0.3	6.9	7.5	9.4	3.1	8.1	16.7
Memorandum										
Net financial flows	13.1	11.8	−3.4	4.5	8.2	12.6	17.3	11.1	17.9	19.0
Exceptional financing	6.8	16.2	26.0	16.7	12.5	12.5	8.9	7.9	4.3	5.0
Countries with recent debt-servicing difficulties										
Balance on current account	−24.2	−19.2	−14.0	−24.8	−43.8	−55.7	−57.0	−44.6	−49.0	−49.2
Change in reserves (− = increase)	0.5	−5.2	−22.5	−23.7	−23.2	−21.2	4.3	−21.3	−14.7	−19.5
Asset transactions, including										
net errors and omissions	13.4	−9.3	−14.4	0.2	−2.8	−15.5	−12.6	−7.0	2.2	1.7
Total, net external financing	**10.3**	**33.7**	**50.9**	**48.2**	**69.8**	**92.4**	**65.3**	**73.0**	**61.5**	**67.0**
Non-debt-creating flows, net	12.0	15.7	22.5	16.0	17.9	18.3	20.5	23.2	24.9	28.3
Net credit and loans from IMF	−1.3	−0.5	0.4	−1.0	−1.8	−0.3	−1.1	13.2	...	...
Net external borrowing	−0.3	18.6	28.0	33.3	53.7	74.4	45.9	36.6	36.7	40.6
From official creditors	12.3	15.2	3.4	4.6	−3.8	4.9	0.7	25.8	−2.0	−11.4
From banks	−12.6	−5.7	−4.4	3.1	−6.7	2.8	−29.2	−0.9	0.9	3.3
Other	−0.1	9.0	29.0	25.6	64.2	66.7	74.3	11.7	37.9	48.7
Memorandum										
Net financial flows	22.8	23.4	18.8	30.3	58.8	74.2	58.7	68.9	61.2	65.5
Exceptional financing	25.7	37.7	50.3	33.7	25.1	22.1	20.3	14.3	10.5	12.3
Countries without debt-servicing difficulties										
Balance on current account	0.6	−8.1	−10.1	−18.6	−15.7	−33.2	−7.2	−33.0	−47.3	−56.7
Change in reserves (− = increase)	−12.3	−19.2	−32.0	−35.9	−28.9	−48.0	−58.5	−49.9	−36.3	−57.9
Asset transactions, including										
net errors and omissions	−16.7	−10.1	−5.9	−14.4	−19.9	−24.2	−34.4	−59.1	−48.6	−48.9
Total, net external financing	**28.4**	**37.4**	**47.9**	**68.9**	**64.5**	**105.4**	**100.2**	**142.1**	**132.2**	**163.4**
Non-debt-creating flows, net	13.2	10.3	13.9	16.6	16.6	38.5	45.7	58.0	59.1	81.6
Net credit and loans from IMF	−2.8	−1.0	−2.3	2.2	1.6	0.2	0.3	−0.7	...	...
Net external borrowing	17.9	28.1	36.3	50.1	46.3	66.8	54.2	85.1	74.0	82.6
From official creditors	5.3	5.6	4.4	15.7	8.0	15.1	3.6	6.8	5.6	4.3
From banks	10.4	11.1	9.8	13.6	20.1	20.0	8.3	41.8	26.1	30.7
Other	2.2	11.4	22.1	20.8	18.1	31.6	42.3	36.5	42.2	47.6
Memorandum										
Net financial flows	19.6	27.6	43.9	59.9	49.9	93.8	81.0	113.9	83.4	114.2
Exceptional financing	0.1	0.2	0.1	0.5	2.3	10.3	−1.8	4.1	5.2	3.9

Table A35 *(concluded)*

	1988	1989	1990	1991	1992	1993	1994	1995	1996	1997
Other groups										
Small low-income countries										
Balance on current account	−15.6	−12.6	−9.1	−9.4	−10.7	−13.2	−11.8	−13.5	−17.4	−18.4
Change in reserves (− = increase)	1.2	−1.1	−3.5	−7.7	−0.3	−4.8	−6.7	−1.7	−0.8	−1.9
Asset transactions, including net errors and omissions	0.5	−2.6	0.9	7.7	4.1	3.0	1.1	0.9	1.1	2.7
Total, net external financing	**13.9**	**16.3**	**11.7**	**9.5**	**6.9**	**15.0**	**17.4**	**14.3**	**17.0**	**17.6**
Non-debt-creating flows, net	2.8	8.0	13.6	5.0	4.6	5.1	4.1	6.3	5.6	6.4
Net credit and loans from IMF	−0.6	−0.2	−0.6	0.4	0.5	—	0.9	0.5	...	...
Net external borrowing	11.7	8.5	−1.3	4.1	1.8	9.9	12.4	7.4	11.2	12.1
From official creditors	9.6	7.2	−2.3	4.1	−1.1	4.1	3.6	4.9	4.0	−4.2
From banks	−0.6	−1.3	−0.3	−0.2	−2.9	−2.1	0.5	0.7	0.3	0.5
Other	2.7	2.6	1.3	0.2	5.9	8.0	8.3	1.8	6.9	15.8
Memorandum										
Net financial flows	13.3	10.5	−2.0	4.0	6.7	13.2	17.1	11.7	16.9	17.7
Exceptional financing	5.2	14.0	20.8	15.3	11.6	11.6	9.3	7.2	4.4	5.1
Least developed countries										
Balance on current account	−5.9	−5.5	−6.5	−7.7	−7.7	−7.3	−5.8	−7.6	−9.0	−9.1
Change in reserves (− = increase)	—	−1.0	0.1	−4.3	2.4	−0.8	−2.0	−0.2	0.8	0.3
Asset transactions, including net errors and omissions	−0.5	−0.6	—	5.5	−1.5	1.6	0.4	0.6	0.3	1.4
Total, net external financing	**6.4**	**7.0**	**6.4**	**6.5**	**6.8**	**6.5**	**7.5**	**7.1**	**7.8**	**7.3**
Non-debt-creating flows, net	0.5	1.2	1.2	2.6	2.5	2.6	1.6	0.9	1.6	1.6
Net credit and loans from IMF	−0.2	−0.3	−0.4	0.1	0.2	−0.1	0.2	0.5	...	...
Net external borrowing	6.0	6.2	5.5	3.8	4.2	4.0	5.7	5.7	6.1	6.3
From official creditors	5.0	4.8	5.3	5.5	0.1	2.8	3.6	4.9	3.6	−4.8
From banks	−0.5	0.7	0.5	0.3	—	−0.1	−0.8	—	0.1	0.1
Other	1.5	0.7	−0.2	−2.0	4.0	1.3	2.9	0.8	2.5	11.1
Memorandum										
Net financial flows	2.2	2.1	1.7	0.7	—	−0.1	1.3	2.3	4.3	3.1
Exceptional financing	4.2	4.6	4.8	5.7	6.8	6.6	6.2	4.9	3.5	4.2

[1]For definitions, see footnotes to Table A33.

Table A36. Developing Countries: Reserves[1]

	1988	1989	1990	1991	1992	1993	1994	1995	1996	1997
					In billions of U.S. dollars					
Developing countries	**252.9**	**276.2**	**325.9**	**398.2**	**422.4**	**484.5**	**562.1**	**634.3**	**688.9**	**749.5**
By region										
Africa	10.8	12.7	17.6	21.3	18.7	20.2	25.8	27.1	29.6	32.4
Asia	158.6	168.5	194.3	238.8	239.8	275.3	347.9	394.4	436.8	481.0
Middle East and Europe	52.4	61.6	65.6	72.1	75.1	79.8	83.2	85.8	83.6	84.9
Western Hemisphere	31.1	33.3	48.3	66.0	88.8	109.2	105.2	126.9	139.0	151.2
Sub-Saharan Africa	6.6	7.2	8.6	9.9	10.2	11.3	13.7	15.2	16.2	16.7
Four newly industrializing Asian economies	111.4	117.7	126.3	143.6	152.7	165.5	189.7	207.7	222.8	237.3
By predominant export										
Fuel	43.6	46.9	54.0	57.0	47.1	47.1	48.9	46.2	47.3	52.6
Nonfuel exports	209.3	229.3	271.8	341.2	375.3	437.4	513.2	588.1	641.6	696.9
Manufactures	136.0	142.9	163.9	196.0	181.0	197.6	254.4	296.5	327.9	357.3
Primary products	13.9	14.0	20.9	26.6	33.6	38.8	49.1	50.1	52.9	54.1
Agricultural products	6.8	5.3	8.8	11.8	15.7	19.5	21.5	23.2	26.0	27.2
Minerals	7.2	8.7	12.1	14.9	17.8	19.3	27.6	26.9	26.9	26.9
Services, income, and private transfers	8.8	10.7	12.3	17.2	24.3	27.1	28.2	29.7	31.0	32.6
Diversified export base	50.6	61.7	74.6	101.4	136.5	173.9	181.5	211.8	229.8	252.9
By financial criteria										
Net creditor countries	107.9	105.0	100.1	112.2	109.2	109.6	118.0	122.4	128.1	133.1
Net debtor countries	145.0	171.3	225.8	286.1	313.2	374.9	444.1	511.9	560.8	616.5
Market borrowers	100.5	116.7	160.0	199.7	214.6	262.4	308.7	372.4	411.9	450.6
Diversified borrowers	29.3	37.5	42.4	55.8	63.8	73.6	88.9	92.2	100.5	115.8
Official borrowers	15.2	17.1	23.4	30.6	34.8	39.0	46.5	47.3	48.5	50.0
Countries with recent debt-servicing difficulties	39.9	49.4	71.8	99.3	125.6	149.4	149.0	170.9	186.4	206.0
Countries without debt-servicing difficulties	105.1	121.9	153.9	186.8	187.6	225.6	295.1	341.0	374.4	410.5
Other groups										
Small low-income economies	8.5	9.8	13.7	19.6	23.2	28.0	33.6	35.9	37.5	39.5
Least developed countries	7.5	7.7	9.1	11.0	11.8	13.1	15.7	16.5	16.4	16.1

Table A36 (concluded)

	1988	1989	1990	1991	1992	1993	1994	1995	1996	1997
	Ratio of reserves to imports of goods and services[2]									
Developing countries	**33.6**	**32.8**	**34.1**	**37.2**	**35.2**	**37.1**	**38.6**	**36.8**	**35.6**	**34.5**
By region										
Africa	12.7	14.3	17.9	21.9	18.3	20.3	24.9	22.5	23.0	23.7
Asia	39.8	37.1	37.5	40.2	35.2	35.6	38.3	35.2	33.8	32.8
Middle East and Europe	32.1	34.1	32.2	31.8	31.8	33.8	37.8	35.5	33.0	29.5
Western Hemisphere	29.3	28.3	35.7	42.9	49.0	55.5	46.7	52.7	53.3	53.8
Sub-Saharan Africa	17.0	18.4	19.9	22.8	23.2	26.5	32.4	31.9	32.3	31.2
Four newly industrializing Asian economies	48.3	44.6	41.9	41.0	38.7	38.0	37.3	32.8	30.9	29.4
By predominant export										
Fuel	34.1	34.0	35.2	32.7	26.3	28.7	34.5	30.6	30.3	28.3
Nonfuel exports	33.5	32.6	34.0	38.1	36.8	38.4	39.1	37.4	36.1	35.1
Manufactures	44.6	41.9	43.5	44.8	35.8	34.4	37.9	36.3	35.1	33.8
Primary products	26.2	25.5	35.1	39.7	42.6	46.8	52.7	47.7	46.3	43.9
Agricultural products	21.1	16.8	25.6	28.6	31.2	35.8	34.7	35.2	35.9	34.6
Minerals	33.9	37.5	48.1	57.1	62.9	67.7	88.5	69.0	64.0	60.1
Services, income, and private transfers	19.5	22.7	25.4	32.4	41.4	44.5	45.6	45.0	43.6	43.9
Diversified export base	22.8	23.6	23.6	29.8	36.0	41.1	37.1	36.2	34.9	34.5
By financial criteria										
Net creditor countries	87.0	77.1	67.6	61.1	54.8	55.3	60.0	55.2	53.9	52.4
Net debtor countries	23.1	24.3	28.0	32.3	31.3	33.9	35.3	34.1	33.1	32.2
Market borrowers	25.6	26.0	30.7	32.8	30.7	33.7	34.0	34.5	33.4	32.3
Diversified borrowers	19.8	22.9	23.2	33.0	33.9	34.9	38.3	32.2	31.7	31.6
Official borrowers	17.3	18.3	22.4	28.0	30.3	33.2	38.5	34.4	32.4	31.5
Countries with recent debt-servicing difficulties	19.2	21.8	28.9	38.9	43.3	48.5	43.5	45.1	44.9	43.9
Countries without debt-servicing difficulties	25.1	25.5	27.6	29.6	26.4	28.3	32.2	30.4	29.2	28.3
Other groups										
Small low-income economies	12.2	13.5	17.1	23.1	26.4	31.0	36.0	33.5	31.8	31.3
Least developed countries	25.6	25.5	28.5	33.8	35.6	38.3	44.0	40.7	37.4	34.7

[1]In this table, official holdings of gold are valued at SDR 35 an ounce. This convention results in a marked underestimate of reserves for countries that have substantial gold holdings.

[2]Reserves at year-end in percent of imports of goods and services for the year indicated.

Table A37. Net Credit and Loans from IMF[1]

(In billions of U.S. dollars)

	1988	1989	1990	1991	1992	1993	1994	1995
Developing countries	**−4.1**	**−1.5**	**−1.9**	**1.1**	**−0.2**	**−0.1**	**−0.8**	**12.5**
By region								
Africa	−0.3	0.1	−0.6	0.2	−0.2	0.2	0.9	0.8
Asia	−2.4	−1.1	−2.4	1.9	1.3	0.6	−0.8	−1.5
Middle East and Europe	−0.5	−0.2	−0.1	—	0.4	—	0.4	0.3
Western Hemisphere	−0.9	−0.2	1.2	−1.0	−1.6	−0.9	−1.3	12.9
Sub-Saharan Africa	−0.2	−0.4	−0.3	—	—	−0.2	0.5	0.6
By predominant export								
Fuel	0.2	1.7	1.9	0.5	−0.5	−0.8	0.4	−0.2
Nonfuel exports	−4.3	−3.2	−3.8	0.6	0.3	0.6	−1.2	12.7
Manufactures	−0.6	−0.1	−0.5	−0.5	0.3	—	—	−0.1
Primary products	−0.4	−0.9	−0.8	−0.9	−0.1	1.1	0.6	2.3
Services, income, and private transfers	−0.3	−0.2	−0.3	—	0.1	0.1	—	−0.1
Diversified export base	−2.9	−2.0	−2.3	1.9	0.1	−0.6	−1.9	10.6
By financial criteria								
Net creditor countries	—	—	—	—	—	—	—	—
Net debtor countries	−4.1	−1.5	−1.9	1.1	−0.2	−0.1	−0.8	12.5
Market borrowers	−1.4	0.2	0.7	−1.2	−1.6	−1.2	−0.7	13.4
Official borrowers	−0.8	−0.2	−1.1	0.3	0.3	−0.3	0.5	0.2
Countries with recent debt-servicing difficulties	−1.3	−0.5	0.4	−1.0	−1.8	−0.3	−1.1	13.2
Countries without debt-servicing difficulties	−2.8	−1.0	−2.3	2.2	1.6	0.2	0.3	−0.7
Other groups								
Small low-income economies	−0.6	−0.2	−0.6	0.4	0.5	—	0.9	0.5
Least developed countries	−0.2	−0.3	−0.4	0.1	0.2	−0.1	0.2	0.5
Countries in transition	**−0.5**	**−0.3**	**0.3**	**2.4**	**1.6**	**3.7**	**2.4**	**4.7**
Central and eastern Europe	...	...	...	2.4	0.5	2.0	0.5	−1.3
Excluding Belarus and Ukraine	...	...	...	2.4	0.5	2.0	0.2	−2.7
Russia	...	...	...	—	1.0	1.5	1.5	5.5
Transcaucasus and central Asia	...	...	...	—	—	0.2	0.3	0.6
Memorandum								
Total, nonindustrial countries								
Net credit provided under:								
General Resources Account	−4.429	−2.542	−1.885	2.520	0.644	3.374	0.594	15.633
Trust Fund	−0.669	−0.509	−0.365	−0.069	—	−0.060	−0.014	−0.015
SAF/ESAF	0.551	1.232	0.688	1.070	0.733	0.253	0.998	1.619
Disbursements at year-end under:[2]								
General Resources Account	31.996	28.639	29.028	31.821	31.217	34.503	37.276	53.275
Trust Fund	1.177	0.627	0.296	0.226	0.217	0.157	0.153	0.141
SAF/ESAF	1.205	2.440	3.363	4.499	5.041	5.285	6.635	8.343

[1]Excludes industrial countries' net credit from IMF. Includes net disbursements from programs under the General Resources Account, Trust Fund, SAF, and ESAF. The data are on a transactions basis, with conversions to U.S. dollar values at annual average exchange rates.

[2]Converted to U.S. dollar values at end-of-period exchange rates.

Table A38. Summary of External Debt and Debt Service

	1988	1989	1990	1991	1992	1993	1994	1995	1996	1997
					In billions of U.S. dollars					
External debt										
Developing countries	**1,147.2**	**1,176.0**	**1,255.0**	**1,340.7**	**1,409.9**	**1,525.1**	**1,654.7**	**1,790.2**	**1,878.2**	**1,990.7**
By region										
Africa	203.9	211.1	224.2	234.0	232.7	242.1	253.9	271.1	281.1	292.3
Asia	324.1	341.2	366.2	406.4	448.2	496.1	570.9	636.2	695.4	766.3
Middle East and Europe	203.5	205.9	227.4	247.6	255.7	280.1	281.9	288.3	290.3	297.0
Western Hemisphere	415.6	417.9	437.1	452.6	473.3	506.9	547.9	594.6	611.3	635.2
By financial criteria										
Net creditor countries	20.3	19.9	17.6	28.3	30.7	33.7	35.4	34.1	34.4	38.8
Net debtor countries	1,126.9	1,156.1	1,237.3	1,312.4	1,379.2	1,491.4	1,619.3	1,756.1	1,843.8	1,952.0
Market borrowers	521.1	521.5	545.2	592.7	643.2	708.3	787.0	880.5	934.4	1,001.6
Diversified borrowers	362.1	377.1	411.4	430.6	451.0	487.6	519.5	550.6	574.2	604.2
Official borrowers	243.6	257.5	280.7	289.1	285.0	295.5	312.8	325.1	335.2	346.1
Countries with recent debt-servicing difficulties	716.5	739.2	787.2	811.5	827.0	868.9	927.3	987.0	1,012.8	1,045.9
Countries without debt-servicing difficulties	410.3	416.9	450.1	500.9	552.2	622.5	692.1	769.2	831.1	906.1
Countries in transition	**144.6**	**153.0**	**202.6**	**209.9**	**212.2**	**229.1**	**245.1**	**269.2**	**286.3**	**310.2**
Central and eastern Europe	...	...	...	114.5	105.1	114.8	119.5	132.6	143.8	153.1
Excluding Belarus and Ukraine	...	...	...	114.5	101.1	110.2	111.1	122.5	131.9	139.9
Russia	...	...	...	95.3	105.4	110.4	119.8	129.4	132.9	144.6
Transcaucasus and central Asia	...	...	...	0.1	1.7	3.9	5.8	7.2	9.6	12.6
Debt-service payments[1]										
Developing countries	**140.0**	**143.5**	**149.7**	**159.9**	**182.5**	**193.8**	**214.8**	**267.5**	**248.5**	**255.6**
By region										
Africa	23.2	26.3	30.7	30.1	29.3	25.5	22.3	33.0	31.7	34.1
Asia	42.9	45.8	45.7	46.8	55.1	61.2	67.7	85.5	90.8	98.8
Middle East and Europe	17.7	18.6	17.4	19.8	23.8	24.8	34.2	32.7	33.0	29.6
Western Hemisphere	56.2	52.7	55.9	63.2	74.4	82.3	90.7	116.3	93.1	93.1
By financial criteria										
Net creditor countries	2.8	3.7	3.5	2.7	2.9	2.8	5.8	7.2	7.0	4.3
Net debtor countries	137.2	139.8	146.2	157.2	179.6	191.0	209.0	260.2	241.6	251.3
Market borrowers	80.1	79.0	82.6	90.8	102.9	117.2	127.8	156.5	141.3	151.6
Diversified borrowers	39.2	40.5	42.7	44.5	51.3	49.7	57.3	77.1	70.9	72.5
Official borrowers	18.0	20.2	20.8	21.8	25.5	24.2	23.9	26.7	29.4	27.2
Countries with recent debt-servicing difficulties	75.4	74.2	77.8	85.1	100.9	106.0	110.7	148.2	122.3	123.8
Countries without debt-servicing difficulties	61.8	65.6	68.4	72.1	78.7	85.0	98.3	112.0	119.3	127.4
Countries in transition	**26.8**	**26.3**	**31.5**	**28.1**	**22.0**	**14.7**	**17.9**	**23.0**	**27.2**	**27.3**
Central and eastern Europe	...	...	...	11.8	9.4	9.6	14.3	18.2	18.3	18.5
Excluding Belarus and Ukraine	...	...	...	11.8	9.4	9.4	12.3	16.5	16.4	16.5
Russia	...	...	...	16.3	12.6	5.0	3.0	3.2	7.7	7.5
Transcaucasus and central Asia	...	...	...	—	0.1	0.1	0.6	1.6	1.2	1.3

173

Table A38 (concluded)

	1988	1989	1990	1991	1992	1993	1994	1995	1996	1997
	In percent of exports of goods and services									
External debt[2]										
Developing countries	**148.7**	**135.4**	**127.0**	**128.8**	**122.6**	**124.2**	**117.5**	**107.0**	**100.4**	**95.1**
By region										
Africa	256.7	248.4	228.3	243.8	241.5	259.0	266.6	252.4	241.3	236.2
Asia	78.3	73.5	70.1	68.4	66.1	65.9	63.5	58.1	55.6	54.1
Middle East and Europe	138.4	119.1	110.8	131.0	124.9	141.0	137.3	127.7	122.3	110.5
Western Hemisphere	317.5	284.6	268.5	279.9	276.8	277.9	263.8	242.9	229.7	222.8
By financial criteria										
Net creditor countries	15.0	12.6	9.7	15.2	15.2	16.8	17.0	14.6	13.7	14.7
Net debtor countries	177.5	162.8	153.5	153.6	145.7	145.3	135.1	122.0	113.9	106.8
Market borrowers	121.1	107.9	98.3	97.4	93.8	94.3	88.0	81.3	76.1	72.5
Diversified borrowers	257.1	239.5	243.2	264.9	257.7	259.0	245.5	221.4	210.2	186.7
Official borrowers	376.4	365.1	336.3	340.6	324.5	335.2	329.5	299.1	283.7	275.5
Countries with recent debt-servicing difficulties	332.8	306.3	299.5	325.7	315.7	318.4	305.5	276.5	258.8	236.4
Countries without debt-servicing difficulties	97.8	88.9	82.9	82.8	80.6	82.6	77.3	71.1	67.7	65.4
Countries in transition	**67.0**	**72.7**	**103.7**	**118.3**	**135.6**	**127.4**	**122.1**	**108.4**	**104.9**	**105.1**
Central and eastern Europe	...	...	...	144.4	119.5	113.7	107.1	93.0	92.5	91.3
Excluding Belarus and Ukraine	...	...	...	160.3	129.2	134.2	117.8	99.7	99.1	97.3
Russia	...	...	...	154.8	183.4	169.4	155.4	142.8	134.7	138.2
Transcaucasus and central Asia	...	...	...	0.2	15.2	28.8	48.3	47.3	50.9	55.3
Debt-service payments										
Developing countries	**18.1**	**16.5**	**15.1**	**15.4**	**15.9**	**15.8**	**15.3**	**16.0**	**13.3**	**12.2**
By region										
Africa	29.3	31.0	31.2	31.3	30.4	27.2	23.4	30.7	27.2	27.5
Asia	10.4	9.9	8.7	7.9	8.1	8.1	7.5	7.8	7.3	7.0
Middle East and Europe	12.0	10.8	8.5	10.5	11.6	12.5	16.6	14.5	13.9	11.0
Western Hemisphere	42.9	35.9	34.4	39.1	43.5	45.1	43.6	47.5	35.0	32.7
By financial criteria										
Net creditor countries	2.1	2.4	1.9	1.4	1.4	1.4	2.8	3.1	2.8	1.6
Net debtor countries	21.6	19.7	18.1	18.4	19.0	18.6	17.4	18.1	14.9	13.7
Market borrowers	18.6	16.4	14.9	14.9	15.0	15.6	14.3	14.4	11.5	11.0
Diversified borrowers	27.8	25.7	25.3	27.4	29.3	26.4	27.1	31.0	26.0	22.4
Official borrowers	27.8	28.6	25.0	25.7	29.0	27.4	25.2	24.5	24.8	21.6
Countries with recent debt-servicing difficulties	35.0	30.7	29.6	34.1	38.5	38.8	36.5	41.5	31.3	28.0
Countries without debt-servicing difficulties	14.7	14.0	12.6	11.9	11.5	11.3	11.0	10.4	9.7	9.2
Countries in transition	**12.4**	**12.5**	**16.1**	**15.8**	**14.1**	**8.2**	**8.9**	**9.3**	**10.0**	**9.3**
Central and eastern Europe	...	...	...	14.8	10.6	9.5	12.8	12.7	11.8	11.0
Excluding Belarus and Ukraine	...	...	...	16.5	12.0	11.4	13.1	13.4	12.3	11.5
Russia	...	...	...	26.5	21.9	7.7	3.9	3.6	7.9	7.2
Transcaucasus and central Asia	...	...	...	—	0.6	0.8	4.9	10.5	6.1	5.6

[1]Debt-service payments refer to actual payments of interest on total debt plus actual amortization payments on long-term debt. The projections incorporate the impact of exceptional financing items.

[2]Total debt at year-end in percent of exports of goods and services in year indicated.

Table A39. Developing Countries—by Region: External Debt, by Maturity and Type of Creditor

(In billions of U.S. dollars)

	1988	1989	1990	1991	1992	1993	1994	1995	1996	1997
Developing countries										
Total debt	**1,147.2**	**1,176.0**	**1,255.0**	**1,340.7**	**1,409.9**	**1,525.1**	**1,654.7**	**1,790.2**	**1,878.2**	**1,990.7**
By maturity										
Short-term	187.6	206.4	218.7	241.3	264.7	290.3	321.6	378.2	415.8	458.9
Long-term	959.6	969.6	1,036.3	1,099.4	1,145.2	1,234.7	1,333.1	1,412.0	1,462.4	1,531.9
By type of creditor										
Official	527.9	555.6	611.5	650.5	656.5	690.6	734.0	776.3	776.8	770.4
Banks	438.4	431.0	411.7	432.9	446.7	464.2	453.1	498.9	518.6	554.0
Other private	180.9	189.4	231.8	257.2	306.6	370.3	467.6	515.0	582.8	666.4
By region										
Africa										
Total debt	**203.9**	**211.1**	**224.2**	**234.0**	**232.7**	**242.1**	**253.9**	**271.1**	**281.1**	**292.3**
By maturity										
Short-term	28.4	28.7	29.0	28.5	26.2	25.4	26.5	31.6	35.1	38.4
Long-term	175.5	182.3	195.2	205.5	206.5	216.7	227.4	239.5	246.0	253.9
By type of creditor										
Official	127.3	134.7	149.1	156.7	161.3	168.8	177.2	185.1	184.8	176.8
Banks	57.9	55.7	58.2	57.4	52.6	52.4	51.3	54.8	56.2	56.8
Other private	18.8	20.6	17.0	19.8	18.8	20.9	25.3	31.1	40.1	58.7
Asia										
Total debt	**324.1**	**341.2**	**366.2**	**406.4**	**448.2**	**496.1**	**570.9**	**636.2**	**695.4**	**766.3**
By maturity										
Short-term	58.6	68.8	66.7	76.4	90.0	98.7	128.0	171.3	200.3	234.1
Long-term	265.5	272.4	299.6	330.0	358.1	397.4	442.9	464.9	495.1	532.2
By type of creditor										
Official	183.5	187.2	199.4	211.3	226.1	248.0	274.8	282.7	290.7	298.7
Banks	92.0	103.6	108.0	119.9	136.3	148.8	169.5	216.3	244.7	276.2
Other private	48.7	50.4	58.9	75.2	85.8	99.3	126.6	137.2	160.0	191.4
Middle East and Europe										
Total debt	**203.5**	**205.9**	**227.4**	**247.6**	**255.7**	**280.1**	**281.9**	**288.3**	**290.3**	**297.0**
By maturity										
Short-term	40.1	45.7	48.4	50.1	56.4	70.7	63.3	67.7	66.7	67.6
Long-term	163.4	160.2	179.0	197.5	199.3	209.4	218.6	220.5	223.7	229.4
By type of creditor										
Official	103.5	112.0	121.3	126.5	113.0	115.8	117.0	117.6	114.2	110.4
Banks	41.8	47.4	45.8	55.3	63.1	65.9	68.2	65.4	63.3	65.7
Other private	58.3	46.5	60.3	65.9	79.5	98.4	96.7	105.3	112.9	120.9
Western Hemisphere										
Total debt	**415.6**	**417.9**	**437.1**	**452.6**	**473.3**	**506.9**	**547.9**	**594.6**	**611.3**	**635.2**
By maturity										
Short-term	60.5	63.1	74.6	86.3	92.0	95.6	103.8	107.5	113.8	118.8
Long-term	355.2	354.8	362.5	366.4	381.3	411.3	444.1	487.1	497.6	516.4
By type of creditor										
Official	113.7	121.8	141.6	156.0	156.1	158.0	165.0	190.9	187.2	184.4
Banks	246.7	224.2	199.7	200.4	194.6	197.2	164.0	162.3	154.4	155.3
Other private	55.2	71.9	95.7	96.3	122.5	151.7	219.0	241.4	269.8	295.5
Sub-Saharan Africa										
Total debt	**102.1**	**106.1**	**118.5**	**127.8**	**132.0**	**135.6**	**144.4**	**154.3**	**159.6**	**164.7**
By maturity										
Short-term	8.7	8.5	9.0	9.8	10.3	12.7	13.4	15.8	17.7	19.3
Long-term	93.3	97.6	109.5	118.0	121.7	123.0	131.0	138.5	141.9	145.4
By type of creditor										
Official	79.8	82.9	94.2	101.4	105.2	109.6	115.9	124.0	126.0	120.0
Banks	13.7	13.7	15.8	15.5	16.1	15.8	15.9	16.9	16.7	16.8
Other private	8.6	9.5	8.5	10.9	10.7	10.3	12.6	13.4	16.8	27.9

Table A40. Developing Countries—by Analytical Criteria: External Debt, by Maturity and Type of Creditor

(In billions of U.S. dollars)

	1988	1989	1990	1991	1992	1993	1994	1995	1996	1997
By predominant export										
Fuel										
Total debt	**159.7**	**170.3**	**180.1**	**197.2**	**204.0**	**218.2**	**215.4**	**213.2**	**210.5**	**210.5**
By maturity										
Short-term	27.3	29.2	26.5	33.1	33.0	41.9	36.8	33.6	29.6	27.4
Long-term	132.4	141.1	153.6	164.1	171.0	176.2	178.6	179.5	180.9	183.1
By type of creditor										
Official	44.3	52.5	58.3	60.1	60.7	65.1	67.8	67.6	65.1	63.8
Banks	66.3	66.8	44.2	52.7	51.2	52.9	50.0	50.7	51.1	53.1
Other private	49.2	51.0	77.5	84.4	92.1	100.2	97.6	94.9	94.2	93.6
Nonfuel exports										
Total debt	**987.5**	**1,005.7**	**1,074.9**	**1,143.5**	**1,205.8**	**1,306.9**	**1,439.3**	**1,577.0**	**1,667.7**	**1,780.2**
By maturity										
Short-term	160.3	177.2	192.2	208.2	231.7	248.4	284.8	344.5	386.2	431.5
Long-term	827.2	828.5	882.7	935.3	974.2	1,058.5	1,154.5	1,232.5	1,281.5	1,348.7
By type of creditor										
Official	483.6	503.1	553.1	590.4	595.8	625.5	666.2	708.6	711.7	706.6
Banks	372.1	364.1	367.5	380.3	395.6	411.4	403.0	448.2	467.5	500.8
Other private	131.8	138.4	154.3	172.8	214.5	270.1	370.1	420.2	488.6	572.8
Manufactures										
Total debt	**116.2**	**112.0**	**111.9**	**127.8**	**142.7**	**157.8**	**195.8**	**236.5**	**262.5**	**292.5**
By maturity										
Short-term	36.9	46.7	48.1	52.1	59.4	63.6	85.3	114.5	124.6	135.0
Long-term	79.3	65.3	63.9	75.7	83.3	94.2	110.5	122.0	137.9	157.5
By type of creditor										
Official	31.3	30.9	32.1	34.6	30.9	31.9	36.5	38.2	39.6	40.7
Banks	46.4	57.0	53.2	55.0	61.5	66.4	70.3	82.4	91.7	100.3
Other private	38.5	24.2	26.7	38.1	50.4	59.4	89.1	115.8	131.2	151.5
Primary products										
Total debt	**202.9**	**213.3**	**224.8**	**236.5**	**243.7**	**250.8**	**274.0**	**287.1**	**294.4**	**307.5**
By maturity										
Short-term	30.1	33.1	32.5	37.8	41.5	34.5	38.0	38.5	42.2	46.1
Long-term	172.8	180.2	192.4	198.7	202.2	216.3	236.0	248.6	252.1	261.4
By type of creditor										
Official	105.2	112.3	127.2	136.8	138.6	148.7	156.9	167.0	169.6	163.1
Banks	65.8	63.3	61.9	60.9	61.4	59.3	65.8	71.0	64.4	64.1
Other private	31.9	37.8	35.7	38.9	43.7	42.8	51.2	49.1	60.4	80.3
Agricultural products										
Total debt	**135.8**	**146.3**	**153.6**	**163.0**	**167.1**	**170.9**	**186.7**	**195.0**	**202.2**	**211.8**
By maturity										
Short-term	18.9	20.3	22.8	28.0	28.5	20.5	22.4	21.5	23.9	26.6
Long-term	116.9	126.1	130.8	135.0	138.5	150.4	164.3	173.4	178.3	185.2
By type of creditor										
Official	68.5	73.3	81.5	88.6	90.1	98.9	103.6	112.6	115.8	116.9
Banks	47.7	47.7	45.5	44.2	44.4	41.4	46.7	50.3	47.7	46.6
Other private	19.6	25.3	26.7	30.3	32.5	30.5	36.4	32.0	38.7	48.3
Minerals										
Total debt	**67.1**	**67.0**	**71.2**	**73.5**	**76.7**	**79.9**	**87.3**	**92.2**	**92.2**	**95.7**
By maturity										
Short-term	11.2	12.8	9.6	9.8	13.0	14.0	15.6	17.0	18.4	19.5
Long-term	55.8	54.2	61.6	63.7	63.7	65.9	71.6	75.2	73.8	76.2
By type of creditor										
Official	36.7	39.0	45.7	48.2	48.5	49.8	53.3	54.4	53.8	46.3
Banks	18.1	15.6	16.4	16.7	16.9	17.8	19.1	20.7	16.7	17.5
Other private	12.3	12.5	9.1	8.6	11.2	12.3	14.8	17.0	21.7	31.9

Table A40 *(continued)*

	1988	1989	1990	1991	1992	1993	1994	1995	1996	1997
Services, income, and private transfers										
Total debt	**75.2**	**82.2**	**90.0**	**91.5**	**88.3**	**92.2**	**94.6**	**93.1**	**92.1**	**94.1**
By maturity										
Short-term	18.6	19.3	16.2	11.0	12.4	13.4	16.1	16.1	16.5	16.8
Long-term	56.5	63.0	73.9	80.5	75.9	78.8	78.6	77.1	75.6	77.3
By type of creditor										
Official	56.6	62.6	69.8	71.4	63.4	62.6	62.1	63.5	64.1	64.6
Banks	13.0	14.1	13.8	15.9	19.5	20.5	20.9	19.7	17.2	17.8
Other private	5.6	5.5	6.4	4.1	5.4	9.2	11.6	9.9	10.8	11.8
Diversified export base										
Total debt	**593.2**	**598.1**	**648.1**	**687.7**	**731.1**	**806.1**	**874.8**	**960.3**	**1,018.7**	**1,086.1**
By maturity										
Short-term	74.6	78.1	95.5	107.3	118.3	137.0	145.4	175.5	202.8	233.5
Long-term	518.6	520.0	552.6	580.4	612.7	669.1	729.4	784.8	815.9	852.6
By type of creditor										
Official	290.5	297.4	324.1	347.6	362.9	382.3	410.7	439.8	438.3	438.1
Banks	246.9	229.7	238.6	248.4	253.2	265.2	246.1	275.1	294.2	318.7
Other private	55.8	71.0	85.4	91.7	115.0	158.6	218.1	245.4	286.2	329.3
By financial criteria										
Net creditor countries										
Total debt	**20.3**	**19.9**	**17.6**	**28.3**	**30.7**	**33.7**	**35.4**	**34.1**	**34.4**	**38.8**
By maturity										
Short-term	22.8	21.6	20.2	23.8	24.0	27.2	29.3	32.5	35.5	38.8
Long-term	−2.5	−1.7	−2.5	4.4	6.7	6.4	6.0	1.5	−1.1	—
By type of creditor										
Official	2.1	1.6	1.5	1.5	1.9	2.1	2.4	2.4	2.3	2.3
Banks	18.1	18.2	16.3	26.8	29.8	32.7	35.5	35.7	35.5	38.1
Other private	0.1	0.1	−0.1	—	−1.0	−1.2	−2.5	−4.0	−3.4	−1.6
Net debtor countries										
Total debt	**1,126.9**	**1,156.1**	**1,237.3**	**1,312.4**	**1,379.2**	**1,491.4**	**1,619.3**	**1,756.1**	**1,843.8**	**1,952.0**
By maturity										
Short-term	164.8	184.8	198.6	217.5	240.6	263.1	292.3	345.6	380.4	420.1
Long-term	962.1	971.3	1,038.8	1,094.9	1,138.5	1,228.3	1,327.0	1,410.5	1,463.4	1,531.9
By type of creditor										
Official	525.8	554.0	610.0	649.1	654.6	688.5	731.6	773.9	774.5	768.1
Banks	420.3	412.7	395.4	406.2	416.9	431.5	417.6	463.2	483.1	515.9
Other private	180.8	189.3	231.9	257.2	307.6	371.5	470.1	519.0	586.2	668.0
Market borrowers										
Total debt	**521.1**	**521.5**	**545.2**	**592.7**	**643.2**	**708.3**	**787.0**	**880.5**	**934.4**	**1,001.6**
By maturity										
Short-term	89.3	104.9	123.4	142.0	161.2	177.3	205.1	241.9	264.4	290.1
Long-term	431.8	416.6	421.8	450.7	482.0	531.1	581.9	638.6	670.0	711.5
By type of creditor										
Official	132.4	139.9	157.5	175.2	170.8	178.6	189.8	217.6	216.8	215.6
Banks	293.3	283.2	258.0	266.6	277.2	287.0	260.9	301.3	316.7	340.7
Other private	95.5	98.4	129.7	150.9	195.2	242.8	336.2	361.5	400.9	445.3
Diversified borrowers										
Total debt	**362.1**	**377.1**	**411.4**	**430.6**	**451.0**	**487.6**	**519.5**	**550.6**	**574.2**	**604.2**
By maturity										
Short-term	54.3	56.3	54.1	55.0	60.2	65.4	64.2	78.8	88.5	99.7
Long-term	307.8	320.8	357.3	375.5	390.8	422.2	455.3	471.7	485.7	504.5
By type of creditor										
Official	199.0	205.0	220.7	233.8	245.2	265.0	284.5	290.4	290.4	290.4
Banks	97.7	101.2	108.8	111.6	115.5	120.0	127.3	131.4	136.3	145.0
Other private	65.4	70.8	81.9	85.2	90.3	102.5	107.7	128.7	147.5	168.8

Table A40 *(concluded)*

	1988	1989	1990	1991	1992	1993	1994	1995	1996	1997
Official borrowers										
Total debt	**243.6**	**257.6**	**280.7**	**289.1**	**285.0**	**295.5**	**312.8**	**325.1**	**335.2**	**346.1**
By maturity										
Short-term	21.1	23.7	21.0	20.4	19.3	20.5	23.0	24.9	27.5	30.2
Long-term	222.5	233.9	259.7	268.7	265.7	275.1	289.8	300.2	307.8	315.9
By type of creditor										
Official	194.4	209.1	231.8	240.1	238.6	244.8	257.3	265.8	267.2	262.0
Banks	29.3	28.3	28.6	28.0	24.3	24.5	29.3	30.4	30.2	30.1
Other private	19.9	20.1	20.3	21.1	22.1	26.2	26.2	28.8	37.8	53.9
Countries with recent debt-servicing difficulties										
Total debt	**716.5**	**739.2**	**787.2**	**811.5**	**827.0**	**868.9**	**927.3**	**987.0**	**1,012.8**	**1,045.9**
By maturity										
Short-term	102.0	106.4	115.1	126.3	129.5	130.1	141.2	150.2	161.0	169.4
Long-term	614.5	632.8	672.1	685.2	697.5	738.9	786.1	836.8	851.7	876.5
By type of creditor										
Official	299.0	324.3	368.0	393.9	394.5	406.1	424.0	457.6	453.6	442.1
Banks	307.0	283.6	258.9	258.0	245.9	241.3	214.4	216.0	210.3	212.4
Other private	110.6	131.4	160.3	159.7	186.5	221.5	288.9	313.3	348.8	391.4
Countries without debt-servicing difficulties										
Total debt	**410.3**	**416.9**	**450.1**	**500.9**	**552.2**	**622.5**	**692.1**	**769.2**	**831.1**	**906.1**
By maturity										
Short-term	62.8	78.3	83.5	91.2	111.1	133.1	151.1	195.4	219.3	250.6
Long-term	347.6	338.6	366.7	409.7	441.0	489.4	540.9	573.7	611.7	655.4
By type of creditor										
Official	226.8	229.8	242.0	255.2	260.2	282.4	307.6	316.3	320.9	326.0
Banks	113.3	129.2	136.5	148.2	171.0	190.2	203.2	247.2	272.8	303.5
Other private	70.2	57.9	71.7	97.5	121.0	149.9	181.2	205.7	237.4	276.6
Other groups										
Small low-income economies										
Total debt	**221.7**	**236.4**	**258.8**	**268.3**	**261.7**	**275.2**	**291.4**	**304.3**	**314.6**	**325.5**
By maturity										
Short-term	19.1	23.3	20.0	19.5	18.1	18.4	21.9	24.2	26.7	29.2
Long-term	202.6	213.1	238.9	248.8	243.6	256.7	269.5	280.1	287.9	296.2
By type of creditor										
Official	172.3	187.6	209.2	217.8	215.0	223.3	234.0	243.3	246.0	241.5
Banks	29.1	28.8	30.4	29.6	26.1	26.5	32.4	34.4	34.3	34.6
Other private	20.4	19.9	19.3	20.9	20.6	25.4	25.1	26.6	34.3	49.3
Least developed countries										
Total debt	**91.7**	**96.0**	**108.0**	**116.0**	**117.2**	**123.5**	**134.6**	**142.8**	**148.9**	**154.5**
By maturity										
Short-term	6.0	7.0	7.2	7.9	8.3	8.9	9.8	12.3	14.2	16.2
Long-term	85.7	89.0	100.8	108.1	108.9	114.6	124.8	130.5	134.7	138.3
By type of creditor										
Official	75.8	79.7	91.6	97.7	97.6	102.6	111.4	118.4	121.5	116.6
Banks	6.7	6.9	7.7	7.3	7.2	7.3	11.6	12.2	12.1	12.1
Other private	9.3	9.4	8.8	11.0	12.3	13.6	11.6	12.2	15.3	25.7

Table A41. Developing Countries: Ratio of External Debt to GDP[1]

	1988	1989	1990	1991	1992	1993	1994	1995	1996	1997
Developing countries	**36.4**	**34.5**	**33.9**	**34.3**	**32.6**	**32.0**	**32.0**	**30.8**	**29.6**	**28.3**
By region										
Africa	60.2	63.1	60.3	65.2	62.0	66.6	70.5	65.3	65.8	64.9
Asia	23.2	21.9	22.5	23.3	22.9	22.4	24.1	22.9	22.3	22.1
Middle East and Europe	36.6	37.3	35.3	36.7	33.6	34.3	32.0	28.2	25.6	22.0
Western Hemisphere	48.6	43.5	41.1	40.0	38.4	37.0	35.1	37.1	36.6	35.8
Sub-Saharan Africa	80.4	85.9	89.4	100.2	100.0	109.5	132.7	124.9	114.8	107.0
Four newly industrializing										
Asian economies	12.5	11.0	9.7	9.6	9.5	9.2	10.6	13.0	13.7	14.3
By predominant export										
Fuel	35.7	37.4	35.7	38.6	35.8	37.2	32.2	26.5	24.6	20.5
Nonfuel exports	36.6	34.1	33.6	33.6	32.1	31.3	32.0	31.5	30.4	29.6
Manufactures	13.9	11.6	11.6	11.9	11.7	11.3	13.7	13.9	13.8	13.9
Primary products	62.1	75.3	62.0	53.6	46.6	42.8	41.8	39.4	36.3	33.4
Agricultural products	55.0	75.4	57.4	49.1	41.4	36.6	35.9	34.3	31.5	28.7
Minerals	84.0	75.0	75.0	67.3	64.6	67.0	64.9	57.4	54.2	52.2
Services, income, and										
private transfers	47.3	75.4	79.0	79.6	65.5	60.9	57.0	57.1	52.2	49.2
Diversified export base	43.0	37.5	36.9	38.8	38.7	39.4	38.8	39.7	39.3	38.8
By financial criteria										
Net creditor countries	7.3	6.1	4.8	7.1	6.9	7.3	7.3	6.5	6.3	6.7
Net debtor countries	39.3	37.6	37.1	37.4	35.5	34.7	34.6	33.2	31.8	30.2
Market borrowers	30.3	27.0	26.6	26.9	26.3	26.1	26.9	27.2	26.6	26.3
Diversified borrowers	47.1	45.7	44.0	46.5	44.9	43.8	42.4	38.3	35.8	32.0
Official borrowers	64.3	80.4	79.2	75.5	66.3	62.3	58.3	52.6	49.3	45.3
Countries with recent debt-										
servicing difficulties	55.8	54.8	52.5	51.2	46.9	43.6	40.0	39.2	37.1	33.8
Countries without debt-										
servicing difficulties	25.9	24.1	24.5	26.0	26.1	27.0	29.3	27.7	27.1	26.9
Other groups										
Small low-income economies	66.6	86.3	86.0	83.0	71.5	67.5	62.4	56.2	52.8	48.2
Least developed countries	76.3	73.7	72.4	71.3	59.4	52.6	49.4	46.4	41.0	35.5

[1]Debt at year-end in percent of GDP in year indicated.

Table A42. Developing Countries: Debt-Service Ratios[1]

(In percent of exports of goods and services)

	1988	1989	1990	1991	1992	1993	1994	1995	1996	1997
Interest payments[2]										
Developing countries	**9.1**	**7.8**	**6.9**	**7.0**	**6.6**	**6.5**	**6.2**	**6.3**	**6.1**	**5.8**
By region										
Africa	12.5	13.3	12.4	12.5	10.7	10.5	10.5	10.9	12.2	12.5
Asia	4.8	4.4	4.1	3.7	3.5	3.3	3.3	3.4	3.1	3.0
Middle East and Europe	5.3	4.1	3.1	5.1	5.6	5.8	5.2	5.5	6.0	5.2
Western Hemisphere	25.2	19.8	17.6	18.0	17.6	18.5	17.7	18.2	17.5	17.3
Sub-Saharan Africa	11.9	11.3	10.5	10.9	9.8	10.2	10.1	13.0	11.5	11.9
Four newly industrializing Asian economies	1.7	1.6	1.6	1.3	1.1	0.9	1.0	0.8	0.8	0.7
By predominant export										
Fuel	4.7	4.8	4.0	5.0	4.4	4.5	4.1	4.8	6.0	5.8
Nonfuel exports	10.0	8.5	7.6	7.4	7.0	6.8	6.4	6.5	6.1	5.8
Manufactures	2.6	2.5	2.4	2.4	2.5	2.3	2.4	2.5	2.3	2.2
Primary products	16.0	12.4	12.8	12.9	11.1	11.1	12.3	12.1	12.6	13.6
Agricultural products	17.7	12.6	14.0	14.0	12.4	12.2	15.0	14.0	14.9	14.8
Minerals	13.7	12.2	11.0	11.4	9.3	9.2	8.0	9.1	8.8	11.6
Services, income, and private transfers	11.1	8.3	5.3	8.8	12.0	9.5	6.6	7.0	8.0	5.7
Diversified export base	18.5	15.6	13.6	13.3	12.2	12.4	11.5	11.5	10.7	10.0
By financial criteria										
Net creditor countries	1.5	1.7	1.3	1.0	1.0	1.0	1.2	1.1	1.0	0.8
Net debtor countries	10.8	9.2	8.2	8.3	7.8	7.6	7.0	7.2	6.9	6.5
Market borrowers	9.9	7.9	7.0	6.6	6.4	6.4	5.8	6.1	5.7	5.5
Diversified borrowers	12.0	11.1	10.8	12.9	11.3	10.7	10.6	10.6	10.2	9.1
Official borrowers	13.9	13.6	10.6	11.5	11.6	11.0	10.7	9.7	11.6	10.5
Countries with recent debt-servicing difficulties	19.4	15.8	13.9	16.1	15.8	16.2	15.3	15.3	15.4	14.4
Countries without debt-servicing difficulties	6.4	5.8	5.4	5.1	4.8	4.5	4.3	4.5	4.1	3.9
Other groups										
Small low-income economies	15.7	15.6	11.5	12.8	12.7	11.6	11.4	9.4	11.6	10.6
Least developed countries	10.3	10.1	8.6	9.6	8.5	8.3	9.0	10.1	10.3	9.7

Table A42 *(concluded)*

	1988	1989	1990	1991	1992	1993	1994	1995	1996	1997
Amortization[2]										
Developing countries	**9.0**	**8.7**	**8.2**	**8.3**	**9.3**	**9.3**	**9.1**	**9.7**	**7.2**	**6.5**
By region										
Africa	16.7	17.7	18.8	18.8	19.7	16.7	12.9	19.8	15.0	15.1
Asia	5.6	5.5	4.7	4.1	4.6	4.8	4.3	4.4	4.2	4.0
Middle East and Europe	6.7	6.7	5.4	5.3	6.0	6.7	11.5	9.0	7.9	5.8
Western Hemisphere	17.7	16.2	16.8	21.1	25.9	26.6	25.9	29.3	17.4	15.4
Sub-Saharan Africa	16.1	15.2	12.7	12.4	13.5	13.3	12.0	14.3	12.0	11.3
Four newly industrializing Asian economies	2.5	1.9	1.6	1.1	0.9	1.3	0.7	0.9	1.0	1.0
By predominant export										
Fuel	9.0	7.9	8.2	8.8	8.1	9.4	13.1	9.1	8.0	6.6
Nonfuel exports	9.0	8.9	8.2	8.3	9.5	9.3	8.6	9.7	7.2	6.5
Manufactures	2.9	3.2	2.4	1.7	1.7	2.0	1.7	1.8	1.8	1.7
Primary products	18.1	17.5	19.2	17.7	17.1	18.1	16.5	27.0	16.8	14.2
Agricultural products	26.7	25.7	24.8	21.9	21.3	21.4	20.7	32.4	18.2	16.7
Minerals	6.6	7.1	11.1	11.5	11.0	12.8	9.7	18.4	14.5	10.1
Services, income, and private transfers	8.7	9.4	7.3	7.5	13.9	12.4	7.1	8.2	9.4	4.6
Diversified export base	15.4	14.6	13.9	15.7	18.9	18.0	17.8	19.1	13.6	12.8
By financial criteria										
Net creditor countries	0.6	0.7	0.6	0.4	0.4	0.4	1.7	2.0	1.8	0.8
Net debtor countries	10.8	10.5	10.0	10.1	11.2	11.0	10.4	10.9	8.1	7.3
Market borrowers	8.7	8.4	7.9	8.3	8.6	9.2	8.5	8.3	5.8	5.5
Diversified borrowers	15.8	14.7	14.5	14.5	18.0	15.7	16.5	20.4	15.8	13.3
Official borrowers	13.8	15.0	14.4	14.2	17.4	16.4	14.5	14.9	13.3	11.1
Countries with recent debt-servicing difficulties	15.6	15.0	15.7	18.1	22.8	22.7	21.2	26.2	15.8	13.6
Countries without debt-servicing difficulties	8.3	8.2	7.2	6.8	6.7	6.8	6.7	5.9	5.6	5.3
Other groups										
Small low-income economies	15.9	18.2	14.0	14.3	19.1	17.6	15.4	15.8	13.2	11.4
Least developed countries	12.5	15.0	15.0	15.3	17.2	13.8	10.9	15.0	11.6	11.0

[1]Excludes service payments to the IMF.

[2]Interest payments on total debt and amortization on long-term debt. Estimates through 1995 reflect debt-service payments actually made. The estimates for 1996 and 1997 take into account projected exceptional financing items, including accumulation of arrears and rescheduling agreements. In some cases, amortization on account of debt-reduction operations is included.

Table A43. IMF Charges and Repurchases to the IMF[1]

(In percent of exports of goods and services)

	1988	1989	1990	1991	1992	1993	1994	1995
Developing countries	**1.2**	**1.0**	**1.0**	**0.8**	**0.6**	**0.6**	**0.4**	**0.6**
By region								
Africa	2.1	2.2	1.7	1.3	1.2	1.2	0.9	2.8
Asia	0.8	0.5	0.5	0.4	0.2	0.1	0.2	0.2
Middle East and Europe	0.4	0.2	0.1	0.1	—	—	—	0.1
Western Hemisphere	3.1	3.0	3.2	3.0	2.7	2.6	1.5	1.6
Sub-Saharan Africa	4.5	4.7	3.3	2.5	2.1	1.6	1.1	6.6
By predominant export								
Fuel	—	0.1	0.1	0.3	0.5	0.6	0.4	0.6
Nonfuel exports	1.4	1.2	1.2	0.9	0.7	0.6	0.4	0.5
By financial criteria								
Net creditor countries	—	—	—	—	—	—	—	—
Net debtor countries	1.5	1.3	1.2	1.0	0.8	0.7	0.5	0.6
Market borrowers	1.0	0.9	1.0	0.8	0.7	0.7	0.4	0.4
Official borrowers	3.2	3.0	2.6	1.9	1.3	1.2	0.7	2.9
Countries with recent debt-servicing difficulties	2.7	2.6	2.6	2.5	2.2	2.1	1.4	2.0
Countries without debt-servicing difficulties	0.9	0.6	0.5	0.4	0.2	0.2	0.2	0.2
Other groups								
Small low-income economies	3.8	3.5	2.7	1.8	1.5	1.1	0.8	3.4
Least developed countries	3.5	4.8	3.9	2.8	1.7	1.4	0.9	9.2
Countries in transition	**0.4**	**0.2**	**0.2**	**0.1**	**0.5**	**0.4**	**1.2**	**1.5**
Central and eastern Europe	...	...	...	0.3	0.8	0.5	1.9	2.4
Excluding Belarus and Ukraine	...	...	...	0.3	0.9	0.7	2.3	2.7
Russia	...	...	...	—	—	0.1	0.2	0.3
Transcaucasus and central Asia	...	...	...	—	—	—	0.1	0.3
Memorandum								
Total, in billions of U.S. dollars								
General Resources Account	10.139	9.317	10.119	8.768	8.070	7.548	8.283	12.922
Charges	2.288	2.317	2.530	2.431	2.301	2.229	1.737	2.861
Repurchases	7.851	7.000	7.589	6.337	5.768	5.319	6.546	10.061
Trust Fund	0.673	0.513	0.367	0.070	—	0.063	0.015	0.015
Interest	0.004	0.004	0.002	0.001	—	0.003	—	—
Repayments	0.669	0.509	0.365	0.069	—	0.060	0.014	0.015
SAF/ESAF	0.003	0.007	0.013	0.021	0.055	0.151	0.329	0.586
Interest	0.003	0.007	0.013	0.021	0.022	0.025	0.024	0.034
Repayments	—	—	—	—	0.033	0.126	0.305	0.552

[1]Excludes industrial countries. Charges on, and repurchases (or repayments of principal) for, use of IMF credit.

Table A44. Summary of Sources and Uses of World Saving

(In percent of GDP)

	Averages		1989	1990	1991	1992	1993	1994	1995	1996	1997
	1974–81	1982–88									
World											
Saving	24.9	22.4	23.4	23.0	22.6	22.0	22.0	22.9	23.4	23.5	23.9
Investment	25.0	23.2	24.3	23.8	23.5	23.3	23.3	23.7	24.0	24.4	24.9
Industrial countries											
Saving	23.2	20.9	21.5	20.8	20.4	19.3	19.1	19.6	20.0	20.2	20.7
Private	21.3	20.2	18.9	18.9	19.3	19.4	19.6	19.5	19.5	19.3	19.3
Public	1.8	0.7	2.6	2.0	1.1	−0.1	−0.5	0.1	0.4	0.8	1.4
Investment	23.2	21.4	22.3	21.7	20.8	20.2	19.4	20.0	20.2	20.4	20.8
Private	18.6	17.4	18.5	17.8	17.0	16.2	15.4	16.2	16.5	16.6	17.1
Public	4.5	4.0	3.8	3.9	3.8	4.0	4.0	3.9	3.7	3.8	3.7
Net lending	—	−0.5	−0.7	−0.9	−0.4	−0.8	−0.3	−0.4	−0.2	−0.2	−0.1
Private	2.7	2.8	0.4	1.0	2.3	3.2	4.2	3.3	3.1	2.7	2.2
Public	−2.7	−3.3	−1.2	−1.9	−2.8	−4.0	−4.6	−3.7	−3.3	−3.0	−2.3
Current transfers	−0.4	−0.4	−0.4	−0.4	−0.2	−0.4	−0.4	−0.5	−0.4	−0.5	−0.5
Factor income	0.5	0.1	0.1	—	−0.1	−0.5	−0.2	−0.2	−0.1	−0.2	−0.2
Resource balance	−0.1	−0.2	−0.4	−0.4	−0.1	—	0.3	0.3	0.3	0.5	0.5
United States											
Saving	20.3	17.6	16.7	15.7	15.8	14.5	14.3	15.2	15.8	15.9	16.7
Private	18.2	17.2	15.0	15.0	15.8	15.6	14.7	14.5	14.7	14.5	15.2
Public	2.1	0.4	1.7	0.7	0.1	−1.1	−0.4	0.7	1.1	1.4	1.4
Investment	20.4	19.8	18.6	17.4	15.8	16.0	16.5	17.7	17.8	18.0	18.8
Private	17.1	16.3	15.2	13.9	12.4	12.7	13.3	14.6	14.7	15.0	15.8
Public	3.3	3.5	3.4	3.5	3.4	3.3	3.2	3.1	3.1	3.0	3.0
Net lending	−0.1	−2.2	−1.9	−1.6	—	−1.5	−2.2	−2.5	−2.0	−2.1	−2.1
Private	1.1	0.9	−0.2	1.1	3.3	2.9	1.4	−0.1	—	−0.5	−0.5
Public	−1.2	−3.1	−1.7	−2.7	−3.3	−4.4	−3.6	−2.3	−2.0	−1.6	−1.5
Current transfers	−0.3	−0.5	−0.5	−0.6	0.1	−0.5	−0.5	−0.5	−0.4	−0.5	−0.5
Factor income	0.8	0.7	0.2	0.3	0.4	−0.4	−0.5	−0.4	−0.1	−0.4	−0.5
Resource balance	−0.6	−2.4	−1.7	−1.4	−0.5	−0.6	−1.1	−1.5	−1.5	−1.2	−1.1
European Union											
Saving	22.7	20.4	22.0	21.4	20.0	19.0	18.4	19.4	20.3	20.4	20.9
Private	22.1	20.9	21.0	21.4	21.0	21.2	21.4	21.9	22.4	21.9	21.5
Public	0.7	−0.5	1.0	0.1	−1.0	−2.2	−2.9	−2.6	−2.1	−1.5	−0.6
Investment	22.6	20.1	22.0	21.8	21.2	20.1	18.2	18.9	19.4	19.4	19.7
Private	18.4	16.9	18.8	18.5	18.0	16.9	15.1	16.0	16.8	16.8	17.2
Public	4.3	3.2	3.1	3.2	3.1	3.2	3.1	2.8	2.6	2.6	2.5
Net lending	0.1	0.3	—	−0.3	−1.1	−1.1	0.2	0.5	0.9	1.0	1.2
Private	3.7	4.0	2.1	2.8	3.0	4.3	6.3	5.9	5.5	5.1	4.3
Public	−3.6	−3.7	−2.1	−3.2	−4.2	−5.4	−6.1	−5.4	−4.7	−4.1	−3.2
Current transfers	−0.8	−0.4	−0.5	−0.5	−0.5	−0.5	−0.5	−0.6	−0.4	−0.6	−0.6
Factor income	0.5	—	0.3	0.1	−0.1	−0.3	−0.2	−0.1	−0.1	0.1	0.1
Resource balance	0.5	0.7	0.2	—	−0.5	−0.3	0.9	1.2	1.4	1.5	1.7
Japan											
Saving	32.4	31.2	32.2	32.1	32.5	32.0	32.7	31.5	30.8	31.5	31.4
Private	28.8	26.2	22.7	21.9	23.0	23.6	26.9	25.5	25.6	26.5	25.6
Public	3.6	5.0	9.5	10.3	9.6	8.5	5.8	6.1	5.2	5.0	5.8
Investment	32.4	28.7	31.3	32.3	32.1	30.7	29.7	28.7	28.6	29.6	29.3
Private	23.0	21.3	24.9	25.7	25.5	23.3	21.1	20.0	19.9	20.4	20.6
Public	9.4	7.4	6.4	6.6	6.6	7.5	8.5	8.7	8.7	9.2	8.7
Net lending	—	2.5	0.9	−0.2	0.4	1.3	3.0	2.8	2.1	1.9	2.1
Private	5.7	4.9	−2.2	−3.9	−2.5	0.3	5.8	5.5	5.6	6.2	5.0
Public	−5.8	−2.4	3.1	3.7	3.0	1.0	−2.7	−2.6	−3.5	−4.2	−2.9
Current transfers	−0.1	−0.1	−0.1	−0.2	−0.3	−0.1	−0.1	−0.1	−0.2	−0.2	−0.2
Factor income	−0.2	0.2	−0.2	−0.6	−0.8	−0.8	0.9	0.9	0.8	1.0	1.2
Resource balance	0.2	2.5	1.3	0.6	1.6	2.2	2.3	2.1	1.5	1.1	1.1

183

Table A44 *(continued)*

	Averages		1989	1990	1991	1992	1993	1994	1995	1996	1997
	1974–81	1982–88									
Developing countries											
Saving	26.7	22.5	25.0	25.3	24.4	25.1	25.8	27.4	27.9	27.9	28.0
Investment	26.7	24.3	26.1	25.8	26.1	26.9	28.5	28.6	29.0	29.5	29.8
Net lending	—	−1.8	−1.1	−0.6	−1.7	−1.8	−2.8	−1.2	−1.1	−1.6	−1.8
Current transfers	1.0	1.0	1.3	1.3	1.2	1.5	1.3	1.3	1.2	1.1	1.0
Factor income	−1.1	−2.0	−1.9	−1.8	−1.7	−1.6	−1.5	−1.2	−1.3	−1.3	−1.2
Resource balance	0.2	−0.8	−0.5	—	−1.2	−1.7	−2.6	−1.2	−1.1	−1.4	−1.6
Memorandum											
Acquisition of foreign assets	3.6	0.5	1.2	2.5	1.6	1.4	2.0	2.9	2.9	2.0	2.0
Change in reserves	1.8	0.1	0.5	1.7	2.2	1.2	1.3	2.0	1.6	1.1	1.2
By region											
Africa											
Saving	29.9	19.1	18.4	18.6	19.0	16.7	15.1	17.4	18.1	17.7	18.0
Investment	32.1	22.8	21.5	19.3	21.2	20.9	19.6	21.1	22.4	22.2	22.6
Net lending	−2.2	−3.6	−3.1	−0.8	−2.2	−4.3	−4.4	−3.7	−4.3	−4.5	−4.6
Current transfers	2.0	2.7	4.5	4.7	4.7	4.9	4.9	4.9	4.5	4.2	3.9
Factor income	−1.1	−3.8	−4.7	−3.9	−4.2	−4.9	−5.1	−3.4	−2.8	−4.0	−4.2
Resource balance	−3.1	−2.5	−2.9	−1.7	−2.7	−4.2	−4.2	−5.2	−6.0	−4.7	−4.4
Memorandum											
Acquisition of foreign assets	1.7	0.4	0.8	1.4	0.2	−1.9	0.2	1.4	−0.4	0.4	0.5
Change in reserves	0.7	—	0.9	1.6	1.8	−1.8	0.4	1.7	0.4	0.6	0.5
Asia											
Saving	26.5	26.9	29.2	29.9	30.4	30.6	32.4	33.9	34.2	34.0	33.7
Investment	27.7	27.8	30.2	30.4	30.5	31.0	34.1	34.2	34.7	35.1	35.1
Net lending	−1.3	−0.9	−1.0	−0.4	−0.1	−0.5	−1.7	−0.3	−0.5	−1.1	−1.4
Current transfers	1.2	0.8	0.5	0.5	0.9	0.9	0.8	0.9	0.8	0.8	0.8
Factor income	−0.7	−0.5	−0.7	−0.6	−0.8	−0.7	−0.5	−0.5	−0.4	−0.2	−0.3
Resource balance	−1.8	−1.2	−0.8	−0.3	−0.2	−0.7	−2.0	−0.8	−1.0	−1.7	−1.9
Memorandum											
Acquisition of foreign assets	1.3	1.4	1.0	2.2	3.6	1.9	2.7	4.9	4.3	3.1	3.1
Change in reserves	1.2	1.0	0.6	1.8	2.5	1.1	1.8	3.3	1.9	1.4	1.6
Middle East and Europe											
Saving	35.4	17.8	20.5	21.5	15.1	20.9	18.6	20.5	20.3	19.1	19.3
Investment	25.4	22.5	21.8	22.9	24.1	24.8	24.1	20.7	21.3	21.0	21.1
Net lending	10.0	−4.7	−1.3	−1.4	−9.0	−4.0	−5.5	−0.2	−1.0	−1.9	−1.8
Current transfers	1.1	1.1	2.5	2.0	−0.5	2.1	1.5	1.0	0.9	0.6	0.5
Factor income	−0.1	−0.9	0.4	−0.9	−0.6	−0.4	−0.5	0.2	−0.2	−0.8	−0.1
Resource balance	9.0	−4.9	−4.1	−2.5	−7.9	−5.7	−6.5	−1.4	−1.6	−1.7	−2.2
Memorandum											
Acquisition of foreign assets	12.0	−0.6	2.9	2.0	−5.6	0.1	0.1	−1.2	−1.0	−0.7	−0.6
Change in reserves	6.0	−1.5	1.5	1.5	2.0	3.1	0.1	0.7	0.4	—	0.1
Western Hemisphere											
Saving	20.7	19.0	21.2	19.9	18.1	17.9	17.2	18.0	18.4	19.0	19.8
Investment	24.0	19.8	21.7	20.2	19.4	20.5	20.5	21.0	20.2	20.8	21.5
Net lending	−3.3	−0.8	−0.5	−0.3	−1.3	−2.7	−3.3	−3.0	−1.7	−1.8	−1.8
Current transfers	0.2	0.5	0.9	1.1	1.2	1.2	1.0	1.0	1.2	1.1	1.0
Factor income	−2.2	−4.3	−4.4	−4.1	−3.3	−3.2	−3.2	−3.1	−3.6	−3.6	−3.3
Resource balance	−1.4	3.1	2.9	2.7	0.8	−0.7	−1.1	−0.9	0.7	0.7	0.5
Memorandum											
Acquisition of foreign assets	2.1	−0.4	0.7	3.7	1.7	1.9	1.9	0.5	2.3	0.8	0.9
Change in reserves	0.4	−0.2	−0.1	1.6	1.7	1.6	1.3	−0.7	1.6	1.0	1.0

Table A44 *(continued)*

	Averages		1989	1990	1991	1992	1993	1994	1995	1996	1997
	1974–81	1982–88									
By predominant export											
Fuel											
Saving	44.0	19.1	19.7	24.2	21.1	20.9	17.5	21.0	21.1	20.5	21.2
Investment	31.1	23.3	21.3	20.4	24.8	26.5	23.2	20.6	20.9	20.6	21.5
Net lending	12.9	−4.3	−1.6	3.8	−3.8	−5.6	−5.7	0.4	0.2	−0.1	−0.3
Current transfers	−2.2	−2.0	−1.8	−2.6	−3.1	−1.9	−2.1	−1.8	−1.8	−1.6	−1.5
Factor income	1.0	−1.2	−2.0	−0.6	0.1	−2.4	−2.2	−1.6	−1.4	−2.8	−2.1
Resource balance	14.2	−1.0	2.2	7.0	−0.7	−1.3	−1.3	3.7	3.4	4.2	3.3
Memorandum											
Acquisition of foreign assets	12.0	−2.0	−0.3	4.2	−2.2	−3.7	−2.6	−0.5	−1.4	−0.1	−0.2
Change in reserves	7.0	−2.5	1.6	2.4	0.5	−1.5	−1.2	0.3	−0.4	0.3	0.6
Nonfuel exports											
Saving	23.1	23.0	25.6	25.4	24.8	25.6	26.7	28.0	28.6	28.6	28.6
Investment	25.7	24.4	26.7	26.5	26.3	26.9	29.1	29.4	29.9	30.3	30.6
Net lending	−2.6	−1.4	−1.1	−1.1	−1.5	−1.3	−2.4	−1.4	−1.3	−1.7	−1.9
Current transfers	1.6	1.4	1.7	1.7	1.7	1.9	1.7	1.6	1.5	1.4	1.3
Factor income	−1.6	−2.1	−1.9	−2.0	−1.9	−1.5	−1.4	−1.2	−1.2	−1.2	−1.1
Resource balance	−2.7	−0.7	−0.8	−0.8	−1.2	−1.7	−2.7	−1.8	−1.5	−1.9	−2.1
Memorandum											
Acquisition of foreign assets	1.9	0.9	1.3	2.2	2.1	2.0	2.5	3.3	3.3	2.2	2.2
Change in reserves	0.7	0.6	0.4	1.6	2.4	1.6	1.6	2.1	1.8	1.2	1.3
By financial criteria											
Net creditor countries											
Saving	48.9	27.0	24.5	25.7	10.2	19.4	19.4	19.9	22.4	22.4	23.1
Investment	26.0	23.0	21.2	21.1	22.2	23.0	23.4	21.2	22.2	22.1	22.7
Net lending	22.9	4.1	3.3	4.6	−12.0	−3.7	−4.0	−1.3	0.3	0.3	0.4
Current transfers	−6.9	−5.5	−5.9	−7.9	−14.1	−5.6	−6.2	−5.7	−5.6	−5.2	−5.1
Factor income	1.1	3.1	3.1	3.6	2.5	1.8	1.9	1.8	3.0	2.3	3.1
Resource balance	28.7	6.5	6.1	8.9	−0.3	0.1	0.3	2.6	2.9	3.2	2.5
Memorandum											
Acquisition of foreign assets	22.0	4.5	1.9	4.2	−10.7	−1.0	−2.3	0.2	−1.5	0.6	0.7
Change in reserves	7.7	1.4	—	−1.5	3.1	1.2	−2.3	0.7	0.8	0.9	0.8
Net debtor countries											
Saving	25.3	22.2	25.0	25.2	25.2	25.5	26.1	27.8	28.2	28.2	28.3
Investment	26.7	24.4	26.4	26.1	26.4	27.1	28.8	29.0	29.4	29.9	30.2
Net lending	−1.4	−2.1	−1.4	−0.9	−1.1	−1.7	−2.7	−1.2	−1.2	−1.7	−1.9
Current transfers	1.5	1.3	1.7	1.8	2.0	1.9	1.7	1.7	1.6	1.4	1.3
Factor income	−1.3	−2.3	−2.2	−2.1	−1.9	−1.8	−1.7	−1.4	−1.5	−1.5	−1.4
Resource balance	−1.6	−1.2	−0.9	−0.5	−1.2	−1.8	−2.7	−1.5	−1.3	−1.6	−1.8
Memorandum											
Acquisition of foreign assets	2.4	0.2	1.1	2.4	2.3	1.5	2.2	3.1	3.1	2.1	2.1
Change in reserves	1.4	0.1	0.6	1.9	2.2	1.2	1.6	2.0	1.6	1.1	1.2
Market borrowers											
Saving	27.4	26.2	28.7	29.6	29.2	29.2	30.6	32.6	32.6	32.4	32.2
Investment	29.3	26.6	28.9	28.8	29.4	30.4	33.1	33.0	32.7	33.0	33.1
Net lending	−1.9	−0.4	−0.3	0.8	−0.3	−1.2	−2.4	−0.5	—	−0.6	−0.9
Current transfers	0.4	0.3	0.5	0.5	0.5	0.6	0.6	0.6	0.6	0.6	0.6
Factor income	−1.7	−2.4	−1.9	−1.5	−1.1	−1.5	−1.3	−1.2	−1.5	−1.4	−1.3
Resource balance	−0.6	1.7	1.2	1.8	0.4	−0.3	−1.7	0.1	0.8	0.2	−0.2
Memorandum											
Acquisition of foreign assets	2.6	0.6	1.5	3.7	3.1	2.2	2.7	4.5	5.0	3.3	3.2
Change in reserves	0.9	0.3	0.7	2.3	2.1	1.1	1.5	2.6	2.5	1.5	1.5

Table A44 (concluded)

	Averages 1974–81	1982–88	1989	1990	1991	1992	1993	1994	1995	1996	1997
Official borrowers											
Saving	21.3	14.0	14.8	14.5	14.8	15.7	13.6	14.5	14.8	14.6	15.4
Investment	26.0	19.7	19.3	18.6	19.3	19.3	18.6	18.6	19.1	19.5	20.3
Net lending	−4.6	−5.7	−4.5	−4.1	−4.4	−3.6	−5.0	−4.1	−4.3	−4.9	−4.9
Current transfers	5.1	5.1	7.0	8.0	9.2	8.2	7.5	6.6	6.2	5.5	5.2
Factor income	−2.1	−2.4	−2.1	−4.0	−5.0	−3.2	−3.8	−3.0	−2.7	−2.9	−3.0
Resource balance	−7.7	−8.3	−9.5	−8.0	−8.6	−8.6	−8.7	−7.8	−7.8	−7.4	−7.1
Memorandum											
Acquisition of foreign assets	1.9	−0.4	1.8	1.6	0.5	−0.7	1.0	1.5	−0.6	−0.5	−0.3
Change in reserves	0.8	0.1	—	2.2	3.0	1.7	1.7	1.7	0.1	0.2	0.4
Countries with recent debt-servicing difficulties											
Saving	23.9	17.6	19.8	18.6	17.1	17.6	16.4	17.3	17.9	18.2	18.9
Investment	25.9	20.3	21.1	19.9	19.5	20.3	20.0	20.4	20.1	20.6	21.5
Net lending	−2.1	−2.7	−1.4	−1.3	−2.4	−2.7	−3.6	−3.2	−2.2	−2.5	−2.6
Current transfers	1.4	1.7	2.8	3.3	3.3	3.0	2.7	2.4	2.4	2.1	2.0
Factor income	−1.5	−4.0	−3.8	−4.4	−3.8	−2.9	−3.1	−2.6	−2.9	−2.9	−2.8
Resource balance	−1.9	−0.3	−0.4	−0.3	−1.9	−2.9	−3.2	−2.9	−1.7	−1.6	−1.8
Memorandum											
Acquisition of foreign assets	2.9	−0.5	1.4	3.1	1.4	1.0	1.8	0.7	1.6	0.7	0.7
Change in reserves	1.5	−0.3	0.3	2.0	2.1	1.8	1.3	0.1	1.2	1.0	0.9
Countries without debt-servicing difficulties											
Saving	26.6	25.6	28.2	29.1	29.7	29.6	31.0	32.9	32.9	32.6	32.3
Investment	27.4	27.3	29.6	29.7	30.1	30.7	33.3	33.1	33.7	34.0	33.9
Net lending	−0.8	−1.7	−1.4	−0.6	−0.4	−1.1	−2.2	−0.2	−0.7	−1.4	−1.6
Current transfers	1.6	1.1	1.0	0.9	1.4	1.3	1.2	1.3	1.2	1.1	1.1
Factor income	−1.1	−1.0	−1.1	−0.8	−0.9	−1.3	−1.0	−0.8	−0.9	−0.8	−0.8
Resource balance	−1.3	−1.8	−1.2	−0.6	−0.9	−1.2	−2.5	−0.7	−1.1	−1.6	−1.8
Memorandum											
Acquisition of foreign assets	2.0	0.8	1.0	1.9	2.9	1.8	2.4	4.2	3.8	2.7	2.7
Change in reserves	1.3	0.4	0.8	1.8	2.2	1.0	1.7	3.0	1.8	1.2	1.4
Countries in transition											
Central and eastern Europe excluding Belarus and Ukraine											
Saving	34.1	31.9	30.3	29.7	23.2	19.1	16.0	18.6	18.8	18.5	19.1
Investment	31.2	30.9	29.5	28.9	24.8	21.0	19.6	19.8	21.3	22.0	22.7
Net lending	2.9	1.1	0.9	0.8	−1.6	−1.9	−3.6	−1.2	−2.5	−3.6	−3.6
Current transfers	1.0	1.2	1.3	1.7	0.6	2.1	1.4	1.4	0.8	0.7	0.6
Factor income	5.5	0.1	−0.8	−0.3	−3.0	−8.4	−1.9	−1.8	−2.6	−2.6	−2.2
Resource balance	−3.6	−0.2	0.4	−0.6	0.7	4.4	−3.0	−0.8	−0.6	−1.6	−1.9
Memorandum											
Acquisition of foreign assets	−0.7	1.6	1.9	2.9	2.2	7.0	−0.3	3.1	5.1	2.6	1.4
Change in reserves	−0.6	0.8	1.7	1.0	1.3	6.4	3.1	4.0	6.0	2.5	1.5

Note: The estimates in this table are based on individual countries' national accounts and balance of payments statistics. For many countries, the estimates of national saving are built up from national accounts data on gross domestic investment and from balance-of-payments-based data on net foreign investment. The latter, which is equivalent to the current account balance, comprises three components: current transfers, net factor income, and the resource balance. The mixing of data sources, which is dictated by availability, implies that the estimates for national saving that are derived incorporate the statistical discrepancies. Furthermore, errors, omissions, and asymmetries in balance of payments statistics affect the estimates for net lending; at the global level, net lending, which in theory would be zero, equals the world current account discrepancy. Notwithstanding these statistical shortcomings, flow of funds estimates, such as those presented in this table, provide a useful framework for analyzing development in saving and investment, both over time and across regions and countries. Country group composites are weighted by GDP valued at purchasing power parities (PPPs) as a share of total world GDP.

Table A45. Summary of Medium-Term Baseline Scenario

	Eight-Year Averages		Four-Year Average 1994–97	1994	1995	1996	1997	Four-Year Average 1998–2001
	1978–85	1986–93						
	Annual percent change unless otherwise noted							
Industrial countries								
Real GDP	2.6	2.5	2.4	2.8	2.1	2.0	2.6	2.7
Real total domestic demand	2.4	2.5	2.4	3.0	2.1	2.0	2.5	2.6
GDP deflator	7.3	3.7	2.1	2.0	2.2	2.1	2.2	2.1
Real six-month LIBOR (in percent)[1]	5.3	3.2	3.2	2.8	3.6	3.3	3.2	3.2
World prices in U.S. dollars								
Manufactures	2.8	5.5	3.2	3.2	10.2	−1.4	1.0	1.0
Oil	. . .	. . .	−1.1	−6.8	9.5	1.3	−7.3	1.0
Nonfuel primary commodities	−0.1	2.1	4.5	13.6	8.5	−1.4	−1.7	2.2
Developing countries								
Real GDP	4.3	5.3	6.2	6.4	5.9	6.3	6.4	6.5
Export volume[2]	0.6	8.6	10.5	10.6	11.3	9.8	10.5	8.6
Terms of trade[2]	2.2	−2.1	−0.2	0.3	−0.1	−0.9	−0.3	−0.2
Import volume[2]	3.7	8.5	10.1	8.4	11.6	9.5	11.0	8.6
World trade, volume[2]	**3.8**	**5.7**	**7.8**	**9.2**	**8.8**	**6.2**	**7.0**	**6.6**
World real GDP	**3.2**	**3.1**	**3.8**	**3.7**	**3.5**	**3.8**	**4.3**	**4.5**

	Four-Year Average 1986–89	1989	1993	1994	1995	1996	1997	2001
	In percent of exports of goods and services							
Developing countries								
Current account balance	−3.0	−1.2	−8.3	−4.8	−4.7	−5.0	−5.1	−4.3
Total external debt	159.2	135.4	124.2	117.5	107.0	100.4	95.1	78.9
Debt-service payments[3]	19.8	16.5	15.8	15.3	16.0	13.3	12.2	10.3
Interest	10.2	7.8	6.5	6.2	6.3	6.1	5.8	4.5
Amortization	9.6	8.7	9.3	9.1	9.7	7.2	6.5	5.8
Memorandum								
Net debtor countries								
Current account balance	−6.0	−3.8	−8.7	−5.4	−5.4	−5.9	−5.8	−5.0
Total external debt	193.7	162.8	145.3	135.1	122.0	113.9	106.8	86.3
Debt-service payments[3]	23.9	19.7	18.6	17.4	18.1	14.9	13.7	11.5
Interest	12.3	9.2	7.6	7.0	7.2	6.9	6.5	5.0
Amortization	11.5	10.5	11.0	10.4	10.9	8.1	7.3	6.5

[1]London interbank offered rate on U.S. dollar deposits less percent change in U.S. GDP deflator.

[2]Data refer to trade in goods only.

[3]Interest payments on total debt, plus amortization payments on long-term debt only. Projections incorporate the impact of exceptional financing items. Excludes service payments to the IMF.

Table A46. Developing Countries—Medium-Term Baseline Scenario: Selected Economic Indicators

	Averages			1994	1995	1996	1997	Average 1998–2001
	1978–85	1986–93	1994–97					
	Annual percent change							
Developing countries								
Real GDP	4.3	5.3	6.2	6.4	5.8	6.3	6.4	6.5
Export volume[1]	0.6	8.6	10.5	10.6	11.3	9.8	10.5	8.6
Terms of trade[1]	2.2	−2.1	−0.2	0.3	−0.1	−0.9	−0.3	−0.2
Import volume[1]	3.7	8.5	10.1	8.4	11.6	9.5	11.0	8.6
By region								
Africa								
Real GDP	2.2	2.0	3.9	2.4	3.2	5.3	4.5	4.5
Export volume[1]	0.3	2.2	3.8	−1.2	5.4	7.0	4.4	4.2
Terms of trade[1]	1.9	−4.6	0.2	−0.8	0.9	—	0.7	—
Import volume[1]	0.6	−0.3	6.0	3.4	10.7	4.2	5.6	4.1
Asia								
Real GDP	6.5	7.6	8.3	8.8	8.4	8.2	7.7	7.7
Export volume[1]	8.0	12.6	12.7	14.1	13.6	11.7	11.2	10.2
Terms of trade[1]	0.1	−0.2	−0.4	−0.1	0.1	−0.9	−0.7	−0.3
Import volume[1]	8.5	12.3	12.7	12.5	15.2	12.1	11.0	10.0
Middle East and Europe								
Real GDP	2.2	3.5	2.6	0.7	3.7	3.1	3.8	4.4
Export volume[1]	−7.4	4.9	5.4	4.1	3.7	2.2	11.9	3.8
Terms of trade[1]	5.4	−4.1	−0.9	0.4	−4.6	0.6	0.1	0.4
Import volume[1]	2.4	3.0	3.2	−9.1	4.9	3.7	14.9	4.4
Western Hemisphere								
Real GDP	3.0	2.5	3.4	4.7	0.9	3.1	4.8	4.9
Export volume[1]	5.0	5.4	9.4	8.5	11.3	9.4	8.4	6.7
Terms of trade[1]	−1.6	−3.0	0.9	2.9	3.2	−3.0	0.5	—
Import volume[1]	−1.9	8.9	7.7	13.0	3.0	5.1	10.0	6.8
By financial criteria								
Countries with recent debt-servicing difficulties								
Real GDP	2.8	2.5	3.5	4.3	1.6	3.7	4.9	4.9
Export volume[1]	1.6	4.2	10.0	6.2	11.1	8.4	14.3	6.7
Terms of trade[1]	0.8	−4.1	0.5	1.2	2.6	−2.1	0.3	—
Import volume[1]	−0.1	3.9	9.0	9.2	6.4	5.7	15.0	6.7
Countries without debt-servicing difficulties								
Real GDP	5.7	6.9	7.7	7.7	8.0	7.7	7.3	7.4
Export volume[1]	4.1	10.6	12.2	13.9	13.3	11.1	10.5	9.6
Terms of trade[1]	1.9	−0.7	−0.2	1.3	−1.3	−0.7	−0.1	0.1
Import volume[1]	6.5	9.7	11.8	10.6	14.4	11.3	10.8	9.7

Table A46 *(concluded)*

	1985	1989	1993	1994	1995	1996	1997	2001
	In percent of exports of goods and services							
Developing countries								
Current account balance	−3.7	−1.2	−8.3	−4.8	−4.7	−5.0	−5.1	−4.3
Total external debt	158.4	135.4	124.2	117.5	107.0	100.4	95.1	78.9
Debt-service payments[2]	21.6	16.5	15.8	15.3	16.0	13.3	12.2	10.3
Interest payments	12.1	7.8	6.5	6.2	6.3	6.1	5.8	4.5
Amortization	9.5	8.7	9.3	9.1	9.7	7.2	6.5	5.8
By region								
Africa								
Current account balance	−1.0	−8.7	−8.5	−10.7	−14.4	−12.7	−12.1	−9.3
Total external debt	199.9	248.4	259.0	266.6	252.4	241.3	236.2	206.0
Debt-service payments[2]	34.8	31.0	27.2	23.4	30.7	27.2	27.5	24.9
Interest payments	12.5	13.3	10.5	10.5	10.9	12.2	12.5	10.2
Amortization	22.2	17.7	16.7	12.9	19.8	15.0	15.1	14.7
Asia								
Current account balance	−5.4	1.1	−1.6	—	−1.5	−2.3	−2.6	−3.0
Total external debt	109.3	73.5	65.9	63.5	58.1	55.6	54.1	48.9
Debt-service payments[2]	13.7	9.9	8.1	7.5	7.8	7.3	7.0	6.3
Interest payments	7.1	4.4	3.3	3.3	3.4	3.1	3.0	2.6
Amortization	6.5	5.5	4.8	4.3	4.4	4.2	4.0	3.6
Middle East and Europe								
Current account balance	−4.0	−1.5	−18.6	−5.0	−6.5	−6.4	−6.1	−2.2
Total external debt	93.5	119.1	141.0	137.3	127.7	122.3	110.5	94.8
Debt-service payments[2]	9.7	10.8	12.5	16.6	14.5	13.9	11.0	9.2
Interest payments	4.8	4.1	5.8	5.2	5.5	6.0	5.2	4.2
Amortization	4.9	6.7	6.7	11.5	9.0	7.9	5.8	5.0
Western Hemisphere								
Current account balance	−1.5	−3.9	−24.6	−22.7	−13.4	−13.1	−13.2	−11.2
Total external debt	319.1	284.6	277.9	263.8	242.9	229.7	222.8	188.1
Debt-service payments[2]	45.1	35.9	45.1	43.6	47.5	35.0	32.7	29.2
Interest payments	31.7	19.8	18.5	17.7	18.2	17.5	17.3	13.5
Amortization	13.4	16.2	26.6	25.9	29.3	17.4	15.4	15.7
By financial criteria								
Countries with recent debt-servicing difficulties								
Current account balance	−6.4	−8.0	−20.4	−18.8	−12.5	−12.5	−11.1	−8.6
Total external debt	300.0	306.3	318.4	305.5	276.5	258.8	236.4	190.8
Debt-service payments[2]	39.4	30.7	38.8	36.5	41.5	31.3	28.0	23.8
Interest payments	24.0	15.8	16.2	15.3	15.3	15.4	14.4	11.0
Amortization	15.5	15.0	22.7	21.2	26.2	15.8	13.6	12.7
Countries without debt-servicing difficulties								
Current account balance	−7.6	−1.7	−4.4	−0.8	−3.0	−3.9	−4.1	−4.0
Total external debt	123.4	88.9	82.6	77.3	71.1	67.7	65.4	57.1
Debt-service payments[2]	17.3	14.0	11.3	11.0	10.4	9.7	9.2	8.0
Interest payments	8.4	5.8	4.5	4.3	4.5	4.1	3.9	3.3
Amortization	9.0	8.2	6.8	6.7	5.9	5.6	5.3	4.7

[1]Data refer to trade in goods only.

[2]Interest payments on total debt plus amortization payments on long-term debt only. Projections incorporate the impact of exceptional financing items. Excludes service payments to the IMF.

World Economic and Financial Surveys

This series (ISSN 0258-7440) contains biannual, annual, and periodic studies covering monetary and financial issues of importance to the global economy. The core elements of the series are the *World Economic Outlook* report, usually published in May and October, and the annual report on *International Capital Markets*. Other studies assess international trade policy, private market and official financing for developing countries, exchange and payments systems, export credit policies, and issues raised in the *World Economic Outlook*.

World Economic Outlook: A Survey by the Staff of the International Monetary Fund

The *World Economic Outlook,* published twice a year in English, French, Spanish, and Arabic, presents IMF staff economists' analyses of global economic developments during the near and medium term. Chapters give an overview of the world economy; consider issues affecting industrial countries, developing countries, and economies in transition to the market; and address topics of pressing current interest.

ISSN 0256-6877.
$34.00 (academic rate: $23.00; paper).
1996 (May). ISBN 1-55775-567-1. **Stock #WEO-196.**
1995 (Oct). ISBN 1-55775-467-5. **Stock #WEO-295.**
1995 (May). ISBN 1-55775-468-3. **Stock #WEO-195.**
1994 (May). ISBN 1-55775-381-4. **Stock #WEO-194.**

International Capital Markets: Developments, Prospects, and Policy Issues

This annual report reviews developments in international capital markets, including recent bond market turbulence and the role of hedge funds, supervision of banks and nonbanks and the regulation of derivatives, structural changes in government securities markets, and recent developments in private market financing for developing countries

$20.00 (academic rate: $12.00; paper).
1995 ISBN 1-55775-516-7. **Stock #WEO-695.**
1994. ISBN 1-55775-426-8. **Stock #WEO-694.**

Staff Studies for the World Economic Outlook
by the IMF's Research Department

These studies, supporting analyses and scenarios of the *World Economic Outlook*, provide a detailed examination of theory and evidence on major issues currently affecting the global economy.

$20.00 (academic rate: $12.00; paper).
1995. ISBN 1-55775-499-3. **Stock #WEO-395.**
1993. ISBN 1-55775-337-7. **Stock #WEO-393.**

Issues in International Exchange and Payments Systems
by a Staff Team from the IMF's Monetary and Exchange Affairs Department

The global trend toward liberalization in countries' international exchange and payments systems has been widespread in both industrial and developing countries and most dramatic in Central and Eastern Europe. Countries in general have brought their exchange systems more in line with market principles and moved toward more flexible exchange rate arrangements in recent years.

$20.00 (academic rate: $12.00; paper).
1995. ISBN 1-55775-480-2. **Stock #WEO-895.**

Private Market Financing for Developing Countries
by a Staff Team from the IMF's Policy Development and Review Department led by Steven Dunaway

This study surveys recent trends in private market financing for developing countries, including flows to developing countries through banking and securities markets; the restoration of access to voluntary market financing for some developing countries; and the status of commercial bank debt in low-income countries.

$20.00 (academic rate: $12.00; paper).
1995 (November). ISBN 1-55775-526-4. **Stock #WEO-1595.**
1995 (March). ISBN 1-55775-456-X. **Stock #WEO-994.**

International Trade Policies
by a Staff Team led by Naheed Kirmani

The study reviews major issues and developments in trade and their implications for the work of the IMF. Volume I, *The Uruguay Round and Beyond: Principal Issues*, gives an overview of the principal issues and developments in the world trading system. Volume II, *The Uruguay Round and Beyond: Background Papers*, presents detailed background papers on selected trade and trade-related issues. The study updates previous studies published under the title *Issues and Developments in International Trade Policy*.

$20.00 (academic rate: $12.00; paper).
1994. *Volume I. The Uruguay Round and Beyond: Principal Issues*
ISBN 1-55775-469-1. **Stock #WEO-1094.**
1994. *Volume II. The Uruguay Round and Beyond: Background Papers*
ISBN 1-55775-457-8. **Stock #WEO-1494.**
1992. ISBN 1-55775-311-1. **Stock #WEO-1092.**

Official Financing for Developing Countries
by a Staff Team from the IMF's Policy Development and Review Department led by Anthony R. Boote

This study provides information on official financing for developing countries, with the focus on low- and lower-middle-income countries. It updates and replaces *Multilateral Official Debt Rescheduling: Recent Experience* and reviews developments in direct financing by official and multilateral sources.

$20.00 (academic rate: $12.00; paper)
1995. ISBN 1-55775-527-2. **Stock #WEO-1395.**
1994. ISBN 1-55775-378-4. **Stock #WEO-1394.**

Officially Supported Export Credits: Recent Developments and Prospects
by Michael G. Kuhn, Balazs Horvath, Christopher J. Jarvis

This study examines export credits and covers policies in major industrial countries.

$20.00 (academic rate: $12.00; paper).
1995. ISBN 1-55775-448-9. **Stock #WEO-595.**

Available by series subscription or single title (including back issues); academic rate available only to full-time university faculty and students.

Please send orders and inquiries to:
International Monetary Fund, Publication Services, 700 19th Street, N.W.
Washington, D.C. 20431, U.S.A.
Tel.: (202) 623-7430   Telefax: (202) 623-7201
Internet: publications@imf.org